D1563610

Shakespeare, Line by Line

A Reader's Companion

Arthur Bernstein

Independently published

Printed in United States of America

ISBN 9781096303848

This book is dedicated to my father,

Jack Bernstein,

who, having been denied a formal education

as a young man, devoted himself to Shakespeare

in his adult years and instilled in me a similar passion.

Preface

This book grew out of a course that I've been teaching in the adult education component of Stony Brook University for the past fourteen years. I am an Emeritus Professor of Computer Science at the University. I started teaching the course when I retired. I had enjoyed teaching, but I didn't want to continue in computer science, or any other science. After a career of over forty years in technology, I wanted to involve myself in something else and, rather arbitrarily, chose *King Lear* as the subject of the first iteration of the course. I knew little about the play, but it had always interested me. That first semester was a success. I enjoyed learning and teaching and the students enjoyed participating.

The course quickly grew into a regular offering. I renamed it *Tragic Theater* and each semester I would cover a different set of tragedies drawn from the entire repertoire of Western theater, from the early Greeks to Absurd Theater. Inevitably, Shakespeare's plays figured prominently. They soon dominated the course, which I expanded to include his history plays and his comedies. I've spent many hours preparing the lectures and this book is an attempt to preserve those lectures and to make them available as a companion for anyone reading his plays.

Shakespeare's plays are difficult, not simply because the vocabulary and style are unfamiliar, but because he went far beyond simply telling a story. The plays express his ideas about human nature, about the functioning of society and about man's place in the universe. My goal in this book is to discuss these ideas and show how they are embedded in the plays. I leave the explanation of the vocabulary and individual phrases to the notes that are generally provided in a good edition of the plays.

The analysis I present is largely based on the extensive literature of Shakespearean criticism. My goal was to gather together the interpretations of some of the leading Shakespearean scholars and to integrate them into a single coherent discussion. Of course, there is no one authoritative interpretation of a play, and in cases where thoughtful interpretations differ widely, I present multiple views. Among the scholars represented you'll find Harold Bloom, A. C. Bradley, Harold Goddard, Harley Granville-Barker, Stephen Greenblatt, William Hazlitt, Jan Kott, Wilbur Sanders and Mark Van Doren. The two series of books, *Modern Critical Interpretations* and *Bloom's Modern Critical Interpretations,* edited by Harold Bloom, were extremely helpful. There is a volume in these two series for each of the plays discussed here, and each volume contains a set of essays by a variety of other leading scholars. Finally, the Arden edition of each play has a substantial introduction to that play, which I have used. I've inserted references to these sources throughout the book so the reader can get a fuller treatment of the ideas that I've presented.

In class, I generally spend about three sessions lecturing on each play and then show a video recording of a production. The students read the play before the first lecture and we go through it in class together, moving from beginning to end, stopping to discuss passages that I've selected either because the poetry is beautiful or because the dialogue plays a significant role in bringing out Shakespeare's meaning.

My intention in writing this book is to provide these notes for use in a similar way as a companion for a reader. Hence, the discussion of a play in this book is broken into a sequence of segments whose length varies from a single sentence to a page or more. Each segment is labelled with the location of the passage in the play to which it relates. In order to make the book useful as a companion to a variety of editions of the plays, the labelling takes two forms. The first uses the line numbers of the Arden editions, so that a label takes the form (*act, scene, line*). Successive references within the same segment are abbreviated as (*line*). Although line numberings might differ from one edition of Shakespeare's plays to another, the Arden numberings will generally bring the reader close to the line in a different edition of the play. To make the reference easier to use for other editions, however, the label also includes the first few words of the passage referenced.

I use the Arden edition of the plays in class not only because of their comprehensive introductions, but also because of the extensive notes that appear on each page explaining the meaning of words and phrases.

TABLE OF CONTENTS

Acknowledgments

This book is based on the work of a number of scholars who have labored over the years to try to understand Shakespeare's remarkable plays and relate them to their lives and the times in which they lived. I would like to acknowledge my dependence on this work, without which my book would have been impossible. The bibliography lists all the texts that I have used, but I would like to single out the work of a few scholars whose work was particularly helpful and influenced large sections of what I have written. Foremost among them is Harold Bloom, who not only edited the two series *Modern Critical Interpretations* and *Bloom's Modern Critical Interpretations,* which include volumes about each of the plays discussed here, but whose book *Shakespeare, The Invention of the Human*, provides an encyclopedic exploration of the playwright's work that puts it in the context of Western literature. Harold Goddard's two volume book, *The Meaning of Shakespeare,* was no less useful in providing a down-to-earth, readable and personal response to the plays. A. C. Bradley's book, *Shakespearean Tragedy,* contains an accessible, deep and detailed analysis of Shakespeare's four major tragedies and Jan Kott's book *Shakespeare, Our Contemporary* was particularly helpful in relating *King Lear* to modern philosophical thought. Mark Van Doren's book, *Shakespeare*, contains short essays that quickly capture the spirit of each play. Finally, the editors of *The Arden Shakespeare* included in each volume extensive introductions to each play and detailed notes explaining obscure passages. This material was invaluable.

Chapter 1

Some Related Information

Shakespeare's plays need no recommendation. The poetry embedded in the dialogue and the humanity of the characters have been apparent to readers for four hundred years. The plays occupy a central position in Western literature, alongside of the Bible. And yet they are not easily accessible; they have to be read carefully in order to be fully appreciated. This is partly due to the fact that the English language has changed with the passage of time and partly because the way that life was lived in the years surrounding 1600 were different than they are today. Wars were fought differently, people recreated differently, and the necessities of life were assembled under different constraints. Hence, the reader of today is not as well prepared as the theater-goer of Shakespeare's time to understand the nuts and bolts of what is going on. The best editions of the plays provide a great deal of help in overcoming this problem. Unfamiliar words and phrases are explained and context that the reader might lack is provided in explanatory notes.

All of this, however, is only a first step. The notes help us to understand individual sentences, not the play as a whole. Shakespeare thought deeply about the psychology of each of his characters, about the relationships between his characters and about the world his characters inhabited. His thoughts on these subjects, rather than the stories that he tells, are at the heart of the plays. This is where his genius is located, and this is why the plays do not grow old. The emotions that make us human and the fundamental challenges that we face in life have not changed. We recognize ourselves in his characters, our joys and frustrations, and the limitations that all of us must accept. This explains the subtitle of the encyclopedic book on Shakespeare written by the great scholar Harold Bloom, *The Invention of the Human*.

Of course, Shakespeare doesn't tell us plainly what he's thinking. This is art, not philosophy. And it might not even be the case that he has consciously organized his thoughts on a particular subject. He was, however, a keen observer of life and he presents to us what he has seen. He places his characters in situations that force them to expose their feelings and to choose appropriate responses to situations that they face. We might not share these feelings or make the same choices, but we recognize them as genuine, as human. And as the action unfolds, we learn about life, we are inspired by the nobility of the characters and we are comforted by the realization that the difficulties and losses we experience in our lives are shared by others.

Readers will respond differently to a particular play, drawing their own conclusions, sympathizing with different characters, deducing life lessons and attempting to understand what Shakespeare had in mind when he wrote the play. Interpretations will differ depending on the personality and experiences of the reader. Although there's no single correct interpretation, each thoughtful one has some value and many such have been developed by scholars over the years.

This book is an attempt to integrate the analysis of many of the best Shakespearean scholars into a coherent discussion and then to relate that discussion to particular points in the dialogue. The dialogue justifies the discussion and the discussion, in turn, clarifies the dialogue. The discussion is presented as a sequence of short comments tied to the dialogue by act, scene and line numbers. The book is thus organized so that it can serve as a companion to a reader of a play, offering a possible interpretation of difficult passages as the reader progresses through the play.

To better understand and appreciate the plays it's helpful to equip oneself with a little background. Some English history is essential to an understanding of the history plays. A few words about poetic structure adds to one's appreciation of why the plays read so well. Shakespeare's towering achievement can be found in his mature tragedies and they, to some extent, have a common structure. It's worth understanding what that structure is and seeing how he builds upon it to create each play. Finally, it's interesting to learn a little about Shakespeare himself and the state of theater at the time the plays were written. Information of this sort is supplied in this chapter.

A Bit of English History

Figure 1, *English Monarchy, 1327 – 1625,* shows the succession to the English throne starting with the coronation of Edward III in 1327 and ending with the death of James I in 1625. This is the period that covers the events described in the history plays and takes us on through Shakespeare's life. Edward was a member of the Plantagenet dynasty and those of his descendants who ascended the throne are marked in bold face in the figure.

On Edward's death in 1377, his grandson Richard was crowned as Richard II (Richard's father having predeceased him). Richard's reign was a turbulent one. He took actions that alienated a number of members of the nobility, particularly Henry Bolingbroke, the son of the Duke of Lancaster, Edward's brother. Richard exiled Bolingbroke and disinherited him. Bolingbroke ultimately led a rebellion that deposed and murdered Richard and he took the throne as Henry IV in 1399, the first Lancastrian king. His legitimacy, however, was questioned by the Yorkist side of the Plantagenet family and a rivalry developed between the two branches. Henry IV was succeeded by his son, Henry V, who was in turn succeeded by his son, Henry VI. Henry VI was both mentally unstable and regarded as a weak king.

The competition between the Yorkists and the Lancastrians broke into open, sporadic warfare, called the War of the Roses, during Henry VI's reign. Richard Plantagenet, leader of the Yorkist family at that time, and his son Edmund were killed by Lancastrian forces loyal to Henry. Henry was later deposed, and probably murdered as well, by his Yorkist rival Edward Plantagenet, Richard Plantagenet's son. Henry was the last of the Lancastrian monarchs, since his heir and only son, Edward of Lancaster, had been killed in battle. Edward Plantagenet, the next in line for the throne, was crowned in 1461 as Edward IV.

Edward, the first Yorkist king, died in 1483. His eldest son, still a child, became Edward V, but was never crowned. He and his younger brother were consigned to the Tower of London and never emerged. They were presumably murdered there. Richard, Edward's younger brother, took the throne in 1483 as Richard III, since George, another brother older than Richard and the next in line for the throne, had also been eliminated by that time. The responsibility for these murders is not entirely clear, but it is widely assumed that Richard ordered the death of the children. Richard was killed in the Battle of Bosworth Field in 1485. At that point the War of the Roses had succeeded in eliminating the male line in both families, ending the War and the Plantagenet dynasty.

The victor at Bosworth was Henry Tudor, also a descendant of Edward III, but through a female line. He ascended the throne as Henry VII, starting the Tudor dynasty. He was followed by Henry VIII, who was crowned in 1509 and whose reign was a turbulent one from the point of view of religion. Henry's first wife, Catherine, gave birth to a daughter, Mary, but he wanted a son to perpetuate the Tudor dynasty and sought a divorce in order to remarry. As a Catholic, Henry needed the Pope's permission, but the Pope refused so Henry broke with Rome, assumed control of the Catholic Church in England, granted himself a divorce and married Anne Bolyn. Allegiance to the Pope was now forbidden in England since it threatened the legitimacy of Henry's marriage to Anne and any children that she might produce, thus imperiling the royal succession. Henry's church evolved into the Anglican Church, the beginning of the Protestant faith in England. The open practice of Catholicism was forbidden, and Catholic priests were executed.

Anne produced a daughter, Elizabeth. Desperate for a son, Henry had Anne tried for adultery and executed. He then married Jane Seymour, who produced a son, Edward. Seymour died in childbirth and several other wives followed. Henry died in 1547 and Edward, his only son, was crowned as Edward VI. England remained a Protestant country since Edward was a bastard in the eyes of the Catholic Church.

English Monarchy 1327 - 1625

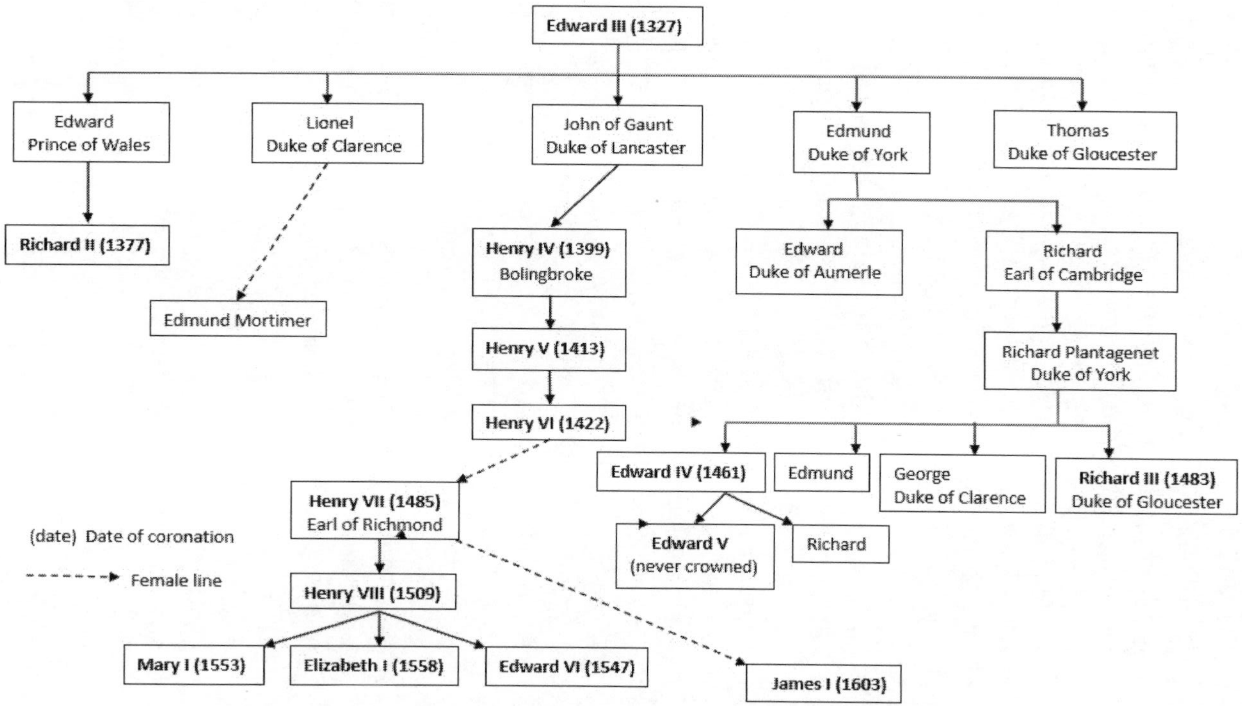

Figure 1

Edward died in 1553 and Mary succeeded him. She returned England to Catholicism since, as the daughter of Henry's first wife, she was Catholic and recognized as legitimate by the Catholic Church. The country once again swore allegiance to the Pope. Mary is often referred to as Bloody Mary in recognition of the harsh measures she took to suppress religious dissent. Mary died in 1558 and Elizabeth took the throne. The country once again broke with the Catholic Church, which considered Elizabeth to be a bastard. The Pope excommunicated her and wanted her deposed. Once again, the open practice of Catholicism was treason, punishable by death.

Shakespeare was born in 1564, a few years into Elizabeth's reign. This was the time of the rise of England as a world power. Catholic Spain attacked Protestant England with the Spanish Armada in 1588. Against all odds, England prevailed and became the dominant sea power of that time.

Elizabeth never married and hence produced no heirs. She died in 1603, ending the Elizabethan period and the Tudor line of monarchs. Henry VIII had tried desperately to preserve the Tudor line, breaking with the Catholic Church and marrying six wives to ensure an adequate supply of male descendants but, in the end, he failed. Elizabeth was succeeded by James, King of Scotland. James' mother, Mary Queen of Scots, was Elizabeth's cousin and a descendant of Henry VII. James' father was a Stuart, so he started the Stuart line of English monarchs and the Jacobean period of English history (James = Jacopo). Although James' parents were both Catholic, he was brought up as a Protestant since his father had been murdered and his mother had been imprisoned and was later executed for treason by Elizabeth. Thus, another religious reversal was avoided.

The Catholic threat to England was real during this early period of Protestant rule, as evidenced by the Gunpowder Plot of

1605, which almost killed King James and most government officials.

James was now both King of England and King of Scotland. As a result, the territory he ruled was divided into two separate countries. Shortly before ascending the English throne he wrote a political handbook for his eldest son warning of the dangers of dividing territory among children, and during his reign he tried to unify the two countries into a larger nation called Britain. He failed in this because the two had long been enemies (Scottish forces were among those defeated at Shrewsbury by Henry IV, as described in *Henry IV Part 1*). As a result, reconciliation was not possible at that time. He is remembered for having sponsored the translation of the Bible into English. That translation is in common use today and is referred to as the King James Version.

Shakespeare used this history as the basis for his eight history plays, which give a fictionalized account of the last of the Plantagenet kings. In chronological order the plays are: *Richard II, Henry IV Parts 1* and *2, Henry V, Henry VI Parts 1, 2* and *3*, and *Richard III*. The latter four were written first and are among Shakespeare's earliest plays. The former four, often referred to collectively as the *Henriad,* were written later and are the product of a more mature playwright. The play *Henry VIII* is thought to be at least in part written by Shakespeare and, if so, is probably his last contribution to the stage.

London Theater in Shakespeare's Time

Morality plays were still being produced when Shakespeare was young, These were essentially secular sermons designed to guide the audience's behavior down the right path. For example, a character named Youth might spend time with another character named Lechery or Sloth or Ignorance and, as a result, bad things would happen until another character named Virtue or Piety came along and straightened things out. The plays were hopelessly didactic and clumsily written. The theater was undergoing a major transition when Shakespeare started his career, but his characters, with their complex psyches, were a sharp departure from anything that preceded them.

At the time Shakespeare arrived in London, around 1590, theaters were a part of the entertainment industry that included brothels, bear baiting and fighting. They were generally frowned upon by the church, which felt that much of what was presented on the stage promoted sinful behavior, and by the city authorities, because of the disorder that often surrounded them. As a result, they were banned by the London authorities and had to be built beyond the city limits, on the south side of the Thames River, to escape municipal control. In the mid-17th Century, not too long after Shakespeare died, theaters were banned throughout the entire country for a period of time by a Puritan government.

Many theaters, including the Globe Theater, consisted of a rectangular, raised stage that was surrounded on three sides by a yard. The yard, in turn, was surrounded by galleries. The stage was covered by an awning and the galleries by a roof to provide protection from the weather, but the yard was open. Galleries had seats that accommodated higher-paying customers. Spectators in the yard stood for the duration of the performance. Theaters were large. The Globe, for example, was octagonal in shape, about 100 feet across. The gallery had three tiers and the theater could accommodate about 3000 spectators.

Scenery had not come into general use at that time, but costumes played an essential role in conveying the theatrical illusion. The stage had no curtain, so playwrights had to write into a play action to clear the stage at the end of a scene. For example, Shakespeare used a funeral march at the end of *Hamlet* to get Hamlet's corpse off the stage.

Theaters had resident acting companies. Actors were all men. Women were not permitted on the stage. Female characters were generally played by boys. Since there was a constant demand for new plays, companies had their own playwrights as well actors. Often, they also had wealthy or noble sponsors. Shakespeare's company was first sponsored by the Lord Chamberlain and was called The Lord Chamberlain's Men. When King James ascended the throne in 1603, he became the sponsor and the name of the company was changed to The King's Men.

Shakespeare

Shakespeare was born in Stratford-on-Avon in 1564. He came from a middle-class family. His parents probably didn't know how to write. He received a basic education (up to about age 16) but didn't go to university. Those who claim that Shakespeare couldn't have written the plays attributed to him point to these facts as evidence. Underlying this attitude is a feeling that an aristocratic upbringing and a college education are required if one is to produce works of genius.

Shakespeare's mother was Catholic. His father was probably a convert to Protestantism. We don't know Shakespeare's religion, but he was probably a non-practicing Catholic. Religion was a touchy business in Shakespeare's time, as the crown alternated between support of the Catholic Church and the

Protestant Church. You didn't want to be caught worshipping God in the wrong way. That might explain why we don't know what Shakespeare's affiliation was and why his plays are generally secular or pagan. He might not have wanted to commit himself in life or on stage.

He married Anne Hathaway when he was 18 years old and she was 26. She was pregnant at the time and a daughter, Judith, was born six months later. Anne gave birth to twins, a son and a daughter named Hamnet and Susanna, a year and a half after that. Hamnet died at age 11, five years before Shakespeare wrote *Hamlet*. Little is known about Shakespeare's life in Stratford. Much of what is known comes from municipal records, like birth and death certificates and the sale or purchase of property.

Shakespeare left his family in Stratford and went to London when he was in his early twenties. He joined the Lord Chamberlain's Men, became an actor and, at some point, began writing plays for the company as well. He spent most of his later life in London, and apparently didn't have much contact with his family. No correspondence survives. He became a shareholder in the Lord Chamberlain's Men and in 1599 the Globe Theater was constructed as their performance space. He made a good living, primarily as a playwright.

The last complete play that Shakespeare wrote is *The Tempest*, which was first performed in 1611. He collaborated on several additional plays, returned to Stratford, and simply stopped writing. He dabbled in real estate in his last years and died in 1616 at the age of 52, a fairly wealthy man. He left the bulk of his estate to his older daughter, with provisions for his younger daughter and his sister. Anne Hathaway isn't mentioned in his will, although the law at the time generally guaranteed that a widow received one third of her husband's estate. Husbands, however, often spelled out this entitlement in their wills, since it was not always enforced. The absence of her name, therefore, raises questions about their relationship. In an addendum to the will he wrote, "I give unto my wife my second-best bed with the furniture".

Shakespeare made no effort to publish his plays. Apparently, plays were not considered significant literature at that time. Some plays, however, appeared in single-play editions called quartos. It's not known whether any of these had Shakespeare's approval. In 1623, after his death, several of his colleagues in the King's Men gathered his plays together and published them in what has come to be known as the First Folio (F). There are significant differences between the two versions of a given play. Modern editions of the plays are generally conflations of the two that are the result of "the exercise of a moderate and quasi-scientific eclecticism" (Bl10 45).

Samuel Johnson, the great 18th Century scholar said: "It doesn't appear that Shakespeare thought his works worthy of posterity or had any further ambition for them than present popularity and present profit. When his plays had been acted, his hope was at an end. ... So careless was he of future fame that, though he retired to ease and plenty, he made no collection of his works, and made no attempt to leave behind authorized copies. Of the plays which bear the name of Shakespeare in the late editions, the greater part was not published till about seven years after his death, and the few which appeared in his lifetime are apparently thrust into the world without the care of the author, and therefore probably without his knowledge."

Shakespeare's Poetry

Shakespeare's plays are written in a combination of prose and poetry. His earliest plays had little to no prose and the poetry tended to be rhymed, but as he matured as a playwright his use of prose increased and blank verse replaced rhyming.

Blank verse consists of unrhymed lines in which the words follow a regular rhythm. Iambic pentameter is the form of blank verse that Shakespeare generally used. A line is broken into five (hence "pent") "feet", each of which generally consists of an unstressed syllable (denoted by * below) and a stressed syllable (denoted by /), called an "iamb", with the unstressed syllable coming first. For example:

When I   do count   the clock   that tells   the time
* / * / * / * / * /

Exceptions to this pattern are permitted, however, to allow some freedom in how the line is to be interpreted. Shakespeare didn't specify how stress is to be placed within a foot. Thus, there is no "correct" reading. The stressed and unstressed syllables might be reversed, or both or neither syllables might be stressed. For example, a reasonable presentation of the opening line of *Richard III* is:

Now is   the win   ter of   our dis   cont ent
/ * * / * * / / * /

Furthermore, an unstressed syllable might be added at the end of the line:

To be   or not   to be,   that is   the ques   tion

* / * / * / / * * / *

Although Shakespeare didn't specify which syllable in a foot was to be stressed, the choice affects the meaning. For example, reversing the stress on the syllables of the foot "that is" gives a different sense to the line.

Scholars have tried to discern a pattern in Shakespeare's choice of which passages he chose to write in prose and which he wrote in poetry. While there seems to be no fixed rule, it's often the case that prose is used for incidental dialogue, and that comic characters – for example Falstaff - and characters whose state of mind is abnormal speak in prose. For example, Lady Macbeth in the sleep-walking scene and Hamlet when feigning madness speak in prose.

Shakespeare's Tragedies

Shakespeare's plays are unexcelled in Western literature, and among them his tragedies are often considered his finest achievements. They form a part of a long sequence of theatrical works, starting with the Greeks and continuing into the present, that attempt to shed light on the most profound questions of human existence. They deal with such issues as what it means to be human, our potential for heroic action, undeserved suffering and the forces that we all face in real life. Although the questions addressed in these plays have changed over the years, there is some consistency to their structure which is worth keeping in mind, especially when reading Shakespeare's contribution to this genre.

To a first approximation a tragic play is one which presents the story of a protagonist who suffers and is brought to some sad ending. In Shakespeare's plays, the protagonist is not an ordinary person. He's generally a member of the nobility. Lear is a king, Hamlet is an heir to the throne, Othello is a general and governor. The horror of the story is thus magnified by the extent of the protagonist's fall. We see that even a great person can't avoid suffering, and this emphasizes our own vulnerability and the powerlessness of man against the forces that oppose him.

Furthermore, the protagonist's fall is not some random event. This is an essential aspect of what tragedy is. If the protagonist suffers for no apparent reason, we learn nothing from viewing his plight. Thus, if a driver obeying the rules of the road gets killed in an automobile accident it's not a tragedy, it's a calamity. On a far grander scale, the slaughter of millions of innocents during World War II is not tragic in the theatrical sense of the word. It's a calamity of historic proportions because it's unrelated to any actions that the victims took.

Tragedy doesn't exist in a random universe. Instead of randomness, tragedy assumes that the rule of cause and effect applies and, furthermore, that a moral order exists to direct our actions. The rule dictates that actions have consequences, and the order might dictate the nature of those consequences. Suffering might be the consequence of deviating from the order, obedience a way of shielding ourselves from disaster. A random universe, on the other hand, is chaotic. Without rules to guide our actions, we cannot hope to shield ourselves. A random universe has been described as one in which God is dead, since it isn't governed by a moral order. There are modern playwrights who focus on the random suffering they see in the world and take this view. More importantly, without moral rules there's no universal standard of right and wrong and we're left with no guidance in deciding how to live our lives. This can yield a sense that life is meaningless. A meaningless life is absurd, and it's this thought that underlies what's called absurd theater.

In contrast to absurd theater, tragedy assumes the existence of an order that we accept as legitimate and that should govern our behavior. That order might be imposed by God, or the gods, or the planets, or society, or the inevitable unfolding of historical forces. The Ten Commandments impose an order and violations are called sins. The legal code imposes an order and violations are called crimes.

The Biblical story of Job sheds light on these issues. Job suffers both physically and mentally, but the mental suffering torments him most. He knows that he hasn't broken God's laws, and hence his suffering threatens his belief in God's justice. The situation is saved from an absurd conclusion because God intervenes and assures Job that there is order in the universe, although man isn't capable of understanding it. Job accepts this on faith, and it is this faith that underlies all the monotheistic religions.

The Renaissance brought with it an emphasis on reasoning and scientific thought that weakened this unquestioning faith. Shakespeare's tragedies reflect this. While they accept the existence of a moral order, there's little in the plays that support the idea that it has a religious basis. Although some of Shakespeare's characters speak in terms of God or heaven, their opinions don't materially influence the view of life that he presents or the evolution of the story. As far as the plays are concerned, the moral order, if it exists, is secular in origin. More importantly, the plays raise the question of whether or not the moral order is just. This lies at the heart of tragedy.

Tragedy addresses the problem of the suffering endured by man. It starts with the assumption that man is not an automaton. He's assumed to have free will and to be responsible for his actions. As a result, a protagonist's suffering is justifiable if it's proportional to the extent to which he has (freely) violated the order. In that case, the suffering is deserved, and the situation isn't tragic. Such suffering is referred to as poetic justice. Robbing a grocery store is a crime. If you do it and as a result you go to jail, that's not tragic - it's justice. It's tragic, however, if you're sentenced to death. We're not surprised that Lear's vanity leads to suffering. The extent of his suffering, however, so far exceeds the foolishness of his actions that we're left wondering how any reasonable order could cause this to happen.

Hence, tragedy doesn't question the existence of suffering in the world. Rather it challenges the notion of poetic justice and asks whether all the suffering we see around us is deserved. And this brings us to the final ingredient in our understanding of tragedy, which concerns responsibility. Shakespeare's protagonists are generally noble figures, but they're not perfect. Othello is credulous, Macbeth is ambitious, Lear has an inflated notion of his importance. These have been referred to as tragic flaws, and they play a role in the protagonists' fall. While we recognize in the protagonists many of our own emotions and desires, they often feel them to a far greater degree and intensity than we do and this, together with their flaws, can lead to unfortunate actions. Lear's excessive vanity leads to chaos in his family and his kingdom. Othello's credulity and jealousy leads to murder, as does Macbeth's ambition.

We're now in a position to elaborate on the very simple description of a Shakespearean tragedy with which we started this discussion. To a greater or lesser extent, his tragedies adhere to the following structure. The play tells the story of a noble protagonist whose view of himself or the world is distorted by an exaggerated character trait. The distortion causes him to violate the moral order and chaos results. He suffers and is dragged struggling to his downfall. In the process, he undergoes a transformation in which he recognizes the distortion. He gains wisdom through suffering. The struggle demonstrates the protagonist's indestructible will, his nobility and the depth of his character. It lends dignity to his life. But it's too late and he dies.

Tragedy deals with what has come to be called the human condition, and by that we mean the very basic circumstances under which we live our lives. Among these are the questions of why we have to die and whether or not there is an afterlife. The circumstance which primarily preoccupies Shakespeare in his tragedies is that of suffering. To what extent is the protagonist responsible for his suffering and to what extent is his suffering the result of an unjust order? Tragedy attempts to challenge the appropriateness of that order. Its harshness becomes clear when one recognizes that there is no appeal from the suffering that occurs. The order is absolute; there's no point asking for pity or appealing for special consideration. We feel that, faulty as he may be, the fault doesn't justify the protagonist's downfall.

The play resonates with us because we see our own suffering acted on the stage and we share the horror of the protagonist's fate with the other members of the audience. The harshness of the human condition and the inevitability of suffering is enacted in a public forum.

Chapter 2

RICHARD III

Background

Richard III is the most popular of Shakespeare's history plays. It was written early in his career, around 1592. He largely followed the history of the period as described in Sir Thomas More's book *History of King Richard III*. More's book has been criticized as being too biased against Richard (ArR3 53) and friendly to his opponent, the Earl of Richmond, who later took the throne as Henry VII, the first Tudor king. Such an orientation would have appealed to Queen Elizabeth, who reigned at the time the play was written, since she was a member – the last - of the Tudor dynasty. As a result, More's description of events was an attractive source for Shakespeare to use as a basis for his play. He manipulated the story he found there for his own dramatic purposes. Whatever the accuracy of the resulting play, its popularity has forever tarnished Richard's reputation.

Richard III is a fictional account of the culmination of a long rivalry for the English throne between two competing royal families within the Plantagenet dynasty: the House of Lancaster and the House of York. These houses consisted of the descendants of two brothers of King Edward III, as shown in Figure 1. It's a complex story involving many characters. Figure 2 is a more detailed depiction of the interrelationships among the Yorkists and the Lancastrians who appear as characters in the play. It will be helpful in following the story. Richmond appears in Figure 1 but not in Figure 2 since he was a Tudor.

The rivalry between the two houses began in 1399 with the deposition and probable murder of Richard II, Edward's grandson, by his cousin Henry Bolingbroke, a member of the House of Lancaster. Bolingbroke ascended the throne as Henry IV. This event fractured the Plantagenet dynasty, often violently, into two competing camps, the Lancastrians and the Yorkists, and resulted in what is called The War of the Roses. The final phase of that war begins just before the opening of *Richard III.*

The last of the Lancastrian kings was Henry VI, the grandson of Henry IV. Richard Plantagenet, leader of the Yorkist family at that time, and one of his sons, Edmund, the Earl of Rutland, were killed by Lancastrian forces loyal to Henry VI. Henry, in turn, was deposed, and probably murdered, by his Yorkist rival Edward Plantagenet, another son of Richard Plantagenet. Henry's heir, and his only son, Edward of Lancaster, was killed as well, thus ending the Lancastrian succession. Edward Plantagenet assumed the throne as Edward IV, the first Yorkist king and the "son of York" referred to in the opening line of the play. These events form the backdrop for the action of the play and explain some of the motivations of the characters. The play opens with the arrival of Henry VI's body for burial and goes on to enact the rivalry for the throne within the Yorkist family.

Richard III

and his Relatives

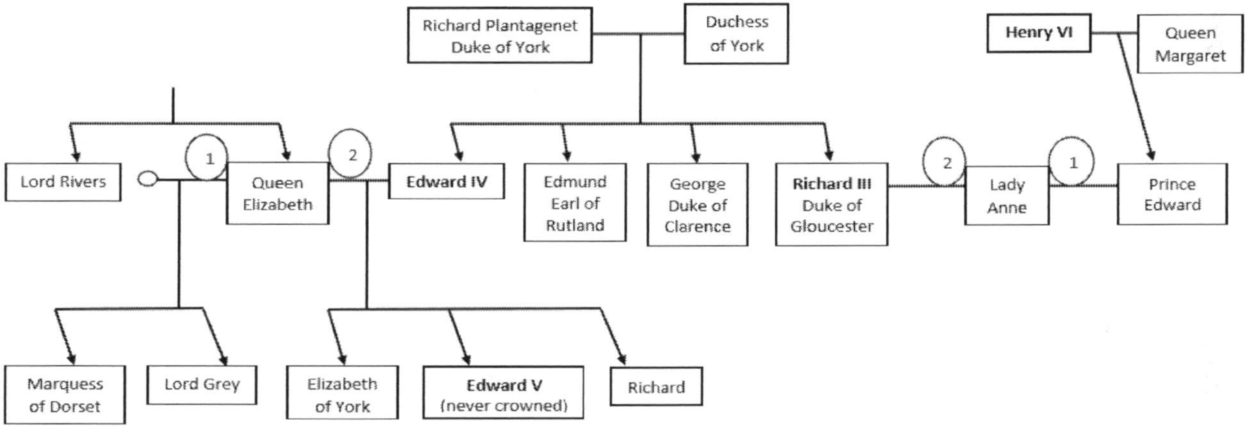

Figure 2

The Play (line numbers from (ArR3))

- (I, I, 1 - 40) Richard's famous soliloquy opens the play poetically and lays out its major points. He speaks of "*our* discontent", although it's apparently his own discontent that concerns him. He refers obliquely and sarcastically to The War of the Roses and the fact that his brother, Edward IV, has brought "glorious summer" to the House of York by capturing the monarchy from the House of Lancaster. Richard was a warrior and regrets that peace has replaced war, since in the current climate his deformity places him at a disadvantage: he can't compete as a lover.

  Richard's deformity was serious, as evidenced by the recent discovery of his skeleton in an unmarked grave under a parking lot near Bosworth Field, the site of his final defeat. Pathetically, he tells us "that dogs bark at me as I halt by them" (23). We sympathize with him, but he uses his deformity to justify crimes that he has and will commit to advance his campaign to mount the throne himself. Most immediately, he has already set a plot in motion against his older brother Clarence, who precedes him as a successor to Edward, using "prophecies, libels and dreams", mechanisms that influence the course of events and that figure prominently in the action to follow.

  Parenthetically, however, it's worth noting that Richard's involvement in Clarence's imprisonment and subsequent murder as described in the play doesn't correspond to the historical record. It was apparently Edward who was responsible for this.

  Richard speaks privately, to the audience. This is a dramatic technique to bring us into the action as co-conspirators, since we know something that the characters on stage do not. Although we're not likely to sympathize with Richard's actions, a bond has been created.

- (I, I, 52) "Yea, Richard ..." - Clarence says that Edward "hearkens after prophecies and dreams", just as Richard had hoped. The prophecy that sends Clarence to the Tower says that the succession is threatened "'G' of Edward's heirs" (39). Clarence's given name is George, so he's implicated, although he's innocent of the charge. Ironically, the guilty party is Richard, whose title also begins with G – Gloucester – so by floating this prophesy he has reflexively implicated himself. Here Richard lies saying that Edward's wife and her brother, Lord Rivers, are responsible for sending Clarence to the Tower (62). The tactic Richard uses of creating hostility among members of the court advances him to his goal of ascending the throne. He commiserates with Clarence and claims that he too is in danger (70). Finally, Richard acts the role of the sympathetic brother (107) and concerned moralist (139). We see in a few introductory lines the outline of Richard's character: schemer, liar, actor.

- (I, II, 14 - 28) "O, cursed be the hand ..." - Anne curses any woman who chooses to marry the man who murdered Henry VI, the first of many curses in the play. The curse becomes reflexive, since Richard was one of the murderers and she later becomes his wife.

- (I, II, 34) "What black magician conjures up this fiend ..." - Anne senses that Richard is acting when he attempts to halt the funeral. The role he plays here is one that displays his dominance. He swears by St Paul who "was associated with demands for deference to authority" (ArR3 151). Richard "manages to enlist, almost magically, the power of the legitimate social order's demands for obedience and deference to hierarchy even while ruthlessly violating such demands himself" (ArR3 15).

- (I, II, 50 – 69) "Foul devil, ..." - Anne is unafraid to challenge Richard to his face, calling him a "lump of foul deformity" (57) and asking God to bring about his death. In response, Richard asks for charity, playing the role of a good Christian (68).

- (I, II, 92) "I did not kill your husband." - Richard sees a marriage to Anne as a useful step in his plan to advance to the throne. Not only is she heir to substantial property (ArR3 147), but "He realizes that in order to substantiate his claims to the position previously held by Henry VI, it is politic to align himself with Henry's daughter-in-law" (Bl20 49), since she was a member of the Lancaster side of the Plantagenet family. The difficulty for him is that he participated in the death of both Henry and Prince Edward (Anne's husband) – a significant impediment to the marriage.

To achieve this goal, Richard acts the role of the abject lover and penitent sinner. First, he denies that he killed Henry (92), but then he admits to the murder (103) saying that Henry is better off in heaven (107). Despite this, he has the gall to suggest that he belongs in bed with her (114). He draws a distinction between the person who sets an act in motion and the agent who performs it (120), saying that the guilty party is really the former. The agent is merely performing a deed that he's forced to do. This is an argument used throughout the play by a variety of characters in order to avoid taking responsibility for their actions. It is central to an understanding of how Richard succeeds in reaching the throne.

In this case, Richard claims, in exaggerated protestations of love, that he was merely an agent and that Anne's beauty was the motivating force that made the murder necessary (182). Finally, he offers his sword to Anne so she can kill him if she won't marry him. Richard demonstrates his considerable wit in this exchange with Anne, a quality he uses throughout his campaign to reach the throne.

Anne isn't fooled (187). But despite the fact that she knows he's putting on an act, she succumbs to his entreaty (195). This can be understood to be the result of the dependent position that all the women in the play find themselves in. They need a protector in an exceedingly violent world. Elizabeth makes this point in the next scene (I, III, 8).

- (I, II, 205) "To take is not to give." - Anne accepts Richard's marriage proposal, but she wants to maintain the fiction that she has preserved her virtue. It's unclear what she is thinking. On the one hand she has stated unequivocally her hatred for Richard, on the other, she's pleased that he has "become so penitent" (222).

- (I, II, 230 - 266) "Was ever woman in this humor wooed?" - Richard gloats at his success in wooing Anne and anticipates her early death (232). His victory is particularly spectacular since he has "no friends to back my suit" (238) and everyone is against him: "All the world to nothing" (240). He describes her dead husband, Prince Edward, who he killed, as "Framed in the prodigality of Nature" (246). The line begs comparison to his description of himself, "Cheated of feature by dissembling Nature" (I, I, 19). He admits that his "all not equals Edward's moiety" (252). Having spoken of his deformed shadow in his opening soliloquy (I, I, 26), he now speaks gayly, "Shine out, fair sun, till I have bought a glass, that I may see my shadow as I pass" (265). One senses his fury at his deformity, his jealousy of those who were born beautiful and a total isolation from normal society.

- (I, III, 8) "The loss of ..." - Elizabeth, Edward's wife, comments on the dependent position that women occupy in the play. Without Edward she would be subject to "all harms". This fact provides some explanation of Anne's willingness to accept Richard's outrageous marriage proposal.

- (I, III, 42 - 53) "They do me wrong, ..." - Richard is indignant, claiming that someone has slandered him to the king. This is another role that he acts. He says that he is "a plain man" who speaks "simple truths". "Nothing can be more characteristic than the turbulent pretensions to meekness and simplicity in this address." (H 144)

- (I, III, 180) "And God, not we, ..." - Richard acts the role of the God-fearing man.

- (I, III, 187 - 232) "What? Were you snarling ..." - Queen Margaret, Henry VI's widow, curses both Elizabeth and Richard: Elizabeth since, with Edward on the throne, she has replaced Margaret as queen; Richard since he murdered both Henry and her son, Prince Edward. All her maledictions come true. Richard mocks her at the end of her curse (232) and substitutes her name for his to make her curse reflexive. “Margaret’s curses have a potential power to anyone secretly sharing her outright belief in magical language – which means everyone but Richard” (Bl20 65). Margaret’s curse includes a wish that Richard be tormented with an inability to sleep, a problem that afflicted Macbeth and that Richard suffers from at the end of the play.

- (I, III, 305 - 307) “I cannot blame her ...” - Richard acts the role of “the wronged man forgiving his enemies” (Sa 89).

- (I, III, 323 - 337) “I do the wrong, ...” - Richard outlines his strategy for creating suspicions among the various factions within the court. He uses religion to hide his plots: “I clothe my naked villainy with odd old ends stol’n forth of Holy Writ and seem a saint when most I play the devil”.

- (I, III, 349 - 354) “Tut, tut, ...” - Among the collaborators in Richard’s pursuit of the throne are those who willingly enact the crimes.

- (I, IV, 9 – 63) “Methoughts that I ...” - Poetry doesn’t reach the same heights in *Richard III* as it does in Shakespeare’s later plays, but Clarence’s description of his dream is an indication of the quality to come. It also displays psychological insight. Clarence’s dream of having been accidently pushed off a boat by Richard and drowning as a result could well mask his fear that Richard is scheming to get rid of him. And the later appearance of Warwick and Prince Edward are a clear indication of his guilt at having betrayed the former and participated in the murder the latter.

- (I, IV, 91 - 94) "I am in this commanded ..." - Brakenbury performs his role in Clarence's murder. He suspects what is about to happen but doesn't ask and takes no action to prevent it. This allows him to avoid responsibility, claiming that he's ignorant and just following orders. This is a trait of the characters in the play that Richard uses in his quest for power.

- (I, IV, 107) "The urging of that word ..." - Murderer 2 hesitates out of fear of God's judgment. Ironically, he's the only one who shows any recognition that murder is immoral. But fear (115) and greed (124) persuade him to continue. He gives a sermon on the impracticality of listening to your conscience (133 – 142), the upshot of which is that having a conscience makes life difficult. "Every man that means to live well endeavors to trust himself and live without it" (141). "Conscience cannot be reconciled with the laws and order of the world", "it is something superfluous, ridiculous and a nuisance" (K 31). Despite this, however, Murderer 1 complains that conscience "even now is at my elbow, persuading me not to kill the Duke" (143). Shakespeare is pointing out both the "discrepancy between the moral order and the order of practical behavior" (K 33) and the fact that our conscience is innate and cannot be discarded.

- (I, IV, 161) "You shall have wine enough ..." - The line refers to the technique to be used to murder Clarence: drowning in a barrel of wine. Murderer 1 says that he and Clarence are both simply men (163), something that Clarence doesn't accept (164), claiming that his royalty makes him different. But the privileges of royalty are not immutable. One's position can change radically. As Murderer 1 says (163), the only thing that's immutable is one's basic humanity.

Like Brakenbury, Murderer 1 evades responsibility for the act he is about to perform by claiming, "My voice is now the King's" (167) – I'm just following orders (Edward had ordered the execution, but it was Richard who sent the murderers to the Tower (242). We learn later (II, I, 87) that Edward had rescinded the order.) Clarence pleads his innocence and appeals to them on the basis of both civil law and God's law, but the murderers point out that Clarence himself is a murderer and amply deserves to die. Furthermore, the king's command is all that counts. Clarence finally argues that in their own self-interest they shouldn't kill him: "they that set you on to do this deed will hate you for the deed" (253). This is a subtle, and often true, observation: The author of a deed can avoid responsibility by blaming the agent. None of Clarence's appeals is met with sympathy, however, and he is murdered as he pathetically pleads for his life (262 – 266).

The episode makes the point that the state operates on the basis of what is useful at a particular moment in time. Neither civil law, religious notions of morality or ethical principles are in control. The mechanisms of the state simply grind on, destroying people arbitrarily. "Clarence has no right to live, the murderers none to kill" (Sa 79).

- (II, I, 32) "Whenever Buckingham ..." - Dying King Edward, in a scene full of hypocrisy, tries to make peace between the Queen's family (Rivers and Dorset), Richard and his followers (Buckingham and Catesby) and Hastings (the king's loyal companion). Buckingham swears an oath that will come back to haunt him (32 – 40) – another reflexive pronouncement. Richard acts the role of a man of peace seeking to reconcile himself with anyone who he has wronged (54 – 73).

- (II, I, 88 - 91) “But he, poor man ...” - Richard cynically hints that a conspiracy is afoot.

- (II, I, 103) “Have I a tongue ...” - Edward belatedly regrets the inhumanity of the government over which he has presided. He speaks of a lack of brotherhood and a lack of justice (122). Immediately on Edward’s departure Richard stokes division within the court (135).

- (II, II, 146 - 150) “My lord, whoever ...” - Richard and Buckingham plot to prevent Elizabeth’s relatives from having influence over the new king, Edward V (150).

- (II, III) An atmosphere of fear pervades the populace.

- (III, I, 6 – 15) “Sweet prince, ...” - Richard acts the role of the wise counselor to his nephew, warning him to beware of “outward show”, the very vice in which he engages in the extreme.

- (III, I, 40 - 43) “God in heaven forbid ...” - Elizabeth and her younger son have requested sanctuary. The Cardinal understands the religious significance of this act and supports their request. Buckingham, however, intervenes with a contrived argument for denying the request (44 -56) and the Cardinal, with Richard looking on and in an abdication of his responsibility, agrees. He says, “you shall o’errule my mind for once”, a wording that allows him to maintain the fiction that he is not complicit in this violation.

He goes with Hastings to snatch the boy from his mother's arms (57). Once again, the failure of the characters surrounding Richard to do what they know to be right enables him to accomplish his ends.

- (III, I, 74 – 83) "But say, my lord, ..." - The Prince asserts that even the unrecorded truth lives for a long time. Richard then hints in an aside that the prince won't live very long. When asked to repeat what he had said, Richard says something different: fame lives for a long time. One possible interpretation of this interchange is that he hopes that his fame as king will be remembered but the events that led him to the throne will not be recorded and quickly forgotten. Richard compares himself to a character in a 16th Century morality play. Characters in such plays personify positive or negative moral attributes and, in this case, Richard boasts that he's like the character 'Iniquity' who equivocates, saying one thing but meaning another.

- (III, I, 161) "Is it not an easy matter ..." - Buckingham's cynicism is evident: He is a party to the plot to put Richard on the throne, a plot that includes the murder of the children, despite acknowledging that York, "so cunning and so young", is wonderful (134).

- (III, I, 181) "Commend me to Lord William." - Richard, forever working the factions that divide members of the court, speaks of the adversarial relationship between Hastings on the one hand, and Rivers, Gray and Vaughan on the other. He says Hastings will be pleased to hear of the latter's execution. He promises Buckingham a substantial reward for his service (194) (but later refuses to make good on this (IV, II, 114)).

- (III, II, 10) "The certifies your lordship ..." - Stanley's dream, like Clarence's, correctly forecasts that Richard is a threat, but Hastings chooses to ignore it (25). The play places a lot of credence on the irrational in predicting and influencing events. Hastings goes on to make an astute political observation: taking the dream seriously and fleeing might make things worse since if Richard knows that they distrust him, he'll have a reason to distrust them. As anticipated by Richard (III, I, 181), Hastings says that he won't mourn the execution of the Elizabeth's relatives despite the fact that they haven't committed a crime (50). He's willing to ignore injustice if it doesn't affect him, although he opposes Richard's plan to take the throne from Edward's son (52). This seals Hastings' eventual execution. He gloats that those who had conspired to condemn him to the Tower are now being put to death and that he is safe (98 - 102).

- (III, IV, 10) "We know each other's faces; ..." - Buckingham says that a man's heart cannot be judged from his face. Despite this, he foolishly trusts Richard and he reassures Hastings that "you and he [Richard] are near in love". Hastings agrees with this evaluation of his relationship with Richard, but he later expresses a different view of the possibility of judging a man's heart from his face, saying "there's never a man in Christendom can lesser hide his love or hate than [Richard]" (51). Unfortunately, he will be proved disastrously wrong. He says that all traitors should be executed and Richard, giving no justification for the action, orders Hastings' execution (75). Too late, Hastings realizes his mistake (87 – 90). The Bishop of Ely observes this order and Lovell and Ratcliffe carry it out, but no one protests. More abdication of responsibility.

Richard is responsible for an impressive number of deaths. He doesn't hesitate to execute those he suspects of not backing him. He has disposed of Rivers and Grey, both in Elizabeth's camp, and Vaughan. Hastings dies because he opposes Richard's plan to usurp the throne. Buckingham will be executed (although he was in open rebellion against Richard, so this is not surprising). Anne dies and the circumstances of her death are not clear. Richard accelerated Clarence's death, and he participated in the murders of both Henry VI and his teen age son, Edward Plantagenet. Shortly his nephews will be killed on his order. The purpose of this carnage is to clear the way for his ascendance to, and strengthen his grip on, the throne. Clearly, he's an exceedingly evil man.

But Shakespeare makes a more important point. Richard couldn't have achieved his goal without the cooperation of the court. The factionalism that he has encouraged works to his advantage. The lies, hypocrisy, abdication of responsibility, and willingness of members of the court to overlook injustice visited on rivals play a vital role in allowing him to act in this way.

- (III, V, 1) "Come, cousin, ..." - Richard asks Buckingham if he can lie and Buckingham responds that he can lie like a great tragic actor. On cue, he lies to the Lord Mayor, saying that Hastings was executed because he had plotted Richard's assassination (38).

After Edward IV's death the throne would naturally go to his son. Richard moves to prevent this by hinting that Edward was a bastard, hence neither he nor his son are entitled to rule, and extolling his own credentials. He enlists Buckingham to speak on this to the populace (72). This is evidence that the approval of the citizens is important. Such approval is irrelevant when succession is controlled by divine right. But this is clearly not the case for Richard and the scene provides evidence of the rising importance of the people's voice in their government.

- (III, VI, 10) "Who is so gross ..." - The scrivener is writing an indictment of Hastings, who has already been executed. He comments on the corruption of the state, but he participates in it. He "is one of the many minor characters who [are] ... not great apostates, nor great cowards, but the small moral casualties of the fray in which others lose their heads" (Sa 83). Although he does nothing, his words give us a small fragment of evidence that resentment against Richard is building. Everyone is afraid to speak out, another social malfunction that enables Richard to control events.

- (III, VII, 2) "Now by the Holy Mother ..." - Buckingham reports that his message at the Guildhall was not enthusiastically received and said that the crowd "looked deadly pale" (25). A sense of fear pervades the populace, a desire not to take sides in a volatile situation and another fragment of evidence that opposition to Richard is building. The atmosphere, however, allows Richard to move forward. Buckingham manipulates the crowd by bringing some followers with him, having them cheer for Richard and then claiming general support for his message (34 - 41): another technique used by political opportunists.

- (III, VII, 94) "See where his grace stands, ..." - Richard stages a press conference using two bishops as props and acting the role of a gentle, pious man who is reluctant to assume the throne. The plan is to get the citizens to beg him to do what he intends to do. Hypocrisy as a tool for political advancement reaches its height in this scene.

- (IV, I, 21 – 25) "I am their mother." - Elizabeth, Anne and the Duchess join forces to oppose the order to separate Elizabeth and her children.

- (IV, I, 97 – 103) "Stay, yet look back ..." - Elizabeth's farewell to her children in the Tower is tender and touching.

- (IV, II) The scene conveys the feeling of both the acceleration of Richard's evil plans and the beginnings of opposition to them. Richard says of his nephews, "I want the bastards dead" (18). Buckingham demurs (24), angering Richard because he demands total loyalty from his entourage, not independent advice (29 - 31). He sends for someone to kill his nephews (34). He speaks vaguely of Anne's coming death and the need to keep her secluded (50). He plans to marry off Clarence's daughter to "some mean poor gentleman" (53) (presumably so her children will not be suitable candidates for the throne). He asks Catesby to help in this, but Catesby shows signs of being less than enthusiastic (56 - 58). Finally, Richard worries that his hold on the throne is weak unless he marries Edward's daughter (his niece) (60).

  Richard shows some sign of understanding the nature of what he has done, which he refers to as sin (64). It's significant that he uses a religious term, since he is a profoundly irreligious man. Although he continues on his murderous path, the word indicates a dawning realization of the enormity of his crimes. The line anticipates similar words used by Macbeth. All this in 65 lines.

- (IV, II, 94 - 105) "I do remember me, ..." - Richard takes prophecy seriously.

- (IV, III, 1 – 22) "The tyrannous and bloody act ..." - Even Tyrrel, who organizes the murder of the princes, is overcome with the horror of the act and the extent of Richard's depravity. Hazlitt credits his words as being "some of those wonderful bursts of feeling, done to the life, to the very height of fancy and nature, which our Shakespear alone could give" (H 146).

- (IV, III, 31 - 43) "Come to me, Tyrrel ..." - Richard isn't satisfied with having killed the children; he wants to hear in detail the "process of their death". He then reviews his progress in solidifying his hold on the throne. Marriage to his niece would cut off the threat that Richmond poses, since Richmond would also like to marry her to advance his claim to the throne. Neither see her as a person. Instead, she is simply a stepping stone for their royal ambitions.

- (IV, IV, 1 – 7) "So now prosperity ..." - Margaret has suffered horribly at Richard's hands, having lost both a husband and a son, and she haunts the play with her hatred and her curses. But she performs a more impersonal function as well. She is "the specially sanctioned spokesman for wronged humanity" (Sa 101). We see this in the opening lines of the scene where she speaks of the inevitable progress of a providence which will bring about Richard's downfall. The implication is that events follow a cycle, evil must be endured, but justice will ultimately follow (73 – 78). This is expressed as a philosophy of history. The progress of providence has two driving forces: an "inner world of conscience where evil brings self-betrayal, and self does self-confound; and in the commonweal where tyranny creates, by its own excesses, the opposition which will overthrow it" (Sa 102).

- (IV, IV, 116) "O thou, well skilled ..." - Elizabeth and Margaret give up their earlier feuding (I, III) and, together with the duchess, they join in condemnation of Richard. Elizabeth asks, "teach me how to curse mine enemies" and Margaret gives a practical and potent response (118 – 123). Although women in the play are always in dependent positions, their power a function of their relationship with powerful men, their curses and prophecies are not without significance in a world that gives credence to mystical forces. The duchess questions the good of words as an answer to calamity and Elizabeth's answer is that "they ease the heart" (127 – 131). The duchess and Elizabeth attack Richard forcefully (137). Only women have the courage to denounce him to his face. He refuses to listen to them, calling for flourishes and drums to drown out their voices (149). The duchess vows never to speak to him again (182) and delivers "my most grievous curse" (188), wishing him death in the battle to come.

- (IV, IV, 150) "Let not the heavens ..." - Richard II was the last king who ascended the English throne in accordance with the rules that govern succession. The legitimacy of his reign was based on the belief that he was anointed by God, and hence he ruled by divine right. He was deposed by Bolingbroke, who could not make the same claim and the legitimacy of his reign and those that followed was threatened as a result. The stability of the government was now based on power and the acquiescence of the nobility and the populace. Shakespeare dealt with this transition in

Richard II. Here we have Richard III, who had murdered Henry VI and carved a bloody path to the throne, outrageously claiming divine right.

- (IV, IV, 170) "Thy school days ..." - Richard's mother's description of his schooldays as "frightful, desperate, wild and furious" leads one to wonder if this was the result of his deformity and/or neglect, and whether it bred in him a need for revenge. As a result, he "suppressed the love instinct in favor of the power instinct, balanced his sense of inner weakness by a show of outward strength ... built up his feeling of superiority, his armor of wit and irony, his creed of self-sufficiency" (Go1 36).

- (IV, IV, 219 – 221) "True, when avoided ..." - Elizabeth rejects the idea of divine predestination by saying that one can choose to reject divine grace and chart one's own course in life. Richard had said something similar in his opening soliloquy: "I am determined to prove a villain" (I, I, 30) (ArR3 351).

- (IV, IV, 281 - 283) "Tell her thou ..." - Elizabeth hints that Richard murdered Queen Anne. Shakespeare chooses to emphasize Richard's villainy here – as if it needed any emphasis. Although, from a historical perspective, there were rumors about Richard's involvement in her demise, it is not known whether they are true.

- (IV, IV, 291) "Look what is done ..." - Richard displays his total indifference to Elizabeth's feelings by suggesting that by marrying her daughter and fathering children with her he will replace Elizbeth's two sons, who he has killed. "A grandam's name is little less in love than is the doting title of a mother" (299). The reasoning recalls a similar situation in the Book of Job in which God replaced Job's children, who had been killed in the test of Job's faith, with new ones.

- (IV, IV, 397) "As I intend ..." - Richard talks of repenting. Sin and repentance, religious concepts, are finally occupying his thoughts. Although this is a sign of some moral growth, he never repents. Elizabeth leaves having shown some sign of relenting and Richard immediately calls her a fool (431).

- (IV, IV, 445 - 456) "Dull unmindful villain, ..." - In contrast to the control over people and events that Richard has demonstrated throughout the play, here he starts to break down.

- (V, I, 11 - 22) "Why then, All Souls' Day ..." - Buckingham recalls that his oath to Edward (II, I, 32) called for his current punishment.

- (V, III, 159) "Richard, thy wife ..." - Anne's ghost visits him in a nightmare and tells him that she "never slept a quiet hour with thee". Thus, we see that, in fulfillment of Margaret's curse, Richard was afflicted by his dreams.

- (V, III, 177 – 206) "Give me another horse!" - Richard wakes in terror crying "Have mercy, Jesu" (178). His statement, "Richard loves Richard, that is, I am I" (183), can be interpreted as a statement of ultimate isolation. In *Henry VI Part 3* he makes the same point more explicitly:

I have no brother, I am like no brother;
And this word "love", which greybeards call divine,
Be resident in men like one another,
And not in me: I am myself alone".

Up to this point, the play has largely concerned itself with the Machiavellian actions Richard had taken to achieve his goal, with little attention paid to the inner world of his consciousness (Sa 82). The lines that follow (184 – 192) are a frenzied attempt by someone who denies any sense of morality to come to terms with a guilty conscience, something Richard hadn't factored into his plans. If one is completely alone in the world, where does guilt come in? Richard is tormented, his soul divided: "Fool, of thyself speak well. Fool, do not flatter" (192). He acknowledges a sense of guilt and suffers because "no creature loves me, and if I die, no soul will pity me" (200). "The man who had deemed himself self-sufficient now finds himself dependent on human love and pity" (Go1 39).

- (V, III, 212- 214) "O Ratcliffe, ..." - Richard admits to Ratcliffe that he has had a "fearful dream" and "I fear". This is a very different man from the one who coldly spoke of his determination to become a villain at the outset of the play. Too late, he recognizes the significance of the qualities that make us human.

- (V, III, 282) "The sun will not be seen today." - The play opened with a pun on the word 'son' who makes "glorious summer". This was the starting point of Richard's rise. Here, as Richard's approaches defeat, the play closes with the information that "The sun will not be seen today".

- (V, III, 307 – 313) "Go, gentlemen, every man ..." - Richard forges ahead in the only way he knows how, urging his followers to ignore "babbling dreams that affright our souls", denigrating conscience as "but a word that cowards use", and urging strength as the guiding force.

- (V, III, 343) "My lord, he doth ..." - It's significant that Stanley doesn't join his forces with Richard's. Richard had drawn his power by commanding others to do his bidding, but Stanley refuses to do this, and this plays a role in Richard's destruction.

- (V, IV, 1 – 7) "A horse, a horse, my kingdom for a horse!" - The pathos of the situation is reflected in this line, since Richard's life has been spent committing every crime conceivable to win a kingdom, and now he's willing to give it away for a horse. He fights courageously, "Daring an opposite to every danger". He is killed, so finally justice is done. We are left to ask if this is God's vengeance or is this "the kind of thing that happens to the kind of person who perpetrates this kind of defiance of the moral order" (Sa 100).

- (V, V, 15) "Inter their bodies ..." - Richmond declares the end of the War of the Roses between the Lancasters and the Yorks, uniting "the white rose and the red" (19), symbols of the two houses. At this point all the male descendants in both families had been killed and, as a result, the Plantagenet dynasty ends. Richmond, a descendant of Edward III, claims the throne. He announces his intended marriage to Elizabeth, Edward IV's daughter (29). While she is clearly a Yorkist, his claim to being a Lancastrian is questionable. The claim is based on the fact that his mother was a great-granddaughter of John of Gaunt, the Duke of Lancaster and the progenitor of the Lancaster line. Hence, his claim to the throne is weak since it is along a female line (see Figure 1).

Discussion

Richard III is one of Shakespeare's early plays and as such doesn't share the qualities he developed later in his career. For one thing, it's short on the poetry that is such an important part of his later plays. Instead, it concentrates on telling a story. More importantly, the play is short on the character development that's a major attraction of his later plays, particularly the tragedies. For these reasons, it is often considered more of a melodrama than a tragedy - a play that draws its strength from plot and physical action over characterization.

Richard explains to us in his opening soliloquy that because he can't be a lover, he's determined to be a villain, and all his actions follow from that fact. We see little of his interior thoughts or feelings. He's no Hamlet, who agonizes over the choice he has to make in avenging his father's death, or Lear, who speaks of his suffering and learns what's most important in life. Although Richard shows some evidence of recognizing the enormity of his crimes at the end of the play, we don't sense any new humanity or regret about the destruction he's caused. He's the same person in Act V as he was in Act I.

Richard is an actor. We're "prompted to marvel at his sheer audacity, his clarity of motive, his ruthless exploitation of the factional and ideological limits that constrain others, his watchful alertness among half-conscious sleep-walkers, egoists, blinkered factionalists and time-servers. Richard may halt, but his social command is deft" (ArR3 17). Hazlitt says he is a "mixture of intellectual vigour with moral depravity" (H 143). Van Doren says, "his energy is mental. ... He is therefore both fearful and fascinating" (VD 24).

Rather than being a study of character, the play is a study of politics and power. "Politics is to [Richard] a purely practical affair, an art, with the acquisition of power as its aim. Politics is amoral, like the art of bridge construction ... Human passions, and men themselves, are clay that can be shaped at will. ... Richard III is not just a name of one of the kings" (K 41). Instead, the play describes the mechanism that moves the world and Richard is the human face of that mechanism. "A terrifying face, in its ugliness and the cruel grimace of its lips. But also, a fascinating face" (K 41). "The implacable steam-roller of history crushes everyone and everything" (K 47), and both Clarence and the murderers and Richard himself are just cogs in this amoral mechanism.

Beyond this bird's-eye view of the workings of the world, there is also a worm's-eye view of the nuts and bolts of the art of political maneuvering. (The following analysis is based on (Gr1)) The play addresses the question: "How could a great country wind up being governed by a sociopath?". It shows us in detail how this over-confident, loathsome, misogynist bully overcame numerous barriers to, against all odds, reach the highest office in the land. It places much of the blame on his enablers, characters who saw clearly his evil nature, but refused or were afraid to oppose it. Their reasons ranged from a sense that they themselves weren't in danger and might benefit from his success to a sense of pleasure that their rivals were made to suffer. The play doesn't depict a violent seizure of power. Instead, there are the lies, the crimes that go unpunished, the fraudulent display of religious piety, the staged political rally, the exploitation of factional divisions, the hint of conspiracy and the slandering of opponents.

Chapter 3

A MIDSUMMER NIGHT'S DREAM

Background

A Midsummer Night's Dream is one of Shakespeare's early plays. Despite that, Harold Bloom says, "It is Shakespeare's first undoubted masterwork, without flaw, and one of his dozen or so plays of overwhelming originality and power" (Bl 148). Harold Goddard says it "is one of the lightest and in many respects the most purely playful of Shakespeare's plays" (Go 74).

The play is organized around four groups of characters, whose stories are largely kept separate through the first four acts and are brought together in Act V. Each group has its own story.

- Theseus, the Duke of Athens and his intended bride, Hippolyta
- the four lovers
- the mechanicals
- the fairies, whose king and queen are Oberon and Titania

On the surface, the play is a light entertainment about love leading to marriage. It describes the events leading up to three weddings, and also describes the troubled marriage of Oberon and Titania. The play was probably written to entertain the guests at some private celebration, perhaps a wedding. But the play also has a more serious side. It illustrates the conflicting roles of reason and imagination in life, where imagination encompasses the irrational, which in the play includes dreams, poetry, love and theater.

The play opens in Athens, the seat of reason, in daytime. Athens is presided over by Theseus, reason's chief exponent, and is the location where conflicts among the lovers are set in motion. In Act II the action moves to the woods and night time, alive with fairies who are presided over by Oberon and Titania. In contrast to Athens, the woods are a symbol of fantasy and imagination. It's a world in which dreams flourish, magic is a tool, the irrational course of love is determined, and inspiration comes to the poet. The players return to Athens in Act V, where the resolution of the conflicts is celebrated.

The Play (line numbers from (ArN))

- (I, I) The theme of marriage is introduced in the first line and is the unifying action of the play. "The fairies have come to Athens to give [the wedding of Theseus and Hippolyta] their blessing; the artisans are preparing their performance ... and the wedding day" is the day that Hermia is to make "the decision expected to settle the outcome of the four lovers' story" (ArN xc).

- (I, I, 7 - 11) "Four days will ..." - Hippolyta speaks of dreaming away the time until her wedding to Theseus takes place. The contrasting roles of dreams and reality – the irrational and the rational - in life is another major theme of the play.

- (I, I, 28 - 38) "Thou, thou, Lysandar …" - Egeus, Hermia's father, accuses Lysander of beguiling Hermia with rhymes (poems) and music, products of the irrational side of nature, and stealing her "fantasy". Fantasy is a product of imagination and hence Hermia isn't behaving reasonably. Egeus, engaging in parental interference that precipitates one of the problems at the center of the play, wants Hermia to marry Demetrius. She objects and asks Egeus to see through her eyes (56). But, as we shall see, eyes can't be trusted.

- (I, I, 65) "Either to die …" - Theseus is a good man and a noble ruler. He's a rationalist who opposes fantasy and imagination and sees love as something that must be subjected to parental control. His dim view of love is confirmed by the fact that he "woo'd [Hippolyta] with my sword" (16). We learn later that he's also a womanizer (although he has apparently given that up). Hence, his role in judging the dispute between Hermia and Egeus can be questioned. His view of the duty a daughter owes to a father makes it clear that he sees a woman as an object to be disposed of. His job is to enforce the law and to cultivate the love of his subjects. To his credit, and in contrast to the choice given to Hermia by Egeus to either marry Demetrius or die, he adds another option – the convent. He exits with Egeus and Demetrius, presumably to try to find a reasonable solution to the problem (114), but unfortunately his mediation doesn't work. The thematic function of this episode is "to dramatize the inability of unaided reason to ensure a tolerable outcome" (ArN civ).

- (I, I, 132 - 149) "Ay me!" - Lysander enumerates various problems that impede the course of love. Shakespeare hints here and in several other places that the unhappiness that the lovers experience is not so much due to outside forces – *i.e.*, parental interference – as due to the follies brought about by love. Here Hermia speaks of one of those follies: abdicating one's judgment to another person: "To choose love by another's eyes" (140).

- (I, I, 168 – 178) "My good Lysander ..." - "The rhetoric of the first eight lines" of Hermia's oath "is neatly undercut by the final couplet, whose jingling and prosaic simplicity collapses the soaring quality of what precedes it" (Bl7 46). Male infidelity is another dimension of the folly of love.

- (I, I, 183 – 204) "Call you me fair?" - The senseless acts that love induces are illustrated at the outset of the play. Helena wants to model herself on Hermia (186), thus foolishly abdicating her judgment to her friend. And folly is also exhibited by Demetrius who, having abandoned Helena, now loves Hermia despite the fact that Hermia hates him: "I give him curses; yet he gives me love" (196).

- (I, I, 226 - 245) "How happy some ..." - The exchange deals with the relationship between the eyes, the mind and love. Helena takes a dim view of the role of the eyes. They present us with reasonable information, but reason doesn't control our actions. "Love looks not with the eyes, but with the mind" (234), a mind that has not "of any judgment taste" (236). The mind, the site of imagination (and desire (K 224)), has the power to transform what the eyes see – perhaps something that is actually "base and vile" - into something that appears to have "form and dignity" (232). We call this love. The operation of the mind should not be confused with reason. The mind's irrational control of love is referred to in the play as "doting", or fixation.

Helena's relationship with Demetrius illustrates this. All of Athens thinks Helena is as fair as Hermia, and Demetrius used to think that as well. But his mind has colored his vision, so that he doesn't see Helena in the same way anymore and now dotes on Hermia. Although Helena realizes that Demetrius' obsession for Hermia is a mistake (230), she admits that she makes the same mistake in obsessing over him. The use of love-juice to anoint the eyes later in the play reinforces the view that eyes and mind can't be trusted.

- (I, I, 246 - 251) "I will go tell him ..." - Love causes Helena to betray her friend, another folly. Finally, Helena looks to "enrich my pain", yet another folly. She's a masochist.

- (I, II) Having introduced the lovers and the Athenians, Shakespeare now introduces the mechanicals, a group of local artisans with theatrical ambitions. Bottom is a weaver. The bottom is the center of a skein on which a weaver's wool is wound. Although portrayed as absurd, he's no simple laughing stock. He shows practical ability and common sense: "He has an urge to be doing ... he sets to work at once", "He gets the preparations for 'Pyramus' off to a good start" (ArN cxv). He provides a stream of advice to Peter Quince, the director: "You are best to call them generally" (2), "First, good Peter Quince say what the play treats on; then read the names of the actors; and so grow to a point" (8), "Call forth your actors by the scroll" (I4). He's full of self-confidence and he's not averse to praising himself. Thus, he says, "I will move storms" (22) (of tears) in acting the hero, and he describes his reciting of some lines as "This was lofty" (35).

He's so eager to act that he tries to get any and all the roles in the play. He's assigned the role of Pyramus, and when Flute tries to avoid the role of Thisbe claiming he has a beard (43), Bottom wants to play that as well. And then he wants to be the lion and is willing to play it in any way required just as long as he gets the part. First, he says that he'll roar so loud that it will make "any man's heart good to hear me" (67), but later promises to "roar you as gently as any suckling dove" in order not to frighten the ladies (77). He uses a more ambitious vocabulary than he can handle: "rehearse most obscenely and courageously" (100).

Bottom is "rather more than equal to any situation ... {his] triumphs ... are unselfconscious: he does not see the difficulty and walks through it" (ArN cxvi). His "imperturbability is not mastery of the situation, but a species of invincible ignorance" (ArN cxvii).

- (II, I) Finally, Shakespeare introduces the fairies. We meet Puck, a "shrewd and knavish sprite" (33), a speedy spirit (like Ariel in *The Tempest*), who enjoys playing practical jokes and who serves Oberon, the king of the fairies. We hear of the feud between Titania, the queen of the fairies, and Oberon, over possession of the changeling child (20). (A changeling is apparently a child that has been substituted by fairies for another child (Bl7 154). It's not clear why the term is used in the play).

- (II, I, 60 - 137) "Ill met by moonlight ..." - Titania and Oberon taunt each other about their respective infidelities: His with Hippolyta, who Titania refers to as "the bouncing Amazon" (70), and hers with Theseus. Titania won't sleep with him anymore (62). As a result of their feud, nature has been disrupted (88 - 117) (ArN cvi). The immediate cause of their anger is Titania's refusal to give the changeling to him for his page (120). The changeling is the son of a votress, a person who was bound to Titania by an oath and who died in childbirth. Titania had vowed to raise the child for her. The description of her relationship with the mother is beautiful poetry (121 – 137). It tells of love between two women and it gives a new dimension to the celebration of love that is the play's main theme. Titania speaks of "a feminine world rich with all the mysteries of fertility, conception, pregnancy, and birth that women can treat with easy familiarity" (Bl7 63). The boy can be viewed as representing this love relationship and it is from this relationship that Oberon is excluded. Oberon wants to possess Titania entirely and by taking the boy he feels he can overcome this separation (Bl7 62). Titania's conduct poses a direct challenge to the early modern view of a good wife held by Oberon, which dictates that she should be chaste, silent and obedient. Titania neither obeys nor prioritizes her spouse. Her bond with the votress and devotion to the changeling are higher priorities and illustrate an alternative marriage arrangement (Bl7 152).

- (II, I, 148 - 175) "My gentle Puck ..." - Oberon plans to overcome Titania by using the juice Cupid uses to anoint his arrows. The juice comes from a flower called love-in-idleness, another name for the wild pansy, but also a barb directed against the vapid lovers who waste their time in love games (Bl7 22). The original target of the arrow was "A fair vestal, throned by the west" (158) This is apparently a tribute to Queen Elizabeth, who might have attended a performance of the play. Cupid aimed at her but missed "and the imperial votress passed on" (163). The juice intended for her is used in the play to control the love relationships of other characters. "It is as though Elizabeth's choice of chastity opens up a cosmos of erotic possibilities for others, but at the high cost of accident and arbitrariness replacing her reasoned choice. Love at first sight, exalted in *Romeo and Juliet*, is pictured here as a calamity" (Bl 159). Oberon sends Puck to get the juice (174).

- (II, I, 188) "I love thee not, therefore pursue me not." - Helena follows Demetrius despite the fact that he asks her not to. She grovels, willing to be beaten and used like a dog (203 - 207). This is more than a folly of love, it's sick.

- (II, I, 249 – 258) "I know a bank ..." - This is "one of the play's most exquisite passages [that provides a transition] from sensuous naturalism to grotesque gusto", perhaps preparing the audience for the transformation of Bottom that follows in the next act (Bl 159).

- (II, I, 260 - 264) "A sweet Athenian lady ..." - Oberon tries to help the Helena/Demetrius coupling by using Puck as his instrument. At Oberon's direction, Puck is to find Demetrius and juice his eyes, and thus redirect his attention to Helena. Unfortunately, Oberon is unaware that there are two young Athenian men in the woods and his instructions aren't sufficient to distinguish Lysander from Demetrius.

- (II, II, 26) "What thou seest ..." - Oberon juices Titania's eyes to punish her opposition to his wishes. He sets up a situation in which she's forced to fall in love with the first thing she sees on waking, perhaps an animal.

- (II, II, 40) "One turf shall serve ..." - Hermia chastely refuses to sleep close to Lysander. Puck misinterprets the fact that they are not embracing in their sleep (75), and concludes that Helena is Hermia and Lysander is Demetrius. As a result, he mistakenly juices Lysander instead of Demetrius (77) and Lysander spurns Hermia and pursues Helena, complicating the love pairings.

- (II, II, 114) "The will of man ..." - Shakespeare mocks the role of reason in controlling love. Lysander explains that he has used reason in switching his affection from Hermia to Helena when in fact the change is due to the juice. Shakespeare here anticipates 20th Century psychology, which has shown that reason is often used to justify choices that are actually made in the unconscious mind.

- (III, I, 8 - 67) "There are things ..." - Since the purpose of theater is to create illusions, it belongs in the realm of imagination. A major theme of the play is the conflict that often arises between imagination and reality in life. Shakespeare illustrates what happens when the two come together by showing the chaos that results when theater tries to imitate reality. The players take each aspect of the performance literally. Their first worry is that the ladies in the audience will be frightened by Pyramus' suicide (10) and that they will therefore need reassurance. Bottom's solution to this problem is that a prologue be written explaining that what is happening on the stage is purely illusion. Consistent with his personality, he offers to deliver the prologue, but more importantly, the solution demonstrates "the deficiency of imagination that lies behind such a laughable conception of theater" (Bl6 49).

  Additional problems must be dealt with. The ladies will be afraid of the lion, the moon must actually shine on the stage (45), and the wall through which Pyramus and Thisbe speak must be solidly in place. Bottom proposes sensible, but hilarious, ways to deal with these problems as well (35 –

72). And Shakespeare adds to the humor by exposing the players' ignorance. Snout says parlous for perilous (12), Bottom substitutes the words defect for effect (38) and odious for odorous (78). Flute throws in the word Jew because it rhymes with hue, (juvenal means young man). He says he is lily-white (87) and in the next line says he's "of color like the red rose", he compares Pyramus to a horse (91) and speaks of Ninny (a fool) instead of Ninus. He also doesn't understand the use of cues (95).

- (III, I, 98 - 137) "If I were fair ..." - On his own initiative, Puck uses his magic on Bottom (ArN cx), transforming his head into an ass's head. Bottom isn't the least bothered by this. He enters with the line "If I were fair". This anticipates Gregor Samsa's transformation in *The Metamorphosis* into a beetle. Both seem to accept their new selves calmly. Although the mechanicals panic and flee when they see him, Bottom is imperturbable and more than equal to the situation.

- (III, I, 124 - 141) "What angel wakes me ..." - Titania awakens and, under the influence of the love-juice, voices her love for Bottom (131), despite the fact that he has and ass's head. In response, Bottom offers wise advice: "To say the truth, reason and love keep little company together nowadays. The more the pity that some honest neighbors will not make friends" (138). His view of love contrasts sharply with Theseus' desire that love be subjected to reason and parental control (I, I, 67). Bottom is unfailingly kind and sweet-tempered (ArN cxvi).

- (III, I, 157 - 167) "Be kind and courteous ..." - Although Titania is intent on getting Bottom into bed, he's more interested in the fairies, who he treats with the utmost courtesy. But Titania is undeterred and tells the fairies to "tie up my love's tongue" (190 - 194). He talks too much, and she has other things in mind.

Shakespeare uses the device of the love-juice to display another dimension of the relationship between reason and imagination. Sexuality clearly plays a major role in a love relationship, but showing the sexual appetite of Hermia or Helena would alter their characters in a way that would violate their chaste nature. That problem doesn't apply to Titania, however. The love-juice not only irrationally directs Titania's attention to Bottom, it also exposes the carnal nature of love (Ko 228). While the play attributes this effect to the juice, the juice is a stand-in for the mind. The message is that the mind not only overcomes the eyes – reason - in shaping our love interest, it drives our sexuality as well.

- (III, II, 88 - 99) "What hast thou done?" - In an attempt to straighten out the love relationships, Oberon juices Demetrius eyes so that he'll return to his earlier love of Helena. The magical power of the love-juice mirrors the compulsive nature, in real life, of the imagination in directing love to unsuitable matches (ArN cxxxiv). Puck enjoys the confusion as well as the lovers' foolish behavior: "Lord, what fools these mortals be!" (115).

- (III, II, 122 – 161) "Why should you think ..." - Helena mocks lovers' vows, another feature of romantic love. Hermia had done the same earlier (I, I, 175). The dialogue displays more than the confusion that the love-juice causes. It displays the real pain that results from misplaced love.

- (III, II, 198 - 219) "Is all the counsel ..." - Helena speaks of the love that had existed between her and Hermia. The play thus celebrates love between two young girls, and this mirrors the relationship between Titania and her votress.

- (III, II, 257) "Away, you Ethiope!" - Although the men are portrayed as more or less interchangeable caricatures, the women, who aren't subjected to the love-juice, are distinguished. They are different physically and temperamentally. "Hermia is spirited and warm-blooded, tender in happy love, hot and militant in anger" (ArN cxi). She's not afraid to fight (298), but at the same time she's sensitive to attacks on what she views as her weak points: her dark complexion (257, 263) and her small stature (295, 328). Helena is much more the lady: very feminine and unwilling to fight (300). She speaks of herself as a "gentle lady" (152) and a "virgin" (160), and of the need to be "maidenly" (217). She's offended that she has to chase Demetrius: "Your wrongs do set a scandal on my sex, we cannot fight for love as men do; We should be woo'd, and were not made to woo" (II, I, 240). On the other hand, she has betrayed Helena's confidence (I, I, 246) and her own self-respect (I, I, 186).

- (III, II, 336) "Now follow ..." - Lysander and Demetrius are brought to the brink of a duel. This is the ultimate chaos that can result from romantic love.

- (III, II, 354) "Thou seest these lovers ..." - On Oberon's order, Puck leads Demetrius and Lysander in a confusing chase in order to prevent them from fighting (396). Puck enjoys the deception. He is a spirit who is "cheerfully amoral, free because never in love, and always more amused than amusing" (Bl6 4). He "has no human feelings, and so no human meaning" (Bl6 5). Bottom, on the other hand, is all human.

- (III, II, 458 - 463) "And the country proverb ..." - Puck delivers his chauvinistic summary of the confusion in the woods: "every man should take his own", "Jack shall have Jill", "The man shall have his mare again".

- In Act III the lovers are manipulated by the fairies with love-juice and led around the woods on false chases. Shakespeare uses the action to make the point that romantic love can lead to folly. The play presents the episode ambiguously as perhaps a dream, perhaps reality. The poet W. H. Auden describes the action as follows:

  > "Hermia and Lysander at the beginning think themselves morally superior, and they're conceited because their love is mutual. Demetrius thinks he's stronger than Helena because he's loved while he himself is unloving. Helena's misfortune makes her spiteful, she betrays Hermia to make everyone as unhappy as she is. Lysander is equalized with Demetrius when he becomes unfaithful and his love is not returned. Hermia is equalized with Helena because her love is not returned. Helena learns not to envy others, and she learns also that being loved isn't so grand. There is a complete reversal. Helena is punished for her spite because she doesn't believe the love offered to her is true, and Demetrius realizes what it is not to be loved. All four now, through similar experiences, have grown up, and it's now possible for them to marry." (Bl7 120)

- (IV, I, 31 - 33) "Truly, a peck of provender; ..." - Bottom is more interested in oats and nuts than Titania's amorous advances. She says that she will "wind thee in my arms", sends the fairies away, and describes how the "female ivy so enrings the barky fingers of the elm". There has been some debate in the scholarly community about whether Titania's love for Bottom is consummated at this point (Bl7 93, 103). Jan Kott says "The slender, tender and lyrical Titania longs for animal love ... [She] drags the monster to bed, almost by force ... The monstrous ass is being raped by the poetic Titania" (Ko 228). Harold Bloom, on the other hand says "It remains ambiguous exactly what transpires. ... does it matter? Does one remember the play for orgiastic bestiality"? (Bl 163)

- (IV, I, 56 - 68) "And she in mild terms ..." - Titania has relinquished the changeling to Oberon. She's been overcome by Oberon, just as Hippolyta was overcome by Theseus. They both accept the fact that a wife should acknowledge the benign superiority of her husband. Oberon arranges that the lovers and Bottom not be able to recall the events in the woods clearly, only "as the fierce vexation of a dream" (68), when they awake.

- (IV, I, 102 - 126) "Go one of you ..." - Mark Van Doren says of these lines: "Had Shakespeare written nothing else than this he still might be the best of English poets. ... The passage sets a forest ringing, and supplies a play with the music it has deserved" (VD 66). "Theseus and Hippolyta [celebrate] the wonderful nonsense of the Spartan hounds, bred only for their baying so that they're 'slow in pursuit'" (Bl 166). He says, "mark the musical confusion of hounds and echo in conjunction", and she responds, "Never did I hear such gallant chiding ... every region near seem'd all one mutual cry. I never heard so musical a discord, such sweet thunder". And then he says, "match'd in mouth like bells, each under each. A cry more tuneable was never hallo'd to, nor cheer'd with horn".

- (IV, I, 142) "How come this ..." - Theseus acknowledges that the lovers have achieved a "gentle concord" in the dream world of the woods, something that has happened without his rational intervention and demonstrates the power of imagination. In violation of his decision in Act I, he simply overrules Egeus and allows Hermia to marry Lysander (178).

- (IV, I, 199 - 217) "When my cue comes, call me and I will answer." - The instant that Bottom wakes from his dream he's ready to start acting. Then he remembers dreaming, but he's both unable and unwilling to describe it (209). Perhaps he's experiencing the same difficulty we all have in recalling a dream. We're left to wonder what he's referring to when he says, "Methought I had". Is he referring to the ass's head or Titania? He has experienced a sublime vision, although he mixes up his senses in trying to convey to us its sublimity: "the eye of man hath not heard, the ear of man hath not seen, ...". The sentence is derived from a line in the New Testament, although the play is set in pre-Christian times (and it borders on blasphemy, since Bottom has just awakened from a dalliance with a fairy). "What Shakespeare has caught here is the miracle of the imagination, the awakening of spiritual life in the animal man" (Go 80) (Bl7 107). "Even within the head of this foolish plebeian weaver a divine light can be kindled" (Go1 177). "The memory of the dream comes back to Bottom in a sort of luminous mist, with clouds of glory trailing from the experience" (ArN cxvii). He sees himself as a great artist. The woman whose death will be celebrated is not identified – perhaps someone in the dream.

- (IV, II, 12) "You must say paragon." - Flute, sensibly, puts down paramours.

- (IV, II, 28) "Masters, I am to discourse ..." - In his excitement Bottom first says he's not going to talk about his dream because, as an Athenian rationalist, dreams mean nothing. But then he says he will. All this despite the fact that he has presumably forgotten it.

- (V, I, 2 – 27) "More strange ..." - Helena had complained (I, I, 232) that the mind has the power to transform the reality that the eyes see from something that is "base and vile" into something that has "form and dignity". Theseus now makes the same point when he says that the lover "sees Helen's beauty in a brow of Egypt" (11), meaning that something beautiful is built out of a trifle.

  Theseus denigrates the lovers' stories as fables. They're constructed from their imagination, and therefore he doesn't believe them. He associates poets and lovers with madmen since they all forsake reality and they all feel that it's enough to think that something is true to make it true. They have the ability to give to "airy nothing a local habitation and a name" (14). In other words, they can take something that is insubstantial and make it real. This is a god-like attribute. Perhaps without meaning to, Theseus' words can be taken as a tribute to the poet's power. "Such tricks have strong imagination" (*i.e.*, the tricks of poets, lovers, and madmen require a strong imagination). "If it would but apprehend some joy" (*i.e.*, imagine it, sense it) "It comprehends some bringer of that joy" (*i.e.*, makes it happen, give it substance, understand it) (19).

Hippolyta, however, senses that there's more to the lovers' stories than fables, since they all report the same events (23). She's more sympathetic to the imaginary world that they describe than he is. She says that they have been "transfigured" – transformed – by their experience, and that is very real. When she says that the events in the woods have "great constancy", she means that they are more than "fancy's images", that they are important and can teach us something. If we think of their stories as poetry and the lovers as poets, then she can be viewed as defending poetry against Theseus' attack.

The lovers' follies illustrate the irrationality of love. This, taken together with Theseus' comparison of lovers and lunatics, argues that the play can be taken as one that censures love for its unreason (ArN cxxxv). But Theseus' attempt to solve the lovers' problems using reason has failed and the final pairing of the lovers was accomplished in the woods, the domain of imagination. Furthermore, Theseus' denigration of lovers as similar to lunatics is balanced by Hippolyta's defense of imagination. Perhaps Shakespeare's view is that expressed by Bottom, which strikes a middle ground by seeing the need for love and reason to be friends (III, I, 137).

- (V, I, 81 - 105) "I will hear the play; ..." - Philostrate says that the play is "nothing" (78), but Theseus kindly insists on hearing it anyway, explaining, "never anything can be amiss when simpleness and duty tender it" (82). Hippolyta says (85) that she doesn't like to see poor people looking bad when they're trying to do something good. Theseus' reassures her (89 – 105). Despite the fact that he doesn't have a high regard for imaginative work, he appreciates the need to respect the effort that the artisans have made to please him. "The kinder we, to give them thanks for nothing". The use of the word "nothing" here harks back to Theseus's earlier reference to poetry as "airy nothing" and anticipates his later statement that we must use our imagination to "amend" what poetry lacks. Theseus's words prepare the stage audience for an amateurish performance and warn them, and us, to be respectful. He speaks eloquently of modesty.

- (V, I, 108) "If we offend ..." - The play within the play is a burlesque on the same theme as *A Midsummer Night's Dream* itself – love and the problem of parental intervention. The production "satirizes the ineptitude of amateur actors; styles of drama which are or should be" outmoded, and the absurdities of mediocre poets (ArN cxviii). For example, one translation of Quince's prologue with the punctuation taken into account comes out as:

> "If we happen to offend you, it's because we want to. We don't want you to think we came here to offend you, except that we want to offend you with our good intentions. Our plan to show off our little bit of talent will wind up getting us executed. Please keep in mind we're only here out of spite. We don't come here with the intention of making you happy. We're absolutely not here to delight you. The actors are ready to come out and make you sorry. By watching their show, you'll find out everything you're likely to know." (nfs.sparknotes.com/msnd/)

Despite its comical intent, however, the play introduces one couple whose fortunes don't end happily. Shakespeare reminds us of yet another dimension of love.

- (V, I, 202 - 203) "Thus have I ..." - Wall justifies his departure with a direct explanation to the audience. Eliminating illusion from a theatrical performance renders it ridiculous. This can be taken as a parody of Theseus's dismissal of the imagination.

- (V, I, 208 - 213) "The best in this kind ..." - Theseus mocks all plays saying that the best are only illusions and the worst are no worse if you use your imagination to fix them. Finally, he says, "If we imagine no worse of them (the players) than they of themselves, they may pass for excellent men" (211). Thus, by using our imagination we can impose a value on something which matches our desire. Theseus uses the word imagination while Helena uses the word mind, but they're both pointing to mechanisms that shape our view of reality.

  This raises the question of who we are. Are we as we appear to others, or is there an essential self, independent of perception (ArN cxxxvii)? Bottom is an example of someone who, despite gross changes to his appearance, views himself as unchanged (III, I, 111). Contrast this with Demetrius' inconsistency in switching his affections from Helena to Hermia (I, I, 110), two women who are equally beautiful.

- (V, I, 311 – 322) "Asleep, my love?" - The traditional comparison of a woman's features to particular flowers is used to describe Pyramus' features, but the flowers and features are mixed up (lily lips, cherry nose) and then the whole passage is made ridiculous by comparing Pyramus' eyes to leeks.

- (V, I, 337) "No, I assure you ..." - When Theseus and Demetrius question something about the play, Bottom steps out of character and courteously explains the proceedings as he had done earlier (181).

- (V, I, 341 – 347) "No epilogue ..." - Theseus views the play with good-natured humor. "As we in the audience watch Theseus watching Bottom pretend to be Pyramus, the extended dramatic perspective forces us to consider the possibility that we too may be only another player audience on another larger stage And if this is the case, then the audience is not only once again reminded by the bad manners of the stage audience of the positive part it must play in making theater work, but it is also being told that its own sense of the real may be no more valid than Theseus's. If his rationalistic scorn of plays and players is called into question by his status as only another player, then perhaps our skepticism about Shakespeare's play is equally compromised, for we stand in the same relationship to the things unknown that the imagination of William Shakespeare has bodied forth as *A Midsummer Night's Dream* as Theseus does to *Pyramus and Thisbe*." (Bl6 51)

  Van Doren summarized the impact of Bottom and his friends: "in their sublime innocence, their earthbound, idiot openness and clarity of soul" they demonstrate that "their creator should become not only the finest of poets but the one who makes the fewest claims for poetry" (VD 67).

- (V, I, 409) "If we shadows ..." - Puck refers to himself as a "shadow" and this puts him in the world of imagination and implicates him in Theseus' dim view of the theater (208): "The best in this kind are but shadows". His concern that we might reprehend the play might refer to the possibility that Protestants in the audience could take offence at the role of fairies, something that was more acceptable under Catholic rule (Bl7 161).

Discussion

If we agree with Theseus' dim view of imagination and the theater, we must conclude that *A Midsummer Night's Dream* is worthless. Anyone who reads the play, however, is bound to come to a different conclusion. Although written early in his career, the play is one of the finest of his achievements and, significantly, it is focused on the world of imagination and dreams. Hippolyta opened the play by speaking of dreaming (I, I, 7). Puck ends the play by telling the audience that the whole play might have been a dream. The lovers referred to their experiences in the woods as dreams (IV, I, 198). Bottom referred to his experience as "Bottom's Dream". Theseus treated the stories told by the lovers as dreams (V, I, 2), although Hippolyta had her doubts (V, I, 23). The fairies have the last word, having taken over the castle and blessed the lovers, and Puck raises the question of whether the entire play is simply a dream in the mind of the audience (V, I, 411). What are we to think? What is a dream and what isn't? We must decide for ourselves.

We can carry the question of what is a dream one step further by asking whether the reality we experience in our daily lives is in fact created by our imagination. As Demetrius suggests, "are you sure that we are awake? It seems to me that yet we sleep, we dream" (IV, I, 192). And this calls to mind Prospero's line in *The Tempest*: "We are such stuff as dreams are made on". Our lives are insubstantial. The play raises the question of what is real and what is imagined and suggests that the irrational insights of the imagination can control our actions. "This world of sense in which we live is but the surface of a vaster unseen world by which the actions of men are affected or overruled" (Go 74). Reason at odds with imagination is the major theme of the play. The play anticipates Freud and his introduction of the role of the unconscious in our lives. Shakespeare seems to be saying that imagination colors our perception and controls our actions to a far greater degree than we realize.

Chapter 4

ROMEO AND JULIET

Background

Shakespeare's plays that end with the death of the protagonist are generally classified as tragedies, and by that measure *Romeo and Juliet* is one of his first plays in that category. The play was written around 1595, roughly seven years into his career as a playwright. Hence, this is early Shakespeare.

Regardless of one's position on whether the play should be considered a tragedy, its popularity cannot be questioned. The story is gripping, and the poetry is superb. The play has been called "a literary monument to the beauty and innocence of youth" (ArRJ 38). William Hazlitt says, "There is a buoyant spirit of youth in every line, in the rapturous intoxication of hope, and in the bitterness of despair" (H 83). And Harold Bloom says that "the play is the largest and most persuasive celebration of romantic love in Western literature" (Bl 90).

The play has served as the the inspiration for Gounod's opera *Roméo and Juliette*, Tchaikovsky's *Romeo and Juliet* overture, and Prokofiev's music for the ballet *Romeo and Juliet.* It was also the inspiration for the Broadway musical *West Side Story* by Bernstein and Sondheim.

The setting is Verona in the second half of July. The heat of the day accentuates the heat of the romance and the aggressive energy that drives the feud that is the subject of the play. The action starts on a Sunday morning and ends at dawn the following Thursday. By packing the story into just a few days, Shakespeare accentuates the impetuosity and the intensity of the lover's emotions. Juliet's fourteenth birthday is only a few weeks away. She is barely out of puberty and Romeo is only a few years older.

The Play (line numbers from ArRJ)

- (Prologue) The play opens with a sonnet that sketches the story. It refers to the lovers as "star-crossed", with the implication that fate has somehow intervened to bring about the tragedy. The role of fate in the story is central to the question of whether the play qualifies as a tragedy, since it hints at the possibility that the lovers are not responsible for what happens.

- (I, I, 1 - 31) The subject of the play is love and violence. Samson and Gregory are retainers in the Capulet household and their conversation is a humorous take on both. They are not anxious to get into a fight and their view of love verges on the pornographic.

- (I, I, 129) "Many a morning ..." - Romeo enters the play as the classic love-sick boy. He keeps to himself, he cries, and he stays in the dark because he's been rejected by Rosaline (166). Love creates chaos in the lovers' minds, and Romeo describes this with a series of oxymorons (174 - 179).

- (I, I, 188 – 192) "Love is a smoke ..." – Here (and again (206)) Romeo describes Rosaline using a romantic ritual often associated with the poet Petrarch. It involves the use of hyperbolic language in the worship of the beloved, false melancholies, and the central role of chastity. This characterizes Romeo's romantic style and is one of the several approaches to love that appear in the play. It distinguishes him from Juliet, who views love differently.

- (I, II, 13 – 18) "Too soon marred ..." - Capulet shows himself to be a caring father. He thinks Juliet is too young to be married and he will not force her to marry anyone that she doesn't like.

- (I, II, 24) "Earth-treading stars ..." - Capulet speaks of the young girls who will attend his ball with a hyperbolic conceit similar to "star-crossed" that ties their beauty to the heavens and is repeated throughout the play.

- (I, III, 2) "Now by my maidenhead ..." - Nurse's first words introduce her character, which is earthy and interested in the sexual dimension of life (96). She says that she was still a virgin at age twelve. Apparently, she lost it shortly afterward. We learn later that Lady Capulet had given birth by age fourteen (72). This tells us that Juliet is poised on the edge of sexual maturity. Nurse's attitude towards sex sets her apart from the Petrarchian model.

- (I, III, 7) "Madam, I am here." - Juliet enters the play as an obedient child. We watch her mature as the play progresses.

- (I, III, 17) "Even or odd ..." - Nurse engages in what is called "memory theater": "moments in which one character's seemingly digressive recollection momentarily displaces dramatic action" (Bl19 148). These digressions serve to both widen the expanse of the play and give us a deeper view of the character. In this case Nurse exposes a "prurient interest in love-business" (VD 58). She remembers how her husband joked that Juliet would be falling on her back when she was older (43). This is an understated version of the more pornographic approach to love taken by Samson and Gregory.

- (I, IV, 1) "What, shall this speech ..." - While Mercutio, a relative of the Prince and not a Montague, might well have been invited to Capulet's party, Romeo and Benvolio are gate-crashers. The party-goers are masked.

- (I, IV, 25 - 94) "Is love a tender thing?" - Mercutio's character is sketched in this scene: he's witty, he's bawdy, and he's a poet. He takes Romeo's innocent description of love as a thorn that pricks the lover and turns it into a reference to intercourse (27). The Queen Mab speech (53) is a long poem about dreams that demonstrates the range of his imagination. The lines are clever and delicate, and it ends on a bawdy note (92), which is characteristic of Mercutio's outlook.

- (I, IV, 106 – 113) "I fear too early, ..." - Romeo has a premonition of the tragedy to come. He alludes to the belief that he's controlled by fate – a reference to the opening sonnet which described the lovers as "star-crossed".

- (I, V, 43 - 48) "O, she doth teach ..." - Romeo is smitten at the first sight of Juliet. This is a part of the romantic ritual to which Romeo subscribes. The passion that he formerly directed towards Rosaline he now abruptly and impulsively redirects to Juliet. He idealizes her using the conceit first introduced by Capulet involving images of light and heavenly bodies. The immediacy of the action signals a transition in Romeo's behavior, who previously was depicted as languishing, moody and sad.

- (I, V, 92 – 105) "If I profane ..." - The first exchange between Romeo and Juliet takes the form of a shared sonnet, emphasizing the harmony that springs up immediately in their feelings towards one another. He kisses her, and she teases him saying, "You kiss by the book" (109). She probably means without feeling. Shakespeare stresses their innocence and purity, and the contrast with both Nurse and Mercutio emphasizes this.

- (II, I) Act II opens with another sonnet describing the situation of the lovers.

- (II, I, 7 - 21) "Romeo, humours, madman, ..." - Mercutio mocks the rituals of romantic love: passion, sighs, poetry, Venus, Cupid. He says that Romeo's love for Rosaline has rendered him virtually dead. His thoughts quickly descend to a reference to Rosaline's genitals and quivering thighs (20) and talk of some "strange nature" having intercourse with her (24). His bawdy humor is a witty version of the conversation that opened the play. It represents the most primitive view of love and it sets the stage for the next scene "where the lyricism of young love reaches one of its loftiest pinnacles in all poetry" (Go1 122).

- (II, II, 1) "He jests at scars ..." - Shakespeare didn't divide his plays into scenes. This was done later by editors. Hence, in the original version one scene simply flowed into another.

This line refers to Mercutio's mocking comments on love that ended (II, I): Mercutio has never been in love and so is not in a position to comment on the pain that lovers experience.

- (II, II, 2 – 9) "But soft, what light ..." - Although Romeo and Juliet are unreserved in their love for each other, they shape that love differently. We see this in the balcony scene. Romeo privately expresses his idealized view of Juliet by comparing her first to the sun and then says that she is the moon's maid (chaste virgin). He wants her to cast off her "vestal livery", presumably her virginity, since "none but fools do wear it". The idealization using the astronomical metaphor continues (15 – 32).

- (II, II, 33 – 49) "O Romeo, Romeo, wherefore ..." - Juliet, thinking that she is alone, questions why Romeo has to be a Montague - "Wherefore art thou Romeo?" - and says that he would be the same person even if he had a different name. She asks, "What's in a name? That which we call a rose by any other word would smell as sweet" (43). "These lines, spoken by a Juliet philosophically sophisticated beyond her years, assert the need to see through to the core of things, past outward trappings" (ArRJ 23). There's no idealization here.

- (II, II, 50) "Call me but love ..." - Romeo reveals himself and says that if she loves him, he will be "new-baptized", no longer Romeo, an act of heroic self-transformation. The feud that separates the two families presumably has old roots and has been inculcated into the minds of the lovers from birth by their parents. As the lovers demonstrate, "there is just one agency powerful enough in youth to defy and cut across this domination of the generations, and that is love" (Go1 119).

- (II, II, 52) "What man art thou ..." - Juliet is taken by surprise by Romeo's presence and is now at a disadvantage since, without knowing how he feels towards her, she has not only revealed her love for him within his hearing (128), but he has acknowledged that he knows it. She cannot play the traditional Petrarchian role of the reluctant lady.

- (II, II, 62 – 69) "How cam'st thou hither, ..." - Juliet, ever practical, worries that Romeo is in danger within the Capulet compound. Romeo, responding with male bravado, says he can fly over walls and he isn't afraid of her relatives. This is a part of the myth of romantic love that Romeo acts out. "Courage, willingness to sacrifice oneself for love, and fidelity, more than long term pleasure or a growing marital relationship constitute success in such a myth" (Bl19 84). "All of these images serve implicitly to exalt the poet-lover in his own imagination ..., as he characterizes himself as empowered, lifted above the earth, by his affection for her and, even more, by her affection for him, as if it were an inspiration from a muse or an act of divine grace. As his lady is made to play a personified role in his imagination, that of ideal Beauty which diminishes by comparison all that is earthly, so is he, by implication, exalted into a mythological role himself, that of Love, the aspiring quester after beauty, given superhuman powers of his own by beauty's powerful influence" (Bl19 83). Thus, egoism is a component of Romeo's love for Juliet. He sees his male image burnished by his love. On the other hand, "Juliet's poetic imagination ... is radically free of this self-regarding concern with her own worthiness or personal attainment but is instead characterized by desires for earthly happiness, sexuality, and day-to-day intimacy" (Bl19 80).

- (II, II, 85 - 106) "Thou knowest the mask ..." - Juliet tries to recoup her position in their relationship by discarding the approved, Petrarchan, form for courtship (88) and moving to the actualities of their relationship. She knows that he loves her, and she recovers her position in the dialogue by so stating (90). But she wants proof. She criticizes the Petrarchan requirement that the woman should hold back when in a romantic encounter by saying "I'll prove more true than those that have more cunning to be strange" (100). She doesn't want him to swear because such oaths are valueless: "At lovers' perjuries they say Jove laughs" (92). She simply asks him to be sincere.

- (II, II, 107) "Lady, by yonder blessed ..." - Romeo attempts to launch into the romantic ritual by swearing by the moon, but Juliet cuts him off (109) and asks him to simply swear by his "gracious self" (113). He starts another hyperbolic sentence and she cuts him off again. Her use of the unadorned and practical word "contract" – an exchange of promises - contrasts sharply with his imagery. She worries that their love is too sudden and will as suddenly disappear, like lightning (119), and her use of that word speaks of the impulsive nature of their love.

That she has achieved parity in the relationship is evident when Romeo asks for "Th'exchange of thy love's faithful vow for mine" (127), a simple and unpretentious request which amounts to an agreement to marry, to which she ultimately replies that her love is as boundless and deep as the sea (133 - 135). She uses the image of falconry to describe how she would like to keep Romeo close to her

(158). Their parting lines are universally known (184 – 187). There is no hyperbolic speech here, just a desire for domestic closeness. Romeo's poetry follows Juliet's departure (188 – 191).

"Her overheard soliloquy in the orchard and the ensuing conversation with Romeo ... show her as a person who is able to speak her own mind, who refuses to be imposed upon by Romeo's Petrarchan rhetoric, and who fights for her right to declare her love in her own words and style" (Bl19 180).

- (II, III, 1 – 26) "Now, ere the sun ..." - Poisons and sleeping potions play a significant role in the play. Here Friar Laurence meditates on the dual nature of herbal concoctions: they contain both the potential for being curative and for being deadly, depending on the degree to which they are used. He sees an analogy between this and inclinations in man (17), who is capable of acting with either grace or "rude will" (24). His message relates to the play if one takes the degree that the substance is used to correspond to the intensity of the feelings between lovers. Modest love is salutary, consuming passion can lead to the lovers' death. In the end, Laurence's analogy fails since their love, although passionate, cannot be described as "rude will". Instead it is celebrated and their death ennobles their life (Bl19 31).

- (II, III, 87) "For this alliance ..." - Despite the anti-Catholic sentiment prevalent in late 16th Century England, Shakespeare seems to have gone out of his way in presenting Friar Laurence as a sympathetic figure. Here we see him trying to solve the problems that separate the lovers and end the feud that divides the families.

Shakespeare's religious affiliation is not known with any certainty, but it's likely that he was brought up Catholic. "It is tempting to view Shakespeare's friars as an implicit declaration of Catholic allegiance – or at the very least sympathy – on his part" (Bl19 72).

- (II, IV, 37 - 45) "Without his roe ..." - Mercutio, with an abundance of wit, mocks both Romeo and romantic love as celebrated by the poet Petrarch (39).

- (II, IV, 85 - 89) "Why, is this not better ..." - Romeo and Mercutio engage in a battle of wits that culminates in Mercutio expressing his pleasure that Romeo has resumed his normal behavior and given up "groaning for love". As he sees it, an interest in sex is natural in man, but not love. He expresses his view of life in bawdy and witty language.

- (II, V, 4 – 17) "O, she is lame!" - Juliet's words speak of the urgency of her passion.

- (II, VI, 9 – 15) "These violent delights ..." - Friar Lawrence urges moderation on Romeo. The play contrasts moderation with the passion of youthful love.

- (II, VI, 24 – 34) "Ah, Juliet, if the measure ..." - Romeo asks Juliet to celebrate their love verbally but, characteristically, Juliet responds saying action speaks louder than words. Words are "ornament", not substance; it's pointless to attempt to measure love with words. Friar Laurence senses their passion and says that he will not leave them alone until they are married. The scene ends with them going to the church.

- (III, I) Mercutio and Tybalt are spoiling for a fight. Tybalt wants to fight Romeo as part of the family feud and because Romeo attended Capulet's party uninvited. But since Mercutio is not a Montague, there's no reason why Tybalt should fight him. Indeed, Tybalt doesn't challenge Mercutio when the scene opens (36). One is led to believe that the feud is simply an excuse to fight. This aggressive stance was displayed by Samson, Gregory, and Benvolio as well, and Shakespeare appears to be saying that their attitude towards violence is part of the make-up of young males, who find it necessary to demonstrate their masculine qualities. When looked at from this point of view, the feud between the Montagues and the Capulets is more a symptom of a broad cultural mindset than the cause of the tragedy. Indeed, Shakespeare never tells us what the feud is all about. He seems to imply that feuding is simply a part of life in Verona.

  Romeo enters and Tybalt tries to goad him into a fight by first calling him "villain" (60) and then referring to him as "boy" (65) (a word that also infuriated Coriolanus). The code that dictates male behavior makes it abundantly clear that insults like that require a forceful response, but Romeo doesn't rise to the bait. As a result of the marriage, Tybalt is now his cousin and Romeo's restraint speaks of his love for Juliet. Since Mercutio is unaware of Romeo's marriage, he is appalled by the restraint, calling it "dishonourable, vile submission" (72) and he initiates a fight with Tybalt on Romeo's behalf. If anyone is responsible for the tragedy that follows, it is Mercutio. Romeo doesn't want to fight Tybalt, and Tybalt had earlier indicated that he had no cause to fight Mercutio (55).

Romeo tries to intervene by drawing his sword but, in the confusion that follows, Tybalt kills Mercutio (85, 105). This is the turning point of the play. Romeo has to choose how to respond. Should he seek revenge for Mercutio's death by fighting with Tybalt or should he refuse to continue the cycle of violence that has plagued the Montagues and the Capulets and place his love for Juliet before masculine honor by making peace with him. Hence, his choice is between the two forces that are the subject of the play, violence and love.

Romeo had, up to this point, been restrained by his love for Juliet, but violence now wins out over love. His masculine instincts are aroused. He says, "my reputation stained" (113) and Juliet's beauty "hath made me effeminate" (116). He reverts to the culturally determined male pattern of behavior (125), challenges Tybalt and kills him. It's hard to fault Romeo for the choice he has made and blame him for the tragic outcome. However, the outcome follows from this. Shakespeare demonstrates the grip that social forces exert on our actions. It's often said that the outcome of the play results from an excess of love, but when viewed in this way it can be described by the opposite: the outcome results from a failure of love (Go1 132).

It's important to note, however, that although Tybalt's death causes Romeo's banishment, Romeo had already violated the tradition of parental rule by marrying Juliet and so some punishment was inevitable.

- (III, II, 1 - 31) "Gallop apace, ..." - Juliet expresses the urgency of her youthful passion in her longing for night and the consummation of her marriage: "Gallop apace, you fiery footed steeds". Sexuality in the play is not restricted to the men. She longs for "love-performing night". She doesn't see night as a metaphor for evil, as in *Macbeth*. Instead she sees it as friendly and "civil" (10), something that will hide the consummation of their union (5). She wants to "learn me how to lose a winning match, played for a pair of stainless maidenhoods" (11), referring to the fact that they are both virgins. Then she says that although she has been sold – married – she has not yet been enjoyed (27). She expresses sexual desire "without ironic undertones of guilt or shame" (Bl19 86). Sex is a part of love, and in that context it is beautiful. This is a far cry from the kiss that they exchanged on their first meeting.

Hazlitt writes, "The character is indeed one of perfect truth and sweetness. It has nothing forward, nothing coy, nothing affected or coquettish about it – it is pure effusion of nature. It is as frank as it is modest, for it has no thought that it wishes to conceal. It reposes in conscious innocence on the strength of its affections. Its delicacy does not consist in coldness and reserve, but in combining warmth of imagination and tenderness of heart with the most voluptuous sensibility" (H 90).

- (III, III, 108) "Art thou a man?" - Friar Laurence challenges Romeo to act like a man, accept responsibility for his actions, and not blame astronomical forces: "Why rail'st thou on thy birth, the heaven and earth, since birth, and heaven, and earth, all three do meet in thee at once" (118). He enumerates Romeo's blessings (134). He proposes a plan that includes a wedding night for the couple in the short term and relief from the banishment in the long term.

- (III, IV, 12) "Sir Paris, ..." - The Capulets have a view of love which involves good marriages and sensible choices. "They are matchmakers, and believe they know best how to put their daughter to bed" (VD 57). Love plays no role in the choice of a husband.

They have chosen Paris to wed Juliet and it now becomes clear why Shakespeare has chosen the name 'Paris' for that character. In his poem *The Iliad,* Homer tells us that the Trojan War was triggered when Paris, a Trojan prince, abducted Menelaus' wife, Helen. Here we see Juliet being given, against her will, in marriage to Shakespeare's Paris. Were this to happen Juliet, like Helen, would be in a bigamous relationship with a man named Paris.

- (III, V, 17) "Let me be ta'en ..." - Male bravado and romantic ritual combine in Romeo's assertion that he's willing to sacrifice his life to satisfy Juliet's desire that he stay past dawn. "Come, death, and welcome! Juliet wills it so" (24). But Juliet, recognizing the dawn, ignores the hyperbole saying, "Hie hence, be gone, away!"

- (III, V, 152) "Thank me no thankings ..." - Juliet begs not to be forced into a marriage (158), but Capulet is adamant. His language has a modern ring to it (152, 160 – 168, 176 - 196). This view of the relationship between the generations is the first of several in Shakespeare's plays. In *Henry IV, Hamlet* and *King Lear,* fathers try to impose their views on reluctant children with varying results.

- (III, V, 214) "Romeo is banished, ..." - Nurse is no better than Capulet in her view of marriage. She advises Juliet to forget Romeo and enter into a bigamous marriage with Paris. Juliet is amazed and, in a line that appears later in *King Lear,* says, "Speak'st thou from thy heart?" (227) Nurse, who had been Juliet's surrogate mother since birth, has deserted her at the moment she is most needed. Juliet, showing courage and determination beyond her years, breaks with Nurse (236).

- (IV, I, 50 - 67) Juliet has been transformed from the obedient child of Act I to the young woman who has been betrayed by her parents and Nurse, and is now prepared to end her life, if necessary, to avoid betraying her husband.

- (IV, II, 17) "Where I have ..." - In an attempt to calm any suspicion about her marriage, Juliet claims to repent her "disobedient opposition" to marrying Paris, and Capulet is so pleased that he moves the wedding up by a day (24). The change contributes to the subsequent tragedy, because the news that Juliet has "died" arrives in Mantua a day earlier, making it more likely that Romeo will hear of this before being reassured by Friar Laurence's letter. It's unclear why Shakespeare included this since, in the end, the letter isn't delivered at all. Perhaps it was done to shorten the time-span of the story and emphasize the sense of haste and impulsive action that characterize the actions of the lovers.

- (V, I, 24) "Is it e'en so?" - Romeo hears of Juliet's "death" and acts impulsively. He decides on suicide and asks Balthasar to hire horses to return to Verona. This haste ultimately leads to the tragedy, since Friar Laurence arrives too late to intervene. The accident that prevented Friar John from delivering the letter is the cause of this sad sequence of events. "Accidents make good incidents, but tragedy determined by them has no significance" (G1 312), and for this reason it's been argued that the play is not a tragedy. While there's merit in this argument, Romeo must take some responsibility for the outcome. His passion and his youth motivated the haste.

- (V, I, 80 - 83) "There is thy gold, ..." - Romeo's comments on the curse of gold – [gold is] "worse poison" - seem more appropriate for a social drama than for a love story. But the grim determination that he exhibits shows us a more mature character than the young man absorbed only with love earlier in the play.

- (V, II, 5) "Going to find ..." - Despite Friar Laurence's best efforts to bring about a happy outcome for the lovers and peace in Verona, fate takes charge. His letter to Romeo is not delivered.

- (V, III, 91 – 105) "O my love, my wife, ..." - Romeo's words to Juliet before he drinks the poison are a far cry from those of the love-sick boy who entered the play a few days earlier. Their poignancy is an indication both that he has matured and that he understands the harsh blows that life can deliver (G1 342). But he dies blaming fate - "inauspicious stars" (111) - for the tragic ending, contradicting Friar Laurence's earlier admonition (III, III, 118). And he still sees himself in the hero's role in the romantic myth that so pre-occupies him (106 – 119). "He measures success in love not as happiness but as achievement and worthiness. ... [He has proved] his constancy in love by dying for his beloved" (Bl19 85). Thus, if his character has been transformed over the course of the play, the transformation is partial.

- (V, III, 170) "This is thy sheath; ..." - "Juliet has so far outgrown Romeo by the end of the play that it seems entirely right that her final act of courage, a 'Roman' suicide, unlike his gentler poisoning, should linger in our minds' eyes". (ArRJ 61)

Romeo and Juliet is, in a number of ways, similar to *Antony and Cleopatra*, one of Shakespeare's last tragedies. Both are love stories that end with the double suicide of the lovers. In both, the female protagonists feign death, bringing about the death of their lovers. And finally, in both cases the suicides ennoble the lovers and make them immortal.

- (V, III, 305) "A glooming peace ..." - Shakespeare didn't want the play to finish on a catastrophic note, so he tacked on an ending in which the families make peace. The final line pays tribute to the fact that Juliet is really the star of the play. It tells us that Romeo was her possession.

Discussion

Scholars have debated whether *Romeo and Juliet* should be considered one of Shakespeare's tragedies. It clearly meets the most basic requirement for this category of plays: the protagonists are dead at the end. Some argue, however, that the play doesn't meet other requirements. Tragedies are supposed to teach us something about the conditions under which we live our lives, the rules that we're expected to obey, and the suffering that follows when those rules are broken. This is often referred to as the human condition. The protagonists of these plays are generally admirable, but imperfect. We recognize their flaws as human and generally share them in some degree. Hence, we identify with them and sympathize with them when they suffer.

In *Romeo and Juliet,* it's difficult to see the protagonists as flawed. Shakespeare goes out of his way to present them as young and innocent. They're passionate in their love, and they act impulsively and hastily as a result. One could argue that these characteristics play a role in the tragic outcome but, given their youth and the purity of their love, it's hard to claim these as flaws. Rather, one wishes that we all could share in such feelings.

The rule of behavior that the protagonists fail to obey is the right of parents to control the lives of their children. Clearly, some such rule is necessary in any society, but the question of how and when the rule should be applied is much more difficult to specify. At what age should a child be allowed to influence the direction of his or her life and in what choices is that influence appropriate? The complexity of this issue is what makes the situation interesting. In the play, Juliet is not quite fourteen years old and she's being forced into a marriage that she opposes. By modern standards this is akin to rape. She is too young and her wishes on so intimate an issue need to be considered. On the other hand, it might be argued that although the rule is harsh it promotes the greater good of the society, since parents generally, although not always, know what's best for their children.

Tragedies thrive in the interaction of the personal flaws and the rules. They raise a number of questions. Is the rule reasonable? How serious is the protagonist's flaw? To what extent does the tragic outcome follow from the action the protagonist takes that violates the rule? Is the suffering experienced by the protagonist proportional to the damage that action has caused? In the play we sympathize with the lovers and feel that Capulet's insistence that Juliet marry Paris is cruel and insensitive. But Juliet's marriage to Romeo is clearly an act of disobedience that violates an important social rule. Finally, the punishment of death is wildly out of proportion to the severity of that act.

The reason that the play's status as a tragedy has been questioned is that it deviates from an important requirement of such plays: the punishment doesn't follow from the disobedience. Romeo dies because Friar Laurence's letter isn't delivered, and Juliet dies because Friar Laurence is frightened by the watch and leaves her in the crypt with Romeo's dead body. Without these accidental events the play might well have ended happily, and we wouldn't have been able to conclude that disobedience brings with it punishment. If the tragic outcome is not related to the protagonist's action, the play teaches us nothing about the human condition. To carry the argument to its logical conclusion, if outcomes aren't connected to actions then they are randomly determined and nothing we do can have an impact on them. This is the premise of absurd theater, not Shakespeare's notion of tragedy.

One further point on the question of whether the play qualifies as a Shakespearean tragedy is worth noting. In the later tragedies, the protagonist comes to a new understanding of himself and the world and is transformed by his suffering. In *Romeo and Juliet,* we see the protagonists mature as they struggle to save their marriage, but there's no evidence that they come to any new understandings. As a result, it's reasonable to think of the play as the product of a playwright in an early stage of his career who is developing the structure of his more mature tragedies.

Chapter 5

RICHARD II

Background

Richard II is "regarded as one of the greatest of Shakespeare's history plays" (ArR 90). It is the first of a sequence of eight plays that Shakespeare wrote that recount English history starting with the reign of Richard II, who took the throne in 1377, and ending with the War of the Roses and the fall of Richard III in 1485. This was the end of the Plantagenet line of kings; the Tudor line was to follow.

The play describes a shattering event in the history of the English monarchy, the deposition of Richard II by his cousin Henry Bolingbroke. In the context of that event, it deals with the nature of the English monarchy and its relationship to Parliament. Some of Richard's contemporaries believed that an English monarch was anointed by God, literally God's agent on earth, and Parliament was subservient to the king. Richard was in this group. In their view, his deposition was not only unthinkable, since it was an act against God, but impossible, since God would defend the king He had placed on the throne. There were others, however, who wanted a more modern state, built on laws and a strong parliament, rather than on an anointed king. They saw "a more contractual relationship between ruler and people" (ArR 18), in which the king "derived his power from the consent of the governed and ... could be removed from office if he failed to redress grievances or abused his power" (ArR 19).

Bolingbroke's act raised two important questions. Is the deposition of a king ever justifiable? What is the role, if any, of Parliament in this situation? In the play, Parliament is convened to approve the change in leadership, displaying its rising power. Shakespeare's sympathies are unclear. He presents positive and negative aspects of both Richard and Bolingbroke in the play.

Richard II is a play about political struggle. It is referred to as a history play since it's based on the historical record. The purpose of a history play was largely moral: it talks about the implications of past events for good or ill. History plays were more than simply entertainments in Shakespeare's time. Many of those attending learned English history through the plays since books were not readily available and education was rudimentary. Unfortunately, the historical record was unreliable, and Shakespeare was writing about events that had happened 200 years earlier. Furthermore, he took liberties with the historical record for dramatic effect by manipulating the events and the personalities and motives of some of the characters to give them tragic weight. As a result, the history described in the history plays is not necessarily accurate. With that in mind, some relevant history beyond that provided in Chapter 1, follows.

Previous History (see Figure 1)

- Edward, Prince of Wales, the eldest son of King Edward III, predeceased his father, so Richard, the Prince's son and the King's grandson, became heir apparent. He took the throne as Richard II in 1377 at age 10, when his grandfather died. The country was ruled by a council of nobles and Richard gradually assumed the reins of power as he grew to maturity.

- Rivalries developed among the nobility in this power vacuum and, feeling threatened, Richard had several arrested, including his uncle, the Duke of Gloucester, who had perhaps conspired against him.
- Gloucester was murdered in prison, perhaps by Thomas Mowbray who was quite possibly acting on orders from Richard. The actual circumstances of his death are unclear.
- Henry Bolingbroke took up Gloucester's cause by attempting to bring Mowbray to justice. He was the son of John of Gaunt, the Duke of Lancaster, Richard's uncle and another of Edward III's sons. Bolingbroke and Mowbray became mortal enemies as a result.
- Richard banished both Bolingbroke and Mowbray, as described in the play. Although his reason for doing so was apparently to keep the peace, he might have had ulterior motives. For one thing, banishment enabled him to confiscate Bolingbroke's property for his own use. For another, he might have wanted to draw attention away from Gloucester's murder, a crime in which he might have played a role. This sets in motion the action of the play.

This history has been given two different spins over the years. One is sympathetic to Bolingbroke, the Lancastrian spin, and the other is sympathetic to Richard, the Yorkist spin. The Duke of York was Edward III fourth adult son and a rival to Lancaster. The Lancastrian spin portrays Richard as "a weak, incompetent and despotic king, extravagantly self-indulgent, deaf to wise counsel, dominated by corrupt and selfish favorites and altogether ruinous to his country ... [whereas Bolingbroke] ... was a justly popular and wronged nobleman, a strong and capable leader, the darling of fortune and destiny, the politically natural successor to Richard, a man who responded boldly to the needs of his time and the savior of the nation" (ArR 24). The Yorkist spin was that Richard was "more victim than villain – a generally devout and well-meaning monarch, misled into wrongful policies and exploited by false and self-seeking friends", while Bolingbroke was an "ambitious, unscrupulous, opportunistic and dissimulating politician" (ArR 24).

The murder of the Duke of Gloucester is the event "which sets up the chain reaction of violence and counterviolence ... that scourges England through half-a-dozen reigns" (Bl3 10) and precipitated the animosity between the Lancastrians and the Yorkists that ultimately led to the War of the Roses at the time of Henry VI. The chaos that followed the murder illustrates the famous line from *Julius Caesar* "the evil that men do lives after them".

One of the characteristics of Shakespeare's later tragedies, such as *Hamlet* and *King Lear,* is the transformation of the protagonist, who comes to a new understanding of himself and the world over the course of the play. We see the beginnings of this in Richard. We also see Shakespeare displaying the beauty of the English language. Shakespeare did not made Richard a great man; instead he made him a poet (VD 68). The play is filled with references to the significance of words, the centrality of the language in life and the importance of conversation.

The Play (line numbers from ArR)

- (I, I, 98 - 108) "Further I say ..." - The play opened (1) with Richard questioning his uncle, John of Gaunt, on the reason Gaunt's son, Bolingbroke, has requested an audience. Here,

Bolingbroke explains, accusing Mowbray of arranging the death of their uncle, the Duke of Gloucester. Since Mowbray was suspected of having acted for Richard, Bolingbroke's challenge is a veiled challenge to Richard himself. Bolingbroke has taken it as his role to avenge Gloucester. It's natural to assume that Gaunt, Gloucester's older brother, would take on this responsibility, but he is unwilling to do so, explaining later that only God can punish the perpetrator of the crime. He tries to dissuade Bolingbroke from fighting Mowbray (160), but Bolingbroke refuses to besmirch his honor by backing away from a fight. A rivalry between Gaunt and his son is hinted.

- (I, I, 173) "Rage must be withstood." - Richard demands that Mowbray and Bolingbroke retract their intention to defend their honor in this dispute over Gloucester's murder. His statement "Lions make leopards tame", has no effect and demonstrates his weakness: he is not a lion. Mowbray eloquently defends the chivalric case for honor (175 – 185). One of the issues addressed in the play is the transition from the old order of chivalry and a God appointed king, to a more cynical view of personal behavior and government.

  Richard responds with a sweeping assertion of royal power, "We were not born to sue, but to command", but he immediately backs down (196 - 201). He demonstrates his inability to control events that threaten his reign.

- (I, II, 1 - 41) "Alas, the part I had …" - Contrary to Bolingbroke's chivalric stance and despite the Duchess of Gloucester's appeal, Gaunt refuses to seek revenge for Gloucester's (Woodstock's) murder. The Duchess essentially accuses him of cowardice (25). In her view, Bolingbroke "has replaced – indeed displaced - his father as the true son of Edward III" (Bl3 91). Gaunt understands that Richard was involved in the murder (38) but he says that it might have been justified (if Gloucester had conspired against the king). Furthermore, Richard is "God's substitute" (37) and Gaunt "will never lift an angry arm against His minister" (40). He feels that it's God's job to deliver justice. As a result, although he's one of Richard's severest critics, Gaunt cannot condone deposition. His view of the monarchy is echoed by several of the characters, but it is "only one aspect of the play's complex political vision" (ArR 18). Shakespeare leaves the question of Richard's guilt unresolved.

- (I, III) The scene is constructed around a formal chivalric ceremony. This is the traditional culture within which Richard thrives and that will be challenged by unadorned political power.

- (I, III, 76) "And furbish new ..." - Bolingbroke's use of the word "furbish" implies that, in his view, Gaunt has let the Lancaster name be tarnished by not avenging his brother's death.

- (I, III, 123 - 138) "Draw near, ..." - Richard stops the list eloquently, but hypocritically. He claims that he wants to avoid bloodshed but, since he's implicated in Gloucester's murder, it's likely that he really wants to avoid further activity related to it by banishing both Bolingbroke and Mowbray. Goddard uses this speech to illustrate the adage "Rhetoric is the art of saying nothing finely" (Go 152).

- (I, III, 154 - 173) "A heavy sentence ..." - The heavier sentence pronounced against Mowbray might be Richard's way of preventing Mowbray from implicating him in Gloucester's murder and Mowbray's surprise might be Shakespeare's way of hinting that he was expecting a reward for doing Richard's will (ArR 49). Mowbray's concern about the suffering he will endure in exile is centered on the loss of the English language, that he loves, as does Shakespeare (VD 69). He speaks of it using a musical metaphor. The centrality of language is a theme in the play. Richard is more a poet than a king. The word "tongue" is used several times. Later, when Richard reduces the period of Bolingbroke's banishment by four years, Bolingbroke asserts, "How long a time lies in one little word" (213 - 215).

- (I, III, 226 - 246) "But not a minute, ..." - As God's anointed king, Richard tends to exaggerate the power of his position. As a reminder of his limitations, when Richard says that Gaunt has many years to live, Gaunt responds with "but not a minute, King, that thou canst give". Later Gaunt speaks of the difficult position that Richard put him in when he asked him to judge his own son. He feels guilty for having agreed to a harsh punishment (236). But other currents might underlie these words: Bolingbroke's desire to avenge Gloucester is a challenge to Richard and tarnishes his father.

- (I, III, 262) "Call it a travel that thou tak'st for pleasure." - Bolingbroke's reply to Gaunt's suggestion is abrupt. He will not "miscall it". He understands that one cannot live in an imagined world. This contrasts with Richard, who is lost in the symbolism of the throne. Gaunt goes on to say that it's possible to turn a bad situation into a good one simply by treating it as an opportunity (275 – 293). But Bolingbroke is unable to see it that way (294 – 303), famously saying "who can hold a fire in his hand by thinking on the frosty

Caucasus?" He is a realist, one of the qualities that makes him an able king. He departs with the patriotic words, "Where'er I wander, boast of this I can, Though banished, yet a true-born Englishman" (309).

- (I, IV, 11 – 52) "Farewell – And, for my heart ..." - Aumerle, a Yorkist and no friend of Bolingbroke's, wishes the word "farewell" carried the power to lengthen Bolingbroke's banishment. Richard describes in dismissive terms how Bolingbroke courts the support of the lower classes (24 – 36), implying the he is a politician and hints that he might have his eye on the throne. If this is a correct interpretation of Bolingbroke's behavior, it points to a new understanding of the monarchy, one which depends on the support of the governed rather than on divine right. Richard then outlines plans to raise money for his Irish war (45 – 52), an act that figures in his deposition.

- (I, IV, 59 - 64) "Now put it, ..." - Richard wishes Gaunt dead so he can confiscate his wealth to fund the Irish war. In so doing, however, he will disinherit Bolingbroke and arouse the anger of the nobility, since it threatens their land as well.

- (II, I, 5 - 30) "O, but they say ..." - Gaunt's poetry uses the metaphor of "harmony" in describing the effect of language. Words are music, and as such can be persuasive. York picks up Gaunt's metaphor, but goes on to condemn the "flatt'ring sounds" and "lascivious metres" of the words that Richard listens to (19). He says that Richard is beyond listening to wise counsel and that he pays attention to ideas or fads "so it be new" (25) – a comment on modern fashion as well. Shakespeare's greatness in no small measure rests on the general applicability of the insights he puts in the mouths of his characters. The bottom line is that language is powerful and can be used in many ways.

- (II, I, 31 – 66) "Methinks I am a prophet ..." - Gaunt predicts that Richard's excesses are ephemeral and will pass. He then launches into his famous patriotic speech praising England's underlying strengths (40). His words do not embrace Richard's belief in God's role in the monarchy. He invokes "a historically oriented nationalism ... a national pride in the virtues and achievements of an historical nation-state, its martial valor, its renown abroad and its strength and independence" (Bl3 18-19). The words were quoted dramatically by Churchill during World War II when England stood alone against Germany. That episode powerfully demonstrated the power of language. It's followed by Gaunt's lament about what England has become under Richard's rule (57 – 66). Together they form a "compelling vision of the past and a passionate denunciation of the present" (Sa 191). (Leasing refers to Richard having "sold, for ready cash, the right of collecting taxes to individuals who are not restrained in their rapacity by the central authority" (Bl3 113).)

- (II, I, 93 - 138) "Now He that made me ..." - Gaunt admonishes Richard for the way he has governed, surrounding himself with flatterers and farming out the powers of the crown to paying clients. He accuses him of Gloucester's murder (128).

- (II, I, 149) "His tongue is now a stringless instrument; ..." - Northumberland announces Gaunt's death with a phrase that essentially says that the difference between life and death is a question of whether one can speak, and the metaphor he uses relates language to music. Richard immediately seizes Gaunt's property (159 - 162).

- (II, I, 171 - 183) "I am the last ..." - York's description of the good prince, Richard's father, hovers "in the background of every scene" (Bl3 42) and serves as a reprimand to Richard's actions.

- (II, I, 189 – 208) "Seek you to seize ..." - York says that hereditary rights are as fundamental as the progress of time or the fact that one day follows another. He tries to occupy a middle ground in the growing antagonism between Bolingbroke and Richard, here warning Richard against further alienating Bolingbroke by taking his property. Furthermore, doing so is foolish since it alienates Richard's own base of support. Once Richard has taken Bolingbroke's inheritance, every noble family in England will say "Who's next?".

- (II, I, 159 - 261) "He hath not money ..." - "Richard's most criminal act, apart from destroying Gloucester and farming the realm, is the 'robbing of the banished' Bolingbroke ... [This violates the law of inheritance] on which the royal title itself depends" (ArR 22).

- (II, I, 277 - 295) "Then thus: I have from ..." - Northumberland reveals that Bolingbroke has raised an army in violation of his oath when he was banished. He's waiting to land until after Richard leaves for Ireland. Northumberland views this as an opportunity to restore England to its former glory, thus hinting that Bolingbroke plans to depose Richard, not just regain his inheritance.

- (II, II, 110 - 115) "Both are my kinsmen." - York is torn between his loyalty to Richard, his anointed king, and his sympathy for Bolingbroke. Both are relatives.

- (II, II, 136 - 138) "Thither will I with you, ..." - Bushy, reflecting the attitude of one who sees the king as wielding absolute power, calls the commons "hateful".

- (II, III, 6 – 20) "And yet your fair discourse ..." - Northumberland and Bolingbroke speak of the power of language to make the time pass quickly.

- (II, III, 87) "Grace me no grace, ..." - York mocks Bolingbroke's reference to him as "my gracious uncle", saying "grace me no grace, nor uncle me no uncle". He refers to Richard as "the anointed king" (96).

- (II, III, 113 - 136) "As I was banished, ... " - Bolingbroke makes the argument that he was banished when he was the Duke of Hereford, but now that Gaunt (his father) is dead, he is the Duke of Lancaster and hence the banishment no longer applies. Although a weak argument, he goes on to eloquently describe the injustice to which he's been subjected.

- (II, III, 141 - 161) "I have had feelings ..." - York opposes the rebels, but finally offers them the hospitality of his castle.

- (III, I, 8 - 15) "You have misled ..." - Bolingbroke's hypocrisy is apparent here. He speaks of Richard, a man he will soon depose and murder, as a "royal king, a happy gentleman in blood and lineaments". He accuses Bushy and Green of sabotaging Richard's marriage, but we see no evidence of a problem in Richard's marriage later in the play. And his later claim (III, III, 18) that he has returned to England simply to reclaim his heritage is also hypocritical, since he is already acting like a king in executing the two.

Bolingbroke and Richard are both hypocrites, and Shakespeare seems to be saying that this is essential for a leader. "Hypocrisy has been called the tribute that vice pays to virtue" (Bl3 116). A leader can't "get hung up on moral principles: the place for moral principles is in what we'd call now the PR job. The reputation of being virtuous or liberal or gracious is more important for the prince than the reality of these things" (Bl3 116). This is one of Shakespeare's points.

- (III, II, 4 - 26) "Needs must I like it well." - Richard overflows with emotional language on arriving back in England from Ireland. In contrast to Bolingbroke, who has summarily ordered the execution of Richard's allies and has gathered up an army, Richard relies on gentle words. He "weeps for joy" and compares his absence to a "long-parted mother with her child". He constantly draws attention to himself and has a penchant for self-dramatization. He's a poet, not a king. He calls upon nature to fight for him (spiders, toads, adders), but he's aware that his audience might think him foolish (23). Carlisle proposes that they rely on God to defend them (27). Richard agrees (36 - 62), "for heaven still guards the right" (62). Richard has put his trust in "the divinity that was thought to hedge kings" (ArR 1) and on the theoretical protections of divine right.

- (III, II, 83) "I had forgot myself." - Richard's reaction to his dire situation constantly changes. First, he's afraid, but when reminded that he's the king he speaks courageously: "am I not king?" and, "is not the King's name twenty thousand names?" Finally, he settles into resignation: "the worst is death, and Death will have its day" (103). "Richard, the man of words, postures, and ceremonial dignity, is defeated by Bolingbroke, the man of action and pragmatic realism" (ArR 3).

- (III, II, 144 – 177) "Of comfort no man speak!" - Richard dramatizes his predicament and luxuriates in self-pity and martyrdom with one of the finest passages in the play (144). His words, "Nothing we can call our own but death" (152) are a testament to the extent to which he has identified himself with the crown. And the dramatization continues with, "For God's sake let us sit upon the ground and tell sad stories of the death of kings" (155). This contrasts with the picture we got of Bolingbroke in the preceding scene: a man of action, decisive and efficient.

  Richard has come to the realization that the crown that he wears is "hollow" (160). It gives the appearance of strength and substance, but within sits death, giving the lie to the appearance. Richard mocks his reign as "a little scene, to monarchize, be feared and kill with looks, infusing him with self and vain conceit" (164) and the sense that he is "impregnable". He ends by renouncing the ceremony he had previously valued so highly, and he identifies with the common man: "For you have mistook me all this while, I live with bread like you, feel want, taste grief, need friends" (175). The fact that Richard has undergone a transformation is underlined by his use of pronouns.

Initially he refers to himself in the royal plurals "we" and "our" but later switches to "me" and "I".

Richard's transformation anticipates a similar transformation of Lear. Both men are kings who have lost their thrones and are facing a dire future. Both come to appreciate the fact that the honor and respect that they enjoyed in their position as king was associated with their office and not with their person. They recognize their bonds with the common man. But there is a big difference between the two monarchs. Lear not only recognizes the humanity he shares with all men but, in addition, he regrets the fact that as king he ignored the suffering and injustice that existed in his kingdom. There is nothing corresponding to this in Richard's words.

The play exposes a general opposition between competing value-systems. "Richard's essentially feudal world, a world of oaths and codes of honor, of titles and of fixed identities, of ritual solemnity and ceremonial beauty, puts heavy stress on the seriousness and potency of words. Bolingbroke, who challenges and overturns that world, brings to bear a more modern, [Machiavellian] and less comely understanding of how meaning is generated. Much of the play's pathos has to do with nostalgia for the break-up of traditional coherences and stabilities implied by the older and more beautiful unity of words and things … the divide between sign and essence that the usurpation opens up wrecks the … unity and married calm of states" (ArR 67).

- (III, II, 178 - 185) "My lord, wise men …" - Carlisle advises that Richard fight to the death: "And fight and die is death destroying Death". In response, Richard once again speaks courageously (188). But York's desertion (200) ends all hope.

- (III, III, 7) "It would beseem ..." - York's ambivalence to the rebellion is shown in his demand that Northumberland refer properly to Richard.

- (III, III, 18) "I know it, uncle, ..." - Bolingbroke claims he's not after the crown: his reference to not opposing heaven's will refers to the fact that Richard is an anointed king. But his determination to redress the wrongs against him is backed by steel and his willingness to use it even if "showers of blood" result (43). York once again speaks his ambivalence (68 - 71).

- (III, III, 72 - 90) "We are amazed, ..." - Northumberland is cast as the radical of the rebellion, unwilling to refer to Richard as king or bowing to him. Richard responds with a dignity and strength which we haven't seen up to this point. Our view of him constantly fluctuates. He is a man in conflict with himself. Having acknowledged his humanity in the previous scene, he here reverts to his view of himself as anointed and calls on God to defend him (77, 85). Shakespeare reminds us that "there is more in any man than may be cramped into a proposition of oral approbations or disapprobation" (Sa 176).

- (III, III, 95 - 100) "But ere the crown ..." - Richard movingly and accurately predicts the chaos of the War of the Roses using gentle images: "the flower of England's face", "maid-pale peace". Northumberland claims that Bolingbroke is only concerned with getting back his property (112) and Richard agrees to grant that (123). He blames his "tongue" for banishing Bolingbroke, an image that speaks of the power of language. He then dramatizes his grief (136 – 141).

- (III, III, 143 - 173) "What must the king do now?" - Richard assumes, correctly, that Bolingbroke has come to depose him, and he enumerates all that he will give up in the process. Self-pity is the dominant emotion. "Once he starts, Richard cannot stop, as in 'a little grave, A little, little grave, an obscure grave'" (Bl 260) and again when he talks of how he and Aumerle will dig their own graves with their tears (167). The performer is aware of his audience and ends with "I talk but idly, and you laugh at me" (171). He is triumphant in his tragedy. And, as in an earlier speech, he starts by referring to himself as "The king" and ends by referring to himself as "Richard". He never stops doing Bolingbroke's work for him: He is the first to use the word "depose" (144) and he essentially offers Bolingbroke the crown before Bolingbroke asks (197).

- (III, III, 177 - 183) "Down, down I come, ..." - Richard and Bolingbroke finally meet and Bolingbroke is in control. He requests that Richard come down to meet him where he waits in the "base court" instead of going to Richard at his superior location. Richard dramatizes his descent.

- (III, III, 196 - 209) "My gracious lord, ..." - Although Bolingbroke claims that he only wants his inheritance back, Richard is ready to give him the throne as well. Richard feels that he has no choice, that power has shifted, but he wants to give the appearance of being in charge. Similarly, Bolingbroke gives the appearance of fealty. He seems unable to admit (perhaps even to himself) the thirst for sovereignty that underlies his self-restraint. That Bolingbroke and Richard acknowledge the new power relationship is evident when Richard says, “Set on towards London, cousin” and Bolingbroke replies “Yea, my good lord”. The destination implies both Bolingbroke’s coronation and the Tower of London for Richard.

The question of whether Richard is deposed by Bolingbroke or willingly abdicates is central: the latter does not violate the hereditary order dictated by God. “Has Richard masochistically delivered up himself and his throne to a hypocritical enemy who would have seized power in any case? Or has Bolingbroke through luck, … a heroic temperament and skillful maneuvering simply placed himself in a position to have greatness thrust upon him? The scene leaves these equivocal questions unanswered. Shakespeare … contrives to promote ambiguous impressions of both antagonists throughout the drama and to manipulate audience responses in such a way as to keep approval and disapproval … in a more or less constant state of flux” (ArR 26).

- (III, IV, 29 - 39) “Go bind thou up …” - “If Shakespeare condemned Richard’s version of divine right, he had just as little use for Henry’s [Bolingbroke’s] doctrine of the strong man. Where that doctrine leads, the rest of the History Plays reveal” (Go 159). The question arises is there no other way? Shakespeare suggests something in this incidental scene. The garden is clearly a metaphor for England and the implication is that the conflict could have been avoided if Richard had cared for his country the way the gardener cares for his garden. Thus, a good gardener encourages the healthy growth of his garden instead of using the garden for his own benefit. The gardener’s words “All must be even in our government" (36) seem to intimate a hint of democracy. And it's significant that this wisdom is put in the mouth of a simple worker.

- (III, IV, 84 - 89) "Their fortunes both are weighed: ..." - The gardener introduces the metaphor of scales (that Richard will use later) to compare the fortunes of Richard and Bolingbroke. In this comparison, Richard is light, standing by "himself and some few vanities", and Bolingbroke is heavy, standing with "all the English peers".

- (IV, I, 1) "Call forth Bagot." - Bagot and Aumerle are the last surviving members of Richard's faction. Here Bolingbroke is trying to find out who killed Gloucester. Bagot accuses Aumerle of doing it and of opposing Bolingbroke (8 - 19).

- (IV, I, 108 - 150) "Great Duke of Lancaster, ..." - York announces that "plume-plucked Richard" has adopted Bolingbroke as heir. In doing so Richard is able to maintain the illusion that an anointed king hasn't been deposed and Bolingbroke is able to say that he mounts the throne "In God's name" (114). But Carlisle refuses to paper over what has happened, saying "God forbid" (115). He subscribes to the notion of an anointed king and bravely denounces the deposition. He speaks truth to power and predicts the bloodshed that will follow if an anointed king is deposed (137).

History shows Carlisle to have been correct: The War of the Roses ultimately engulfed England. His words get him arrested for treason. Bolingbroke agrees that there should be a public transfer of power to create the illusion that Richard has voluntarily abdicated. The play "can be seen to confirm the Machiavellian hypothesis of the origin of princely power in force and fraud" (Bl5 127). Carlisle and Gaunt are spokesmen for the values that are a part of the past that is being swept away by Bolingbroke.

- (IV, I, 155) "May it please you, lords, to grant the commons' suit?" - Northumberland asks his fellow peers that "the terms of Richard's abdication (including the charges against him) be publicly declared in Parliament" (ArR 392), thus demonstrating the power of Parliament to judge the king. In deference to Carlisle's demand (130) and to give an air of legitimacy to the transfer of power, Bolingbroke orders that Richard be present. "Shakespeare clouds the issue of whether Richard can be legally condemned by Parliament by having the King depose himself" (ArR 21), thus removing the matter from Parliament's hands.

- (IV, I, 163) "Alack, why am I sent for ..." - The scene, enacting the deposition of an anointed king, was considered so sensitive that it was "omitted in all editions published in Queen Elizabeth's lifetime" (ArR 392) (K 12). "To show how a king, by taking off his crown, became an ordinary mortal was something one could not permit" (K 357). Richard enters and immediately resorts to sarcasm, his only weapon. He dramatizes his plight by comparing himself to Christ (171). His "volatile stream of words" in this scene "partly conveys his narcissistic delight in the aesthetic pleasures of his own eloquence. ... But the play proves finally that power in the common-sense world lies less in words than in deeds" (ArR 69).

- (IV, I, 181 - 222) "Give me the crown." - Richard, living in a world of symbolism and imagination which tells him that he has been anointed by God, believes he cannot be deposed. In order to maintain that belief, he chooses to abdicate. As a dramatist and a poet who is constantly staging acts in which he plays a central role, he takes center stage and performs the abdication before Parliament. In the process, he forces Bolingbroke to the sidelines (VD 75). He demands that Bolingbroke take one side of the crown while he holds the other to physically demonstrate that Bolingbroke is seizing the crown while, at the same time, he's giving it away. He compares them to the buckets used to fetch water from a well, his full of tears, heavy and down low, and Bolingbroke's successful and up high (184 - 189). But this is a double-edged metaphor since Bolingbroke's empty bucket, "dancing in the air" can be taken to represent a person of no significance (Bl3 117) while Richard's tears have dramatic weight.

Bolingbroke wants to cut Richard short (190), but Richard continues saying that he is giving away his crown but he's keeping his grief (191), something that he revels in. Then he does a riff on his cares (195 – 199) and another on whether he's willing to resign (201 -204), in which he says, "I must nothing be". Richard so fully identifies himself with his crown that he feels that he will lose his entire identity when he gives it up. Lear says something similar. Finally, Richard enumerates all that he's giving away.

- (IV, I, 222 - 252) "No more but that you read …" - Northumberland is the pit bull who moves the deposition forward. Here he "unfurls that all-too-familiar document of the police-state – the prepared confession, drawn up to the specifications of the new regime, not by the accused, but by his accusers, that the souls of men may deem the prisoner worthily condemned, whatever the true facts of the case may be" (Sa 170). He wants Richard to openly confess and thus justify his deposition. Forcing Richard to confess has a political significance since if Richard is innocent of any wrongdoing, then Bolingbroke is guilty of usurping the throne.

By admitting guilt Richard is being forced to leave "a fantasy-world where he is spared the agonies of self-knowledge" (Sa 178). He movingly asks not to be humiliated in this way: "If thy offences were on record Would it not shame thee in so fair a troop to read a lecture of them?" (230) He argues that if all crimes are listed in such a list, the crime of deposition should be included on Northumberland's list. He forces them to take full responsibility for what they are doing by again comparing himself to Jesus and them to Pilate (239) saying, "water cannot wash away your sin". Then he condemns himself (244 - 252) for agreeing to give up the crown, thus abetting the deposition.

- (IV, I, 254 - 267) "No lord of thine ..." - Having given up the crown, Richard says he no longer has a name (259). He has so closely identified himself with his symbolic body that without the crown he feels he is nothing. He resembles Lear in this who says after he has given away the crown, "Does anyone here know me?". Richard asks that a mirror be brought (265) so that he can see who he is now that he has lost his "majesty" (267). Ironically, the royalty that is supposed to be a part of his symbolic body begins to emerge when the symbolic body has disappeared. Instead, it shows itself a part of his natural body (Bl3 122).

- (IV, I, 269) "Read o'er this paper ..." - Northumberland's concern that the commons must be satisfied is an indication of the shift from an absolute to a constitutional monarchy. And Bolingbroke's unwillingness to force Richard to agree that he has committed the crimes he has been asked to confess to can be viewed as either sympathy for Richard or a concern that when he takes the throne, he might similarly be subject to control by the commons.

- (IV, I, 276 - 302) "Give me that glass, ..." - Richard continues his performance with the mirror speech. The mirror "is the best symbol in the play for this Narcissus-King" (Go 157). He comments on the duality of human nature – the inner reality versus the external façade, "truth and vanity, face and mask" (Bl3 28). Richard's youthful façade, seen in the mirror, was a part of the artificiality of his life, one in which he was flattered into believing – like Lear – that he was more than human, and in this was abetted by his "followers in prosperity" (280), the sycophants who praised him. He now realizes his error and smashes the mirror, thus rejecting the façade. The blows that sorrow has struck (278) are a part of the inner reality that does not appear in the mirror.

  Bolingbroke's comment, "The shadow of your sorrow has destroyed the shadow of your face" (292), requires some interpretation. In one such, the first use of the word "shadow" implies that Richard's sorrow is unsubstantial, feigned. Hence, Bolingbroke says that Richard's grief is theatrical, and that theatricality is responsible for the destruction of the image – the second use of the word "shadow" - in the mirror (ArR 410).

  Richard now gleefully picks up the word "shadow" spoken by Bolingbroke: "Say that again ... Ha, let's see" (293). He searches for a way to use it in another riff whose subject is a thought similar to one expressed by Hamlet: "I have that within which passes show, These but the trappings and the suits of woe". His "external manners" are merely a shadow that hides the unseen grief of a "tortured soul" (298). "There lies the substance". The distinction between the inner and the outer self is a theme that runs through several of Shakespeare's plays. He thanks Bolingbroke for giving him the idea for this riff (299). Then he does a riff on Bolingbroke's reference to him as "fair cousin" (305) and on his use of the word "convey". He leaves the scene in triumph. Richard cares more about his poetry and his grief than his crown.

- (V, I, 26 – 34) "What, is my Richard …" - The Queen encourages Richard to go down with a fight.

- (V, I, 37 – 45) "Good sometimes queen, …" - Richard's farewell to his queen is not about her sorrow, but his. "The thought of his own death is delicious pleasure" (VD 77).

- (V, I, 55 – 69) "Northumberland, thou ladder …" - Richard calls Northumberland a "ladder" that the "mounting Bolingbroke" is using to ascend his throne and correctly forecasts Northumberland's treason against Bolingbroke when Bolingbroke is king. These lines are recalled in *Henry IV Part 2.* Northumberland casually accepts guilt for his role in the deposition, an open recognition on his part of the immorality of this exercise of political power.

- (V, II, 18 – 21) "Whilst he, from the one side …" - Once again, we see Bolingbroke polishing his public image.

- (V, II, 23 – 40) "As in a theater …" - One of the finest passages in the play.

- (V, II, 58) "My lord, 'tis nothing." - York discovers Aumerle's plot against Henry in the same way that Gloucester obtains the forged letter from Edmund in the later play, *King Lear*. There's hypocrisy in York's rage against Aumerle's treason, since York had committed treason against Richard. The episode demonstrates that one unlawful act spawns another.

- (V, III, 1) "Can no man tell me …" - Bolingbroke – now King Henry IV - speaks of his "unthrifty" son. The reference is to Prince Hal, the future King Henry V, and the subject of the next few plays of the *Henriad*.

- (V, IV, 1) "Didst thou not mark …" - Exton assumes the role of Henry's "friend" by deciding to murder Richard. Henry tries to avoid responsibility for the act by not explicitly ordering it. It is ironic that the play opened with Henry demanding justice for the murder of his uncle Gloucester and here it closes with him encouraging the same crime.

- (V, V, 1 - 49) "I have been studying …" - Richard's only soliloquy. He needs an audience for his drama, so he starts by creating a mental audience – "a generation of still breeding thoughts" all of them, like himself, discontented (8). And they are in conflict. For example, thoughts of heaven are mixed with those that warn of the difficulty of getting into heaven (12), thoughts of the possibility of wonderful things happening "die in their own pride" (18). Given his situation, thoughts of happiness (content = contentment) "flatter themselves" with the realization that others have suffered as he suffers (23). He alternates between imagining himself a king and a beggar (32) and, when a king, that he is "unkinged" by Bolingbroke (37). Underlying this is the sense that Richard now understands that the meaning of the title "king" has changed. Whereas formerly the meaning of "king" was Richard permanently on the throne by God's decree, now the meaning can change depending on worldly events. Richard ends this passage with the nihilistic statement that happiness can only be achieved in the grave (40).

He then hears music, and this gives him the idea for a riff on keeping time and its importance in both music and life. He ends with an admission that he governed badly: "I wasted time, and now doth Time waste me" (49). Richard is a changed man; he has learned through suffering. He's come to an understanding of his tragedy, but his regret seems more centered on his mismanagement of the government and the loss of the throne than on "what he has allowed himself to become" (Bl3 33).

- (V, V, 84 – 94) "So proud that Bolingbroke ..." - Richard compares himself to his horse Barbary, who didn't protest when Bolingbroke rode him. At first, he's angry at Barbary, but then asks the horse's forgiveness. They both have been "spurr'd, gall'd, and tir'd by jauncing Bolingbroke", and he has behaved "like an ass".

- (V, V, 108 – 112) "That hand shall burn in ..." - Richard reclaims his identity as king and refers to his two bodies: his "body mystical will rise to rejoin the divine source of its sacramental power, while his body natural will sink down and dissolve to earth" (ArR 44).

- (V, VI, 24 - 29) "Carlisle, this is your doom: ..." - Henry shows the noble side of his person. While acknowledging the fact that Carlisle has always been his enemy, he also recognizes that he is an honorable man and punishes him lightly. As usual, Shakespeare's characters are complex; they are human and don't fit easily into simple categories.

- (V, VI, 38) "They love not poison ..." - Henry is careful not to admit that he was the cause of Richard's death. He admits, however, that he's relieved that he's dead, but regrets that the murder brings slander on his head. He cynically punishes Exton for the murder that he implicitly ordered and compares his exile to Cain's after the murder of Abel. "It is ironic that a course of action which he had initiated as the avenger of Abel (I, I, 104) finds him at its conclusion the patron of Cain" (Sa 172). Henry regrets "that blood should sprinkle me to make me grow" (46), an admission that his rise to power went hand in hand with criminal acts. It's reasonable to extrapolate from this Shakespeare's view that "it was inevitable that [Bolingbroke] should shed [blood]", that blood and growth "are inseparably intertwined", and that this inevitability is tied to a sense "of moral misdirection which has hung about the figure of the successful rebel" (Sa 172). Henry later confesses his responsibility by speaking of a trip to the Holy Land "to wash this blood off from my guilty hand" (49).

Discussion

The 19th Century Shakespearean scholar William Hazlitt summarized his feelings about Richard with the following words: "We feel neither respect nor love for the deposed monarch; for he is as wanting in energy as in principle: but we pity him, for he pities himself. His heart is by no means hardened against himself, but bleeds afresh at every new stroke of mischance, and his sensibility, absorbed in his own person, and unused to misfortune, is not only tenderly alive to its own sufferings, but without the fortitude to bear them. He is, however, human in his distresses; for to feel pain, and sorrow, weakness, disappointment, remorse and anguish, is the lot of humanity, and we sympathize with him accordingly. The sufferings of the man make us forget that he ever was a king" (H 111).

Beyond Richard's personal tragedy, the play juxtaposes two flawed characters, Richard and Bolingbroke, and two different philosophies of government, one based on mystical notions rooted in the past and the other based on a more modern view that acknowledges the role that raw power must play in the political sphere and a more contractual relationship between the government and the governed. Bolingbroke was a realist as well as an opportunist, while Richard's world, although imagined, had kept order in the kingdom for centuries. Bolingbroke was a strong and decisive leader; Richard was weak. Both were corrupt. We are left with the question of whether Richard's corruption justifies Bolingbroke's aggression. And, overriding this issue of morality, we see the workings of the political world which dictated that a confrontation between the two would inevitably lead to deposition.

The play conveys the sense that the characters are caught in a grand, amoral mechanism that moves history forward. It is this mechanism that causes Bolingbroke to perform a deed of which he does not approve: "They love not poison that do poison need" (V, VI, 38). Changes to the institutions of government, for better or worse, come about through amoral actions. Bolingbroke is the whirlwind that inevitably rushes into

Richard's vacuum (Go 155). While on a personal level this involves an abdication of responsibility, it carries truth on a historical level. It is on this note that *Henry IV Part 1* starts.

Chapter 6

HENRY IV PART 1

Background

Mark Van Doren said, "no play of Shakespeare's is better than *Henry IV*" (VD 97). The poet W. H. Auden said, "It is difficult to imagine a historical play as good as *Henry IV* will ever again be written" (ArH1 1). Harold Bloom said that Hamlet and Falstaff "are the most intelligent of Shakespeare's persons" (Bl 271), and that Falstaff "speaks what is still the best and most vital prose in the English language" (Bl 275). William Hazlitt said of Falstaff that "this is perhaps the most substantial comic character that was ever invented" (H 117).

The play is a history play, the second in the *Henriad* tetralogy. It picks up the story of the English monarchy from the point where *Richard II* left off. As with Shakespeare's other history plays, the events described in the play are based on the historical record, but are not necessarily accurate. With that in mind, the following points describe the events leading up to the story presented in the play.

Previous History (see Figure 1)

- Bolingbroke, the son of John of Gaunt, forced Richard II to abdicate in 1399. Both Bolingbroke and Richard were grandchildren of Edward III, the previous monarch. The act has been explained in a variety of ways: a product of Bolingbroke's ambition, a repayment for an earlier wrong that Bolingbroke had suffered at Richard's hands, and the result of the fact that Richard was generally felt to be a weak king.

- Bolingbroke took the throne as Henry IV.
- The Percy family, including Worcester, his brother Northumberland and Northumberland's son Hotspur, sided with Bolingbroke in this action.
- Richard was childless, leaving some question as to who should legitimately follow him to the throne. Both Bolingbroke and Edmund Mortimer, another of Edward's descendants, had strong claims. Although Richard had named Mortimer his heir, Mortimer's claim was weak since his descent from Edward was not along a purely male line, whereas Bolingbroke's was.
- It is widely assumed that Bolingbroke played a role in Richard's subsequent murder.
- Mortimer, along with the Percy's, is one of the conspirators who opposes Henry (Bolingbroke) in *Henry IV Part 1*.

This is the background which caused Shakespeare to portray Henry as concerned about his hold on power and fearful that, having usurped the throne, and hence having trampled on the notion of divine right, he was vulnerable to the same treatment. "Henry's presence on the throne threatened the familiar notions that kings rule by divine sanction and that political disobedience is as much blasphemy as it is treason" (ArH1 25).

Henry rules over a nation whose borders are insecure at a time when his legitimacy as king is under attack. The same northern nobles that had helped Henry to the throne, including the Percys, are now joined by England's traditional Scottish enemies in opposing Henry in the north. In the west, there's a threat from Wales, led by Glendower in the play, which is made more ominous by the fact that Glendower's daughter has married Mortimer.

The two *Henry IV* plays center on Prince Harry, called familiarly Hal, Henry's eldest son. In both plays, Hal is the seemingly prodigal prince who must prove himself a worthy heir to his father. The plays weave together two threads: a historical thread based on, but not always adhering to, the real events of this period, and a comic thread centered on Falstaff, which is entirely fictional. There are four major characters: Henry IV, a pragmatic king whose hold on the crown is threatened, the rebel Henry Percy, also known as Hotspur (and not to be confused with his father Henry Percy, Earl of Northumberland), recklessly committed to his chivalric ideals, Falstaff with his outrageous, comic vitality, and finally Hal, who is the focus of these characters' attention.

The play can be viewed as Hal's coming of age story. Henry IV, Hotspur and Falstaff are all, in different ways, attractive to Hal, but each also represents something dangerous for his development as a future king. In some ways, the play resembles the traditional morality play common in Shakespeare's youth with Falstaff, in particular, and Hotspur and Henry IV to a lesser degree, corresponding to characters who tempt Hal. "The play … traces the process by which [Hal] takes for his own some qualities that each models for him, and rejects others" (ArH1 5).

A question that has been much debated by scholars is whether *Henry IV Part 1* and *Henry IV Part 2* should be viewed as two parts of one ten act play, or whether they stand independently as two complete plays. Many scholars now agree that *Part 2* was begun after *Part 1* had achieved its success, that Shakespeare had written *Part 1* to stand on its own, and that he later wrote *Part 2* to take advantage of the earlier play's popularity. (For a more complete discussion of this issue see the Background section of Chapter 7.)

The Play (line numbers from ArH1)

- (I, I, 1) Henry's first words speak of the instability of his reign. In an effort to unify the country and to relieve his guilt over the murder of Richard II, he had proposed a crusade to the Holy Land (19), a wise move "because killing Moslems is so meritorious an act that it wipes out all previous sins" (Bl3 114). But the news he gets of war in Wales (34) makes it impossible to move ahead with such a venture (47).

- (I, I, 77 - 89) "Yea, there thou mak'st me sad ..." - Henry praises Hotspur's devotion to honor and compares Hal to him unfavorably. Hotspur is one of the characters who will influence Hal's behavior as the play progresses. The sequence of monarchs who ascended the throne starting with Henry II and ending with Richard III were all members of the Plantagenet family (88). The Percys were not a part of this dynasty.

- (I, II, 1 - 77) "Now, Hal, what time ..." - Hal and Falstaff have an ambivalent relationship that is played out as a duel of wits. We see this when they first appear on stage. Falstaff is a thief and he fears that when Hal becomes king he might be punished. Many scholars characterize Falstaff as Hal's mentor, and he views Hal almost like his son, but it's not clear whether Hal reciprocates this view. They are clearly friends, but Hal's ultimate rejection of Falstaff in *Part 2* is anticipated in this early interaction.

Hal is on the attack. He questions why, given Falstaff's dissolute life, he has any need for knowing the time of day. Falstaff acknowledges the attack, then parries it. He refers to Hal as "thy grace" and then changes "grace" to "majesty" saying that Hal will not have grace – a word that means salvation (16). He then changes the intent of the word to mean a prayer before meals (19). Hal responds, using the word "roundly", meaning get to the point, but also referring to Falstaff's figure (21). Falstaff then reveals his hope that when Hal becomes king criminals will be treated as "squires of the night" (22), "Diana's foresters", "gentlemen of the shade", "minions of the moon", "men of good government" who are governed by the moon "under whose countenance we steal". In doing so he demonstrates his wit, the overabundance of imagery that flows from his mind, and the breadth of his intelligence. Hal responds by switching his stance: instead of challenging Falstaff's dissolute life he now includes himself in it – he speaks of the "fortune of *us* that are the moon's men" (30). He reveals the two sides of his life – riot and respectability – and we see that he can easily switch from one to the other. He then mentions the gallows and Falstaff quickly changes the subject (38) because he fears that when Hal ascends the throne, he might choose to punish him.

Falstaff then says that Hal has called the hostess "to a reckoning many times and oft" (46), without saying exactly what he means, although a sexual interpretation is reasonable. That moves the subject to the need to pay what one owes (49). This is one of the themes of the play. Hal has always paid Falstaff's bills at the tavern. But commercial reckoning is just a symbol for a more serious form of reckoning – that of paying the price for one's actions. Falstaff's and Hal's riotous behavior and Henry's usurpation of the throne all must be reckoned with and commercial allusions to this appear throughout the play.

Falstaff transitions from "here apparent" to "heir apparent" to introduce what's on his mind, which is the issue of the gallows (56). Falstaff is haunted by his mortality and he relates to Hal both as a friend and as a dependent. His request "do not hang a thief" is not a joke – it's a serious plea. Hal has protected him up to this point, but he wants reassurance that he won't have to forfeit his life in repayment for his actions when Hal becomes king. Both Hal and Falstaff will face a reckoning at some point. Then the conversation shifts from Falstaff being a judge to Falstaff misjudging Hal's meaning and from hanging a man to hanging around in court and from suits in court (lawsuits) to the right of the hangman to get the suits of the condemned. The wordplay ends with Falstaff calling Hal "a sweet young prince" (77).

- (I, II, 76 - 105) "Thou hast the most unsavoury ..." - Falstaff mocks piety. He'd like to buy a good name. The relationship between persons and titles is rooted in *Richard II*. Richard treated the title "king" as a part of his person, meaning that it could only apply to him since only he had been anointed by God. Bolingbroke proved otherwise: "king" applies to him because he had the power to depose Richard and because he has convinced those around him that he deserves that title. Falstaff here further debases the relationship between the title and the person by saying that titles can simply be bought.

The proverb Hal quotes (85) fits the situation: Hal's behavior deserved criticism and Falstaff ignored that criticism. But both Hal and Falstaff understand that the proverb also applies to Falstaff and that he might pay the price if he continues his shoddy behavior (although Hal, as a prince, can escape punishment). Hence, Falstaff is annoyed that Hal quotes Scriptures (86 - 94) and in an outrageous reversal, bemoans the fact that Hal has led him into evil ways. But he follows this by immediately agreeing to commit a new crime, with the explanation that he's simply "laboring in his vocation" (100). Hal introduces Poins with the remark "If men were to be saved by merit, what hole in hell were hot enough for him?" (103) The dialogue in this scene jumps quickly from one jibe to another. The two characters entertain one another with their wit. Falstaff leads the way, but Hal is a good student.

- (I, II, 109 – 116) "Good morrow, sweet Hal." - The image of reckoning appears once again: Falstaff sold his soul and "will give the devil his due".

- (I, II, 185 - 207) "I know you all, ..." – Hal's soliloquy reveals his strategy for ascending to power: he will enjoy immoral behavior now and when he ascends the throne, when he is "wanted", "he may be more wondered at by breaking through the foul and ugly mists of vapours that did seem to strangle him" (191). Hal exhibits a cynical and devious political nature. His time in the tavern world, which the king sees as subverting what should be the goal of ascending the throne as a strong and respected king, is revealed to be Hal's tactic for achieving that goal. It is a "carefully calculated intemperance designed to make his 'reformation' the more extraordinary and compelling" (ArH1 36). He says he will "pay the debt I never promised" (199), meaning that he did not choose the role of king. It's notable that he measures behavior as a credit or a debit that has a transactional, rather than a moral, quality.

The commercial image is related to the fact that Henry does not, and Hal will not, rule by divine right. They hold power by creating artificial identities and managing political capital that is paid and owed. They are counterfeits, a word that is used often in the play and represents another of its themes: a cynical attitude towards those in power. Hal's cynicism extends to his manipulation of Falstaff and this subverts the humanity of their relationship. The tavern world, which can be viewed as a humane alternative to the power-seeking world of the court, becomes merely a staging ground for power. Shakespeare mirrors the dual nature of Hal's personality by alternating tavern scenes with political-military scenes (Go 175).

- (I, III, 5) "I will from henceforth ..." - "To be oneself means to perform one's part in the scheme of power as opposed to one's natural disposition, [which is] what we would normally designate as the very core of the self. Indeed, it is by no means clear that such a thing as a natural disposition exists in the play as anything more than a theatrical fiction" (Bl5 139). The play promotes the Machiavellian view that power is not the result of divine right, but usurpation and assuming counterfeit personalities.

- (I, III, 30 - 64) "But I remember, ..." - Hotspur talks at great length and with great feeling of the aftermath of battle.

- (I, III, 77 - 112) "Why, yet he doth deny ..." - Hotspur and Henry disagree on the subject of ransoming Mortimer. Hotspur is in favor of this, since Mortimer is his brother-in-law. Henry refuses, since Mortimer has a reasonable claim to be Richard's successor. In support of his case, Hotspur's gives a poetic description of Mortimer's bravery in battle (98 - 112).

- (I, III, 159 – 180) "But shall it be that ..." - Hotspur regrets his family's support of Henry in Richard's usurpation. Richard is now "that sweet lovely rose" and Henry a thorn and a canker. Hotspur is troubled by Henry's illegitimate ascension to the crown (171); Worcester and Northumberland are not. He speaks of redeeming the family's banished honor – that is his main concern. Hotspur views honor in religious terms. It is a central motivating force for him, and battle is the way to achieve it.

- (I, III, 186 - 234) "Peace, cousin, say no more ..." - Hotspur is passionate but not practical. He talks a lot and Worcester and Northumberland try to quiet him (186, 198, 207, 214, 225, 233, 234, 254). He seeks situations involving danger and honor (194, 200 - 206) and he mocks Hal (228).

- (I, III, 240) "In Richard's time ..." - A theme of this play, and more importantly *Part 2,* is the role of memory in choosing an action. Here we see Hotspur unable to recall the name of the castle at which he and Bolingbroke met, but he recalls the exact words (250) that Bolingbroke had used to encourage the Percys to join his rebellion against Richard. The difference is that the latter is connected with Hotspur's anger at Bolingbroke and now justifies the rebellion against him. Memory is selective – we choose to remember those things that support the action we want to take.

- (I, III, 256) "Then once more ..." - The Percy's – Worcester, Northumberland, and Hotspur - are the king-makers, having helped to put Bolingbroke on the throne and now planning to replace him with Mortimer. Worcester's plot against Henry involves making peace with the Scots by returning those Scots held prisoner by Hotspur without demanding ransom, making peace with the Welch (Glendower), and making peace with the Archbishop, a member of the York side of the Plantagenet family. Mortimer, next in line for the throne, will be the nominal leader. Thus, a deeper divide develops between the York branch of the Plantagenet family and the Lancaster branch, and this ultimately leads to the War of the Roses.

- (I, III, 281 - 285) "The king will always ..." - Henry is deeply indebted to Worcester and Northumberland and Worcester worries that Henry will always fear that the Percy's aren't satisfied that he's treated them well enough in return, and that they will act against him as a result. The image "pay us home" describes a political act in commercial terms. In contrast to Hotspur (172), Worcester is apparently unconcerned with Henry's legitimacy or with restoring the Percy family's honor. He's concerned with practical issues: Henry will attack them to solidify his hold on the throne. They plot to unite with Glendower (Wales) (290) and Douglas (Scotland) (257) to bring Henry down.

- (II, II, 10 - 34) "I am accursed to rob ..." - Falstaff speaks of his love for Hal (17). He complains about his inability to move (12, 24, 34). This contrasts with Hotspur's imagery (I, III, 200) of flying to grasp honor.

- (II, II, 105) "Falstaff sweats to death and lards the lean earth as he walks along." – Hal's imagery is worth noting.

- (II, IV, 4) "With three or four loggerheads, amongst three of fourscore hogsheads." - The play is about Hal's education on his way to the throne and part of that is his exposure to all elements of society. Here he talks about befriending some members of the laboring class, and in the process sounding "the very bass string of humility". He boasts that he can "drink with any tinker in his own language" (18). What at first appears as fellowship between the top and bottom of society, however, has its practical dimension. He points out that "when I am king of England I shall command all the good lads of Eastcheap" (13). He realizes that he needs to know his subjects in order to rule them. So, counterfeiting is going on here as well.

  Later, he mocks the other end of the social spectrum. Of Hotspur, he says that "he kills me some six or seven dozen of Scots at breakfast, washes his hands and says to his wife 'Fie upon this quiet life! I want some work'" (100). Hal mocks Hotspur's narrow, martial, outlook, claiming that he has reduced life to "honor or death". Hal's view, on the other hand, spans the distance between the tavern and royal society. This broad exposure to life is exactly what Hotspur lacks.

- (II, IV, 152 - 271) "What's the matter?" - Falstaff's "outlandish exaggerations ... are not lies anyone is expected to believe, but evidence of the improvisatory genius that has long delighted his friends" (ArH1 45). 300 marks becomes 1000 pounds (153), two thieves become eleven (210), he evades defending his account of the robbery by refusing to be compelled to do so (229), he out-curses Hal (238), and then explains his cowardice by claiming that he recognized the prince and didn't want to fight with him

(255). The real issue here isn't Falstaff's cowardice, but the way he uses his wit to escape from a difficult situation.

- (II, IV, 387 - 425) "Peace, good pint-pot; ..." - Falstaff plays Henry IV with wit and charm. It is play "in its sweetest and purest sense, an exercise that heals and restores" (Bl 301). He uses the opportunity to defend himself, poignantly calling himself "A goodly portly man". When he speaks of his age as "some fifty, ... inclining to three score" there's the altogether human suggestion of embarrassment. And finally, in his reference to the relationship between a tree and the fruit that it bears, there's a hint of a "forlorn wish that he somehow could be a father to Hal" (Bl15 32). Perhaps he senses Hal's divided feelings towards him.

- (II, IV, 433 – 475) "Swearest thou, ungracious boy?" - In contrast, Hal plays Henry IV with anger and mockery. He isn't joking (435 – 447). Falstaff's words in his own defense are eloquent and exhibit a genial self-love (454 - 467). He's also not joking – he's pleading for Hal's love, particularly when he repeats the phrase "banish not him thy Harry's company". He refers to his openness to life when he says, "Banish plump Jack and banish all the world". Hal's response – "I do; I will" – although presumably in jest, is curt, prophetic, and consistent with his first soliloquy. Falstaff suspects that Hal isn't joking.

  The play within a play foreshadows the play within a play in *Hamlet*. In the latter case, the play's purpose is to catch the "conscience of the king"; in this case, it catches the conscience of the king-to-be (Bl5 15).

- (II, IV, 471) "Out, ye rogue!" - The arrival of the sheriff is significant since Falstaff's arrest could send him to the gallows. Hence, the fact that Falstaff wants to continue the performance demonstrates both his courage, since he's not going to run away, and the importance he places on making his case to Hal.

When Falstaff says, "never call a true piece of gold a counterfeit: Thou art essentially made without seeming so" (478), Falstaff acknowledges that although there are two Hal's - the Hal of the tavern and the Prince – he has an essential core. The sentence is difficult to interpret. Falstaff might mean that loyalty should be, or is, a part of that core and, if so, Hal should, or will, protect him from the sheriff (Bl15 38). (Some commentators think "made" might be a printing error and the word "mad" was intended. In that case the interpretation is that Hal is really the madcap prodigal, not the responsible prince who would turn him in (ArH1 235)).

Hal's answer, "and thou a natural coward without instinct", refers to Falstaff's claim that he instinctively recognized Hal's royalty during the robbery and hence couldn't fight him (263). Hal says that there is an essential Falstaff and he's a coward. He has made the logical premise, which Falstaff refers to as "your major", that because Falstaff fled during the robbery, he must be a coward. Falstaff denies that and the proof is that he is not fleeing from the sheriff: "let him enter" (483).

The play seems to be saying that in the political realm there's no such thing as essential; political power is built on creating counterfeits.

- (II, IV, 508) "It may be so." - Hal assures the sheriff that Falstaff is "answerable" for any crime he's committed. Repayment of money hints at other forms of repayment.

- (III, I, 12 – 67) "I cannot blame him." - Hotspur demonstrates his wit and humor in this verbal battle with Glendower. Shakespeare might be critical of Hotspur's passion for honor, but he gives him substance. He's not a character that is easily mocked. Shakespeare makes him a winning figure, while at the same time bringing out the limitations of his feudal virtues: his lack of tact and judgment, his boyish habit of leaping to conclusions, the noble but also comical way he's carried away by "imagination of some great exploit" (I, III, 198), his indignation at "this vile politician Bolingbroke" (Bl4 60). Van Doren says of him, "It is not ambition that goads him, or any ordinary pride; it is rather a sense of his own superb mettle, a feeling of his strength, a toxin that attacks him because his energy is excessive and finds no outlet in life as most men live it" (VD 102). His warm relationship with his wife shows in his unwillingness to tell her that he's going off to battle (II, III, 86), and in the sexual innuendos (223) and jokes he directs at her (249).

- (III, II, 4 - 63) "I know not whether …" - Henry speaks of Hal's riotous behavior as punishment for his own guilt. His criticism of Hal is concerned with the need to acquire and hold power, not with the morality of Hal's behavior. Henry's actions have demonstrated that power is dependent on strength and popular support rather than derived from divine sanction. He himself has weakened the legitimacy of hereditary succession. Hence, Hal's behavior puts his succession to the crown in jeopardy.

Henry admonishes Hal and describes the strategy he used in his ascent to the crown. Prior to ascending the throne Henry kept himself in the background so that "by being seldom seen I could not stir but, like a comet, I was wondered at" (46), "I stole all courtesy from heaven and dressed myself in such humility that I did pluck allegiance from men's hearts … thus did I keep my person fresh and new" (50).

His behavior contrasted with Richard's – "the skipping king" (60) – who "mingled his royalty with cap'ring fools" and by so doing diluted the respect necessary for maintaining power. Richard believed that he was anointed by God and that his power flowed from this relationship and was unshakable. Henry destroyed this connection and replaced it with one in which power depends on role playing and hypocrisy. Hal's strategy (I, II, 185 - 207) isn't very different from Henry's. Although Henry led a private life and Hal leads a riotous life, both are cynical and hide their true selves, demonstrating that "value can be produced by manipulating appearances – and must be produced that way when it isn't natural or intrinsic" (ArH1 67). It's this hypocrisy that's played on by references to the word "counterfeit". In contrast, Falstaff and Hotspur are what they appear to be.

- (III, II, 92) "I shall hereafter, …" - Hal says that he will "Be more myself", meaning that he will behave in accordance with his birth and position as opposed to his natural inclinations. Hence, he will be a counterfeit. This is a repeat of the king's statement (I, III, 5) and reinforces the Machiavellian idea that one's position in society is managed by creating artificial facades.

- (III, II, 147) "Percy is but my factor ..." - The word "factor" (broker) raises the commercial image. Hal will elevate himself to kingly stature by defeating Hotspur in battle and, as a result, getting credit for being able to defeat all those who Hotspur had previously defeated. The implication is that such stature is not intrinsic to his person.

- (III, III, 24 – 50) "Do thou amend thy face, ..." - Falstaff refers to the parable of Dives in the New Testament, in which a rich man goes to hell for refusing aid to a beggar. The parable comes up later in the play and is clearly on Falstaff's mind, perhaps because he senses that Hal might not protect him from the punishment he deserves. Falstaff's riff on Bardoll's nose moves from one metaphor to another: a lantern in a ship's poop, a *memento mori* (reminder of death), the Burning Bush, a will-o'-the wisp, fireworks, a torchlight procession, a bonfire, a fiery salamander. He overwhelms Bardoll with a torrent of imagery. And this all starts with a Biblical reference: the story of Lazarus, the beggar, who goes to heaven, and the rich man (Dives) who roasts in hell. Thus, Falstaff mocks the Bible.

- (III, III, 124) "What beast?" - Falstaff makes a joke out of the question of whether an otter is a fish or an animal. The sexual connotation (126) is clear, but not to the hostess, who carries the metaphor forward at her own expense (128).

- (III, III, 144) "Why, Hal, thou knowest ..." - Falstaff recognizes that Hal has two distinct personalities, one riotous and one responsible, something that Hal's soliloquy had made clear (I, II, 185) and that Falstaff had pointed out earlier (II, IV, 478). The play on the word counterfeit alludes to this theme of the play and raises the question, "What is real?"

(Go 175). The same ambiguity applies to Henry, the usurper and the responsible king.

- (III, III, 202 – 205) "The land is burning, ..." - Hal speaks patriotically; Falstaff wants his breakfast.

- (IV, I, 96 – 109) "All furnished, all in arms, ..." - Vernon gives a glorious description of Hal and his army marching to Shrewsbury.

- (IV, I, 133) "Die all; die merrily" - Hotspur has no regard for the lives of others in his pursuit of honor.

- (IV, II, 11 - 47) "If I be not ashamed ..." - Falstaff shows his contempt for the whole military enterprise by drafting established men who then buy out their service and substitute beggars – "slaves as ragged as Lazarus" (24), "cankers of a calm world" (29).

- (IV, II, 64 - 66) "Tut, tut, good enough to toss, ..." - Falstaff mocks war and honor when he says his recruits are "good enough to toss ... food for powder [cannon fodder]. They'll fill a pit [grave] as well as better. ... mortal men". The soldiers are there to be killed, and these will do it as well as any. So much for war and honor. Falstaff's disregard for the lives of his soldiers mirrors Hotspur's (IV, I, 133).

- (V, I, 97) "I am content that he ..." - Hal nobly proposes single combat with Hotspur to avoid total war, demonstrating his transformation from an irresponsible prince to a worthy successor to the throne. But Henry overrules him and offers pardon instead. The rebellion is doomed, however, by Northumberland's feigned sickness (IV, I, 16), Mortimer's preference to stay with his wife rather than fight (IV, IV, 22) and Glendower inability to gather his troops in time (IV, I, 125).

- (V, I, 121 – 140) "Hal, if thou see me ..." - The asymmetry of the relationship between Falstaff and Hal is evident. Falstaff is fearful of the coming battle and wants some reassurance, but Hal instead mocks him, saying only a colossus can "bestride" him. Then Falstaff poignantly remarks, "I would 'twere bedtime, Hal, and all well" and Hal cruelly responds, "thou owest God a death". (The pun here is the substitution of the word "death" for "debt" and the resulting reminder of the commercial theme.) Falstaff's wit is evident in his quick comeback to Hal's use of a commercial metaphor: "Tis not due yet" (127). He uses the metaphor to mock honor and his "catechism", as he calls it, contrasts sharply with Hotspur's view. The catechism is blasphemy in a society which worships honor.

- (V, II, 1) "O no, my nephew must not know, ..." - Worcester refuses to convey Henry's offer of pardon out of fear for his own safety. This comes immediately after Falstaff's catechism, showing that honor is no more respected at the court level than it is at the tavern level. Although he acts deceitfully, Worcester's fear is well founded, as demonstrated in *Part 2*. Recall that his brother, Northumberland, has abandoned the rebellion. Thus, one is duplicitous, the other a coward.

- (V, II, 51 - 68) "No, by my soul." - Vernon praises Hal's generosity.

- (V, II, 80) "I cannot read them now." - Hotspur has no time for engaging in life's normal activities, such as reading letters. He says their cause is just (87), each man should do his best (92), and speaks of the battle as an "adventure" (95).

- (V, III, 25) "The King hath many ..." - Henry arranges for counterfeits of himself to populate the field of battle to deflect attacks on his person. This is consistent with the facades that both he and Hal use in their run-up to power.

- (V, III, 54 - 62) "Ay Hal. 'Tis hot; ..." - Falstaff shows his contempt for war: He carries sack instead of a pistol. He disdains Blount's grinning honor: Blount is dead. "Give me life" is his motto. This stands in sharp contrast to Hotspur's cry: "Die all; die merrily" (IV, I, 133).

- (V, IV, 26 - 34) "What art thou, that counterfeit'st the person of a king?" - Douglas can't distinguish the real king from a counterfeit. His question can be taken on two levels: He is trying to find the real king on the battlefield and he also questions Henry's legitimacy on the throne. The implication is that in the political world there's no essential person. Royalty is only a role, and anyone can play it.

- (V, IV, 41) "It is the Prince of Wales ..." - Hal uses the commercial metaphor again, and redeems himself in the eyes of the king (47).

- (V, IV, 76 - 100) "O Harry, thou hast robbed me ..." - Hotspur is willing to accept his death more easily than the loss of the honors he has won (which are passed to Hal on his defeat in combat). He refers to life as "time's fool" (anticipating Macbeth's words, "life is but a poor player"), recognizing the ephemeral nature of both life and honor. Hal's epitaph for Hotspur speaks of him as a gentleman with a "great heart", but also disparages his "Ill-weav'd ambition". He talks of Hotspur's honor going with him to heaven and his disgraces "sleep with thee in the grave". This is the opposite of Marc Antony's assertion that the good that Caesar did will be buried in his grave.

Before Shrewsbury Hal hadn't said much about his own attitude towards honor, but in battle he acted bravely and honorably, he called Hotspur "valiant" before they fought (61) and he treated him respectfully after his death (95). His position on honor stands between that of Falstaff and Hotspur. If Falstaff "selfishly underestimates its value, Hotspur's devotion to it overestimates it. For Hotspur honor is an obsession that overwhelms any other consideration – even success" (ArH1 70).

- (V, IV, 101 - 109) "What, old acquaintance!" - Hal's epitaph for Falstaff is ambivalent. He regrets his death saying, "I could have better spared a better man". But he mocks him as well.

- (V, IV, 110 - 128) "Embowelled? If thou ..." - Falstaff gives a lesson on counterfeiting saying it is better to feign death in order to live than to die. He mocks honor saying, "the better part of valor is discretion", and speaks of the value of life. His lesson reminds us of the different kinds of counterfeiting exhibited in the play, including the counterfeit kings on the battlefield, but more importantly, the counterfeiting that Hal and Henry engage in to gain and hold power. In contrast, Falstaff and Hotspur are not counterfeits. But Falstaff's disdain for honor doesn't prevent him from wanting to take credit for Hotspur's death and thereby being elevated to a higher position (142).

- (V, IV, 137) "Thou are not what thou seem'st" - Hal's line emphasizes the counterfeiting that is central to the play. Falstaff's response, that he's not a "double man", rings true.

- (V, IV, 140) "There is Percy. If your father ..." - Falstaff attempts his most incredible stunt: He claims that he's killed Hotspur. Hal had said (70) that he would "take the budding honors" from Hotspur's crest for his own. But he doesn't follow through on this: he allows the credit for Hotspur's death to go to Falstaff and in the process discounts the honor that comes with this triumph. Both Hal and Hotspur (80) seem to have declared the death of honor as a motivating principle. Hal's behavior at Shrewsbury – his valor in fighting Hotspur and his courage in saving his father - demonstrates another side to his personality.

- (V, V, 25) "Then, brother John of Lancaster, ..." - Hal demonstrates a generous nature by granting Douglas his freedom without demanding ransom and allowing his brother to take credit for the act. This stands in contrast to Hotspur (I, I, 93), who was possessive of his hostage.

Discussion

Falstaff - Commentators have drawn from a long list of unpleasant words to describe Falstaff (Go 175): Glutton, drunkard, coward, liar, lecher, boaster, cheat, thief, rogue, ruffian, villain. George Bernard Shaw said he was a "besotted and disgusting old wretch". He is a fat, old, dissipated and lying knight. He's a man without a superego. "He cheats, he whores, and he eats and drinks to excess" (ArH2 54).

Despite all these negative qualities, however, Falstaff is one of Shakespeare's supreme creations. The explanation of this apparent contradiction is that he behaves "with such joyful abandon and defends himself with such shameless brio that he has acquired a stature beyond that of any other comic character in Shakespeare" (ArH2 54). In the words of William Hazlitt, "Falstaff's wit is an emanation of a fine constitution; an exuberance of good-humor and good-nature; an overflowing of his love of laughter and good-fellowship; a giving vent to his heart's ease, and over-contentment with himself and others" (H 117).

A. C. Bradley speaks of Falstaff as follows: "The bliss of freedom gained in humor is the essence of Falstaff. ... He will make truth appear absurd by solemn statements, which he utters with perfect gravity and which he expects nobody to believe; and honor, by demonstrating that it cannot set a leg; ... and law, by evading all the attacks of its highest representative ...; and patriotism, by filling his pockets with the bribes offered by competent soldiers who want to escape service ...; and duty, by showing how he labors in his vocation – of thieving; and courage, alike by mocking at his own capture of Coleville and gravely claiming to have killed Hotspur; and war, by offering the Prince his bottle of sack when he is asked for a sword; and religion, by amusing himself with remorse at odd times when he has nothing else to do ... These are the wonderful achievements which he performs, not with the sourness of a cynic, but with the gaiety of a boy. ... he offends none but the virtuous and denies that life is real or life is earnest, and delivers us from the oppression of such nightmares, and lifts us into the atmosphere of perfect freedom" (Bl 297).

But there's another side to Falstaff that has fascinated readers: Falstaff instructs us in how to live. He values freedom – "not a freedom in society, but from society" (Bl 276). He's "the representative of imaginative freedom, of a liberty set against time, death, and the state" (Bl 288). He embodies the triumph of imagination over facts (Go 183). He's the man without a superego. He teaches us to enjoy our being (Bl 293) as he enjoys his inventiveness. He pursues "life for the fun of it, rather than life for what you can get out of it" (Go 181).

Falstaff tells us that life has to be more than fulfilling responsibilities. "We all of us beat up upon ourselves; the sane and sacred Falstaff does not, and urges us to emulate him ... Many of us become machines for fulfilling responsibilities; Falstaff is the largest and best reproach we can find" (Bl 313).

Finally, with all his faults, and in contrast to Henry and Hal and the other members of the court, Falstaff is not a hypocrite. He is not a man who intentionally tries to deceive, he is not a man who is seeking power over others. "His humor is directed against everything moral and respectable. For these things impose limits and obligations and make us the subjects of the law and our station and its duties, and conscience and reputation, and other people's opinion, and all sorts of nuisances" (Bl 296). In this sense, he's an aged hippie with sack as a substitute for drugs. He's "a professional soldier long since turned against the nonsense of military glory and honor" (Bl 281). He sees no point in sacrificing his life to support the cause of either Hal or Henry, two equally selfish seekers of power.

Falstaff's presence on the stage forces us to address questions such as: Where does virtue lie? and What is important in life?

There's a negative side to all this. Falstaff is "a knight fallen on hard times, a down-at-heels aristocrat desperate to preserve a shred of dignity" (ArH2 44). He's a man "with a haunted horror of mortality and a desperate need to be loved" (ArH2 54). This leaves him vulnerable. He wants Hal's love. If this is withdrawn, he will be destroyed. All this makes him real, and we sympathize with him.

And he is vulnerable for one other reason. To Falstaff, "order is less important than freedom, patriotism is less valuable than fellowship, honor is less desirable than laughter" (ArH1 49). He has no interest in public values, which he sees as mere cant, masking self-interest as public good (ArH1 50). For these reasons, he must ultimately be rejected by the state since he represents a threat. Rule can't tolerate anarchy (ArH1 39).

Hotspur revels in honor, he is absurdly courageous, and he is "doom-eager" (Bl 308). But he's delightful in a headlong, spontaneous way. He is honest and has the unforced integrity of the great aristocrat and "he speaks the richest, freshest poetry of the play" (Bl4 59). "Shakespeare finds the values and personality of a Hotspur inappropriate for true management, stability, and safety in the world. There isn't enough in Hotspur that seeks life over death. He shows too much willfulness, too great a reluctance to adjust his spirit to the realities of existence" (Bl4 93). A major difference between Hotspur and Hal is that while Hotspur stays rigidly within one persona, Hal moves easily between the dissolute tavern world and the respectable world of the court.

Hal - The play is about the education of Hal. Henry, Falstaff and Hotspur all serve as models of behavior and draw him in different directions. Although Hotspur only interacts with Hal at the very end of the play, he has substantial indirect influence as the model of chivalry and honor. Henry represents responsibility and sobriety. Although he is an effective king and has good intentions, he's also a hypocrite. Falstaff, on the other hand, is the devil who tempts the Prince to riot, but he's "never a hypocrite, rarely ambivalent, and decidedly not a counterfeit" (Bl 277). One way of characterizing the influences of Falstaff and Henry on Hal is the opposition between imagination and authority, between freedom and force, between play and war (Go 186). Shakespeare asks the question "which is the better influence?"

"Hal is Falstaff's masterpiece: a student of genius who adopts his teacher's stance of freedom" (Bl 277). Falstaff teaches Hal "how to transcend the joyless and usurping father without rejecting him" (Bl 294). "Shakespeare gives us more than enough evidence to suggest that part of Hal is a colder hypocrite than even his father" (Bl 291). But despite his cynical side, when Hal ascended the throne he succeeded militarily and presided over a stable government. The play can be viewed as a morality play in which a madcap prince grows up into an ideal king.

King Henry IV usurped, and probably murdered, Richard II, the rightful king. Shakespeare presents him as an ambitious man who sought the throne, but whose motives were not entirely selfish. He recognized that Richard was unsuited to govern and, once having assumed the throne, attempted to govern well. But he was never able to clear his conscience of what he had done. Nowhere in the play do we see him at ease. This lends a sense of tragedy to the play to balance the comedy of the Falstaff plot.

Chapter 7

HENRY IV PART 2

Background

Henry IV Part 1 and *Henry IV Part 2* present a warts-and-all "national epic about England ranging from nobility to riff-raff, from battlefields to brothels, from the city to the countryside, and from high politics to low humor" (ArH2 26). *Part 2* continues the narrative begun in *Richard II* and *Part 1,* and involves many of the same characters.

In contrast to the other plays of the *Henriad*, however, *Part 2* contains relatively little history. Instead, it concentrates on issues that reside at opposite ends of the social spectrum. At the upper end, it dramatizes how the nobility gain and maintain political power. At the lower end, it presents a picture of a social scene which includes a wide range of marginalized characters, such as a tavern hostess and a whore, menials and hangers-on, and country justices and rag-tag recruits (ArH2 3). Finally, Falstaff, who dominated so much of *Part 1* with his humor, intelligence and free spirit, returns to enliven the story and challenge us and the characters on stage with his unique view of how life should to be lived.

Part 2 closely mimics *Part 1* in its form, but this only serves to call attention to their differences. "It is a play more somber in tone, more serious in content than *Part 1*" (Bl5 64). While *Part 1* balances the political scene with some characters whose actions are modelled on the chivalric ideal and some who are simply seeking power, chivalry doesn't play a role in *Part 2,* which centers on the latter group. Machiavelli, rather than King Arthur, serves as a guide. The play "offers policy in place of honour, substitutes disease and death for the celebration of living, and calls into question the official version of history to which *Part 1* more resolutely adheres" (ArH2 5). For example, the confrontation at Gaultree Forest, which is a focus of the play, was apparently a minor skirmish, but Shakespeare exaggerates it, perhaps to "illustrate an unsavoury political calculation alien to the chivalric ethos on display at Shrewsbury" (ArH2 16).

Henry IV Part 2 was written within a year after the completion of *Part 1.* Much scholarly attention has been paid to the question of whether Shakespeare originally set out to write two tightly connected plays or whether *Part 2* was conceived later, perhaps to take advantage of the success of *Part 1* (The following discussion is based on (ArH2 3 – 16)). Arguments can be made on both sides of this issue. Those who argue that *Part 1* was not conceived with *Part 2* in mind point to the fact that although the characters of *Part 1* reappear in *Part 2,* they are changed. For example, the Hostess, who was simply a tavern keeper In *Part 1,* now runs a brothel. Falstaff is older, sicker and hardly interacts with Hal. And Hal's reformation in *Part 1* is forgotten in *Part 2.* The promises he made to his father are forgotten as well, and he once again consorts with his low-born friends. His actions in *Part 2* don't seem to be consistent with a reformation. Had the two play been conceived together, these differences would probably been smoothed over. Finally, *Part 1* has a natural ending: Hal has emerged as a worthy heir to the throne and he and his father have been reconciled.

On the other hand, those who argue that the two parts must have been planned together point to the fact that *Part 2* is unimaginable without *Part 1*: the latter cannot be properly understood, and is rarely performed, without the former. For example, the impact of Hal's rejection of Falstaff at the end of *Part 2* depends on our understanding of the close relationship they exhibited in *Part 1*.

The Play (line numbers from (ArH2))

- (Induction, 1 – 15) The character Rumour sets the stage for much of what underlies the play, namely that we live in a world of, and make decisions based on, bad information. "Expectations, lies, misconstructions, and bad faith govern the play" (Bl5 107). Rumour speaks specifically of situations in which we are misled into believing that we are at peace when war is brewing, as well as situations in which we are misled into mobilizing for war when "some other grief" is at issue (9 – 14). (Rumour doesn't explain what that grief is.) The Tonkin Gulf incident and "fake news" are examples. Rumour's information is amplified by the mob, the "the blunt monster with uncounted heads" (19). Social media plays this role today.

- (I, I, 14) "The King is almost wounded …" - Northumberland is Rumour's first victim. He's told that his son, Hotspur, has killed Hal and that Henry is mortally wounded. This is particularly cruel since he shortly finds out (68) that Hal has killed Hotspur and Northumberland himself is arguably responsible for this since he didn't come to the rebel's aid as he had promised – he is said to have been "crafty-sick" (Induction, 37).

- (I, I, 136 – 160) "For this I shall have ..." - Northumberland calls on his fellow noblemen to continue the fight against Henry and one can speculate that his reasons for doing so include retribution for his son's death, the guilt that he feels knowing that he bears responsibility for it and a sense that only a fight to the death will relieve him of that guilt. The reference to Cain brings to mind the murder of one's close relative.

- (I, II, 1 – 22) "Sirrah, you giant, ..." - Shakespeare introduces Falstaff by showing that he's concerned about his health, that he's poor (Hal pays for his page) and that he's fat and witty (11).

- (I, II, 62) "He, my lord; but he hath ..." - Falstaff thrives on the reputation for valor that he (falsely) won at Shrewsbury. In this scene, he feels confident enough to mock the Lord Chief Justice, who's call to appear in court he had previously ignored (102). The two old men represent poles pulling Hal in opposite directions. The Lord Chief Justice, along with Hal's father, pull Hal towards lawful and responsible behavior, while Falstaff pulls him towards lawlessness and unrestrained freedom. Hal will ultimately have to choose between the two.

  Falstaff tries to divert the conversation from his court appearance and feigns a concern for the Justice's health and his age (98), and in the process Shakespeare again reminds us that sickness is a part of the background of the play (109). The Chief Justice counters by insinuating that Falstaff is hard of hearing (118), that he's poor and fat (141, 144), and that he's old (158). He also accuses him of misleading the Prince (145) – an accusation that is at the heart of the play. Falstaff parries each attack by saying that he excels in virtue, intelligence and wit and nothing else is important and ends with "You that are old consider not the capacities of us that are young" (174). The Justice counters by enumerating all the ways in which age has diminished Falstaff (181). Falstaff admits to only being old in judgment and understanding – two characteristics that are attributed to age.

Falstaff's refusal to succumb to the depredations of aging is a triumph of the life force and has a heroic dimension. The frequent references to age and disease (230) in *Part 2* distinguish it from frequent references to revelry in *Part 1*.

- (I, II, 243) "A pox on this gout, …" - Falstaff will claim his limp is the result of a war injury rather than gout in order to justify (or perhaps enlarge) his military pension (ArH2 57).

- (I, III) The scene shows the uncertainty in the rebel ranks about whether they should engage the King's forces in battle. Mowbray (son of the exiled Mowbray in *Richard II*) says he needs more information (6) in order to make a decision. Hastings leans towards fighting, particularly since Northumberland will be coming (13). Bardolph (no relation to Falstaff's friend) isn't so sure and doesn't want to count on Northumberland (17, 20). Hastings wants to gamble, but Bardolph makes a rational argument that action must be based on a realistic view of the possible outcomes (41 – 62). The Archbishop supports Hastings and urges action (85 - 108). He deplores the fickleness of the multitude whose support cannot be relied on. The play centers around various forms of betrayal by those in power and the imagery is, again, of sickness (99). The nobles "take stock of their experience to make possible wise action and rational planning. However, they often find the most soberly laid plans have only the status of wishes. ... Prudence, which for the rebels means heeding the disastrous example of Hotspur's defeat, only leads to their own" destruction (Bl5 50). The scene illustrates the lack of certainty in human affairs and reinforces Rumour's earlier warning about the uncertainty of information.

- (II, I, 13 - 17) "Alas the day, take heed ..." - Mistress Quickly's dialogue throughout this scene is laced with malapropisms and double entendres. For example, "He stabbed me in mine own house" can be given both a literal and a sexual interpretation, and she says honey-suckle and honey-seed (55) when she means homicidal and homicide. "Her comic attempt to use a vocabulary beyond her [educational level] betrays her bourgeois social aspirations, just as her bawdy puns betray her profession as a brothel-keeper", something she's trying to disavow (ArH2 71, 74).

- (II, II, 45) "But I tell thee, my heart bleeds ..." - Hal is concerned about his father's health. The line speaks positively of his relationship with the king and prepares us for the king's death later in the play.

- (II, II, 104) "I do allow this wen ..." - Hal compares Falstaff to his dog and says that he "allows" him to be in his company, denigrating their relationship.

- (II, III) The point of the scene seems to be to highlight the death of chivalry and honor. Thus, Lady Percy says that Northumberland broke his word (10) when he didn't show up at Shrewsbury to support his son, Hotspur, who was killed as a result. And then she speaks of Hotspur as "the glass wherein the noble youth did dress themselves" (21). Northumberland tries to minimize his culpability in abandoning his son by referring to it as "ancient oversights" (47). His daughter-in-law and wife convince him not to support the Archbishop but instead to flee to Scotland, the opposite of what Hotspur would have done. Shakespeare paints Northumberland, as well as his brother Worcester, as devious characters and, more generally, displays the cynicism of those in power.

- (II, IV, 46) "We catch of you." - The reference is to sexually transmitted diseases and accents the sense of disease that pervades the play. The following exchange (50 – 54) can be interpreted in both a military or sexual sense.

- (II, IV, 114) "I will discharge upon her, ..." - Shakespeare has replaced Hotspur with Pistol, both of whom have built up a reputation around fighting. But while Hotspur is an exemplar of chivalry and a genuine warrior, Pistol is a decadent character, referred to as a "swaggerer", who talks a good game but shows no real abilities in battle. Here he shares a sexual joke with Falstaff. Falstaff has no difficulty besting him in a duel (204) and Bardolph has no difficulty later in ejecting him from the tavern (208). By replacing Hotspur with Pistol, Shakespeare emphasizes the decline of chivalry and the rise of political manipulation, and sets a darker shading on the mood of *Part 2* in contrast to *Part 1*.

- (II, IV, 217 - 236) "Ah, you sweet little rogue ..." - Doll is presented as a sympathetic character: she claims that she loves Falstaff and, in view of his age, says that he should give up fighting (233). Falstaff's response expresses his fear of death (236) and we get the sense that his spirit is finally running down

- (II, IV, 239) "A good shallow young fellow." - Falstaff insults Hal and Poins without realizing that they're listening. Poins' comment on old age is cutting: desire outlives performance (263).

- (II, IV, 246 – 267) "Because their legs ..." - Falstaff's answer to Doll's question demonstrates his quick wit and the depth of his imagination.

- (II, IV, 271) "Thou dost give me flattering busses." - Falstaff complains that Doll's kisses are "flattering busses", an indication that he is no longer sexually attractive. He then says, "I am old, I am old", a fear and sadness that underlies the joy in his life.

- (II, IV, 315) "I shall drive you ..." - Hal charges Falstaff with abusing him. Falstaff defends himself by saying that he didn't know Hal was listening and, using an imaginative lie, he claims he only abused him to "wicked" people (323) and hence he was a "careful friend" (325). He repeats "no abuse" with real fear that he has angered Hal.

This scene corresponds to the robbery scene in *Part 1*, but the mood there was happy. Again, we see a change that lends a more somber feeling to *Part 2* as compared to *Part 1*. In this case, the scene illustrates the complexity of Falstaff's relationship with Hal, which has less of the easy camaraderie than it did in *Part 1*. He needs Hal's protection and recognizes the vulnerability of his position. Falstaff justifies his claim that the Hostess is among the wicked by saying that she suffers flesh to be eaten in her house (348) –

in other words that she runs a whore house – but the Hostess takes this literally and thinks that he's accusing her of selling meat at Lent. Line (351) has a slang interpretation in which she admits Falstaff's charge (ArH2 279).

- (II, IV, 379) "Farewell, hostess; farewell Doll." - Falstaff parodies a thought that will appear later: the notion that suffering is the price of leadership, with the subtext that leaders are entitled to their wealth and power. "The undeserver may sleep when the man of action is called upon" (Bl5 146). Mistress Quickly shows honest emotion in wishing Falstaff well.

- (III, I, 4 – 31) "How many thousand ..." - In a soliloquy that picks up on Falstaff's joking words about the price of leadership, the king, a troubled, weary man, shares his thoughts about sleep in a more serious tone. In the process, Shakespeare asks us to understand the costs of power. "This suffering ennobles, if it does not exactly cleanse, the lies and betrayals upon which this position depends" (Bl5 146). Both King Henry and King Lear refer to their impoverished subjects. Henry's reference is self-serving – he envies their ability to sleep despite their suffering. Lear, on the other hand, expresses his remorse that he hasn't done more to relieve their suffering. Lear is undergoing a transformation, while Henry is not.

- (III, I, 38 – 44) "Then you perceive ..." - Henry and Warwick use the metaphor of sickness to describe England's current troubles. This metaphor is repeated throughout the play, lending it a somber quality.

- (III, I, 45 – 78) "O God, that one might read ..." - Henry is concerned with the past because he is unable to overcome the guilt he feels for deposing Richard. He wants to understand why things have happened. He talks of change being brought about by forces that man can't contend with - the relentless passage of time, the overwhelming power of nature and the random impact of chance. He compares this with the "inconstancy and fickleness of relationships in the political arena" (Bl5 51). The implication is that these too are beyond control. Given this situation, man should be entitled to some relief from feelings of guilt for his actions, and it would not be surprising if the "happiest youth, viewing his progress through [life]... would shut the book and sit him down and die" (54).

Henry is troubled by the fact that Richard's prophesy, that Northumberland would betray him (67) as he had betrayed Richard (although, in fact, he was not present in that scene (*Richard II* (V, I)), has come true. This implies that he believes that there are supernatural forces at work in shaping history. Prophecy in particular is worrisome since it "puts a moral meaning into a reading of history" (Bl5 51), in contrast to the view which stresses chance and the arbitrariness of change. A world governed by prophesy is one in which sin and responsibility play a role, as well as crime and punishment, a view that Henry wishes to avoid, while "fate with its message of alteration relieves man of his moral burden. The question is, which kind of necessity rules our lives" (Bl5 51)?

Henry tellingly misquotes Richard's reference to him at the time of his deposition as "my cousin Bolingbroke" (71), when Richard had actually said "the mounting Bolingbroke" (*Richard II*, (V, I, 56)). The latter is an accusation of predatory ambition, which Henry has selectively forgotten. Henry denies that he intended to depose Richard, saying that he and greatness "were compelled to kiss" (72 - 74), a view that relieves him of his moral burden by appealing to the past as a force in controlling events in the present. Henry's version of the events leading up to his coronation conflicts with that of the rebels who believe that he sought power and gained their support using promises that have not been fulfilled. Hotspur had referred to him as "this forgetful man" (*Henry IV Part 1,* (I, III, 160)).

Warwick has a rationalist take on the subject. "Prophesy is ... no more than correct forecasting based on lived and understood experience" (Bl5 51). In this view, the future is often an outgrowth of the past - "times deceased" (81) - which can't be avoided and hence can be forecast. Henry likes this explanation since it avoids the issue of sin and retribution. It conforms with his view that the deposition couldn't be avoided and asks, "Are these things then necessities?" (92)

Decisions are based both on memory of the past and an accurate picture of the present. Not only do the characters have different recollections of the past, but they are also ignorance of their present situation. Henry incorrectly estimates the size of the rebel's army at 50,000 (96), while a later estimate is 30,000 (IV, I, 22). But the rebels earlier had put their number at 25,000 (I, III, 11).

- (III, II, 1) "Come on, come on, come on; ..." - "The back-biting worlds of court and tavern yield to a world of ... good fellowship" (ArH2 79) in the countryside, as the play broadens its view of English society. Shallow's use of repetition hints at is age. Silence seems to regret his obligation to pay the tuition for his son at Oxford (12) – a problem that persists to this day. Shallow talks of his wild days (15) when he was a young man. It's unclear whether this memory is true or simply the imaginings of an elderly man trying to create an exciting past. The gentle tone of the conversation contrasts sharply with court and tavern dialogue. The conversation turns to mortality (34) which, along with disease, lends a somber mood to the play. Without losing a beat, Shallow talks of the price of cattle (38). "The delicate humor and pathos with which an old man's recognition of mortality is poised against his undimmed will to live are unmatched in Shakespeare's canon" (ArH2 81).

- (III, II, 153) "You may; but if he had ..." - Feeble's interrogation begins on a note of sexual innuendo. Although an unlikely candidate, he shows himself to be one of the few characters in the play with any integrity. He doesn't try to bribe his way out of service but instead says, "We owe God a death" (236) (Hal had said the same thing to Falstaff (*Henry IV Part 1* (V, I, 126))) and agrees to serve.

- (III, II, 214) "We have heard the chimes at midnight." - Falstaff expresses nostalgia for his youth in this famous line.

- (III, II, 244) "Sir, a word with you." - Falstaff's irresponsible behavior isn't without real costs. For example, he abuses the king's recruitment process for his own benefit: He takes bribes to spare men from military service, and he recruits men (*e.g.*, Wart (144)) who he knows to be unable to fight, hence sending them to their deaths.

- (III, II, 301) "Lord, Lord, how subject we old men are to the vice of lying!" - Falstaff speaks of the false information which gets transmitted from one person to another due to lies and a failure of memory. This is a theme of the play and reiterates Rumour's speech in the induction. Falstaff tells us that he intends to extract money from Shallow, showing a harder edge than he had in *Part 1*.

- (IV, I, 54 - 58) "Briefly, to this end: ..." - The Archbishop says that the country is diseased, and the purpose of the rebellion is to "purge the'obstructions which begin to stop our very veins of life". He takes a balanced approach to decision-making involving both a careful evaluation of "the wrongs our arms may do" and "what wrongs we suffer" (68) and an acceptance of the fact that man is dragged along by the necessity of the times (70 – 72). The former involves accepting responsibility for actions taken while the latter is a fatalistic view that allows one to deny responsibility. He argues for war.

- (IV, I, 94 – 129) "My brother general, the commonwealth." - Although the rebels claim that they are confronting the King to heal the state, personal motives are hinted at. The Archbishop may have revenge in mind for the execution of his brother by Bolingbroke (94 – 96). Westmoreland argues that Mowbray has no cause to rebel against Henry because Henry had restored his father's lands to him (110), but Mowbray doesn't see it that way, saying that there was nothing for Henry to restore since the lands were rightfully his. Furthermore, his father's honor had never been stained by Richard. Richard had had no choice but to banish his father because of Bolingbroke's (Henry's) charge that he had murdered Gloucester (113 – 116). Mowbray recalls the scene in *Richard II* in which Richard called off the list between Bollingbroke and his father. He thus intimates that his animus towards Henry is based on the fact that his father had been unable to settle with Henry over Henry's charge that his father had killed Gloucester. Thus, cynical motives are hidden beneath claims that the rebellion is justified for the general good.

- (IV, I, 185) "Fear you not that: ..." - Once again, Hastings is the eternal optimist (I, III, 13). He thinks they should engage in peace talks with the government's forces. Mowbray is not so sure (189 - 196): the king will always be suspicious of them. His position is similar to that of Worcester in *Part 1* (*Henry IV Part 1* (I, III, 281)). He uses the metaphor of corn in the wind and this is picked up in the Archbishop's reply (198 – 210). The Archbishop now agrees with Hastings and says that they should accept the peace offering.

- (IV, I, 232 - 258) "My Lord of York, ..." - Prince John upbraids the Archbishop for using his pulpit to support a political cause and hence implying the God has taken his side in the dispute. This is a technique that has been used through the ages. The cynicism of those in power is a major theme of the play.

- (IV, I, 261) "The time misordered doth, ..." - The Archbishop speaks of man's inability to resist the force of the times and this is consistent with both Warwick's (III, I, 81) and Hastings' prediction of the future (272), which implies that there's a logic that constrains the way history unfolds. Prince John disagrees, saying that Hastings is too shallow "to sound the bottom of the after-times" (278). His point, and perhaps Shakespeare's point, is that we live in a world in which misinformation and faulty reasoning make the outcome of the actions we take difficult to anticipate.

- (IV, I, 334) "Good tidings, my Lord Hastings, ..." - Machiavelli triumphs over chivalry in this scene. Prince John and the rebels agree to a resolution of the rebel's grievances, but once the rebels dismiss their forces they are arrested. John says he didn't break his word because he promised redress of the grievances, but not safety for the leaders of the rebellion, a narrow technicality and a clear violation of the spirit of the agreement. John is "guilty of the most despicable piece of treachery recorded anywhere in these plays" (Go1 191) and he compounds his guilt by attributing this "triumph" to God ((349). Peace has been ignobly achieved; "no one's hands are clean; no one's motives are honorable" (ArH2 106). There are different accounts of the actual events at Gaultree. What is clear is that a battle was not fought and the rebel leaders were executed. Shakespeare has chosen to dramatize the account that emphasizes the duplicity of the King's forces and, along with Northumberland's duplicity, shows the lack of honor on both sides. "The founding of the modern state, like the founding of the modern prince, is shown to be based on acts of calculation, intimidation and deceit" (Bl5 144).

- (IV, II, 84 - 115) "I would you had the wit; ..." - Falstaff powerfully expresses his distaste for Prince John by saying that no one can make him laugh. He goes on to extol the effects of wine, which enhance one's wit and courage.

- (IV, III, 103 - 110) "And wherefore should ..." - Henry bemoans the fact that something bad always accompanies something good.

- (IV, III, 152) "Why doth the crown lie ..." - The troubled relationship between the king and Hal is evident in their interaction over the crown. Hal first comments on the fact that the crown disturbs the king's sleep and compares this with the ease with which a peasant sleeps wearing a simple nightcap (157). The thought is similar to that expressed by the king earlier (III, I, 4). Hal shows little emotion at the thought that his father has died. He places the crown on his head (174), an action that has Oedipal overtones. One is left to "wonder why [Hal], on the discovery of his father's death, did not instantly recall his brother and the nobles who had just gone out" (Go 192).

Hal speaks of his determination to preserve "this lineal honour" (177) of receiving the crown. His determination is evidence that his desire for power matches that of his father and that he's no longer identifying with Falstaff. The reference to "lineal" acknowledges the impact of the usurpation on the legitimacy of Henry's reign.

On waking, and with Hal out of the room, the king speaks of the ingratitude of children using timeless words (195 – 208). In an attempt to defend Hal, Warwick reports that he found him in tears (212), but when Hal returns the king delivers a scalding denunciation, accusing Hal of wishing him dead (222) and of not loving him (234), and expressing his disgust of his son. His speech if full of self-pity and he projects guilt on Hal. But he probably hopes for a reconciliation.

In apologizing for his behavior, Hal claims that he berated the crown for having caused his father's death (288). But this is not what he had said, which was that it prevented his father from sleeping. Hal expresses a love for his father that was not a part of his first speech. This "is not fabricated; we know he has been weeping" (Bl5 55). Yet the feeling of love has been incorporated into his memory "by considerations we can only guess at – regret, tact, manners, shame, calculation. ... The scene leads us away from the simple opposition between the truth and a lie, and towards involvement in the maze of Hal's intention" (Bl5 55). Was he truly angry at the crown or did he take it with pride? "To this riddle there is no clear answer" (Bl5 55). Hal's recollection of what had happened is less a record of facts than a subjective, passionate justification of his action, just as the king's recollection of his role in Richard's deposition was justification of that action. The scene ends with a reconciliation between father and son in which the king speaks of his guilt in usurping Richard and his precarious hold on the throne (312).

- (IV, III, 338) "I cut them off, ..." - Henry exhibits his Machiavellian mindset when he says that he had planned to lead a crusade to the Holy Land as a means of occupying potential rivals and advises Hal similarly "to busy giddy minds with foreign quarrels". And he ends by saying "How I came by the crown, O God forgive", airing his guilt and contradicting what he had said to Warwick and others that he had had no intention of taking the crown from Richard, but that it was forced on him to maintain order (III, I, 72). The contradiction between his guilt and his cynical advice to lead a Holy Land Crusade doesn't seem to bother him. Hal's response is that "You won it, wore it, kept it, gave it to me; then plain and right must my possession be" (349). Thus, Hal avoids his father's guilt by substituting "linear succession for divine right" (ArH2 112) as justification for occupying the throne. It's ironic that Henry, having described his guilt and the chaos that followed his usurpation of Richard, now advises Hal to follow in his footsteps and cynically take up the crusade he intended to lead to Jerusalem.

- (IV, III, 363) "Laud be to God, ..." - Shakespeare mocks the efficacy of prophesy. Henry speaks of the prophesy which predicted that he would die in Jerusalem and discovers that the name referred to a room in the castle, not the city.

- (V, I, 4 – 11) "I will not excuse you." - Shallow's role is to serve as a contrast to Falstaff. He is a thin, dry, doddering old man who has lost all the juices that Falstaff has kept (VD 111). Here Shakespeare captures the repetitive voice of the elderly as opposed to Falstaff's sharp wit. But beneath Shallow's hospitality is a streak of corruption (28). His gracious treatment of Falstaff is at least partly due to his belief that Falstaff will be influential when the Prince takes the throne. This contrasts with the behavior of the Lord Chief Justice.

- (V, I, 62) "It is a wonderful thing ..." - Falstaff comments on the influence Shallow has had on his employees and conversely their influence on him. Shakespeare here reminds us of a central action of the play, the attempts of Falstaff and Henry to influence Hal. Falstaff says that "either wise bearing or ignorant carriage is caught" (73). He goes on to describe his plan for entertaining Hal in the future, making his relationship with Hal seem forced and artificial, rather than spontaneous.

- (V, II, 67) "No? How might a prince ..." - Hal reminds the Lord Chief Justice that he had put him in jail for hitting him and it wouldn't be surprising that now that he is king, he would retaliate. The Chief Justice defends his action and the rule of law (72) and as he does so we're left to wonder what Hal intends to do. But given his reconciliation with his father, it's no surprise that Hal has no intention of retaliating and that he deliberately made the Chief Justice uncomfortable. Perhaps this is a throwback to his tavern mentality. He adopts the Chief Justice as a surrogate father when he says, "you shall be as a father to my youth" (117). Hal has gone through a long education in *Part 1* and *Part 2* in which he has been pulled in opposite directions by Falstaff and his father. His choice of the Chief Justice as his new father is the result of this education and indicates that his father's influence has won out. He speaks of mocking the expectations of the world, thus fulfilling the promise he had made in *Part 1* (*Henry IV Part 1* (I, II, 185)) to throw off his loose behavior.

The Chief Justice shows himself to be incorruptible and plays a role similar to that of Henry and opposite to that of Falstaff in their influence on Hal. But while the Chief Justice is a paragon of rectitude, it would be a mistake to view Falstaff as the opposite. With all his faults, Falstaff represents freedom, a love of life and the importance of joy as a part of living.

- (V, III) The scene celebrates rural plenty and friendship. Silence, who has said hardly anything over the course of the play, is drunk and suddenly bursts into song, celebrating the joys of wine and women. Falstaff is impressed, saying that he didn't think Silence was a drinker (merry = tipsy) and Silence says – perhaps with feigned indignation - that he has been drunk once before this (39).

- (V, III, 121) "Away, Bardolph! Saddle my horse!" - Falstaff is so sure of his relationship to Hal that he feels empowered by Hal's ascension to the throne. This explains the shock he feels later when Hal banishes him.

- (V, V, 13) "This poor show doth better; ..." - Falstaff cynically plans his appearance at the coronation procession to impress the king with his excitement. But instead it's offensive: his outfit is poor and sweat-stained from travelling (24) and he refers to the king as Hal, as if he were still his tavern friend. Some critics see Hal's public rejection of Falstaff as harsh and humiliating, and the mockery of Falstaff's figure is gratuitously cruel. But it also can be seen as a political necessity. Hal now has a responsibility to the state to maintain law and order, and the fact that he has inherited a tarnished crown makes it imperative that he demonstrates publicly his legitimacy and his rejection of his riotous youth.

Furthermore, the punishment, consisting of a banishment together with an allowance which will increase if he reforms his life, isn't as harsh as it might be. The stay in the Fleet that is imposed by the Lord Chief Justice is unexplained, but possibly related to the robbery at Gads Hill and might only be intended to hold him until a court date.

Hal's rejection of Falstaff makes good on his soliloquy in *Part 1* (*Henry IV Part 1* (I, II, 185)) which starts "I know you all, and will awhile uphold the unyoked humor of your idleness". And it's consistent with Freudian psychology. Falstaff is a "surrogate father who must inevitably be the victim of the Oedipal wish of the adopted son to destroy him" (Bl5 58). And finally, it's consistent with modern managerial behavior which dictates that a manager can't be personally friendly with his subordinates, since he has to be able to freely make decisions regarding their employment.

Other critics, however, view the rejection as a betrayal and see Hal as a cynic and, like his father, a cold and unscrupulous political opportunist (Bl5 57): he enjoyed his wild life with his tavern friends, but from the beginning had every intention of throwing them off when he ascended to the throne, having pledged in *Part 1* "I do; I will" (*Henry IV Part 1* (II, IV, 464)) to Falstaff's plea that he not be banished. Here he makes good on that pledge saying, "I know thee not old man". Hal demands, in a high-handed tone, that Falstaff reform his life, ignoring the fact that he has just recently opted to reform his own life. He claims that he despises his tavern life, and in so doing completely rejects all that was good in it.

As politically necessary as the rejection might be, many see it as an "impersonal manifestation of state will, and Falstaff, the all-too-human victim of a callous political system" (ArH2 93). Falstaff is more than just a lawless individual. He embodies the unrestrained enjoyment of life and irrepressible vitality, and his final rejection, which is the victory of social restraint over individual freedom, cannot be viewed without regret.

- (V, V, 87) "Fear no colours." - We are left to wonder about Falstaff's reaction to this rejection. Is he unbowed, and like Charlie Chaplin, does he leave the stage "ready to face another bout with society and chance", his "indomitable humanness" intact (Bl5 61)? Or, is he finally beaten and humiliated? His last words – "My lord, my lord" (92) - seem to indicate that he has been reduced to impotence (Bl5 66). Our acceptance of Falstaff's rejection depends on how we view the play. If we see it as primarily a comedy, then the ending is a shock. If we see it primarily as a play about political power, then the ending is inevitable.

- (V, V, 96) "I like this fair proceeding ..." - Shakespeare allows Prince John, the man who cruelly broke his word to the rebels, to deliver the final assessment of Hal's rejection of Falstaff. The fact that he likes what Hal has done is an indication that Shakespeare does not (Go 205). John goes on to emphasize that Hal does not intend that the punishment be severe.

- (Epilogue) Falstaff was originally called Sir John Oldcastle in *Part 1* and *Part 2*. In contrast to Falstaff, Oldcastle was a real person, a friend of the Prince and someone who participated in his adventures, although there's no evidence that his character was in any way similar to the character portrayed in these plays. England was a Catholic country in Henry IV's time and Oldcastle was active in an effort to reform the Catholic Church. He refused to recant some positions he had taken and was burned at the stake as a result. When the play was written, however, Elizabeth was queen and England was a Protestant country. Although Oldcastle was not attacking Catholicism, he was a reformer and therefore in agreement with some of the current government's positions on religion.

  It is unclear what Shakespeare's motive was in naming a debauched knight after a reformist martyr. It could have antagonized the crown. Alternatively, since Oldcastle was a radical, Shakespeare might have felt that he was supporting the Anglican Church by mocking the contemporary efforts of the radical Puritans who were attempting to reform it. Whatever the motive, however, a court performance of *Part 1* caused an uproar and Shakespeare was forced to change the name of the character to Falstaff.

Discussion

Themes - *Henry IV Part 2* deals with political power and how decisions, which affect the unfolding of history as well as the unfolding of our individual lives, are made. Shakespeare's view is that we make decisions using our memory of the past and our assessment of the present. Based on that information, we use reason to anticipate the effect of each of the choices that we might make on the future and decide accordingly. As Shakespeare shows in the play, each of these components of the decision-making process is flawed.

The past is remembered differently by different actors depending on their own selfish purposes. This severely limits its effectiveness as a guide to decision making. For example, the rebels remember the promises that Henry made to bring them to his side against Richard and which they feel he has subsequently broken, while Henry remembers the Percy's betrayals. Henry remembers that Richard was weak, and this justifies his action in deposing him, while Hotspur remembers that Henry was ambitious. The failure of memory isn't restricted to the great movers of history. Falstaff suggests that Shallow's memory of his early life is more faithful to his vanity than to the truth.

Hal's recollection of his soliloquy at Henry's bedside illustrates a related point. It differs from what he had said. But Hal is neither a liar nor without his own ambitions. His motives are complex and even he might have difficulty understanding them. Shakespeare seems to be saying that what we remember "is less a record of facts than a subjective, passionate justification" of our actions (Bl5 55).

Our assessment of the present can also be inaccurate. Rumor, opinion and lies stand in the way. Worcester intentionally lies to Hotspur in failing to report Henry's offer of pardon in *Part 1*, thus impacting Hotspur's decision to enter the battle. The description of the battle at Shrewsbury given in the first scene of *Part 2* to Northumberland is clouded by confusing reports and, as a result, Henry misjudges the size of the rebel army.

Finally, personalities and desires often overcome reasonable arguments when decisions are being made. For example, Hotspur's foolish thirst for a good fight at Shrewsbury wins out over the reasonable caution expressed by the other rebels when their allies abandon them. A defeat follows. Even when reason prevails, as at Gaultree, and the new set of rebels prudently decide to accept a peace offer from the crown, disaster follows. Thus, reason is no sure guide to action. Henry expresses this view when he describes how chance seems to control natural processes. He sees betrayals, such as Northumberland's betrayal first of Richard and then of himself, as similar to random natural events which defy rational planning.

The play has another significant theme. Shakespeare shows that "actions that should have the effect of radically undermining authority turn out to be the props of that authority. ... moral values - justice, order, civility – are secured paradoxically through the apparent generation of their subversive contraries. Out of the squalid betrayals that preserve the State emerges the 'formal majesty' into which Hal at the close, through a final definitive betrayal – the rejection of Falstaff – merges himself" (Bl5 145).

Henry IV Part 2 is concerned with power: how it is acquired, how it is maintained, and its effect on the people who wield it. It shows "how the assumption of power sets a man apart and sometimes calls for acts which may be necessary and justified on political grounds but are nevertheless distressing when judged by the standards of genial humanity" (Bl5 69).

Characters – For some thoughts on the main characters of the play, see the Discussion section of Chapter 6.

Chapter 8

As You Like It

Background

As You Like It is one of Shakespeare's mid-career plays. Its plot was taken largely from a novel by Thomas Lodge called *Rosalynde* and it's referred to as a pastoral comedy. Pastorals are generally populated by characters who escape the corruption of a rigid royal court for the freedom and good fellowship of an idyllic natural setting, a place where the folly of romance can have its day. In this play the pastoral setting is called the Forest of Arden. It's unclear what Shakespeare meant in naming the play as he did, but freedom from societal restrictions is traditionally one of the pleasures of the pastoral setting: "liberation from clocks and clerics, and from the constraints and conventions of the court" (ArA 90). Hence, *As You Like It*.

The play is often credited with being "one of the supreme achievements of Shakespearean comedy" (Bl12 140). Harold Bloom sees Rosalind, the central character, as one of Shakespeare's greatest creations. "She alone joins Hamlet and Falstaff as absolute in wit" (Bl12 1). "She must be the most remarkable and persuasive representation of a woman in all of Western literature" (Bl12 159).

As in a number of Shakespeare's comedies, sexual confusion is central to the humor and this drew the ire of many who were critical of the theater for encouraging immoral behavior. The problem was magnified by the requirement at Shakespeare's time that all female roles be played by boy actors. "It was felt that cross-dressing excited homoerotic feeling both in the actors on the stage and in the audience" (AlA 9). In the play, Rosalind takes the name Ganymede and impersonates a man throughout most of the play. As Ganymede, she then impersonates a woman. Hence, we have a boy playing a woman (Rosalind) who impersonates a man (Ganymede) who impersonates a woman (Rosalind).

The Play (line numbers from (ArA))

- (I, I, 1) The play opens with Orlando's complaint concerning his treatment by his older brother, Oliver. He says that the animals on Oliver's estate are treated better than he is. Shakespeare here comments on the inequities imposed by the rule of primogeniture (41). Both Oliver and primogeniture are a part of the corrupt civilized world which stands in contrast with the idyllic world of the Forest of Arden.

- (I, I, 105) "She is at court ..." - Shakespeare introduces a reference to the bond that can exist between women. One of the main concerns of the play is to explore the way the characters relate to one another.

- (I, I, 155) "Yet he's gentle ... - Oliver describes Orlando as "gentle". This is an adjective generally associated with women, and hence suggests one of the themes of the play, which is that characteristics that are generally associated with a particular sex need not be restricted to that sex. Oliver's concern that Orlando is "so much in the heart of the world, and especially of my own people" (158) is similar to that of Ricard II's concern about Bolingbroke.

- (I, II, 31 - 42) "Let us sit and mock ..." - Celia and Rosalind debate the role of Nature (the attributes we are given at birth) and Fortune (what the future holds for a person) in shaping a woman's life. Celia regrets that Fortune's gifts are not distributed equally and Rosalind agrees that Fortune doesn't treat women well. Celia feels that Fortune directs beautiful women into an unchaste life and ugly women into a virginal one. Rosalind distinguishes between gifts of Nature, physical appearance and wit, and the role of Fortune, the direction our lives take.

- (I, II, 70 - 78) "Stand you both forth now." - Touchstone asks Rosalind and Celia to "stroke your chins and swear by your beards". Since neither the girls (nor the boy actors playing them) have beards, the oath is meaningless. The point of Touchstone's homily is that if you swear by something you don't have you can't be responsible for the truth of what you have sworn. The example he uses is that of a knight who has sworn by his honor that something is true, but since he has no honor he can't be faulted if the oath is false. That a knight's oath is false is an indictment of the code of chivalry.

  The fact that Rosalind and Celia have no beards draws attention to the sexual ambiguities at the center of the play and harks back to the scene in *A Midsummer Night's Dream* in which Flute tries to avoid playing a woman in the mechanicals' performance of *Pyramus and Thisbe* by pointing out that he has a beard growing in (*A Midsummer*

Night's Dream (I, II, 44)). A touchstone is a hard stone used to test the quality of a sample of a precious metal. The metal is scraped across the stone and the mark left on the stone is an indication of the purity of the metal. Touchstone plays an analogous role by revealing the pretensions that underlie social interactions.

- (I, II, 85) "The more pity that fools ..." - Touchstone anticipates Fool in *King Lear,* whose wisdom Lear ignored.

- (I, II, 104) "Thou loosest thy old smell." - Touchstone farts, Rosalind calls him out and Le Beau is "amazed" by the coarse level of her humor, which seems more male than female. The fact that Rosalind seems to respond like a man gives us a glimpse of her personality as well as Shakespeare's blurring of the difference between men and women.

- (I, II, 238) "Can I not say, I thank you?" - Orlando bemoans the fact that he's unable to respond properly to a woman. He's untrained in romance, something that Rosalind will correct later in the play. Rosalind demonstrates female aggression by adopting the ruse that Orlando had called to her (242). He says that he has been "mastered" by Rosalind (248), someone who is presumably "weaker" (249) than he. This contradicts the macho hierarchy that dictates that the physically stronger sex, the male, always masters the weaker sex, the female.

- (I, III, 74 - 81) "She is too subtle for thee, ..." - Oliver wanted to be rid of Orlando because he's concerned that Orlando is too popular with the people. Here, Duke Fredrick banishes Rosalind for a similar reason. He fears that she outdoes

Celia in popularity. Both cases speak of the rivalries, and the resulting corruption, that flourish in court life.

- (I, III, 111 - 119) "Were it not better, ..." - Rosalind decides to impersonate a man. She says that her heart will remain that of a woman's, but she'll take on a "martial outside, as many other mannish cowards have". She mocks men who only pretend to be courageous and, in the process, blurs the distinction between the sexes. "Just as Rosalind explodes myths of feminine sexuality so ... Orlando revises the binaries of violent masculinity and gentle femininity" (ArA 32).

- (II, I, 1 – 17) "Now, my co-mates ..." - Act I has demonstrated the corruption in court: Duke Senior and Rosalind have been banished, Orlando has been deprived of his inheritance by Oliver and is threatened by Duke Fredrick. The setting now changes to Arden. Duke Senior speaks of the happiness that he derives from living in Arden. He calls his fellow exiles "co-mates and brothers", implying an oppressive hierarchy in court, and he uses the words "peril" and "envy" in describing court life. He says that the harsh weather they experience in Arden serves as a counsellor that reminds them of the realities of life – "what I am" (11) - as opposed to the flattery (10) that permeates court life: "Sweet are the uses of adversity" (12). The passage anticipates Lear's recognition that he was flattered "like a dog" when he was king and only realized his true humanity when foul weather woke him to the fact that he wasn't "ague-proof" (*King Lear* (IV, VI, 96)).

- (II, I, 21 - 43) "Come, shall we go ..." - Duke Senior bemoans the need to kill deer for food, showing himself to be sensitive to cruelty in the world, and in so doing

Shakespeare makes clear that Arden is no paradise. This thought is carried forward by Jaques, who sympathized with a wounded deer (26) "as he [Jaques] lay along Under an oak, whose antic root peeps out upon the brook that brawls along this wood" (29). The description (in the words of 1 Lord) goes so far as to claim that the deer shed tears. Hunting was "under fire from humanists who attacked its cruelty and the aristocratic culture ... which accompanied it" (ArA 53). "In an age of censorship, the pastoral mode provided a way of saying one's dangerous piece with relative safety" (ArA 103).

- (II, I, 54 – 63) "'Ay,' quoth Jaques, ..." - Jaques attacks not only court and country, but "this our life" (60) as well. He apparently is unable to see any good in the world.

- (II, III, 9) "Your praise is come too ..." - Adam observes that men's "graces serve them but as enemies", meaning that some people want to destroy anyone who excels, particularly if they feel themselves as outdone. The message is, don't outdo your boss, a message that was also expressed by Ventidius in *Antony and Cleopatra*. Adam also points out that the old and lame are "in corners thrown" (41) and Orlando says that whereas formerly servants worked out of a feeling of duty, now they're only looking for "promotion" (59 - 62). Adam comments on the corruption of court life. Orlando and Adam, two good people, enter Arden.

- (II, IV, 4) "I could find in my heart ..." - Rosaliind (Ganymede) and Celia (Aliena), two more good people, and Touchstone enter Arden. Rosalind speaks of the difference between men and women. Their trek into Arden could bring a woman to tears, but as Ganymede she must maintain a courageous appearance. Touchstone is contrasted to Adam. The latter works for duty and willingly gives his savings to Orlando, while the former says he will not be happy having to help Celia because she has no money to repay him (12).

- (II, IV, 22) "No, Corin, being old, ..." - Silvius measures the depth of a suitor's love by the number of ridiculous things that he does as a result of loving (27). This is part of the sentimental ritual that is romantic love. Touchstone recounts the foolish things he did when he was in love (43) and concludes that foolishness is an integral part of being in love: "As all is mortal in nature, so is all nature in love mortal in folly" (51), by which he means that lovers are "ready to die for their delusions" (AcA 206). Rosalind compliments him and he responds, "I shall ne'er be ware of my own wit till I break my shins against it" (54).

- (II, IV, 63 - 68) "Holla, you clown!" - Shakespeare illustrates the difference between good and bad manners.

- (II, IV, 74 – 86) "Fair sir, I pity her ..." - Shakespeare introduces another element of social consciousness (in addition to his mention of primogeniture). Corin describes the "bleak prospects for rural living" (Bl12 112). He works for an absentee landlord who exploits the land for profit and threatens to sell it "with no concern for his workers' future prospects; he refuses the ethical responsibilities of his class" (Bl12 113). Rosalind and Celia offer to buy the property and "mend his wages".

- (II, V, 10) "I can suck melancholy out of a song as a weasel sucks eggs." - Shakespeare mocks the melancholy affectation of philosophers.

- (II, VI, 15) "Come, I will bear thee ..." - Orlando treats the ailing Adam with an almost feminine tenderness.

- (II, VII, 24 – 27) "And so from hour to hour ..." - Jaques repeats what Touchstone had said: time progresses and nothing important happens except rotting. The thought asserts the meaninglessness of life and Jaques loves it (but not necessarily Shakespeare (Go 288)). It anticipates Macbeth's words, "Tomorrow, and tomorrow, and tomorrow, creeps in this petty pace from day to day ... signifying nothing" (*Macbeth* (V, V, 19)). Motley is a multi-colored garment traditionally worn by fools.

- (II, VII, 44 - 61) "It is my only suit ..." - Fools are often credited with wisdom and are tolerated when they anatomize someone (*e.g.*, Fool in *King Lear*). By acting the fool, Jaques claims that he can "cleanse the world" with his wisdom, but the duke says he should cleanse himself first (65). Jaques defends himself by saying that he isn't accusing anyone in particular (70) - he directs his wisdom to the world in general.

  Jaques has wit and wisdom but he uses it to enhance his own standing, not as a guide for living his life. He has withdrawn from the world and needs only an audience. "Being out of love with life, Jaques thinks of nothing but himself" (Go 283, 284).

- (II, VII, 88) "Forbear and eat no more!" - Orlando enters with his sword drawn and, under the force of hunger, aggressively demands food. Duke Senior responds by offering the food and says, "Your gentleness shall force more than your force move us to gentleness" (102). Orlando asks, "Speak you so gently?" (107) and the duke says, “sit you down in gentleness” (125). Orlando compares himself to a female deer instead of an aggressive animal. Thus, gentleness, a feminine characteristic exhibited by Duke Senior, wins out over aggressive behavior, a male characteristic.

- (II, VII, 137 - 167) “We are not all alone unhappy.” - Duke Senior makes it clear that suffering exists in and out of Arden. He compares the world to a theater and this has been interpreted as a defense against forces in Elizabethan society which regarded the theater as a threat. Jaques continues the metaphor with his discourse on the seven ages of a man’s life. He speaks of man as a player in a performance: “All the world’s a stage”. He sees life as a series of preordained roles that a man assumes as he ages. This trivializes man’s significance as an individual (Bl12 8).

  Significantly, he omits the roles of husband and father in this progression, perhaps because they suggest relationships with others, something that he does not value. The last of the roles is a second childhood, a “mere oblivion”. It is probably no accident that as soon as he finishes, Orlando enters carrying Adam, who is at the end of his life, but is hardly a child: Adam has made Orlando’s escape possible. Jaques’ speech anticipates Macbeth’s much bleaker evaluation: life’s “a poor player that struts and frets his hour on the stage” (*Macbeth* (V, V, 26)).

- (III, II, 13) “Truly, shepherd, in respect ...” - Corin asks Touchstone his opinion of a shepherd’s life. Touchstone’s answer is a series of contradictions and Corin’s reply (22 – 29) is a series of obvious truths. The contrast is a measure of who these characters are. Corin is a simple, honest man, perhaps reflective of country life, and Touchstone is not above sarcasm and mockery. Touchstone calls him a "natural philosopher", but says that without having lived at court he can't possibly be well mannered and therefore he is damned (33). Corin disputes that by pointing out that what constitutes good manners is relative. It depends on whether you're in court or in the country, hence perspective is involved (43 – 48). But what is absolutely clear is that it is Touchstone who is ill mannered.

Finally, Corin describes the simple contentment he finds in his life, showing himself to be wiser than Touchstone (70 – 74). This can be viewed as 'how he likes it' and thus a reference to the title of the play. His point is an implicit criticism of the envy and ambition that pervades court life. Sensing that it's futile to argue, Corin refuses politely to continue. Touchstone's final mockery shows him to be arrogant and rude (75 – 82).

- (III, II, 85) "From the east to western Inde ..." - Rosalind enters reading a Pertrachian love poem that she has found nailed to a tree by Orlando. Touchstone mocks the poem by composing his own bawdy version of a love poem (98).

- (III, II, 116) "for you'll be rotten ere you be half ripe, ..." - Rosalind's wit stops Touchstone.

- (III, II, 122) "Why should this a desert be, ..." - The verses read by Celia are mocked by Rosalind as a "tedious homily of love" (152) and as having "more feet than the verses would bear" (162) ('feet' refers to the two-syllable metrical unit used to construct a poem). By elevating Rosalind to divine status, the poem becomes impersonal. In typical Petrarchian fashion the author says he is Rosalind's slave

(151). Rosalind doesn't know who wrote the verses and demands that Celia tell her.

- (III, II, 189) "Good my complexion!" - Shakespeare raises the issue of the distinction between the genders and whether one blends into the other. Here Rosalind begs like a young girl for the name of the person who wrote the poems (176 – 204) and then says that just because she's dressed like a man doesn't mean her inner self is masculine. The humor is bawdy (198).

- (III, II, 211 - 243) "Orlando." - Celia finally reveals that the author is Orlando and that he's in the forest. Rosalind has all the characteristics of a young woman in love. She assaults Celia with a torrent of questions and wants an answer in one word (212 - 217). When Celia chides her for interrupting, she says "Do you not know I am a woman? When I think, I must speak" (242). Shakespeare has created a character who is a leader, who is wise, witty and spontaneous, and who is fully feminine.

- (III, II, 269) "Will you sit down with me ..." - Jaques takes pleasure in finding fault with the world, and asks Orlando to join him. Orlando takes pleasure in being in love (275). While Jaques serves to counter the idyllic pretensions of the pastoral setting, Orlando counters Jaques' pretension to wisdom by telling him that he if sees his reflection in the brook he will have found a fool (279).

- (III, II, 287) "I will speak to him ..." - Rosalind, as Ganymede, says she will behave like a "saucy (impudent) lackey" in her relationship with Orlando. Thus, Ganymede becomes a more aggressive, and hence masculine, character than the gentle Orlando. She demonstrates her wit in the interchange about the progress of time (299 - 322).

- (III, II, 353) "I am he that is ..." - Orlando declares his love for Rosalind. She could at this point reveal herself, since his love is what she wants. But first she wants to use her disguise as part of a scheme to cure him of his Petrarchian romantic style. She refers to love as madness and lunacy (384 - 388). Her goal is to rid him of the "false melancholies" and "corrupting idealism" (Bl12 3) that accompanies this take on romantic love. She then describes how she intends to do this, which involves impersonating Rosalind (390 - 410).

- (III, II, 408) "I would cure you, ..." - Rosalind, as Ganymede, convinces Orlando to pretend that she is Rosalind and to make him (Ganymede) the object of his love. This enables her to engage him safely without explicitly expressing her own love. "Thus, the love between the two is rehearsed in the kingdom of the imagination, where all true love begins, before any attempt is made to bring it down to the level of everyday life, a situation that permits both lovers to speak now as boldly, now as innocently, as though they were angels or children" (Go 292). In the process, both homosexual (Orlando/Ganymede) and heterosexual (Orlando/Rosalind) love become an integral part of the play. As the play progresses the audience has to wonder whether Orlando loves Rosalind or Ganymede, and how he can practice new romantic skills with someone he believes to be a man. In addition, the close relationship between Rosalind and Celia can be played as verging on homosexual.

- (III, III, 4 - 13) "Your features, Lord warrant us!" - Audrey makes it clear that she isn't overwhelmed with

Touchstone's looks. And he complains – using bathroom humor - that it's depressing when your joke falls flat (10 – 13). Touchstone mocks the poetry of love which he says expresses a lot of desire (faining) but is full of lies (feigning) (17 – 19). Audrey says she is chaste (honest) and Touchstone says that he wishes she was poetical because poets lie (23) (and hence she's not chaste). She admits she's ugly (foul) (35) and Touchstone says, hopefully, that she might become a slut. Audrey has no pretensions, and neither has any illusions about the other.

- (III, III, 73) "As the ox has his bow, ..." - The relationship between Touchstone and Audrey is the opposite of that between Silvius and Phoebe. Instead of exaggerated sentiment, here we have "love reduced to its lowest common denominator, without any sentiment at all" (Bl12 13). Touchstone compares marriage to the halter worn by an ox when pulling a plow and finds it necessary only because "man hath his desires" (74). Without marriage, they will "live in bawdry" (89). Shakespeare introduces their relationship to show love without any sentiment, a grim alternative. "Romantic participation in love and humorous detachment from its follies, the two polar attitudes which are balanced against each other in the action as a whole, meet and are reconciled in Rosalind's personality ... she remains always aware of love's illusions while she herself is swept along by its deepest currents" (Bl12 14).

- (III, III, 76 - 81) "And will you, being a man ..." - Jaques, the wise man, and Touchstone, the fool, serve the purpose of "scraping the veneer off the surface of pastoral pleasure" (ArA 106) and reminding us of the hard realities of life. Here, Jaques counsels Touchstone that he should get a real priest to perform his marriage to Audrey and Touchstone mocks him by saying that if his marriage is not performed properly it will be easier for him to get out of it at a later time if he so wishes (82). This is an attitude that is hardly appropriate for an idyllic setting or supportive of romantic bonds. Touchstone is simultaneously Jaques' adversary (fool vs. philosopher) and his ally (ArA 110).

Wise fools play an important role in several of Shakespeare's plays. Their presence serves as a comment on the social situation in which they are embedded and the characters that surround them. If wisdom comes from fools the implication is that the world around them is foolish. "If the world has come to stand on its head, one can adopt the right attitude to it only by turning somersaults ... The world makes clowns of everybody, except clowns" (K 284). This is the basis of the attraction that Jaques feels for Touchstone.

- (III, IV, 2) "Do, I prithee, but yet have ..." - Rosalind bemoans the fact that Orlando is late. Celia tells her that in her disguise as a man she doesn't have the luxury to cry, thus reminding her of her own words earlier in the play (II, IV, 4). "The social and cultural constructions of gender ... are the equivalent of a wardrobe of garments to be put on and off at will" (ArA 12, 14). The blurring of boundaries between male and female are at the heart of the play.

- (III, IV, 48) "If you will see a pageant ..." - Corin invites Rosalind and Celia to observe Silvius – "the pale complexion of true love" and Phoebe – "the red glow of scorn and proud disdain".

- (III, V, 1) "Sweet Phoebe, do not scorn me, ..." - Silvius is an advocate of romantic love in its sentimental form. He pleads with Phoebe not to scorn him. He imagines her his executioner. Phoebe mocks his claim that she's capable of killing him (20) with looks. In doing so she aligns herself with Rosalind, who has a similar attitude toward romantic hyperbole. Rosalind attacks Pheobe for being cruel (36) and Silvius for being weak (50). Theirs is another form of romantic love relationship: female scorn and male abasement. Rosalind ends by advising Phoebe "Sell when you can, you are not for all markets" (61). She scorns "the exaggerations of conventional sentiment" (Bl12 12).

- (III, V, 86) "Why, I am sorry for thee, ..." - Phoebe refers to Silvius as "gentle", another male with feminine characteristics. She takes Rosalind's advice and accepts his love, but she does so reluctantly, saying that it is a "neighborly" act (91). This is love without passion (94 – 99).

- (III, V, 110 – 136) "Think not I love him ..." - Phoebe's description of Ganymede displays both a clear-eyed understanding of Ganymede's flaws as well as a veiled admission of her love for him. This is love without illusions.

- (IV, I, 4) "I am so; I do love it ..." - Melancholy is Jaques' persona – he loves "it better than laughing". Rosalind is unimpressed and says that extreme melancholy and extreme laughing are abominable. To Jaques' assertion that "'tis good to be sad and say nothing", Rosalind replies "Why then, 'tis good to be a post" (9). Her wit outpaces his. He's a scholar of melancholy and demonstrates this foolishness by enumerating seven different varieties (10 - 18). And then Rosalind delivers the final blow (24 – 26): "I'd rather have a fool to make me merry than experience to make me sad."

- (IV, I, 86 - 99) "No, faith, die by attorney." - Rosalind (Ganymede) attempts to cure Orlando's foolish view of romantic love. Here she mocks his claim that he'll die if he can't have Rosalind. She says that he won't die (perhaps some sort of a proxy – "attorney" - will die) and in fact no man has ever died of love: "men have died from time to time, and worms have eaten them, but not for love" (98). In other words, death is real, but it is not the result of unrequited love. Rosalind is witty, but in a benign way. It's not that she doesn't love romance, it's just that she can't ignore the foolishness that comes with it. Her disguise as Ganymede enables her to safely express her love (102 - 115).

- (IV, I, 135) "For ever and a day." - Rosalind mocks Orlando's promise with a realistic assessment of marriage. She says that "maids are May when they are maids, but the sky changes when they are wives" (138) and then proceeds to describe the various ways she will torment her husband once she marries (136 – 146). She wants love to be "independent of illusions" without being any the less intense. She wants to inoculate love "against life's unromantic contradictions" (Bl12 17). She describes this kind of behavior as wise and says, "the wiser, the waywarder" (150). She says that a woman's wit is irrepressible (151 – 154), and then demonstrates that by turning the conversation to sex (157). The conclusion that can be drawn from this discussion is that a woman can always outmaneuver her husband (162 - 164).

- (IV, I, 167) "Alas, dear love, I cannot ..." - In a show (perhaps feigned) of romantic hyperbole, she claims that she can't do without Orlando's presence. Celia suggests (189) that she debases the female sex by pleading with Orlando to return at the time he's promised and threatens to strip Rosalind naked to demonstrate to all that Ganymede is a woman.

- (IV, II) The illusion that the Forest of Arden is pure and idyllic compared to the outside world is challenged in this scene in which the killing of a deer is celebrated.

- (IV, III, 28) "I say she never did ..." - Rosalind cannot accept that Phoebe has written the love letter that Silvius, who has taken the role of Phoebe's servant, delivers to her. She says, "This is a man's invention" and "Women's gentle brain could not drop forth such giant-rude invention" (33). In fact, the letter turns out to be a lot of romantic hyperbole and Rosalind seems to be saying that a woman is incapable of writing such tripe.

- (IV, III, 103 – 115) "Under an oak, whose boughs ..." - The Forest of Arden is not the Garden of Eden. Duke Senior made this clear when he spoke of the harsh weather that the residents of Arden had to deal with (II, I, 5). We also saw this in the celebration of the hunt in (IV, II) and now we see it here. The snake and the lion pose a threat to life. Touchstone and Corin (III, II, 13) had addressed the relative advantages of country and court life but their conversation yielded no clear resolution. While criticizing court life, Shakespeare seems to want to make it clear that he doesn't see nature as a uniformly positive alternative to life in civilization.

- (IV, III, 156) "Why, how now, Ganymede ..." - Rosalind faints and as a result comes close to betraying her gender. On awakening she says, "I would I were at home" (a line that recalls Falstaff's "I would 'twere bedtime, Hal, and all were well" (*Henry IV Part 1* (V, I, 125)). Oliver says that she lacks a man's heart. She tries to disguise the faint by claiming that she faked it. It's apparent that she can't continue to masquerade as Ganymede (163).

- (V, I, 30) "Why, thou sayst well." - Touchstone quotes an aphorism stating that a fool thinks he's wise, but a wise man knows himself to be a fool. This is a criticism of Jaques, who thinks he's wise.

- (V, II, 31 - 40) "For your brother and my sister ..." - The romance of Celia and Oliver demonstrates another of love's trajectories – love at first sight.

- (V, II, 49) "I can live no longer by thinking." - Orlando's complaint is reminiscent of Bolingbroke's response to Gaunt (*Richard II* (I, III, 294)) that thinking on the "frosty Caucasus" doesn't enable him to hold fire in his hand. Here, however, the words mark a turning point in the play. Orlando has been playing at love, but that will no longer sustain him. Realizing that Orlando is ready for real love, Ganymede responds by saying that she will produce Rosalind, "human as she is", meaning not the "paper paragon of Orlando's halting sonnets" (Bl12 68).

- (V, II, 73) "Youth, you have done me ..." - Phoebe complains of Rosalind's "ungentleness". Rosalind responds that to be "ungentle" is her intent. Silvius comment, "love is all made of sighs and tears" (80), is an indication that he still subscribes to the Petrarchian model of romance. Shakespeare makes the point that women need not be gentle and romantic love is foolish.

- (V, IV, 43 – 101) "If any man doubt that, ..." - Touchstone demonstrates his wit in a series of exchanges. First, he mockingly enumerates what it means to be a gentleman (44 - 47). Then he refers to the couples waiting to be married as "country copulatives" (55) and speaks of virginity in an ugly girl as a "pearl in your foul oyster". Finally, he discusses the stages through which a simple discourtesy can be built into a major insult (68 - 81) and shows how, through use of the word 'if', a fight can be avoided (89 - 101). He ends with, "much virtue in 'if'". In the middle of all of this he reminds Audrey to watch her posture (69).

- (V, IV, 114) "To you I give myself, for I am yours." - Although Rosalind has orchestrated the marriage of all four couples, once the ceremony starts she submits to her father and Orlando, gives up the power and independence she has wielded throughout the play and joins the conventional, patriarchal family structure. Her conversion is necessary to meet the requirements of pastoral comedy, but it's unclear whether Shakespeare approved of this.

- (V, IV, 157) "And to the skirts of this wild wood ..." - Duke Fredrick no sooner enters Arden than he undergoes a conversion, discards his evil ways and gives the kingdom back to Duke Senior. Taken together with Oliver's conversion and the four marriages, the play ends on a false, but happy, note that conforms to the pattern of a pastoral comedy. Shakespeare's comedies aren't completely different from his tragedies. They don't eliminate the unpleasant, they just eliminate the tragic ending.

Discussion

As You Like It challenges conventional thought on a number of fronts, all related to sexuality. First, and perhaps most significantly, Shakespeare has created in Rosalind a character who breaks the stereotype normally associated with women. She dominates the play with her independence and wit. "Feminist thought has highlighted the audacity and originality of Shakespeare's conception of Rosalind, analyzing the ways in which the play participates in an Elizabethan questioning of attitudes to women. ... Rosalind is witty, voluble, educated and imaginative; spirited and energetic; a woman who faints at the sight of her lover's blood; an imperious shepherd; a powerful magician who arranges the marriages at the end of the play; and a saucy boy who returns to speak the epilogue" (AlA 9). But Shakespeare goes beyond that, to show that these qualities do not preclude a healthy appetite for heterosexual love.

Secondly, the play is an exploration and critique of love in its various forms. Shakespeare gives us four couples whose attitude towards courting and marriage differ, and asks the question, "Which of these make sense?" Romantic love, as practiced by Orlando, is Shakespeare's main target and Rosalind mocks it with enthusiasm as a part of a process to reform his courting technique. While love-at-first-sight, illustrated by the Oliver/Celia pairing, largely escapes Shakespeare's critical pen, the relationship between Silvius and Phoebe does not. It centers on unrequited love. It's a hopeless situation, characterized by cruelty on one side and self-abasement on the other and it takes an artificial dramatic device to resolve it. And finally, we're shown Touchstone and Audrey, a truly novel pairing based on the total absence of illusion. She is simple and unattractive and knows it; he chooses her because he needs the comfort of a woman and the peace of not having to worry about her being unfaithful.

Finally, Shakespeare is interested in contrasting masculine and feminine characteristics and asks the question "are men inherently masculine and women inherently feminine?" (ArA 31) He shows us Rosalind, who is self-confident, capable of taking on leadership roles, willing to challenge men to get her way and successful in masquerading as a man. And on the other hand, he shows us Orlando and Duke Senor, who display a gentle and accommodating nature which is at odds with the stereotypical male macho persona. At the very least, Shakespeare seems to be saying that there is a wide range of masculine characteristics and a wide range of feminine characteristics with a significant overlap between the two.

Chapter 9

JULIUS CAESAR

Background

Julius Caesar is Shakespeare's most political play. It was written in 1599 when Queen Elizabeth's reign was coming to an end. Elizabeth had no descendants, so there was growing concern about the succession to the throne and the political turmoil that might occur on her death. This was compounded by the religious division in the country and the very real threat to her life posed by the Catholic Church. A play about a similar transition in Roman history was bound to be of interest to the London audience. *Julius Caesar* "evokes strong feelings of recognition and concern during any time marked by high anxiety about the public's future, by revelations of self-justifying evil connivance among powerful men in whom the public has placed its trust, and by ambitious, prideful, incautious decisions on the part of leaders. These conditions would appear to be even more pronounced and worrisome for present-day audiences than for Shakespeare's own. Thus, the play has a special capacity to connect with contemporary moods encompassing failure, loss, hurt, or impending disaster" (Bl16 5).

The play is based closely on the history contained in Plutarch's book *Parallel Lives* and hence can be considered one of Shakespeare's history plays. But the story it tells of Brutus' life is clearly tragic, and so the play is more often considered one of Shakespeare's tragedies. It was the first play performed at the Globe Theater.

The Roman Republic was formed around 500 BCE to replace the monarchy that had previously ruled Rome. In the early days of the Republic, society was divided by ancestry (birth) between patricians and plebeians and, in an overlapping fashion, by wealth and political privilege. The government was a complex form of democracy whose rules evolved, giving more and more power to the plebeians over time. The Senate, consisting of several hundred senators, was the highest legislative body and the office of Consul was the highest executive office. In addition to certain administrative, legislative and judicial powers that consuls wielded in Rome, they were military commanders. Each consul headed up an army and was assigned by the Senate to a region over which he had absolute control. A consul's absolute power did not extend to Rome, however, where the Senate was in control. Consuls usually served in pairs so no one person could completely dominate the government. The office of tribune was created to represent the interests of plebeians.

Office holders were elected for a one-year term. Eligibility to vote for a particular office depended on a variety of things, such as economic status, class, tribe, place of residence. Women and slaves could not vote. There was no constitution. Although nominally democratic, the voting system was rigged in favor of the rich, but equality under the law eventually became a guiding principle.

Hence, the Roman Republic was a combination of monarchy, aristocracy and democracy. The consuls were the monarchical element. The senate, which controlled finances and oversaw the law, represented the aristocratic element. The people were the democratic element. They elected the government officials, made the final decision on going to war and acted as a judicial court for major offences (*SPQR* 188).

The peaceful politics implied by this structure began breaking down in the late Republic. Social struggles resulted in a blurring of class distinctions. In 287 BCE, plebeians and patricians were declared equal under the law. Hence, plebeians could vote and assume public office. For example, Augustus, the emperor who took control when the Roman Republic was transformed into the Roman Empire, was a plebeian.

Even with the reforms, political power was monopolized by the richest social echelon. Public offices were generally filled by members of a competitive elite, and in the interest of preventing any one person from assuming dictatorial control, charismatic individuals were suppressed by peer-group pressure.

Julius Caesar rose through the military ranks and eventually was elected consul in 60 BCE. He was sent to Gaul where he achieved military success. The Senate, fearing Caesar's growing power and popularity with the masses, demanded that he relinquish control of his legions. He refused and returned to Rome with his army. The Rubicon, a river whose location is no longer known for certain, was one of the last barriers he had to cross on his return. Once he had done so he was in open violation of the Senate. He was fifty-one years old at that time. He was opposed by Pompey the Great, another powerful consul, and in the ensuing conflict Pompey was defeated.

Pompey retreated to Egypt, which was ruled by the Greek Ptolemaic dynasty.

Ptolemy had been a general in the Greek army headed by Alexander the Great. In that capacity he had been given control of Egypt, and he and his heirs continued to rule there after Alexander's death. Greece went into a decline after Alexander's death. Egypt, although nominally independent, became a client state of Rome.

Caesar followed Pompey into Egypt but found when he arrived there that Pompey had been assassinated by the Egyptians. They feared Caesar and didn't want to be seen as sheltering his enemy. Caesar supported Cleopatra, a member of the Ptolemaic royal family, in her bid to become Queen of Egypt and began a romantic relationship with her. She later gave birth to a child who she claimed was Caesar's son.

After the defeat of Pompey, Caesar was appointed dictator in Rome with Marc Antony as his second in command. He ruled for five years and, in 44 BCE, was assassinated in a conspiracy led by Brutus and Cassius in the name of liberty. Although many agreed that the tyrant had to go, most Romans preferred the reforms that he instituted - which included support for the poor, overseas settlements and occasional cash handouts - to Brutus' fine-sounding ideas of liberty. Having no legitimate children by Roman law, Caesar had previously designated his grand-nephew, Octavius as his heir. Octavius was inducted into the Senate and later became a consul.

By the time these events were unfolding the tradition of rational policy-making and debate that had prevailed during the Roman Republic had eroded, and violence was increasingly taken for granted as a political tool. Without this tradition the Senate couldn't function as a political force. Octavius allied himself with Antony and, avenging the murder of his great-uncle, defeated Brutus and Cassius at Philippi in 43 BCE. Octavius, Antony and Marcus Lepidus, anther general, took over the government of Rome, calling themselves the Second Triumvirate. This was the end of the Roman Republic and the beginning of the Roman Empire. When the Triumverate disintegrated a few years later, Octavius became the sole ruler, taking on the name and title Emperor Augustus.

To a large extent *Julius Caesar* follows this history, but it ignores Caesar's involvement in Egypt and collapses the time between his return to Rome from Gaul and his assassination. The play opens with Caesar entering Rome after the defeat of Pompey.

The Play (line numbers from (ArJ))

- (I, I) The play opens with Marcellus and Flavius, two tribunes, telling the plebeians celebrating Caesar's final victory over Pompey's forces that they should be at work. The tribunes think it unseemly that Romans should be celebrating the defeat of Pompey, a fellow Roman and a great general. Shakespeare probably had a message in this. The issue is the political role of the plebeians. Although they represent the plebeians, the tribunes believe that politics is the realm of the patricians, who participate in a deliberative process in the context of a representative government. They fear the power of the mob and see the plebeians as primarily economic entities. Hence, they demand that the plebeians that they meet on the street go back to work and fulfill their proper role. Caesar, on the other hand, cultivates plebeian support for his political aspirations. For him, political discourse occurs in mass rally's, not in face to face conversations in the Senate (Bl16

152). He's a populist who draws his power directly from the people.

- (I, I, 33) "Wherefore rejoice?" - Marcellus reminds us that Pompey, who had recently been defeated by Caesar, was a popular figure and that Caesar now had a clear path to be officially recognized as king (75). Marcellus and Flavius oppose this.

- (I, II, 6) "Forget not in your speed, ..." - The scene introduces us to the major characters. Calpurnia, Caesar's wife, is unable to conceive and this casts some doubt on Caesar's virility. Antony reminds us of Caesar's absolute power (10). Caesar shows his disdain for the supernatural (24) in words that convey male decisiveness. In this case, he ignores the famous warning, "Beware the Ides of March" (18). There is a strong bond between Brutus and Cassius (33, 44). Male bonding characterizes several of the relationships in the play.

- (I, II, 48) "Then, Brutus, I have much mistook ..." - Cassius begins his campaign to bring Brutus into a conspiracy against Caesar.

- (I, II, 52) "No, Cassius; for the eye ..." - Brutus voices one of the insights that Shakespeare scatters throughout his plays: "For the eye sees not itself but by reflection". These insights apply universally and enrich his plays. Here, the thought is that we lack the ability to evaluate ourselves and depend on the judgment of others. Cassius responds that Brutus needs a mirror so that he can appreciate his own worth.

- (I, II, 63) "Into what dangers ..." - Brutus senses Cassius' intent and his words indicate that he has had similar thoughts: "I do fear ..." (79). He speaks of his love of Caesar (82), another male bonding (in addition to Cassius and Titinius, and Antony and Caesar). He also speaks of his honor (86 - 89). This is central to his view of himself and he doesn't hesitate to let us know that he is an honorable man. He states his credo: "I love the name of honor more than I fear death" (89). As the play progresses it becomes clear that Brutus is more devoted to ethical abstractions than he is to practical affairs (STA 127).

- (I, II, 92 - 131) "Well, honour is the subject ..." - Cassius is jealous of Caesar's power. He sees Caesar as no better than himself. Thus, his motive in promoting the conspiracy goes beyond his concern for Roman liberty. He describes two incidents in which Caesar was weak: he nearly drowned in the Tiber and he behaved poorly when he was sick (100).

- (I, II, 134 - 160) "Why, man, he doth bestride the narrow world like a colossus ..." - Cassius describes Caesar in his famous speech. The play makes clear that Caesar is not without his weaknesses, but here Shakespeare reminds us that Caesar was truly an exceptionally powerful figure. Cassius speaks of two names, Brutus and Caesar (141), and introduces the notion that a name is distinct from the man it identifies. The former represents the idea of the man, the latter the man himself. The name "Caesar" brings to mind a powerful leader, but the man himself has weaknesses. Cassius is encouraging Brutus to think of his own name as representing something similar. In Brutus' case that would be his courage and honor. One theme of the play concerns the difficulty of enacting the political or moral ideal that one's name represents.

Cassius' jealousy of Caesar is complemented by his love for Rome. He ends with, "there was a Brutus once ..." (158), a reference to Brutus' ancestor who defeated the tyrant Tarquin, an act that ended the Roman monarchy and was instrumental in creating the Roman Republic.

- (I, II, 182) "The angry spot doth ..." - The games are over, and both Caesar and Cicero are angry as they emerge from the stadium. Cicero, a senator, a republican, a prominent intellectual and a major political actor, opposes Caesar's ambitions.

- (I, II, 191 - 213) "Let me have men ..." - Caesar, whose instincts are sharp, says that he wants to have bodyguards about him, men who "sleep a-nights". The implication is that those who are on a normal sleep cycle aren't plotting conspiracies and hence can be trusted to protect him. Thus, in his view, sleeplessness and evil are connected. He's suspicious of Cassius because Cassius thinks and reads too much, because he's a keen observer of human nature, and because he doesn't smile or listen to music. Falstaff had a similar complaint against Prince John in *Henry IV Part 2*. Caesar says he doesn't fear Cassius, but "if my name were liable to fear" he's the man he would avoid (198). He refers to himself as "my name" rather than "I" because he's speaking of his image, which is courageous, not of his human self, which shows signs of weakness. Caesar recognizes that Cassius is a jealous man (207). The passage ends with two conflicting thoughts on two successive lines that remind us of the two Caesars: he again refers to his courageous image by speaking of himself in the third person, "for always I am Caesar" (211), and he admits to frailty by telling Antony that he's deaf in one ear.

- (I, II, 234 - 249) "I can as well be hanged ..." - Caska, a nobleman, describes the offer of the crown made by Antony to Caesar. It appears to Caska that Caesar wanted to accept the offer, but for some reason, he refused it. Perhaps he hoped that the crowd would ultimately force it on him and he could then claim that he had no choice but to accept it. The scene is reminiscent of a similar scene in *Richard III* in which Richard stages a meeting with a group of citizens who are concerned about the succession to the throne. The difference between the two plays is that in *Richard III* the citizens are manipulated by Richard's followers into offering Richard the throne, whereas here Caesar's support seems to be spontaneous. An alternate explanation for why Caesar refuses the crown is that he might simply want to demonstrate to the Senate his sway with the people and force the Senate to crown him. Either way the scene demonstrates the political strength of the people, Caesar's dependence on it, and hence his populist leanings. Caska expresses his disdain for the lower classes, calling them rabble (243). And he gives us further evidence of Caesar's frailty: he has epilepsy (253).

- (I, II, 273) "If Caesar had stabbed ..." - Caska says that the mob so adores Caesar that they would not be put off if he killed their mothers.

- (I, II, 283) "it was Greek to me" - Caska mocks Cicero, and by extension it can be argued that Shakespeare is mocking intellectuals. We also learn that the two tribunes who opposed Caesar have been "put to silence", an ominous expression that could mean that they had been killed or simply that they had lost their position as tribunes. This is an indication of extra-legal actions and the decline of the Republic.

- (I, II, 307 - 321) "Well, Brutus, thou art noble: ..." - Cassius' soliloquy anticipates similar thoughts expressed by Iago in *Othello*. Cassius has both a political and a personal motive for promoting the conspiracy: He's a patriot, but he's also jealous of Caesar and senses that Caesar doesn't like him (312). Noble minds, like Brutus', can be manipulated by ignoble ones, like his own. And that's what he intends to do. Honorable men, like Brutus, can be persuaded to do anything for the sake of honor. Finally, Cassius speaks of "the great opinion that Rome holds of his name" (317), once again referring to the distinction between a man and his public image. Both Cassius and Brutus are portrayed as courageous patriots, but whereas Brutus is not motivated by personal animus, Cassius is and he's devious.

- (I, III, 15 - 33) "A common slave ..." - Reason was an underpinning of the Republican Rome. The Republic's deterioration is hinted at by the number of appeals in the play to supernatural explanations of worldly events. Here Caska talks of fantastic happenings that cannot be explained rationally (29). Cicero dismisses this (34), saying that a man can interpret things in a manner that has nothing to do with the purpose of the things themselves. Shakespeare goes on to illustrate this: Caska interprets the storm as either "civil strife in heaven" or a warning that the gods are unhappy with the respect that they are getting from "the world" (11). Cassius, on the other hand, sees it as a warning from the gods concerning the threat posed to Rome by Caesar (72).

- (I, III, 85 - 88) "Indeed, they say ..." - The Senate intends to crown Caesar.

- (I, III, 142 - 148) "Be you content." - Cassius' continues his campaign to bring Brutus into the assassination plot. The conspirators need Brutus because "he sits high in all the people's hearts" (157 - 160).

- (II, I, 4) "I would it were my ..." - Brutus associates sleep with an untroubled mind, a notion that both Henry IV and Macbeth expressed. Sleep is associated with goodness and nature; the conspiracy is evil and unnatural.

- (II, I, 10 - 34) "It must be by his death: ..." - Brutus tries to justify his decision to join the conspiracy. He says, "He would be crowned: How that might change his nature, there's the question." His concern is that Caesar will become a tyrant, although he admits that he hasn't observed "when his affections swayed more than his reason" (20). That it's difficult to extrapolate from the man he is today to the tyrant he might become in the future is expressed in the line "And since the quarrel will bear no colour for the thing he is, fashion it thus: that what he is, augmented, would run to these and these extremities" (28). Brutus here anticipates our modern concern for public relations.

  The question of the transformation of an individual as he acquires power is raised in *Henry IV.* Had Falstaff considered this question he might not have been surprised by his treatment when Hal assumed the throne as Henry V.

  Brutus is clearly unsure of himself. In deciding for the conspiracy, however, he displays the Stoicism that governs his life: his emotional bond to Caesar must give way to the rational justification for the assassination. More generally,

Stoics focus on logic as a tool for understanding oneself and the world, virtue as the ultimate good, and self-control as a means of achieving virtue. They attempt to rigidly control their emotions and to be superior to feelings of pleasure and pain. Thus, while Caska is frightened by the lightning and Cassius sees warnings from the heavens about the future of Rome, Brutus simply finds the lightning helpful since it allows him to read (44).

- (II, I, 61 – 69) "Since Cassius first did whet ..." - Brutus, like Macbeth, speaks of the mental torment that is experienced between the time of the conception of a crime and the time of its execution. Loss of sleep is a part of this (88). The point is made again by Portia (251) and with respect to Lucius, whose innocence allows him to enjoy the "honey-heavy dew of slumber" (228).

- (II, I, 77) "O conspiracy, Sham'st thou ..." - As in *Macbeth*, evil thrives at night.

- (II, I, 113) "No, not an oath." - Brutus, ever idealistic and impractical, objects to the swearing of an oath and the inclusion of Cicero in the conspiracy (149). These are probably mistakes, but his objection to the assassination of Antony is the decision that ultimately dooms the conspiracy (161). Cassius, an incisive judge of human nature, sees Antony as a "shrewd contriver" (157). Brutus says that he opposes only the spirit (name) of Caesar (166), not the man himself, and that the spirit contains no blood. His conclusion that they must draw blood – kill the man - to kill the spirit is the point at which his reasoning goes wrong. He sees a difference between carving him up as a dish for the gods and hewing him as a carcass fit for hounds (171). It's undoubtedly the case that Caesar would not have appreciated the difference. Brutus sees their act as one of sacrifice, not butchery: Caesar must be sacrificed in the cause of saving Rome; hence the assassination serves an ideal and is not murder. Cassius, ever the realist, sees the danger in this idealistic strategy.

Underlying Brutus' rationalizations is an attempt to minimize the violence, in the hope that the assassination can be justified as an honorable act. What Brutus misses is that murder, whether of one person or several, cannot be justified.

- (II, I, 194) "For he is superstitious ..." - Cassius claims that Caesar has become superstitious and that he appreciates flattery (205) – other weaknesses.

- (II, I, 236 - 301) "Not for yours neither." - Shakespeare gives Portia only a few lines but she comes across as a character with depth, wisdom and strength. She could easily be expanded into the protagonist of her own play. She worries about her husband's health and well-being. She wants to be included in all aspects of his life and to know his secrets. She's not afraid of asserting herself (244). "She speaks without coquetry of her 'once-commended beauty'" (270) (G2 378). She has a healthy notion of how a husband and wife should relate to one another and asks, "Dwell I but in the suburbs of your good pleasure?" (284) and, if so, says she is a harlot, not a wife. And, finally, although she admits she's 'only' a woman (291), she says she is strong and speaks of her "constancy" (298). She shows him a self-inflicted wound which demonstrates her ability to withstand pain, an ideal valued in the Stoic approach to living.

Portia understands that eating and sleeping are associated with goodness, health and nature. Brutus is deprived of them and the symbolism tells us that the conspiracy is evil, sick and unnatural. Portia goes on to describe the intimacy that should exist in a good marriage (279).

- (II, II, 5) "Go bid the priests ..." - In contrast to Brutus, Caesar is concerned with supernatural forces. He speaks of his courage (10 – 12, 41 - 48), and in doing so he refers to his image (name) not his person and, in the well-known quote, he speaks of his attitude towards death (32 – 37). He had planned to go to the Senate, but when Calpurnia begs him not to, he quickly reverses himself and blames the reversal on Calpurnia (55). He now speaks of himself as "I" rather than "Caesar" (62), since he understands that his decision smacks of cowardice and is unworthy of his image. He carefully explains to Decius that it's not that he cannot or dare not go to the Senate, but that he will not. He is unwilling to accept his decision as a sign of weakness.

- (II, II, 126) "Good friends, go in, ..." - In an effort not to endorse any of the characters in the tragedy, Shakespeare shows a friendly side of Caesar by having him invite the conspirators in for a glass of wine.

- (II, IV, 8) "I have a man's mind, ..." - Portia again appeals to the Stoic principle of constancy. She wants to emulate Brutus. In this case, keeping a secret, placing a barrier between her heart and her tongue (also (II, I, 290)).

- (III, I, 47) "Know, Caesar doth not wrong ..." - Caesar's self-regard reaches a peak just prior to his assassination. He says he "doth not wrong" (47), that he is as "constant as the Northern star" (60) and that he is the only one who is "unassailable" in his position (68). This is a central tenet of Stoic philosophy, the ability to rationally decide a course of action and to be unaffected by emotion or turmoil in carrying it out. He suggests his place among the gods with his reference to Mt. Olympus (74). This is the Caesar image and it "may seem a little foolish, yet if we see only foolishness, we are wrong. We must observe both Caesars, keep both ever in mind: one physical and weak, the other all but supernatural in spiritual power, a power blazing in the fine hyperboles of his egocentricity" (STA 121). The Caesar image is more powerful than Caesar the man, and it is this that Brutus comes to fear. It is something that Caesar the man tries to live up to and that outlives him after his death. His dominance in Rome is demonstrated by the fact that he has the power to decide the fate of a citizen without consulting anyone (73).

- (III, I, 77) *"Et tu, Brute?"* - The phrase is not taken from Plutarch: It is Shakespeare's invention.

- (III, I, 78) "Liberty! Freedom! Tyranny is dead!" – Cinna's cry has to be understood in the context of the times. The conspirators were not claiming to set up a new democratic government. Rather they were simply trying to preserve the *status quo* and prevent Caesar from dominating the patricians as well as the plebeians. It was patrician liberty, not plebeian liberty, that was really at stake. This is the midpoint of the play and Caesar is already dead. Hence, he's clearly not the protagonist. Shakespeare probably named the play for him to bring in an audience, but the protagonist of the play, the tragic hero, is Brutus.

- (III, I, 148 – 150) "O mighty Caesar!" - Antony doesn't seem to distinguish between Caesar the man and Caesar's image.

He loved a unified individual and hence can see no justification in his assassination.

- (III, I, 167) "yet see you but our hands ..." - Brutus tries to distinguish his body from his spirit. His hands have done the bloody work, but his heart was pure in its intentions. This is the same distinction that Brutus tried to make about Caesar: The goal was to kill Caesar's ambitious spirit, not to kill him. The question of whether the mind can be separated from the body has concerned philosophers for ages. Shakespeare seems to say that it can't.

- (III, I, 231) "You shall, Mark Antony." - Against the advice of Cassius, Brutus consents to let Antony give a funeral oration. This is another mistake, as demonstrated by Antony's soliloquy shortly afterward (254). William Hazlitt said this of the play: "the whole design of the conspirators to liberate their country fails from the generous temper and over-weening confidence of Brutus in the goodness of their cause ... Thus, it has always been. Those who mean well themselves think well of others ... That humanity and honesty which dispose men to resist injustice and tyranny render them unfit to cope with the cunning and power of those who are opposed to them." (H 24)

  Antony cannot see beyond the act to the principle that motivated it. In his view Caesar was murdered and there can be no justification. He cynically sets out to incite "domestic fury and fierce civil strife" (263) and predicts that "mothers shall but smile when they behold their infants quartered" (267). He vows to "let slip the dogs of war" (273). The play doesn't make clear if his motive is purely revenge for the murder of a good friend or whether self-interest – his own advancement – is involved (Bl16 97). In either case, Antony doesn't hesitate to bring chaos to his beloved Rome. It can be argued that Brutus' mistake was not the savagery of the murder, but that he was not savage enough. If he had dealt more forcefully with Antony, the chaos might have been avoided and the Republic saved.

- (III, II, 8 - 10) "I will hear Brutus speak." - Shakespeare inserts a small exchange which supports the idea that he attempts to give a balanced portrayal of the plebeians. They intend to listen to both Brutus and Cassius and compare their justifications for the assassination, a reasonable strategy that gives the conspirators a fair hearing.

- (III, II, 13 – 34) "Romans, countrymen and lovers, ..." - Brutus' funeral oration is written in prose. It's simple, logical and unemotional. The crowd approves. Ironically, one of the plebeian's cries, "Let him be Caesar" (51), raising the question of whether the crowd deserves the liberty that the assassination was meant to provide.

- (III, II, 74 – 108) "Friends, Romans, countrymen, ..." - Antony's funeral oration is written in blank verse. It's emotional and designed to arouse the crowd against the conspirators. He brings Caesar's body to the podium for this purpose. He mocks Brutus' claim to honor and his attribution of ambition to Caesar by constantly repeating these two words. They are the central words of the two speeches: Honor characterizes Brutus' Stoic philosophy and ambition is the sole crime that Caesar is charged with.

Antony says that Caesar wept for Rome and that his heart is in Caesar's coffin. His use of the word "brutish" (105) is a veiled reference to Brutus and a comment on his nature. He takes a dramatic pause claiming he needs to control his emotions. He produces Caesar's will (130) but says that he won't read it because it will inflame the crowd. He then waits for the crowd to beg him to read it and he ultimately does so. His strategy here is to create a personal connection between Caesar and the plebeians, in contrast to Brutus' rational argument. He repeatedly tells the crowd that he will not give them reasons for opposing the conspirators, but then does exactly that. The result is that the crowd is completely swayed against the conspirators.

- (III, II, 214) "For I have neither wit, ..." - The merit of Brutus' sober words is completely overshadowed by the techniques Antony employs in presenting his argument. These techniques are part of the toolbox used by populist politicians. Shakespeare dramatizes "the power of speech to stir men's blood". The two orations and the crowd's response to them demonstrate the "importance of public performance in winning and maintaining political power" (Bl16 122). Antony's cynicism is evident in his remark: "Now let it work. Mischief, thou art afoot: Take thou what course thou wilt" (251). He has deliberately provoked mob violence without any idea of what will follow.

It has been frequently argued that the crowd's reversal of its support for Brutus after Antony's speech is an indication of its fickleness. This indictment is strengthened by the similar reversal of support for Pompey that was denounced by Murellus (I, II, 33). But were this true, one would have to assume that had Antony spoken first the scene would have ended with the crowd supporting Brutus, an unlikely outcome.

Romans had conflicting motivations. On the one hand they appreciated the measure of participation in governing that they enjoyed and the guarantee of equality under the law. These are things that Brutus claimed were threatened by Caesar. On the other hand, they supported Caesar for his military success in expanding Rome's empire abroad and for the reforms that he had supported that worked to their advantage at home.

- (III, III) Whereas Antony could have used his speech to "define a political program" or to demand that the conspirators face justice (Bl16 154), he has instead unleashed senseless mob violence, as shown in this scene. It's interesting that it is a poet who is attacked. And this is immediately followed (IV, I) by the corrupt bargains made by Antony, Octavius and Lepidus who now control Rome. Their misappropriation of Caesar's money is dwarfed by their plan to murder opposition figures. This involves a cynical trade: Lepidus will agree to the murder of his brother if Antony agrees to the murder of his nephew. Then Antony and Octavius discuss how they will dispose of Lepidus (IV, I, 12) so that the Roman world can be divided in two instead of three. The chaos of the mob is matched by the cruelty of the rulers.

- (IV, III, 1) "That you have wronged me ..." - The quarrel scene illustrates the tangle into which Brutus' notion of honor leads him. He berates Cassius for taking bribes (9) and Cassius, essentially admitting bribery, replies that it's foolish to be dealing with such issues before a battle (7). The argument becomes petty. They debate who is a better soldier (30) and Cassius backs down, unwilling to further anger Brutus (56).

Brutus says that his honor prevents him from raising money through extortion, but it doesn't prevent him from demanding the money that Cassius has obtained in that way. Brutus ironically claims that he is "strong in honesty" (67).

We see here, in a small interchange, the flaw that is central to his tragedy. Brutus is so sure of his own rectitude that he can't imagine that his actions – taking tainted money - could possibly be wrong. Cassius' emotional nature, as opposed to Brutus' logical nature, is revealed in this scene. He loves Brutus and bemoans the fact that Brutus isn't able to overlook his faults, as friends should (85). He dramatically offers up his life, claiming that he is weary of the world because Brutus doesn't love him (95), and he charges Brutus with loving Caesar more than himself (105). And then, with the first sign of forgiveness on Brutus' part – Brutus admits that although he generally behaves like a lamb, he's prone to sudden bursts of anger (115) - Cassius quickly responds, "Give me your hand" and they reconcile like lovers. Cassius says "O, Brutus!"

The contrast between their natures is demonstrated in the exchange over Portia's suicide (145). (Plutarch says that she committed suicide by swallowing burning coals.) Whereas Cassius is emotional, Brutus is a Stoic, unemotional and detached. In a few lines he explains the circumstances of her death, but not a word about how it has affected him.

From a theatrical point of view Brutus' Stoicism has the effect of blunting him as a tragic hero, since it prevents him from being affected by the actions in the play. "Nobility has numbed him until he cannot see himself for his principles" (VD 160). It's been said that Shakespeare is more interested in character than in plot and from this point of view one can see the limitations of the play as compared with his later tragedies. Hamlet, Lear and Macbeth are tormented characters, and it's this torment that makes them human and that Shakespeare so brilliantly portrays on the stage. Brutus' reticence, however, keeps us at a distance and diminishes our involvement in the play.

"Cassius has profound understanding, a rich personality. He is very sincere. He claims, rightly, to have nothing in him of the flatterer or scandalmonger ... His seriousness makes him somber, gloomy, ashamed of all trivialities. Smiles, plays, music – all are barred. Instead, we have knowledge of men, books, restlessness of temperament" (STA 135). Shakespeare seems to have taken pains to give a balanced picture of Cassius. Although he deliberately manipulated Brutus into joining the conspiracy and was partly motivated by jealousy, he is Brutus' loyal friend and sincerely affected by Portia's death. Shakespeare gives the same balanced treatment to Caesar by showing the weakness behind this extraordinary man, and to Brutus by showing the basic decency and morality that exists besides his inflated pride.

- (IV, III, 171) "That by proscription ..." - The end of the Republic is confirmed by the murder of seventy senators, Cicero among them. His death is significant since he was a leading advocate of the tradition of rational policy making and debate that characterized republican Rome.

- (IV, III, 194) "Well, to our work alive." - Brutus' strategy of attacking Antony's forces at Philippi turns out to be bad. He justifies it with the familiar words "There is a tide in the affairs of men which, taken at the flood leads on to fortune" (216). The quarrel scene ends with Brutus referring to

Cassius as "good brother" (235), evidence of a more emotional dimension to Brutus' character. More evidence of this is shown in Brutus' loving relationship to Lucius, who embodies the "care-free purity of youth" (263) (STA 130).

- (IV, III, 250) "Look, Lucius, here's the book ..." - Brutus can't find his book and he's forgetful. This is a reminder of his frailty and the fact that this paragon of honor has a mortal side just as Caesar, the paragon of a soldier, has his. It also tells us that Brutus is a reader. There are also references to his philosophy (IV, III, 143), (V, I, 100) and his schooling (I, II, 295), (V, V, 26). Shakespeare wants us to know that Brutus is an intellectual. Yet his plans for the conspiracy and for the battle at Philippi prove to be foolish. Poets appear twice in the play and are ineffective and treated poorly. All this raises the question of whether Shakespeare had an anti-intellectual bias (STA 265)

- (IV, III, 273) "How ill this taper burns" - It's not clear whether the ghost is real or, at least at a subconscious level, Brutus is simply troubled. What is clear, though, is that although Caesar the man is dead, his spirit lives on. In contrast to Macbeth who, after the murders of Duncan and Banquo, suffers from guilt, guilt isn't a factor in Brutus' conscious mind and he doesn't respond to the ghost with either terror or remorse. He is a Stoic. Caesar's murder was consistent with his notion of a personal, logical morality and it is this alone that guides his actions. He recognizes no moral absolutes in the universe that demand his obedience and he doesn't fear that he has offended the gods.

From a practical point of view, however, he would have been better served if he had recognized that political actions must justify themselves, not his concept of morality.

Lucius, the personification of innocence, delivers Shakespeare's last word on the subject, "the strings, my lord, are false" (289), words that can be interpreted to mean that the simple notion of right and wrong cannot be denied – murder is wrong under any circumstances. Brutus, however, doesn't get the message; he thinks that Lucius is referring only to the instrument.

- (V, I, 76) "You know that I held ..." - Cassius claims that his philosophical outlook has shifted. Omens are sent by the gods, and whereas he had previously scorned them, he now gives them some credence. This is consistent with his emotional nature and contrasts with Brutus' view.

- (V, I, 100) "Even by the rule of ..." - Brutus is prepared to accept the outcome of the battle with Stoic reserve. He will not resort to suicide to avoid a future of suffering. Being led through Rome in chains, however, violates his notion of honor, something he will not do.

- (V, I, 114 - 125) "And whether we shall meet again, ..." - Brutus and Cassius part for the last time.

- (V, III, 5) "O Cassius, Brutus gave the word ..." - Another military error made by Brutus.

- (V, III, 45) "Caesar, thou art revenged ..." - Cassius misconstrues Titinius' fate, as Cicero had predicted earlier, and commits suicide as a result. He gives Caesar credit for having brought about his defeat. The references cannot be to Caesar the man, but to the idea of Caesar. Brutus confirms this (94) (V, V, 17, 51). Caesar's ghost at Philippi symbolizes the triumph of his spirit over the conspirators.

- (V, V, 31 – 52) "Farewell to you; ..." - Brutus "is sincere throughout. He unwaveringly pursues an ethical ideal" (STA 131, 133). Many critics consider him "one of the most noble and lovable figures" Shakespeare ever created (Go1 310) and almost everyone in the play thinks highly of him, including his enemy, Antony, who says, "This is the noblest Roman of them all" (69 - 76). But others see a different Brutus: He was a fool to pursue an ethical ideal in and for itself, unrelated to the time and people around (STA 134). And he was "an egotist, an unconscionable prig ... A man should have no more acquaintance with his virtue than a woman with her beauty" (Go1 311).

Discussion

The protagonists in Shakespeare's major tragedies generally exhibit two important characteristics: despite their heroic proportions, their character is flawed in a way that leads to a tragic conclusion and, during the struggle which is the action of the play, they come to a new understanding of themselves and how life is to be lived. As a result, they rise to nobility.

Brutus is the protagonist of this play and his flaw is his belief in his own rectitude. Trusting in that rectitude, he convinces himself that the end of saving Rome from tyranny justifies the means, Caesar's assassination. Unfortunately, there is no evidence that he comes to realize that the assassination was unjustified and has led to chaos. He expresses no regret, nor has he been transformed. His final words concern the glory he will achieve in his suicide (36) and an admission that Caesar has triumphed: "Caesar, now be still, I killed not thee with half so good a will" (V, V, 51). Ironically, having started with the desire to kill Caesar's spirit without killing the man, the play ends with Caesar's spirit killing him.

The play addresses the question: What happens when one does evil to advance a good cause? In this case, the cause is republican government and the evil is the use of assassination as a political instrument. The answer to the question is chaos. "Those who oppose imperialism with force run the risk of being no better than the imperialists themselves" (Go1 330).

Chapter 10

Hamlet

Background

Hamlet is the first of Shakespeare's mature tragedies. It was written in 1601, in the middle of Shakespeare's career as a playwright. It is a huge play and for that reason rarely performed in its entirety. It was probably based on an earlier play, referred to as the *Ur-Hamlet* (that might have been written by Shakespeare), which has since disappeared. Shakespeare's eminence in all of Western literature is indisputable, as is *Hamlet*'s eminence among Shakespeare's plays. Beyond that, the character Hamlet has achieved an eminence that exceeds the play itself. He is regarded as virtually human, with a life outside the play, and has been the subject of psychological analysis.

More than any other of Shakespeare's plays, *Hamlet* is about its main character. Although the play doesn't lack physical action, it is the mental action, his thoughts and the debates that he has with himself, that are at the heart of the play. Shakespeare presents to us the inner life of this intelligent and noble man at a moment when a crisis has called into question his most fundamental values. It is this focus on a man's inner life that distinguishes the play from the literature that precedes it and that makes the play modern. In placing his focus there, Shakespeare anticipates psychology and Freud and sheds light on our own inner lives.

Although the play's focus on Hamlet's mind was unusual at the time it was written, it is the nature of that mind that engages us because "it abounds most in striking reflections on human life, and because the distresses of Hamlet are transferred ... to the general account of humanity" (H 65). The play places Hamlet in a situation that forces his thoughts to touch on a variety of issues and as a result we see him in a number of different guises. He is the political actor forced to maneuver against a deadly adversary; "the moralist, unable to draw a clear-cut line between good and evil; the intellectual, unable to find a sufficient reason for action; the philosopher, to whom the world's existence is a matter of doubt" (K 62). He struggles to come to an understanding of the issues with which he has to deal and, in these struggles, we see our own lives. This is the basis of the play's universality and of the eminence that it has achieved.

There is no version of the play in Shakespeare's hand that we can point to as official. There are three main printed versions: the first Quarto (Q1), the second Quarto (Q2), and the Folio (F). The play was probably first performed around 1601, Q1 is dated 1603 and Q2 is dated 1604. F is dated 1623, after Shakespeare's death in 1616. It's not known how these editions are related to what Shakespeare actually wrote.

Q2 and F are similar but there are significant differences – several thousand words out of a total of roughly twenty-eight thousand. Q1 is quite different from either of the other two. It's a little over half the size. Some scholars think that Q1 is a first draft by Shakespeare; others think it may be a reconstruction, perhaps a bootlegged version, based on a stage production. In any case it's generally discounted as an acceptable version of the play. F, coming later than the other two, might have been based on later revisions, perhaps made by Shakespeare. In any case, both Q2 and F are considered authoritative. Published versions of the play are often the product of an editor who has conflated Q2 and F. Both Q2 and F are considered too long for a stage production and might have been intended by Shakespeare for readers.

The Play (line numbers from (ArH))

- (I, I, 2) "Stand and unfold yourself" - The introductory exchange sets the theme of the play: an exploration of man's – particularly Hamlet's - inner life. Hamlet reminds us of this later when he says that he has "that within which passes show" (I, II, 85).

- (I, I, 59) "Such was the very armour ..." - King Hamlet was a warrior king. He fought the Poles and he killed Fortinbras Sr. (85). A contrast with Hamlet (the son) is intended here. His fight with Fortinbras Sr. was arranged as fair, single combat with an agreement that the winner would be awarded certain contested lands. Fortinbras Jr., angry at this loss of his father and of his inheritance, wants the lands back. This explains Elsinore's concern about a possible attack. Both Fortinbras Jr. and Hamlet have lost fathers and the former's aggressive behavior serves as a contrast to the latter's more passive stance.

- (I, II, 65 - 73) "A little more than kin, ..." - Hamlet's first words demonstrate his wit and intellect. He does this throughout the play. In this case, he both rejects his kinship to Claudius and implies that Claudius has been unkind. His dress indicates that he is still in mourning for his father, but also serve as a rebuke of Claudius and a rejection of his marriage to Gertrude.

- (I, II, 76 - 85) "'Seems', madam – nay it is, ..." - Hamlet distinguishes his inner life from his outward appearance. A similar distinction was made by Richard (*Richard II* (IV, I, 295)).

- (I, II, 129 - 159) **First soliloquy**: "O that this too too solid [sallied in Q] flesh ...." - Hamlet wishes for death. Only religion keeps him from it. Life has no interest for him. It's full of evil. Hamlet is a man who is perpetually arguing with himself and Shakespeare gives us those arguments in his soliloquies. The soliloquy is the main device that Shakespeare uses to expose Hamlet's inner life. They carry the play. They dramatize Hamlet's consciousness and they form the basis of the analyses that scholars have made of Hamlet's character. His upset centers on his mother's hasty marriage to his unworthy uncle (at this point he doesn't know that his father has been murdered). He expresses disgust at her insatiable sexuality (156). He idealizes his father, comparing him to Hyperion, the Greek sun-god, and he idealizes the relationship his parents had had. He magnifies his father's protective concern for her, her attachment to him and her grief at his funeral. This idealization leads Hamlet to find Gertrude's betrayal of his father unforgivable. Hamlet then generalizes this condemnation to all women: "frailty they name is woman". This may explain his change in attitude towards Ophelia later in the play. He compares himself mockingly to

Hercules, a man of action, indicating that he views himself as a basically contemplative man.

Shakespeare's ability to portray his characters' interior life, its agendas, emotions and even internal conflicts, demonstrates his genius. It's what gives his characters complexity and depth. For example, in this soliloquy he interrupts himself at several points: "nay, not so much, not two", "heaven and earth, Must I remember", "Let me not think on it", "O God, a beast that wants discourse of reason … ". These interruptions suggest that powerful emotional pressures are breaking through his conscious train of thought against his will, revealing an internal struggle. Hamlet refers to aspects of his interior life on several occasions that he deliberately refrains from telling us about. Thus, he speaks of "actions that a man might play, But I have that within which passes show" (I, II, 84) and "I have within me something dangerous" (V, I, 251).

- (I, II, 160) "I am glad to see you well …" - Hamlet greets Horatio in an open, friendly and humorous way. This is a glimpse of an earlier Hamlet, before the murder, and is different from the way he interacts with other characters in the play. We learn that Hamlet was a student in Wittenberg.

- (I, II, 179 - 181) "Thrift, thrift, Horatio …" - The line is an example of Hamlet's wit. His reaction to his mother's hasty wedding is similar to how he would feel if he met his "dearest foe" in heaven: both terrible events. The comparison is an indication of the importance of imaginings about the afterlife in Hamlet's mind. We get a new view of him in his dialogue with Horatio. He is generous and open – perhaps reflecting his nature before the murder - not grieving and melancholy. We'll see different Hamlet's as the play progresses.

- (I, II, 185) "I saw him once ..." - When Horatio refers to Hamlet's father as "goodly king", Hamlet responds that "'A was a man, take him for all in all". The stress is on "a man". Hamlet's open and friendly personality is evident in his impatience with distinctions of rank.

- (I, III, 57 - 79) "And these few precepts in thy memory ... " - Polonius is a tiresome, meddlesome character, but here he gives good advice on how one should behave. This is another measure of Shakespeare's genius: He makes even minor characters three dimensional.

- (I, III, 109) "My lord, he hath importuned ..." - Ophelia says that Hamlet "importuned me in honorable fashion". This is a glimpse of Hamlet in earlier times.

- (I, III, 114 - 134) "Ay, springes too catch woodcocks - ..." - Ophelia is told to break off with Hamlet (and she does (II, I, 106)). This, perhaps, explains Hamlet's later cruelty toward her. Ophelia obeys her father. Although the demands that have been made are far different, this serves as a contrast to Hamlet's inability to obey his father.

- (I, IV, 17 - 38) "This heavy-headed revel ..." - The passage is difficult to parse, but gives insight into Hamlet's character. He deplores Claudius' drunkenness, he expresses concern for the breakdown of reason, he recognizes that a person's birth should not be held against him, he's concerned about appearances and he makes an acute observation about human nature: small defects in a man's character can obscure all his virtues. Perhaps Shakespeare is pointing to a "tragic" flaw in Hamlet's character. His sense that small imperfections dominate great good implies a desire for perfection in what he does and this can lead to an inability to decide to do anything. Hence, action is paralyzed. The passage demonstrates Hamlet's concern for moral and rational behavior, his generosity, and the analytical nature of his mind.

- (I, IV, 40) "Be thou a spirit of health ..." - Hamlet doesn't know if the ghost comes from heaven or hell. This is the first indication that Hamlet might have doubts about the message he will get from it.

- (I, V, 25) "- Revenge his foul and most unnatural murder!" - The ghost reveals that he was murdered by Claudius (39), something Hamlet apparently suspected (40), and he demands revenge. He speaks of murder as foul even in the best of circumstances, yet he asks Hamlet to murder Claudius. This is the central dilemma of the play. From this point on the play describes the contest in Hamlet's mind over whether revenge is morally justifiable and the contest between Hamlet and Claudius over whether or not revenge will be achieved.

- (I, V, 42) "Ay, that incestuous, that adulterate beast ..." - The ghost hints that Gertrude might have been unfaithful during his lifetime. He claims that he satisfied Gertrude sexually (56) and Hamlet shouldn't punish her since she'll be punished in heaven (85) and by her own guilt.

- (I, V, 76) "Cut off even in the blossoms ..." - Since King Hamlet didn't get a chance to confess his sins before dying, he's confined to purgatory. This is an example of the strong role of religion in shaping the action.

- (I, V, 92) "O all you hosts of heaven, ..." - Hamlet goes through several cycles of passion followed by lethargy. This is the beginning of the first (see also (29)): he vows to "sweep to my revenge" and thus rejects his earlier thought (I, IV, 40) that the ghost comes from hell.

- (I, V, 98 - 104) "Yea, from the table of my memory ..." - Hamlet sees a conflict between his intellectual life and his need for action.

- (I, V, 137) "It is a honest ghost ..." - At this point Hamlet accepts the ghost's story, but his doubts as to whether the ghost is a manifestation of the devil recur later.

- (I, V, 149) "Swear." - The ghost's voice comes from under the stage. Perhaps this indicates hell. According to some commentators, Shakespeare frequently associates what is morally wrong with what is physically low (Go 341). Hence the stage direction can be interpreted as a clue to Shakespeare's view of blood revenge.

- (I, V, 165 - 170) "There are more things in heaven ..." - Hamlet places a limit on how much philosophy can do. He speaks of feigning madness (an "antic disposition") and some of his actions from this point until his return from England exhibit madness. Scholars debate whether this is real or feigned. Some think it unlikely that Shakespeare wanted us to think that Hamlet is mad (HC 194). Others think the madness is a combination of both acting and the effects of the devastating news and awful responsibility that have suddenly been thrust upon him. "Of the feigned madness of Hamlet there appears no adequate cause, for he does nothing which he might not have done with the reputation of sanity." (SJ)

- (I, V, 186) "The time is out of joint; ..." - Hamlet curses the fact that it is his responsibility to set right a terrible wrong. As will become apparent later in the play, blood revenge would be the immediate response if Laertes or Fortinbras were faced with his situation, and he would not be agonizing at this point. But Hamlet's sensibilities run in a different direction and from this point on he is a divided man.

- (II, I, 1 - 71) "Give him this money ..." - Polonius demonstrates his tedious nature. He is a man who "meddles his way to his doom" (Ba1 66). He is in this scene "manifestly modified from that of the earlier scene, with its terse dispensing of sound worldly wisdom" (Ba1 66). He sends Reynaldo to spy on Laertes.

- (II, I, 74) "My lord, as I was sewing ..." - Ophelia's description points to Hamlet's madness, but more likely this is feigned, an example of "antic disposition" (Ba1 67).

- (II, II, 6) "Sith nor th'exterior ..." - Claudius speaks of the inward and the exterior man. A major concern of the play is that we have an interior ("that within that passeth show") and an exterior life, and that they might be quite different.

- (II, II, 15) "To draw him on ..." - Guildenstern and Rosencrantz are sent to spy on Hamlet. Polonius has just sent Reynaldo to spy on Laertes. Shortly Ophelia will be sent to spy on Hamlet (III, I) with Polonius and Claudius secretly watching. And in the bedroom scene, Polonius is again secretly watching. A pattern of duplicity pervades the action.

- (II, II, 86 – 95) "My liege and madam, ..." - Polonius demonstrates what it means to be tedious by denouncing it.

- (II, II, 165) "But look where sadly ..." - Hamlet enters, reading. This emphasizes his intellect.

- (II, II, 227 - 231) "Then you live about her waist ..." - Hamlet enjoys sexual banter.

- (II, II, 259 - 276) "I will tell you why." - Hamlet tells of his melancholy. His recognition of the beauty of the world and the wonder of man tells us something of his outlook prior to his current troubles. But this no longer brings him happiness. In describing man, he speaks of reason and apprehension – qualities that are of importance to him. Hamlet's depression is the opposite of his passion after seeing the ghost: He has descended into the lethargy that ends his first cycle of mood swings. "Through all he says there is threaded the longing to be free from the corrupt realities of life" (Ba1 73).

- (II, II, 315) "I am but mad north-north-west." - Hamlet mocks his antic disposition.

- (II, II, 359) "You are welcome, masters, welcome all." - Hamlet's warmth in welcoming the players is a reflection of his earlier self, and contrasts with the cruelty he demonstrates towards Ophelia, Gertrude, Rosencranz and Guildenstern. The joke about the voice of the "young lady" (362) relates to the fact that female characters were played by boys.

- (II, II, 383) "One speech in't I chiefly loved - ..." - Hamlet chooses the speech describing how Pyrrhus kills Priam. Pyrrhus was Achilles son and he punished Priam because Achilles was killed in the Trojan War and Priam was the king of Troy at that time. Hence, Pyrrhus is a son whose father has been killed and Priam bears some responsibility. The situation is similar to Hamlet's, although Achilles wasn't murdered and in contrast to Pyrrhus, Hamlet can't bring himself to kill Claudius. The speech stands as an admonishment to Hamlet that he has yet to do what his father has demanded. Hamlet's recollection of the speech tells us something about his personality: He is interested in the arts and he is capable of performing (404). Hamlet also wants to hear about Hecuba and how she mourned for Priam (439). This contrasts with Gertrude's reaction to Hamlet's father's death.

- (II, II, 466 - 470) "God's bodkin, man, much better!" - An example of Hamlet's generosity and his insight into human nature.

- (II, II, 480) "Very well. Follow that lord - ..." - Hamlet's directive to "mock him not" is another example of his humanity and the complexity of his relationship to Polonius, the man who might have become his father-in-law.

- (II, II, 485 - 540) **Second soliloquy**: "O, what a rogue and peasant slave am I ..." - The soliloquy gives us another (I, II, 129) view of the conflict going on in Hamlet's mind. First, he imagines what the Player would do if he were in Hamlet's place and concludes that "he would drown the stage with tears ..." (495). Interestingly, he doesn't say that he would resort to murder. Hamlet is divided on what he should do and here he simply expresses a desire to confront Claudius, not kill him (perhaps he's hoping that Claudius will undergo a redemptive transformation). This can be viewed as a part of Hamlet's struggle against the blood revenge course of action. Hamlet berates himself for inaction. Then he attacks Claudius (515). Then he attacks himself again for substituting a verbal attack on Claudius for physical action (517).

Finally, Hamlet summons his rational side to develop a plan to test the ghost's story: "About, my brain!" (522). He argues with himself and then defers revenge saying that he needs more evidence before acting in order to determine whether or not the ghost was sent by the devil. The plan involves more delay and although the soliloquy started with Hamlet feeling disgusted with himself, he's quite happy by the end because he has a plan to take action. He seems to have shaken off his melancholy. These examples all raise the question "Do we take Hamlet at his word?"

- (III, I, 49) "How smart a lash ..." - Claudius refers to Polonius' line (46) about feigning piety. Claudius is not simply a villain: He regrets his crime. "It is plain that he becomes a criminal not through viciousness, but through weakness" (Go 364).

- (III, I, 55 - 91) **Third soliloquy**: "To be or not to be – that is the question; ..." - It's not clear whether the question concerns suicide or revenge ("take up arms"). Hamlet's feelings about death are "precisely where he was at the time of his first soliloquy" (Br 132) (I, II, 129). He's introspective and rational and thinks through his choices. He talks about the difficulty of making a choice and how that choice might have implications that extend to the afterlife. The lines, "Conscience does make cowards ..." (82) and "The pale cast of thought ..." (84) are indicators that Hamlet's passion has again cooled. He registers an awareness of thoughts' power to paralyze action.

"The soliloquy is a classic expression of the wearying effect upon a sensitive spirit, of the daily injustices and ignobilities and misfortunes of life" (Sa1 48). Interestingly, Hamlet makes no mention of the ghost and, in fact, seems to deny its existence when he says that "no traveler returns" after death (78).

- (III, I, 92) "My lord, I have remembrances ..." - The fact that Ophelia returns Hamlet's gifts - and perhaps his suspicion that she's being used by Polonius against him (129) - might be what motivates Hamlet's attack on her in the play scene.

- (III, I, 138) "wise men know well enough ..." - Hamlet's words speak of misogyny: women make men into monsters. He threatens Claudius (146).

- (III, I, 149 - 160) "O, what a noble mind ..." - Ophelia speaks of Hamlet's past virtues, but Claudius recognizes that Hamlet is a threat and that he's not crazy (163).

- (III, II, 1) "Speak the speech, ..." - Some critics consider the advice to the players as extraneous, but interesting. Hamlet criticizes "barren spectators" who interrupt when "some necessary question of the play is being considered" (40). But he will commit exactly that indiscretion shortly.

- (III, II, 64) "And blest are those whose blood and judgment are so well co-meddled that they are not a pipe for Fortune's finger to sound what stop she please. Give me that man that is not passion's slave and I will wear him in my heart's core ..." - Hamlet admires Horatio's ability to temper passion (blood) with judgment, something that he is unable to do. By Fortune he means the arbitrary force that controls future events. Passion is the necessary force that underlies all action, but it must be controlled if action is to be effective. Without control a man is no more than passion's slave (Bl2 51).

- (III, II, 76 - 80) "If his occulted guilt ..." - Hamlet's plan will determine the origin of the ghost.

- (III, II, 108) "Lady, shall I lie in your lap?" - Hamlet's sexual jokes are crude, particularly since Ophelia is portrayed as young and innocent. But his love for her prior to the opening of the play is genuine. She says this (I, III, 109) and Hamlet talks of his love later (V, I, 258). Both Polonius and Laertes warn Ophelia to be wary of Hamlet for the wrong reason: that he (using his royal position) might try to take advantage of her sexually. Hamlet treats her poorly, but it's not in his character to do anything like that. His reasons have only to do with the murder and his mother's marriage, in which Ophelia plays only an incidental role. He suspects that Ophelia is cooperating with Polonius and Claudius against him. "His conduct to Ophelia ... is that of assumed severity only. It is the effect of disappointed hope, of bitter regrets, of affection suspended, not obliterated, by the distractions of the scene around him!" (H 68)

- (III, II, 129) "What means this, my lord?" - The play within a play is similar to the morality plays that were popular prior to Shakespeare's time. They made no attempt to be realistic, but instead presented a moral lesson and involved characters who represented various forms of virtue and vice. *The Murder of Gonzago* did this in the context of the story of a murder. Hamlet could be using the play in its traditional fashion, to illustrate immoral behavior and encourage repentance. This isn't unreasonable since both Gertrude and Claudius have some regret for their actions. This would be the use of art, rather than revenge, to resolve a crime (Go 361). More likely, however, he's using the play to establish Claudius' guilt as a stepping stone to revenge.

- (III, II, 173) "In second husband ..." - Player Queen denounces a wife who takes a second husband.

- (III, II, 182 - 189) "Purpose is but the slave to memory, ..." - Player King discusses the relationship between thought and action. He doesn't question his wife's sincerity. He simply points out that action is blunted by time and once passion subsides, purpose is lost. This clearly relates to Hamlet's situation. He then goes on to say that all is accident: desire and destiny are unrelated (205). "Our thoughts are ours, their ends none of our own" (207). There is also a worthwhile comment on making friends (201 - 203): someone who's not desperate for a friend has an easier time making one than someone who is. This is another example (in addition to Polonius' advice to Laertes) where minor characters speak wisdom.

- (III, II, 237) "This is one Lucianus, ..." - *The Murder of Gonzago* describes the murder of a duke by a character named Lucianus. Hamlet says, however, that Lucianus "is *nephew* to the *king*". He has introduced his own relationship to Claudius (nephew) and he has substituted king for duke. This suggests that he is a threat to Claudius. Hamlet "tells all" (254), exactly what he criticizes the players for doing in the dumb show. He doesn't let the play speak for itself, but practically accuses Claudius of murder. He uses the play to convict Claudius and as a prelude to blood revenge, and he sets in motion a disastrous sequence of events (*e.g.*, by killing Polonius Hamlet creates an enemy in Laertes). Hamlet's rising passion has blunted the use of the play as a mechanism for encouraging regret and moving Claudius to confess and perhaps taking steps towards redemption.

- (III, II, 380) "Now could I drink hot blood ..." - After the play Hamlet is once again passionate. His triumph at the *Mousetrap* is the turning point. But his purpose is again blunted in the prayer scene and the closet scene.

- (III, III, 11) "The single and peculiar life ..." - Rosencrantz and Guildenstern provide reasonable justification for being concerned about Hamlet's behavior: a public figure needs to protect himself. Thus, even the evil characters in the play have some justification for their actions.

- (III, III, 36 - 72) "O, my offence is rank: ..." - Claudius' remorse seems genuine. He recognizes his guilt and looks for relief in prayer but realizes that he cannot repent if he still possesses "those effects for which I did the murder" (54). He debates repentance – presumably giving up "those effects" – and can't decide what to do. Although their situations are different his words, "I stand in pause where I shall first begin and both neglect" (42), are applicable to Hamlet. We feel some sympathy for him and realize that perhaps there are grounds for redemption and an alternative to blood revenge. This gives added dimension to the play. Implicit here is a belief in heaven and hell, and rewards and punishment in the afterlife. He touches on the Cain/Abel story, speaks lines similar to Lady Macbeth about washing his hands clean of blood and similar to King Lear about the corruption of justice by money.

- (III, III, 73 - 96) "Now might I do it." - Hamlet delays revenge due to concerns about Claudius' afterlife (93). His concern here mirrors the Ghost's earlier complaint that he was "Cut of even in the blossoms of my sin" ((I, V, 76) and perhaps is motivated by it. He requires absolute justice and perfect revenge (H 66). Killing Claudius in prayer will not punish him adequately. This demand for perfection is a failure of the rational mind. "It is the youthful nobility which refuses to compromise between the self and the world" (Bl2 72).

By the start of the 17th Century religion was under attack and being replaced by reason as a guide to action. The play might be interpreted as Shakespeare's view of the quandary of a man caught between the two. Hamlet is clearly a reasonable and thoughtful man. But he's also concerned with the supernatural. Earlier he had said that God has "fixed his canon 'gainst self-slaughter" (I, II, 132) and that punishment in the form of dreams might be a part of the afterlife (III, I, 65). The ghost represents the supernatural world demanding action, although Hamlet doesn't know whether to trust it or whether it's been sent by the devil - and reason provides no help. "While *Hamlet* certainly cannot be called ... a 'religious drama', there is in it nevertheless both a freer use of popular religious ideas, and a more decided ... intimation of a supreme power concerned in human evil and good, than can be found in any other of Shakespeare's tragedies" (Br 174).

Another interpretation of Hamlet's explanation of the delay is that it might be an unconscious excuse. Although on a conscious level Hamlet believes he ought to kill the king, on an unconscious level he might believe that he ought not to do so. "A man's consciousness is the merest surface of his self" (Go1 370). Whatever the reason for the delay, however, it causes the final tragedy, since if Claudius were killed at this point none of the deaths that follow would have occurred. The irony is that Hamlet delays because he thinks Claudius is praying, when in fact Claudius has apparently given up on prayer (97).

- (III, IV, 17 - 19) "Come, come, and sit you down." - Hamlet wants Gertrude to see into herself. This reflects his own attempt to understand himself. Self-understanding is central to the play.

- (III, IV, 22) "How now! A rat!" - Hamlet's triumph in the play scene is followed by two devastating mistakes: not killing Claudius in the prayer scene and killing Polonius in error. In both cases, appearances have misled him: Claudius wasn't praying and Polonius, not Claudius, was behind the arras. In the first case, excess reason was the problem, in the second impulsive action. The killing of Polonius demonstrates that Hamlet's hesitation in the prayer scene was not because of an inability to act.

- (III, IV, 28) "As kill a king?" - The queen doesn't know that King Hamlet was murdered. Hamlet comes close to telling her here. It's strange that Gertrude doesn't ask for an explanation of Hamlet's insinuation nor does Hamlet ever question her on her involvement in the murder. One gets the feeling that Hamlet is more concerned with Gertrude's sexual relationship with Claudius than with the murder. Hamlet's lack of contrition for killing Polonius is testament to the change that has occurred in him – from sensitive and chivalrous (Ba1 103) to cruel and brutal.

- (III, IV, 53) "See what a grace ..." - Hamlet mind runs to extremes. Here (as in (I, II, 140)) he compares his father to the sun-god.

- (III, IV, 66) "You cannot call it love, ..." - Hamlet is obsessed with sex's role in motivating Gertrude's actions (and, perhaps, women's actions in general). The Ghost spoke of the dignity of his love and his virtue while using the word "lust" in referring to Gertrude and saying that she sated herself with him in his "celestial bed" and then proceeded to "prey on garbage" (I, V, 56) (meaning Claudius). Hamlet had alluded earlier to her sexual appetite (I, II, 156). He now says that at her age sexual urges are controllable, but then contradicts himself saying perhaps that's not so (81): desire "canst mutine in a matron's bones". He says that she lives "in the rank sweat of an enseamed bed" (90) – hence her appetite isn't so weak. This is another example of the internal conflict going on in Hamlet's. Note, however, that these accusations coming from Hamlet and his father, two characters who believe they've been wronged, may be biased.

- (III, IV, 100) "Save me and hover o'er ..." - The fact that Gertrude doesn't see the ghost raises the question of whether the ghost is a figment of Hamlet's imagination. But we saw earlier that Horatio and the guards did see the ghost, so we must conclude that Shakespeare meant us to treat the ghost as real.

- (III, IV, 155) "O throw away the worser part ..." - While Hamlet has been merciless in denouncing Gertrude's actions, there's something beautiful in his loving response to the Queen's surrender. His words, "when you are desirous to be blessed I'll blessing beg of you" (169), anticipate Lear's (*King Lear* (V, III, 10)). Hamlet seems to be more devastated at his mother's fall than he is at his father's murder and he wants desperately to raise her. This raises Freudian questions.

- (III, IV, 159 - 166) "That monster Custom, ..." - While custom can make repeated evil seem acceptable, it can also cause us to get into the habit of repeating good acts: "for use almost can change the stamp of nature" (166).

- (III, IV, 184) "Make you to ravel all this matter out ..." - Hamlet asks Gertrude not to reveal to Claudius that he's not mad. She promises not to do so (196) and she doesn't (IV, I, 7).

- (III, IV, 205) "Hoist with his own petard, ..." – The phrase means to get caught in your own trap, and is a reference to the use of mines in tunnels (blown up by your own bomb).

- (IV, I, 13) "It had been so with us ..." - Gertrude doesn't reveal that Hamlet was attempting to kill the king when he killed Polonius. She has shifted her loyalty from Claudius to Hamlet.

- (IV, III, 14) "Without, my lord, guarded, ..." - Hamlet is under guard. As a result of his inaction he has gone from threatening the life of the king to becoming a prisoner.

- (IV, IV, 26) "This is th'impostume ..." - Hamlet wisely points out that too much wealth and peace generate war. This points to two extremes, senseless action on the one hand and Hamlet's inaction on the other.

- (IV, IV, 31 - 65) **Fourth soliloquy**: "How all occasions do inform against me ..." - The fourth soliloquy is similar to the second (II, II, 485) and shows that Hamlet hasn't progressed: "There too he was stirred to shame when he saw a passionate emotion awakened by a cause [an actor playing a role] which, compared with his, was a mere eggshell" (Br 141). Man, capable of large discourse, which allows him to take into account the past and future, and with godlike reason, is but a beast if he is incapable of acting. Hamlet blames bestial oblivion for his failure to kill Claudius. He emphasizes "thinking too precisely on th'event", which recalls his refusal to kill Claudius because he was at prayer. Although the opportunity for revenge was at hand, he had demanded that an additional condition be met. Thinking is one part wisdom and three parts cowardice. This illustrates the thought "conscience doth make cowards of us all" (III, I, 82). He claims not to know (42) why, despite his godlike reason, he hasn't acted. These are the thoughts that explain his inaction.

  Hamlet then goes on to mock Fortinbras' "divine ambition" (48) that motivates him to fight for an "eggshell" (52). He talks about greatness (52): one shouldn't act without thought, but action is called for when honor is at stake. This seems to be a middle ground in balancing thought and action. Having mocked Fortinbras, however, he draws a conclusion which is precisely the opposite of what one expects: thoughts that aren't bloody are worthless (65). The irresistible pull of blood revenge has won out. This internal debate yields a negation of all he has believed in until now: his admiration of Horatio's mix of blood and judgment (III, II, 64). Hamlet's inability to act would be a joke if the stakes were small. It's tragic when reason doesn't motivate action and the stakes are large. (Ba1 253)

- (IV, V, 129 - 135) "How came he dead?" - In contrast to Hamlet, Laertes wants immediate revenge.

- (IV, VII, 57) "Will you be ruled by me?" - Shakespeare contrasts Hamlet to Laertes on several issues. Whereas Hamlet endlessly debates what action he should take, Laertes immediately opts for revenge (IV, V, 134). Whereas Laertes has no problem giving up his independence to Claudius without even knowing what Claudius wants him to do (57), Hamlet chafes at his lack of freedom. We see this at a number of points in the play. Laertes says of Hamlet that his "will is not his own" when he warns Ophelia not to be taken in by Hamlet's advances (I, III, 17). In the Folio edition, Hamlet explicitly says that Denmark is a prison (ArH 466). His father's call for revenge binds Hamlet to a job that he doesn't want to do. Hamlet wants to be his own master. One must not be 'passion's slave' or 'a pipe for Fortune's finger'" (III, II, 66). He resents the thought that someone would presume to know his stops (III, II, 356).

- (IV, VII, 109 - 124) "But that I know love ..." - Claudius' says that although Laertes passion for revenge is rooted in love, love cools over time. And, too much of a good thing, even love, can die of its own excess (115). Hence, Laertes should respond to this situation quickly (this is similar to (III, II, 182)).

  Hamlet suffers from this syndrome, although in his case delaying is only the symptom. It's the thinking that causes the delay that is the underlying problem. Claudius wants to get right to the point when he says, "to the quick of the ulcer" (121). He agrees that murder in church is a possible option – he doesn't have Hamlet's scruples. He outlines his plot against Hamlet (125). Claudius uses Hamlet's generous nature in planning his death (132), just as Iago uses Othello's generous nature in plotting his destruction. Note that Hamlet has no comparable revenge strategy; Claudius' death in Act V is unplanned.

- (IV, VII, 161) "One woe doth tread on another's heel, ..." - The news of Ophelia's death gives occasion for both Gertrude and Laertes (186) to show their better sides.

- (V, I, 26) "Why, there thou sayst, ..." - The gravediggers talk casually of death and mock how a person's rank affects religious practice.

- (V, I, 142 - 146) "Why, because 'a was mad." - The gravedigger jokes about the sanity of the English.

- (V, I, 154) "How long will a man lie i'th' earth ere he rot?" - Hamlet and the gravedigger banter about death. Hamlet considers the evanescence of life and the emptiness of fame in pointing out that Alexander's dust might be plugging up a bung hole (193). The conversation here has an earthiness, emptiness and resignation that makes it quite different from Hamlet's talk of death earlier in the play. Hamlet's words, "O! that this too too solid flesh ... ", and "To be or not to be ... ", were rational, abstract contemplations that didn't face the reality of death. They were attempts "to resolve the riddles of passion and action" (Bl2 61). They were the speech of a man who struggles against "the admission of his own radical impotence to master his destiny; not of a man to whom the very idea of a destiny ... is grotesque; not of a man mortified in the flesh by the knowledge of his nothingness" (Bl2 61). Man is not in control, he cannot "take up arms against a sea of troubles and by opposing end them". Alexander and Caesar were men of action but look where their actions got them. Hence, action is largely pointless. The change in tone of the talk about action and death is an indicator of the change that has occurred in Hamlet's outlook. He is now resigned to the emptiness of life.

- (V, I, 233) "Sweet to the sweet." - Gertrude's words at the grave add dimension to her character. She's capable of tenderness.

- (V, I, 235 – 243) "O, treble woe ..." – Laertes words at the grave express explosive anger and grief.

- (V, I, 243 - 252) "What is he whose grief ..." – Hamlet responds in frustration at what he feels to be Laertes' over-dramatic expression of grief. He has no patience for a public performance of private emotions.

  His next words - "This is I, Hamlet the Dane" (246) - go beyond performance. They are an indication that he has moved beyond his penchant for privately analyzing his actions. They are a public assertion of his own significance, that he is a person to be contended with. And he continues with a warning: "For, though I am not splenative rash, yet have I in me [*i.e.,* the inner man] something dangerous" (250). There's a calculated menace here that's different from the threat of impulsive action. Hamlet is a changed man since his return and he's capable of violent acts.

- (V, I, 258) "I loved Ophelia - ..." - Hamlet's protestation that he loved Ophelia more than 40,000 brothers is excessive and certainly not borne out by his treatment of her during the play.

- (V, II, 4 - 10) "Sir, in my heart ..." - Hamlet has some reservations about the use of reason - deep plots (9) - and its relationship to action. Sometimes, rash action (6) and chance "serves us well". Thus, the fact that he couldn't sleep on the boat (chance) made it possible for him to steal (a rash action) the letter Rosencranz and Guildenstern were carrying. But then he goes a step further: "there's a divinity that shapes our ends, rough-hew them how we will" (10). No matter how we try to set the general course of our lives, we're not in control.

And then, chance intervened a second time: Hamlet had his father's signet ring in his pocket (48) and this made it possible for him to seal the forgery. In both cases, Hamlet identifies chance with divinity, but it is a divinity drained of religious concepts such as sin, punishment or doing God's will (Br 145). Instead, it is more akin to the supernatural force referred to elsewhere as Fortune.

Hamlet is preoccupied with the question of thought and action. He sees that too much thought can impede action and too little thought can result in men fighting over eggshells. He sees that if action is not taken quickly enough the passion that motivates it will dissipate. He sees that rash action sometimes serves us well. He admires Fortinbras' ability to act when honor is at stake, but he also admires Horatio for not being "passion's slave". And finally, we reach this point in the play where he resigns himself to fate: divinity is in control. What we are seeing here is a debate going on in Hamlet's mind. This is a thoughtful man who considers all possibilities. We are observing how his, and by extension our, mind works. Shakespeare is not providing any simple answers.

- (V, II, 57) "They are not near my conscience." - Hamlet dispatched Rosencranz and Guildenstern without any pangs of conscience. This is what happens when minor characters (baser nature) insinuate themselves in a fight between two powerful opponents (59). The action demonstrates Hamlet's capacity for villainy, since they might have been unaware that they were carrying Hamlet's execution order (Ba1 143) (Br 102). The cruelty of Hamlet's act is mitigated, however, by the fact that he knew that they were working for Claudius and the decisiveness of the act is evidence that Hamlet has a new attitude towards action. He's tired of questioning.

- (V, II, 62 - 66) "Does it not, think thee, ..." - Hamlet questions whether revenge is morally justifiable in his situation, and whether killing Claudius can be done with a clear conscience. Note that he includes the charge that Claudius has assumed the throne (election) which is rightfully his.

- (V, II, 67) "Your lordship is right welcome ..." - Osric is played as a fop and Hamlet ridicules him.

- (V, II, 190) "Thou would'st not think ..." - Hamlet doesn't seem to have any plan for his revenge and has reverted to a passive stance. He intimates his reluctance to enter the duel – perhaps sensing the disaster that will follow and that he's doing something that violates his natural inclination against blood revenge. He rejects superstition (augury) and returns to his feelings about man's impotence (10) when he says: "There is special providence in the fall of a sparrow" (197): Our plans and analysis are of no consequence, death comes when it will, and God controls everything. This is similar to Player King's comments (III, II, 205), but Player King simply says that our wills and our fates are unconnected, not that outcomes are under divine control.

Hamlet's statement "Readiness is all" anticipates Edgar's statement "Ripeness is all" (*King Lear* (V, II, 11)). This is serenity and acceptance, not despair. Apparently, revenge is no longer motivating him. Bloom feels that whereas King Hamlet was the authority figure in the first four acts, pushing Hamlet to action, Hamlet has transcended that in Act V and now allows destiny to take its course. Goddard sees this differently. He explains the change in Hamlet's attitude by saying "In proportion as our will declines, our belief in destiny mounts. When we are compelled to confront the consequence of some weak or bad act of our own, the easiest way to escape a sense of sin is to put the blame on fate ... or as we are more likely to do today, on heredity, environment, our bringing up, or just 'tough luck'" (Go 378).

- **Christianity** intrudes in a minor way in the play. King Hamlet is apparently Catholic, since he complains of being in purgatory and having died without last rites. Similarly, Hamlet's hesitation to kill Claudius while he is praying points to Catholicism. Shakespeare demonstrates a "nostalgia for the residual pull of Catholicism in a world in which the old religion continued to make its presence felt" (JS 131), despite the fact that he is treading on dangerous ground in Protestant England. On the other hand, Hamlet, Horatio, Rosencranz and Guildenstern have all studied in

Wittenberg, where Luther nailed his theses to the church door and ushered in the Protestant Reformation (But Laertes wants to return to Catholic France (I, II, 51).), and the play is set in Protestant Denmark. Hamlet talks of a "divinity that shapes our ends" and "providence in the fall of a sparrow" which is neither one nor the other. So, the play has a Christian setting, but is neither a wholly Protestant nor a wholly Catholic work (Bl 391).

- **The Several Hamlets** - Some say that Hamlet is insane, but that doesn't seem defensible. His soliloquies are clearly not crazy, his interactions with most of the characters in the play are completely rational, and his crazy interludes have been foretold by him as a deliberate "antic disposition". Furthermore, a play about an insane man tells us little about ourselves and it's doubtful that Shakespeare would have wasted his time writing it.

  We get several other views of Hamlet. There's the Hamlet prior to the King's murder, and therefore prior to the opening of the play, whose generosity, friendliness and honesty we now see only in snatches: in his interactions with the players and Polonius (II, II, 359, 466, 480), with the gravediggers and Horatio, and when he first welcomes Rosencranz and Guildenstern. Ophelia praises his character (III, I, 149) and the early expression of his love. Horatio, the honest, rational man, speaks of him in the highest terms. Laertes' dying words say he was "noble", and Fortinbas says, "He was likely to have proved most royal".

  Another Hamlet is the disillusioned, melancholy, grieving man who we meet when the play opens. And finally, there's the hardened Hamlet who returns from England. "He is a changed man: mature rather than youthful, certainly quieter ... Perhaps the truth is that he is at last himself, no longer afflicted by mourning and melancholia, by murderous jealousy and incessant rage. Certainly he is no longer haunted by his father's ghost. It may be that the desire for revenge is fading in him" (Bl1 2). "And while he still regards his maligned mother as a whore, he has worn out his interest there also" (Bl 431). Disinterestedness dominates; he feels that "he is in the hands of Providence" (Br 144). He's transcended the passions of the first four acts and come to a new sense of himself. He seems to have detached himself from life (Bl 431). But the die has been cast. His actions have made a confrontation with Claudius inevitable and now he's caught in the flow.

- (V, II, 204) "Give me your pardon, sir." - Hamlet apologizes to Laertes, claiming that he didn't kill Polonius, rather his madness did. While Laertes' acceptance of the apology (221) is clearly disingenuous, the sincerity of the apology itself is greatly debated. It "has struck editors and commentators since at least Samuel Johnson in 1765 as disingenuous: Hamlet is clearly using his assumed or supposed madness as an excuse for his behavior" and the "fact that Hamlet talks in generalities and doesn't spell out the crimes with which he is charged seems, to say the least, evasive" (ArH 449). But Goddard says that the apology consists of "words that ring with sincerity" (Go 378) and Van Doren claims (VD 167) that it is one of the few places in the play where he speaks with true sincerity. According to Van Doren, most of his other interactions are spoken for a calculated effect. "We may not assume ... that he believes what he says. ... This noble mind whose harmony was once like sweet bells rung in tune, this courtier, soldier scholar whose disposition has hitherto been generous ... is not himself" through the majority of the play. "With the exception of Horatio there is no person in the play for whose benefit he has not conceived and studied a part" (VD 168).

Hamlet's claim that madness killed Polonius parallels the gravedigger's discussion of whether Ophelia committed suicide (V, I, 15) (Go 375). The gravedigger says that if the water came to Ophelia then the water killed her and she's not a suicide. While he is mocking the distinction between Christian and non-Christian burial, a more serious point underlies these two deaths. In both cases death is being connected to psychological forces. Hamlet's supposed madness is related to the internal conflict between action and thought with which he wrestles. Shakespeare might be hinting at the complexity of our psyche and suggesting that it involves two warring forces: the id (action) and the superego (thought).

- (V, II, 294) "No, no, the drink, ..." - Gertrude dies a better woman than she had lived. She feels remorse for her marriage to Claudius, she loves her son and doesn't betray him to Claudius and her sorrow at Ophelia's grave is genuine.

- (V, II, 309) "Here, thou incestuous, damned Dane!" - Hamlet describes Claudius as being "incestuous" in Q2. This seems to be Hamlet's motivator. But the word "murderous" has been added in F (ArH 136). Hamlet kills Claudius in a spontaneous response to Gertrude's death that is not inconsistent with the attitude of resignation to the force of destiny and the passive stance he has adopted since returning from England.

- (V, II, 323) "Thou livest: report me ..." - Hamlet's concern that his story be told makes the point that, despite our inability to control our destinies, the integrity of a life – as determined by actions - is important (Bl2 64) and ought to be preserved. His interest in his reputation is at odds, however, with his overall detachment. His reference to death as "felicity" (331) echoes his mood in the third soliloquy (III, I, 55) where he deplores the "thousand natural shocks that flesh is heir to".

- (V, II, 364 - 370) "So shall you hear ..." - Horatio sums up the result of King Hamlet's demand for revenge. Much of the carnage has "Fallen on th'inventors' heads": Rosencranz and Guildenstern, Laertes and Claudius were all "hoist on their own petard".

- (V, II, 379 - 387) "Let four captains bear Hamlet like a ..." - Hamlet is treated like a warrior and the last word of the play is "shoot". This ending is ironic: "Hamlet, who aspired to nobler things, is treated at death as if he were the mere image of his father" (Go 381). The implication is that "Human existence will be what it was before Hamlet lived" (VD 171).

Discussion

Hamlet's Personality - "No theory of Hamlet's character will ever satisfy all men" (Go 331). There's no single key that reveals it. Each has some truth, but more importantly, they reflect the complexity and depth of the character. With that in mind, much has been written about him.

That Hamlet is an intellectual is obvious from his conversation and wit. He's a student and he's interested theater. He's also interested in philosophy, but he recognizes its limitations and is open to a wider view (I, V, 165). He's moral and idealistic: he's disgusted with his uncle's drunkenness (I, IV, 8), he loathes his mother's sensuality, he's contemptuous of Osric's pretentiousness, he's indifferent to external show as opposed to inner feelings (I, II, 85) and he's impatient with distinctions of rank and wealth (I, II, 186).

And Hamlet is no wilting lily. He threatens to kill anyone who prevents him from going with the ghost, he can scarcely speak to Claudius without an insult or to Polonius without a gibe, he insults his mother harshly, he kills Polonius, he steals Rosencranz and Guildenstern's letter, he's the only one to board the pirate ship, he fights Laertes at Ophelia's grave and again in the final scene, and he kills the king. Much of this is impulsive and justified, but Hamlet is also capable of, or driven to, villainy. It's hard to justify his treatment of Ophelia, his lack of regret in the killing of Polonius, and the murder of Rosencranz and Guildenstern. As one major critic puts it: "That this grossness and brutality should be induced on a soul so pure and noble is profoundly tragic" (Br 104).

Why Doesn't Hamlet Act? – *Hamlet* revolves around the murder of Claudius; *Macbeth* revolves around the murder of Duncan. Hamlet learns of his father's murder in Act I but doesn't get the revenge on Claudius that his father demands until Act V. And even then, the revenge is not a planned action, but an impulsive reaction to the death of both Gertrude and Laertes, and his own impending death. In *Macbeth,* on the other hand, the murder of Duncan takes place at the beginning of Act II. The difference between the two plays is that in *Macbeth* Shakespeare is interested in studying the effect of the deed on the protagonist, whereas in *Hamlet* he's concerned with the protagonist's struggle to convince himself that the deed should be done.

A number of reasons have been proposed to explain why Hamlet delays. None are entirely convincing, but each sheds some light on Hamlet's inaction and, more importantly, tells us something about the forces and emotions that affect our own behavior.

- **Melancholy** – Hamlet is often referred to as the "melancholy Dane", and one explanation is that his inaction is caused by the melancholy into which he's thrown by his mother's marriage. He idolized his parents and their relationship, and is shocked that his mother could have so quickly married someone so inferior to his father, exposing both her shallowness and her sensuality. The subsequent shock of discovering that his father was murdered and that his mother was adulterous throws him into a mental state that inhibits action.

  The weakness of this view is that Hamlet demonstrates that he's not incapable of action. Much of this action, however, "does not proceed from ... deliberation and analysis, but is sudden and impulsive, evoked by an emergency in which he has no time to think" (Br 106). Thus, it's more accurate to say that he seems incapable of performing the central action of the play: taking revenge on Claudius. But that task would be hard for anyone, regardless of melancholy. He has to kill an anointed king and afterwards justify the deed to Gertrude and the world, and the only evidence he has that Claudius is a murderer is the word of a ghost, who most of the characters haven't even seen and none have heard (Ba1 247).

- **Psychological Analysis** - The Freudian interpretation (Go 343) says that it would be normal for Hamlet to have repressed childish wishes to kill his father and marry his mother because his father is a competitor for his mother's love. But it's hard to see why repressing his desire to kill his father impedes his ability to kill Claudius. The interpretation explains this by pointing out that Hamlet recognizes that Claudius has enacted those childish wishes (Go 343), hence killing Claudius is akin to killing himself.

  At the most basic level, our thoughts and actions are the product of the electrical and chemical properties of neurons in the brain. In an attempt to come to grips with the enormity of the problem of understanding the workings the brain when examined at this level, Freud proposed that the brain be analyzed at a higher level of abstraction involving such constructs as the id and the ego. While there is undoubtably value in examining the workings of the brain at both these levels, it's a distraction from trying to understand what Shakespeare had in mind. They trace everything to electrical or chemical interactions or to unconscious and infantile fantasies. But they have nothing to say about Hamlet's imagination or his genius or his effort to "transcend the morality of his time" (Go 345), all of which operate at a still higher level of abstraction, the level at which life is lived. Shakespeare has created a man who is engaged in a dramatic battle, "the perennial attempt of life, in the face of forces that would drag it backward, to ascend to a higher level" (Go 345). That battle cannot be properly addressed by Freudian analysis.

  A related psychological analysis (Go 357, 372) explains Hamlet's attacks on Polonius, Ophelia and Gertrude as expressions of his own self-loathing. In this interpretation, Hamlet sees both Polonius and King Hamlet as parents who demand obedience from their children. He subconsciously hates his father for demanding revenge and projects that hatred onto Polonius. Similarly, he places himself in the same category as Ophelia, since both are children who are being coerced to obey their fathers. He hates himself for this obedience and projects that hatred onto Ophelia. In addition, he regards Ophelia's actions as a betrayal of her relationship to him, just as Gertrude's actions were a betrayal of his father. He is angry at Gertrude and projects that anger onto Ophelia. Finally, Hamlet is portrayed as a man who has focused his life on philosophy, religion and art, as opposed to sensuality. He sees Gertrude as embodying sensuality in her relationship to Claudius and rejects her as he has rejected sensuality in his own life.

- **Moral Scruples** - (Bl2 12) Most critics take it as given that it was Hamlet's duty to revenge his father. But the play can be viewed as Shakespeare's attack on revenge morality. Hamlet is presented as a cultured, thoughtful, high minded and imaginative person. At one point he questions whether murdering Claudius is morally justifiable (V, II, 62) and we are left to wonder if he is suited for such an action. Imagine Jesus being asked to commit a murder (Go 333).

  In contrast to Hamlet, his father was a warrior, accustomed to violence. His father demands revenge and the influence of a father over his child is demonstrated in Polonius' relation to Laertes and Ophelia. Since Hamlet has idealized his father, his influence is especially strong. Hamlet is torn by a demand that is so contrary to his nature. He says so explicitly: "O cursed spite that ever I was born to set it right!" (I, V, 186). King Hamlet is Hamlet's authority figure, but he acts like a devil in urging his son to serve a cause in which his son doesn't believe, and to follow the tradition of violence that he has embraced and is embedded in society (GS xxii).

Hamlet must make a choice between blood revenge and dealing with the crime in a more peaceful way. The latter alternative is not so far-fetched, since we've seen that Claudius is wracked with remorse. This is the central dilemma of the play. Hamlet is "a divided man won to the side of violence only after a protracted struggle" (Go 338). Hamlet's "delay, then, instead of giving ground for condemnation, does him credit. It shows his soul is still alive and will not submit to the demands of the father without a struggle" (Go 341). That he could become "a dealer in coarse death was both his tragedy and the world's" (VD 172).

More generally, the play demonstrates "how bloodshed ... brings on the very thing it was intended to avert, how ... force begets force and vengeance begets vengeance" (Bl2 15). By the end of the play only Horatio and Fortinbras are alive, and King Hamlet's "conquests have been for nothing ... Fortinbras, his former enemy, is to inherit the kingdom! Such is the end to which the Ghost's thirst for vengeance has led" (Bl2 23). We have a choice Shakespeare seems to say: philosophic and religious values or war (Go382).

- **Roles** - As in *King Lear*, several family stories are woven together in *Hamlet*. Three of the characters in the play, Hamlet, Laertes and Fortinbras, are sons, each of whom must deal with their father's death. Laertes and Fortinbras are proponents of unfettered action and Hamlet, the introspective man, is contrasted with them. Hamlet's father and Laertes' father were murdered, and revenge is called for; Fortinbras' father was killed in fair combat and the issue is not revenge. Both Laertes and Fortinbras act aggressively, but they're motivated differently. Laertes' actions are motivated by revenge: he's the straight, hard-charging revenge hero. Fortinbras' actions are motivated by honor. Shakespeare has Fortinbras and his army parade across the stage so that Hamlet can reflect on what motivates Fortinbras' actions. He is, Hamlet says, "with divine ambition puffed" (IV, IV, 48).

Underlying an action are the reasons which explain it, the feelings which accompany it and a role which is a framework for performing it. A role provides an outline of what a person must say and do and orchestrates his behavior dramatically for public consumption. It provides a paradigm for the person's personality in displaying his intentions. Laertes takes on the revenge role and this calls for revenge rhetoric (IV, V, 129 - 135) and revenge theatrics. In the burial scene, he jumps into Ophelia's grave and demands to be buried with her (V, I, 240). Similarly, Fortinbras takes on the honor role, which involves going to war and jeopardizing thousands of lives for an eggshell.

Men find the revenge and honor roles satisfying because they lead to virile actions. "They combine maximum dramatic satisfaction with the irrefutable reality that only bloody death can supply" (Bl2 96). Death makes role playing more real. The gravedigger, on the other hand, makes fun of death and thus essentially ridicules the role playing that leads to it. For him dead is dead, and dying in pursuit of honor or revenge has no value.

Hamlet finds role playing an artificial substitute for the underlying feelings that accompany an action and is reluctant to engage in it. Once you realize that you're playing a role, and that the role is a self-serving facade, its attraction fades. At least it does for Hamlet. Early in the play he distinguishes between one's inner emotions and the external façade one presents to the world by disparaging the mourner's role and the resulting "actions a man might play" (I, II, 84) as opposed to the feelings "within which passes show". His comments on the Priam/Hecuba speech also deal with the artificiality of role playing: "What's Hecuba to him?" (II, II, 494).

Beyond the artificiality of role playing, Hamlet is also concerned with its aesthetics. In his instructions to the players he indirectly comments on how one ought to play a role. He demands elegance, restraint and dignity, and deplores actors who overact (III, II, 1). "He objects to passionate rhetoric because to him it typifies bestial unreason. The conventional revenger ... responds mechanically to circumstances, beating his breast in grief ... Such a man is Fortune's pipe, the puppet of his circumstances, and the prisoner of his own passion ..." (Bl2 123). Hamlet mocks Laertes for overplaying the revenge role (V, I, 243). He competes with him in overblown rhetoric, claiming that his love exceeds that of forty thousand brothers (V, I, 258), and scolding him by saying he can out-rant him (V, I, 273) (Bl2 126). And he mocks Osric for overplaying the courtier's role (V, II, 78).

Hamlet is ambivalent about the honor role that Fortinbras has adopted. On the one hand, he sees it as vanity. Honor instigates wars for pleasure and glory. It's a manufactured purpose: "Rightly to be great is not to stir without great argument" (IV, IV, 52). But on the other hand, he admires Fortinbras, refers to his ambition as "divine" (IV, IV, 48) and understands the need "greatly to find quarrel in a straw when honour's at the stake".

The dilemma for Hamlet is that although he finds role playing dishonest, he lacks a framework within which he can take the action demanded of him. Reason alone doesn't do this. It provides a motive, but not the mechanism within which the motive can flower into action. Hamlet, the rational man, is capable of action, but the actions he takes are generally "impulsive, evoked by an emergency in which he has no time to think" (Br 106). Killing Polonius and Claudius, boarding the pirate ship, stealing the letters are reflexive actions, not choreographed by a role. Their timing is controlled by external events and they aren't embroidered with artificial drama. More considered actions are enabled by role playing, something Hamlet dislikes. He has a reason for killing Claudius, but he lacks a role through which he can act and hence he delays.

- **Thought and Action** - Does thought inhibit action? Can you think too much? Hamlet's attitude evolves on this subject and through the soliloquies Shakespeare allows us to view the debate that goes on in his mind. Hamlet is articulate and imaginative. He has studied philosophy, he is an amateur actor, he is an expert swordsman and he has thought deeply about issues of right and wrong and life and death. Above all, he's introspective, examining his own behavior and mercilessly critical of his failings, and he urges Gertrude to do the same (III, IV, 18). In the second soliloquy Hamlet sees thought as an essential precondition to action. His words, "About, my brains!" (II, II, 522) expresses a determination to enlist thought in the service of action and he proceeds to outline a plan to use the players to get evidence of Claudius' role in the murder.

In the third soliloquy he takes a different position. He recognizes that thought has the power to paralyze action. He says, "conscience does make cowards of us all" and "the native hue of resolution is sicklied o'er with the pale cast of thought" (III, I, 82). One critic says that the play "is intended to show how a calculating consideration which aims at exhausting ... all the relations and possible consequences of a deed, cripples the power of acting" (Schlegel, quoted in (Br 105)). This view is supported by Hamlet's own words. Earlier, after hearing from the ghost, he says "I'll wipe away ... all saws of books ... and thy [King Hamlet's] commandment all alone shall live" (I, V, 98).

Nietzsche took this description one step further, giving the issue an existential twist, and claimed that knowledge, rather than thought, inhibits action. Although an action can have an immediate effect, that effect is transient and can't change anything in the eternal nature of things. Thus, it's ridiculous that we should be asked "to take up arms against a sea of troubles ..." or to set right a world that's "out of joint". These goals are unachievable, and knowledge of this fact dampens our ardor for acting on their behalf. "Knowledge kills action; action requires the veils of illusion ... true knowledge, an insight into the horrible truth, outweighs any motive for action" (Nietzsche, quoted in (Bl 394)).

In the fourth soliloquy Hamlet seems to have come to a middle ground on the subject. He notes that, in contrast to beasts, man is possessed with "godlike reason" which should not be allowed "to fust in us unused" (IV, IV, 38). He then he proceeds to argue with himself. While beasts cannot be expected to respond to an event, since they live in "bestial oblivion", man might fall into the same trap for the opposite reason: "some craven scruple of thinking too precisely on th'event" (IV, IV, 40). Hamlet is deeply concerned with his behavior, its morality and its impact, and he sees this as being a hindrance to action.

Hamlet admires Fortinbras' ability to act spontaneously, without the need to analyze all aspects of what he does. There is both approval and a note of criticism in his description of Fortinbras as being with "divine ambition puffed" (IV, IV, 48): Fortinbras might have an inflated view of the worthiness of what he sets out to do, but it enables him to take on major challenges. He'll risk his life and the lives of others "even for an eggshell". Hamlet sees himself as torn between two poles. The first asserts, "Rightly to be great is not to stir without great argument" (IV, IV, 52), meaning actions have to be justified by serious thought. The second asserts, "But greatly to find quarrel in a straw when honour's at stake" (IV, IV, 54), meaning that when honor is involved thought should not be an impediment. Swayed by Fortinbras' example, the soliloquy ends with Hamlet adopting the second pole: "My thoughts be bloody, or be nothing worth" (IV, IV, 65). He's willing to subdue any thought that blocks his path to revenge.

This, however, isn't Hamlet's last word on the subject. After returning from England, there's resignation: "there's a divinity that shapes our ends, rough-hew them as we will" (V, II, 10). He concludes that actions are forced on us no matter what we think or how we try to shape our lives. "Readiness is all" (V, II, 200).

In the end, Hamlet has looked at the issue of thought and action from multiple points of view, presenting arguments on all sides. He gives no answers, nor should we expect any. There are no easy answers; there's some truth in all of Hamlet's thoughts on the subject. It's sufficient to see the doubts and difficulties that we all privately experience in our lives opened up on the stage for all to share.

A related issue is the need to act promptly once a course of action is chosen. The Player King says "Purpose is but the slave to memory, Of violent birth but of poor validity" (III, II, 183). Hamlet validates this when the ghost reappears: He admits that his passion has lapsed (III, IV, 104). Claudius also agrees, saying "That we would do we should do when we would", because we might be dissuaded if we wait (IV, VII, 116). "Nothing could bring out with greater force the melancholy perception that the whole play has dramatized. Action traps the actor in the labyrinth of concealed evil: inaction in the toils of time and the lapse of passion" (Bl2 59).

Chapter 11

OTHELLO

Background

As with many of his plays, Shakespeare took a ready-made story as the basis of *Othello,* in this case a short story by an author named Cinthio. *Othello* was written after *Hamlet* but before *King Lear* and *Macbeth.* Two early editions of the play were published after Shakespeare's death: A Quarto edition (Q) and the version that appears in the Folio (F). There are numerous, mostly small, differences between the two editions. For example, many of the profanities that appear in Q have been deleted in F. It's conjectured that the profanities were Shakespeare's and the deletions were done to avoid problems with censors. For example, the first word of the play, "Tush", is a mild oath that doesn't appear in F.

Othello is a Moor, a group of Arabs and Berbers living in the land west of Egypt along the North African coast. The region was referred to as Barbary, which is the source of the word "barbarian". The skin color of Moors ranges from olive to black. They had conquered Spain during the Middle Ages but were finally defeated and, around 1525, were offered the choice of conversion to Christianity or expulsion. Converts were called Moriscos and were regarded with suspicion, since their adherence to Christianity was questionable. Their position in society was similar to that of Marranos, those Jews who, having been offered a similar choice a few years earlier and electing to stay, converted.

Othello was written shortly after a state visit to London by the ambassador of the King of Barbary and his retinue and hence the Moors were in the news at the time. Also, a book describing the character of the Moors and written by a Moorish author had been translated into English by this time and might well have influenced Shakespeare. It made the following claims: "Most honest people they are, destitute of all fraud and guile", "very proud and high minded, and wonderfully addicted unto wrath", "they are so credulous that they will believe matters impossible which are told them", and finally "no nation in the world is so subject unto jealousy, for they would rather lose their lives then put up any disgrace in the behalf of their women" (JL 40). These characteristics relate closely to Othello.

At the time of the play, Venice was a city state with an empire and a powerful navy. It was also "regarded as the pleasure capital of Europe" (ArO 9), a fact that relates to the action in the play. The Ottoman Empire had been advancing into Eastern Europe for hundreds of years. As a part of this, the Turks took Cyprus from Venice in 1570 – an event of the recent past when Shakespeare wrote the play. Although Othello isn't a Turk, his non-Christian background and African roots put him in a similar category.

The Play (line numbers from (ArO))

- (I, I, 1 - 32) The first few lines of the play tell us that Iago has been taking money from Roderigo and that he resents being passed over by Othello for promotion to lieutenant (10). Othello has given the position to Cassio who, Iago feels, is inferior to him in military experience. His description of Cassio as "bookish" and "Meer prattle without practice" indicates that his anger has a flavor of class resentment and his accusation that Cassio knows no more about battle than a spinster reminds one of the description of the major-general in *The Pirates of Penzance*. (The word "ancient" means ensign.)

- (I, I, 41 - 64) "I follow him to serve ..." - Iago admits, "I am not what I am", meaning that he sets out to deceive and hence his inner and outer selves differ. He's similar in this respect to Hamlet and Hal in *Henry IV*. The question of whether other characters exhibit the same split personality and under what circumstances is one of the issues of the play. Iago's view of life is the Hobbesian one: he will get what he wants by any means. He adheres to no notion of morality. This is reminiscent of Edmund in *King Lear*.

  Iago's analysis of the master/servant relationship is similar to the one given by Orlando (*As You Like It* (I, III, 56 – 62)), who distinguishes between servants who feel they have a duty to serve their masters and those who do so for their own advancement. Iago makes the same distinction, putting himself in the latter category and claiming that only such servants have any "soul" (spirit).

- (I, I, 65) "What a full fortune ..." - "The most dramatic reactions to Othello's blackness within the play are those of

Iago and Roderigo in the opening scene" (Bl9 47). Roderigo refers to Othello as "thicklips" (65) and says that Desdemona is held in the "gross clasps of a lascivious Moor" (124). Iago's comments reduce the relationship between Othello and Desdemona to sex in the crudest terms. He pictures sex as a "violent, bestial overpowering of a woman by a man which degrades both" (Bl8 92). Speaking to Brabantio he says, "an old black ram is tupping your white ewe" (87), a "devil" will make a "grandsire of you" (90), your daughter is "covered with a Barbary horse" (110) and "your daughter and the Moor are now making the beast with two backs" (115). In Iago's words, Othello's "blackness connotes ugliness, treachery, lust, bestiality and the demonic", and this was apparently the reigning stereotype of the African on the Elizabethan stage. "This poisonous image of the black man ... informs Othello's judgment of himself" (Bl9 47).

- (I, I, 116) "Thou art a villain!" - When Brabantio calls Iago a villain, Iago responds by calling Brabantio a "senator" (117), demonstrating his resentment of class distinctions.

- (I, I, 134) "an extravagant wheeling stranger of here and everywhere." - Roderigo's describes Othello as rootless and unstable.

- (I, II, 18 - 30) "My services, which I have done ..." - Othello speaks in his own defense. He has provided good service to the government. He comes from a royal family. He has given up his free life for his love of Desdemona. Iago swears by Janus, the two-faced god (33).

- (I, II, 50) "Faith, he tonight ..." - Iago once again expresses his sexual view of the love between Othello and Desdemona by saying that Othello "hath boarded a land carract" (a treasure ship)".

- (I, II, 59) "Keep up your bright swords ..." - This oft quoted, menacing, monosyllabic line illustrates Othello's calm, commanding presence. It stands in contrast to his loss of control later in the play. These are the opposite poles of his personality.

- (I, II, 62 - 81) "O thou foul thief, ..." - Brabantio compounds his racism – "the sooty bosom of such a thing as thou" (70) – by accusing Othello of gaining Desdemona's love through magic, presumably a technique practiced in Africa.

- (I, III, 18) "This cannot be, ..." - The Turk's maneuver in heading for Rhodes instead of Cyprus is a deception included to give us a clue to Iago's behavior: The Turks external actions hide their real intent (Go 81).

- (I, III, 63) "For nature so preposterously ..." - Brabantio sees Desdemona's choice of Othello as unnatural. He sees nature, by which he means inbred inclinations rather than rational thought, as controlling many of our decisions. In this case, nature normally dictates that a person should choose a mate of the same race. Thus, nature operates in the social sphere.

- (I, III, 77 - 107) "Most potent, grave, ..." - Othello exhibits a measured and rational response to Brabantio's wild charges (60) that he has stolen Desdemona, corrupted her with spells, medicines and witchcraft, and entered into a marriage that is unnatural. He doesn't hesitate to remind those present of his long military experience (84). Brabantio continues his attack (95 – 104) by first describing

Desdemona as a “maiden never bold, Of spirit so still and quiet that her motion Blushed at herself”, and repeating his charge that their relationship violates the claims of nature. Apparently, Desdemona is very young: 15 or 16 (ArO 42). Iago later says, “She that so young ...” (III, III, 212).

- (I, III, 129 - 170) “Her father loved me, ...” - Othello describes his courtship of Desdemona, which started with a tale of his adventures as a military hero. It’s apparent from this description that Desdemona was no wilting lily - she encouraged Othello and practically proposed to him (165 – 167) In one of his more poetic speeches, Othello concludes “She loved me for the dangers I had passed and I loved her that she did pity them” (168). This is hardly the basis for an enduring love. The implication is that they didn’t know each other very well and this, in addition to the fact that they differed in age, race and background, could be a factor in explaining why Othello is so quick to doubt her fidelity later in the play and she is unable to see that her defense of Cassio is a provocation. Also, the fact that he was attracted to her because she was overwhelmed by the story he told of his life, indicates a narcissistic component in his personality. Their marriage might well be an unstable match because it was based on inadequate information (Bl8 26).

- (I, III, 180 - 189) “My noble father ...” - It’s apparent that Brabantio’s earlier description of Desdemona (95 – 106) is inaccurate. He doesn’t know his own daughter. Her strength is demonstrated by the force of her response to Brabantio. She asserts that her duty is to her husband, words that are similar to Cordelia’s description of how she will view her duty to her husband and her father when she marries in *King Lear*.

- (I, III, 190 - 220) "God be with you, I have done." - Brabantio backs off. The Duke tries to council him to accept the marriage. But Brabantio mocks the Duke by comparing his loss of Desdemona to the Duke's loss of Cyprus: just as he shouldn't bemoan the former, the Duke shouldn't bemoan the latter. His message is that words don't heal such major losses. Brabantio discounts the power of words to affect our emotions, but the play demonstrates otherwise.

- (I, III, 230 - 235) "The tyrant custom, ..." - Othello often speaks of himself in overblown terms.

- (I, III, 249 - 260) "That I did love the Moor, to live with him ..." - Desdemona may be chaste, but she has a "healthy, casual acceptance of sexuality" (Bl8 88). In the sentence, "My heart's subdued even to the very quality of my lord" (252), the words "very quality" which appear in (F) have replaced the more sexually expressive words "utmost pleasure" in Q. Some argue that her embrace of sexuality "awakens the deep current of sexual anxiety in Othello" (Bl8 55) because he sees it, as did orthodox Christianity at that time, as akin to adultery. Both the Protestant and Catholic Churches viewed excessive sexual pleasure in marriage as sinful. In this view, Othello destroys Desdemona both for her openness to sex and for awakening such feelings in himself.

  When Desdemona says that "I saw Othello's visage in his mind" she might mean that she "overlooked his blackness in favor of his inner brilliance" (Bl8 11), implying that she has some of the same racial hang-ups as other Venetians. She then demands to be allowed to go to Cyprus despite the danger (260) so that she's not made to sacrifice the "rites for which I love him". It's "possible ... to see Desdemona as the strongest, the most heroic person in the play" (ArO 43).

- (I, III, 261 -301) "Let her have your voice." - Othello gives his view of sex. It's ironic that someone who is driven to distraction by sexual jealousy later in the play places so little importance on consummating his own marriage. He says he's not a young man and his sexual appetite has waned. He asks the Duke to grant Desdemona's wish to go to Cyprus because she wants it, not because he's lusting after her. He doesn't seem upset at the disruption of his wedding night: He agrees to leave for Cyprus "With all my heart" (279). The Duke, without intending insult, says Othello's virtue contradicts his blackness (290) – a typical Venetian view of blacks. Brabantio warns Othello that Desdemona might betray him as she has betrayed her father (294) – a warning that haunts Othello later. Othello divides up the hour he has left with Desdemona before departure between 'love' and 'instruction' (299). "If that 'hour' is literal, then 'love' will be lucky to get twenty minutes of the overbusy general's time" (Bl 459).

- **Race -** (Bl9 43) Othello is a black man in a white society who complicates an already difficult situation by marrying a white woman. Miscegenation was no less a hot topic then than it is today, so the question of the role played by race in the play must be addressed. Commentators disagree on the view Shakespeare took of this subject. Some argue that race is not a major factor in the play. Othello is simply a man who faces a situation with which we can all sympathize. He happens to be black, but we're all brothers under the skin and race doesn't determine what happens in the play. It's hard to accept this position. The subtitle of the play, *The Moor of Venice,* puts the black/white issue front and center.

More importantly, Othello's race clearly affects how he's viewed by others and how he views himself.

Hence, most commentators agree that race is a major issue. They can be divided, however, into two groups. Those who view the Moor negatively think that he's a savage who has disguised himself in a thin veneer of Western civilization which he discards as the play progresses. If this is taken one step further, by attributing Othello's savagery to his African roots, then this is racist theater. It's difficult to reach this conclusion, however, since Othello is so obviously a courageous and noble figure capable of deep love and tenderness. Those who view the Moor positively, on the other hand, think that Shakespeare intended to discredit the negative Elizabethan stereotypes of Africans. By presenting an essentially sympathetic portrait of Othello, Shakespeare is an author ahead of his time in his willingness to challenge racism (ArO 29, 31).

Some commentators suggest that Shakespeare wanted us to view Othello as a representative of all Africans and was interested in showing us what happens when a black man takes on some elements of European civilization (Br 186). In other words, Shakespeare was acting as a sociologist interested in a cultural problem. But extrapolating from this we might conclude that the point of *Hamlet* is to tell us something about the character of Danes and the point of *Julius Caesar* is to tell us something about the character of early Romans. This doesn't seem likely. Each of Shakespeare's protagonists was a particular individual, not a typical representative of some group of people. Race matters in the play, but it doesn't determine Othello's essential character (Bl9 45).

- (I, III, 306 – 358) "I will incontinently drown myself." - Roderigo threatens suicide over his inability to possess Desdemona, and Iago castigates him for not being more self-centered (314), a quality that Iago values. Roderigo bemoans the fact that he doesn't have the will power (virtue) to control his desire for her (319). Iago dismisses this. His philosophy is similar to Edmund's in *King Lear*: We are master of our fate. We are driven by sensual and emotional urges - he speaks of the "blood and baseness of our natures" (329) - and this can lead to vice and folly. This extends Brabantio's view of nature as controlling aspects of the social order (95) to individual behavior and places a moral judgment on it. Fortunately, these urges can be held in check by reason, but the balance between the two is easily disturbed. Iago disturbs that balance in Othello. The speech is reminiscent of Hamlet's words to Horatio: "blest are those whose blood and judgment are so well co-meddled that they are not a pipe for Fortune's fingers to sound what stop she please. Give me that man that is not passion's slave and I will wear him in my heart's core" (*Hamlet* (III, II, 64)).

  Iago takes a coldly rational view of life. Emotions should be held in check. Love is simply a byproduct of lust (332). Women are sex objects and sexual predators. Othello, being a Moor, will tire of Desdemona (347) and Desdemona's love for Othello will fade "when she is sated with his body" (350). Then she'll look for a younger man and Roderigo will have his chance. Iago sees no role for love as a binding force in their relationship.

- (I, III, 385 - 402) "I hate the Moor ..." - Iago speaks of his hatred of Othello and justifies that by saying that he suspects that Othello has had sex with Emilia. His plan for revenge is based on his estimate of the characters of the people he will manipulate. This touches on a theme of the play: the difficulty one has in understanding someone else. Iago has no difficulty doing this, Othello does. Iago judges that Cassio has a "smooth dispose" and that will make it possible to frame him as a seducer. And he judges that Othello "is of a free and open nature" and "thinks men honest that but seem so". Iago mocks this and concludes that he can "be led by th' nose as asses are". These comments also indicate that Iago is not so evil that he doesn't recognize the goodness in others.

Iago improvises his plot. Commentators speak of him as an artist, a playwright, writing a play in real time and doing so by controlling his characters.

- **Othello** - Shakespeare presents Othello to us as "dark and grand ... no longer young and now grave, self-controlled, steeled by the experience of countless perils, hardships and vicissitudes, at once simple and stately in bearing and in speech, a great man, naturally modest but fully conscious of his worth, proud of his services to the state, unawed by dignitaries and unelated by honors, secure, it would seem, against all dangers from without and all rebellion from within. And he comes to have his life crowned with the final glory of love ... [His] mind, for all its poetry, is very simple. He's not observant. ... He is quite free from introspection and is not given to reflection" (Br 189). He's prone to trusting people. First, he puts all his faith in Desdemona, later he puts it in Iago. In his trust, he's all-or-nothing. In his love, he's passionate and total.

  Othello is also a man of contrasts (VD 192). He can be both monstrous and tender, a soldier and a lover, a man who is both superior to passion and its slave. He's a Christian with a pagan background and a black man who is married to a white woman. He's a person attempting to assimilate into a culture other than the one of his forebears, a "permanent outsider" (Bl8 45), a stranger from another world. This can lead to misunderstandings, since different cultures often lack a common language (ArO 28). It might explain his dependence on Iago to interpret the actions of his Venetian wife and the attitude towards sex and fidelity in Venice. It also might explain resentments against him, especially since he's a black governor who outranks the Europeans he governs. As in Shakespeare's other tragedies, Othello's high position in the government is symbolic of his inner nobility.

From a dramatic point of view, Shakespeare portrays Othello and Desdemona as opposites: Venetian versus. African, young versus. old, innocent and pure versus. rough and military. Although they are both Christian, it's hinted that his parents were pagan (III, IV, 57) and the play doesn't specify whether or not he's a Morisco or was born a Christian. In either case, however, in contrast to Desdemona he would not have been fully integrated into Venetian society.

Finally, there's much debate among Shakespearean scholars as to whether Othello could be played by either a black or an olive colored actor. Roderigo refers to him as the "thicklips" (I, I, 65) and Othello himself and others refer to him as black, but there are arguments to be made to the contrary, since he could have had Arabic roots. The prevailing opinion, however, is that Shakespeare chose to emphasize his difference from Desdemona by making him black. This is important in understanding Desdemona's character. She's shown to be as "simple and innocent as a child, ardent with the courage and idealism of a saint, radiant with that heavenly purity of heart which men worship" (Br 201). The fact that, without any notion of universal brotherhood – she's not a civil rights activist - she fell in love with someone so different is a testament to how extraordinary she is.

Othello is the opposite of Hamlet. Exchange "Othello and Hamlet in one another's plays and there would be no plays. Othello would chop Claudius down as soon as the ghost had convinced him [of Claudius' guilt], and Hamlet would have needed only a few moments to see through Iago and to begin destroying him by overt parody" (Bl8 1).

- **Iago -** It is unclear what Iago's motives are in setting out to destroy Othello. He speaks of several reasons for this: his resentment against Othello for appointing Cassio to the position that he felt he deserved, his desire to take that position from Cassio, and his suspicion that Othello has had sex with Emilia. More generally, he seems to hate and envy Othello and to resent social privilege.

  Some commentators, however, take a different view. They think there are too many motives for his hatred. They speak of the "motive-hunting of motive-less malignity" (Colerige (ArO 33)). "His motives ... make him a credible human being, provided that we refrain from searching for a master motive, one that unlocks all the rest" (ArO 41). No passion, love or lust motivates him. His pleasure comes from manipulating others. Iago is an artist whose medium is life and whose style is evil. Like any other artist, he enjoys his art for art's sake (Ba 105).

This is the ultimate evil – evil without reason, cold revenge, the union of intellect and hate. In Iago "Shakespeare reveals, ... that unrestrained intellect, instead of being the opposite of force and an antidote for it, is force functioning on another plane" (Go 79). Iago is a complete cynic with respect to goodness. His is a "cynicism which consists not of denying that good men exist but of saying that better men do also – men who like himself can take the measure of nobility and thereby be above it" (VD 195). Iago is the "most terrific indictment of pure intellect in the literature of the world. ... The intellect, as all the prophets have divined, should be the servant of the soul. ... the moment the intellect sets up a claim of sovereignty for itself it is the slave in revolt ... Lucifer fallen" (Go 76). Iago has no soul.

- (II, I, 5 – 17) "Methinks the wind hath spoke ..." - Shakespeare makes his storm out of poetry.

- (II, I, 80) "Make love's quick pants ..." - Cassio hopes that Othello will arrive safely in Cyprus so that he can consummate his marriage.

- (II, I, 97) "Let it not gall ..." - Cassio refers to his breeding in his show of courtesy to Emilia, and Iago refers to this later (167) in a mocking way. The passages seem to emphasize Iago's resentment over their class difference.

- (II, I, 112 - 122) "and housewives in ... your beds!" - Iago engages in sexually suggestive banter and Desdemona encourages him (117). The exchange shows that she's not naïve. She speaks about hiding her real feelings, something that Iago does constantly (122) and is central to the play.

- (II, I, 139 - 158) "What miserable praise hast ..." - In a playful exchange, Desdemona asks Iago to praise "foul and foolish" women. His response is essentially that they're no worse than "fair and wise" women. She then asks what he has to say of a truly deserving woman who wasn't afraid to hear what malice itself would say of her. She is speaking of herself, but unbeknownst to her, malice is Iago. He composes a poem on the fly enumerating the merits of a deserving woman and demonstrates his wit and intelligence as well as an understanding of what deserving means (Go 84).

- (II, I, 167) "He takes her by the palm; ..." - Iago, the reasonable man, develops a plot in stages as the action in the play progresses. Here he plots to ensnare Cassio using the fact that Cassio is a gentleman who observes the courtesies of his class. Iago finds this appropriate, since he resents the class distinctions that work against him.

- **Time** - The play takes place over a period of roughly 36 hours, starting in the middle of a day in Venice and ending at the end of the next day in Cyprus. Some of its action takes place in real time – the action takes the same amount of time as the acting. At other points, time is radically compressed. Thus, minutes stand for the hours it would ordinarily take for three ships to be successively sighted and docked and their passengers brought ashore, all in the midst of a raging storm. Shakespeare crowds "into one intense theatrical experience the mysterious evolution of states of feeling that can, and do if spread over days or weeks in the real world, lead human beings from confidence to perplexity to doubt to surrender to breakdown" (Bl9 99). Apparently, Shakespeare is not concerned with time. "The play's essential action lies in the processes of thought and feeling by which the characters are moved and the story is forwarded. ... [Shakespeare is] concerned with fundamental passions, and its swift working demands uncumbered expression" (Ba2 30).

- (II, I, 179) "O my fair warrior!" - Othello calls Desdemona a warrior. A possible explanation of this can be found in Othello's description of his courtship in which she was drawn to him by his description of the adventures he had experienced (I, III, 146): "She wished that heaven had made her such a man" (I, III, 163). Shakespeare tells us that Desdemona is not a wilting lily, that she's stronger than she appears and that she's "in love with danger" (Go 83).

- (II, I, 181 – 193) "It gives me wonder ..." - Othello is a romantic, as seen in the way he imagines the glories of military life and adventure, and the way he speaks of his love for Desdemona. Here, he hints at a "preference for a perpetually unconsummated courtship" (190), with the implication that "marriage and consummation naturally pose a threat to this idealistic love" (Bl8 85). He ends on a pessimistic note – that from here on out it's downhill - which she corrects with her optimism. He's childlike in his language, referring to Desdemona as "Honey" and "my sweet" (203). In the previous scenes Iago and Roderigo had painted Othello in the worst possible light. Here, Shakespeare pulls a switch on us and shows us a man with the most loving sensibilities. In this way, he prepares the audience for the misjudgments that will follow.

- (II, I, 220 - 249) "Mark me with what violence ..." - Iago once again reassures Roderigo that Desdemona will tire of Othello. He views her as being motivated by innate sexual urges (225) rather than love. He says that Desdemona's "eye must be fed" (223), and that she needs someone who possesses "loveliness in favour, sympathy in years, manners and beauties". There is some truth in this analysis, but the problems that arise in her marriage to Othello have more to do with their inability to understand one another than with natural urges.

- (II, I, 255) "Lechery, by this hand: ..." - Iago sees lechery in innocent actions. Thus, touching the palm of Cassio's hand is a prologue to lust.

- (II, I, 284 - 310) "That Cassio loves her, ..." - Iago continues to develop his plot in real time based on an evaluation of the people he will manipulate. In his view, it's not unreasonable that Cassio and Desdemona could be suspected of loving one another and that Roderigo is trash that can be easily manipulated. Iago speaks positively of Othello, "a constant, loving, noble nature", who he believes will prove to be a "most dear husband". But Othello's good sense won't be sufficient to protect him from jealousy.

  Note that at this point Iago's goal seems to be to torment Othello in order to get Cassio's position, not to kill anyone. He again speaks of his suspicions that Othello and Cassio have had sex with Emilia, although there's no other indication in the play that this is so. Iago's soliloquies are not like Hamlet's. In Hamlet's case, they expose an inner debate, whereas Iago's soliloquies simply inform the audience of his plans. Othello has only two soliloquies and they don't give us much insight to his inner life.

- (II, III, 1 – 3) "Good Michael, look you to the guard ..." - In a few lines Shakespeare gives us an inkling of Othello's personality – a disciplined soldier and an affectionate superior officer. He confirms that his marriage wasn't consummated in Venice (9).

- (II, III, 14 - 26) "Our general cast us thus ..." - Iago views the relationship between Othello and Desdemona through the lens of sex and Cassio parries this by speaking of her purity. The exchange demonstrates the social distance between them.

- (II, III, 159) "What is the matter here?" - Iago has arranged for a fight between Cassio and Roderigo that will once again interrupt the wedding night, this time on Cyprus, and will also discredit Cassio. Othello demonstrates his commanding presence (168). With a parody of Othello and Desdemona in mind, Iago has the gall to describe Cassio and Roderigo as friends who are "like bride and groom divesting themselves for bed" (176).

- (II, III, 200 - 205) "Now, by heaven, ..." - Othello speaks of passion taking control of his better judgment. These are the two sides of his character – a passionate core held in check by judgment. His words echo a similar thought spoken by Iago (I, III, 327).

- (II, III, 248 - 254) "All's well now, sweeting, ..." - Othello accepts with remarkable equanimity a second arousal from his wedding bed: "Tis a soldier's life". Furthermore, it's not clear whether at this point Othello goes back to bed with Desdemona or goes with Montano to tend to his wounds. Shakespeare leaves unresolved the question of whether Othello and Desdemona consummate their marriage.

- (II, III, 258) "Reputation, reputation, ..." - Cassio speaks of the loss of his reputation and Iago belittles its importance

(264). Iago's view is that ambition and self-advancement are the only things that are important, everything else can be sacrificed to that. This is consistent with his earlier lecture to Roderigo (I, III, 320) in which he spoke of the importance of reason and self-control in mastering passion and in which he denigrates love.

- (II, III, 331 – 357) "And what's he then ..." - Iago takes an artist's pride in the beauty of his plot: Cassio will enlist Desdemona to plead his case to Othello while he insinuates to Othello that Desdemona does so because she lusts after Cassio. And he will get Emilia to prod Desdemona to do the pleading (378). Finally, he'll arrange for Othello to see Cassio enlisting Desdemona's intervention. This is a pivotal point in the play. Up until now, Iago has simply been trying to get Cassio's position. But now he goes further and makes "the net that shall enmesh them all" (357). Iago speaks of working by wit (intelligence) rather than by witchcraft (367) (that which Othello has been accused of doing) and of the pleasure he has in devising his plots (374). This is evil for its own sake, for how will destroying Othello's marriage advance Iago's interest?

- (III, III, 19) "Do not doubt that: ..." - Desdemona speaks assuredly of her determination. She radiates strength.

- (III, III, 34) Iago can't destroy Othello directly. Rather he brings about Othello's self-destruction by carefully planting seeds of suspicion in his mind. A close analysis shows Iago's evil brilliance.

    - (34) "Ha, I like not that." - He introduces a note of confusion. By denying that Cassio snuck away (38) he introduces the idea that that's exactly what he did.

- (70) "What, Michael Cassio that came ..." - He overhears a piece of information, then uses it later in a question he innocently asks (93) to bring Cassio to Othello's mind in a compromising way. The word "harm" colors the question (97).

- (101 – 120) "Indeed?" - He teases and annoys Othello by dangling the words "honest", "think", "indeed" and refusing to explain their use.

- (127) "For Michael Cassio, ..." - He shifts from "sworn" to "think" and says, "men should be what they seem" (130), intimating some doubt about Cassio's honesty.

- (140) "As where's that palace whereinto foul things sometimes intrude not?" - He says that he has some "vile" thoughts, thoughts that might not be true, and that this is not unusual. He insinuates that they have some sexual content by referring to them as "uncleanly". By not revealing them he claims that he's protecting Othello from troublesome imaginings (155). He knows that this will only motivate Othello to probe further.

- (158 - 163) "Good name in man and woman, ..." - He speaks of the importance of reputation to both "man *and woman*", suggesting that his thoughts concern reputation and bringing the conversation closer to Desdemona. He contradicts his earlier position (II,

III, 258) that belittled reputation: "Who steals my purse steals trash ... ".

- (167) "O beware, my lord, of jealousy!" - He introduces the words "jealousy" and "cuckold" into the conversation in a general way to suggest the self-destructive passion he's trying to introduce.

- (180) "Think'st thou I'd make ..." - Othello declares that he's immune to jealousy, but he's clearly taken the bait. His defense of himself - that Desdemona chose him in spite of his appearance - implies some inner insecurity related to his race (190). This is related to Desdemona's words "I saw Othello's visage in his mind" and Brabantio's words that she fell in love with someone that she "feared to look on" (I, III, 99).

- (200) "Look to your wife, ..." - Iago is now blunt, pointing a finger at Desdemona. He backs that up by talking about the adulterous ways of the Venetians and the fact that Desdemona deceived Brabantio (209). Note that he has shifted the conversation from Cassio's honesty to Desdemona's honesty.

- (230) "Long live she so; ..." - Iago insinuates that Othello simply "thinks" that Desdemona is honest. Othello recognizes the unnaturalness of their union: "nature erring from itself" (231). Iago uses this to suggest that she is capable of doing strange things, pointing out that she rejected other proposals where the suitor matched her geographical origin (clime), race (complexion), and class (degree). He uses the word "rank" to hint at a sexual basis for her action and hints that there's something perverse about it. Othello defers to Iago's judgment (246, 264), perhaps because he's unfamiliar with Venetian culture and in addition he's a soldier, not a courtier.

- **Sex –** This is the turning point of the play. Othello's mind has been poisoned with the idea that Desdemona has had sex with Cassio and all his actions and thoughts are now preoccupied with this issue and the passion that accompanies it. Othello's "sexual jealousy is a passion like no other. It is pathological ... Facts and reason are its playthings" (Ba 113). Macbeth is also a passionate man, but it's ambition that motivates him, and ambition is not in itself ignoble. Jealousy, on the other hand, brings with it a sense of shame and for this reason it's often hidden.

  Assuming that he hasn't consummated the marriage, Othello could have easily resolved any doubts he had about Desdemona's chastity by simply having sex with her. If she's a virgin, then Iago is exposed. If not, then she has clearly cheated. The only way there could be any doubt about her chastity is if the marriage had been consummated and sufficient time has elapsed since then for her to have had an affair. But the collapsed time of the play doesn't allow for that. Shakespeare has sacrificed plausibility in the interest of dramatic power.

- (III, III, 262 - 283) "This fellow's of exceeding honesty ..." - Othello considers two reasons that might have caused Desdemona to deceive him: that as a black man and a soldier he's not sufficiently skilled to manage the social conventions of Venetians, and that he's old. The former trivializes the racial issue and the latter might be evidence of sexual anxiety. Both reasons evade the deeper source of his anxiety: that his attempt to assimilate as a Venetian has failed and that Desdemona has deceived him simply because he's black. He's unwilling to admit this because it would leave him with only two options: "to embrace his blackness and hurl its beauty and its power in the face of his enemies ... or to internalize [Venetian society's] image of him [as a savage] and yield to self-loathing. Either choice would proclaim his complete alienation" (Bl9 55). Embracing his blackness would force him to accept the fact that he's an outcast and to abandon his view of himself as a Venetian.

Othello then goes on to blame the female appetite for sex, saying it's beyond control (272). He also asserts, without any justification, that privileged men are destined to be plagued by unfaithful wives (279). Both explanations allow him to ignore the possibility that the problem is his color. And then Desdemona enters and he says, "If she be false, O then heaven mocks itself" (282). At stake for Othello is more than just simple jealousy. It's his faith in women and his view of himself as a member of Venetian society. He uses astronomical images (90, 282) to convey the extent of his concern.

- (III, III, 291) "Your napkin is too little." - The handkerchief is a key symbol in the play. It's a trivial object, but the outcome of the play turns on it. This, of course, is no accident on Shakespeare's part. Its loss and its recovery by Emilia are the first interventions by fate that determines the tragic outcome. It is ironic that Desdemona, in an act of love, loses it and, in the end, it is the object that condemns her to death. "Was there ever a better demonstration that everything may depend on anything?" (Go 86).

- (III, III, 324 - 332) "I will in Cassio's lodging ..." - Iago muses on the progress of the poison that he's administered to Othello and he's proud of its effect (332 - 336). He "salutes both his own achievement and the consciousness that Othello will never" enjoy life again (Bl 467).

- (III, III, 348 - 362) "I had been happy ..." - Othello is a little over-dramatic. He romanticizes war eloquently as a "majestic order" (Bl8 30). This contrasts with the chaos into which his life is descending (92). He demands "ocular" proof to convince himself of Desdemona's adultery, proof that can't be disputed. When Iago asks for further clarification (399), he uses the crudest image to refer to the evidence, thus sticking in the knife and causing the desired pain: "Death and damnation".

- (III, III, 386 - 393) "By the world ..." - Othello is completely bewildered. F says, "Her name" (389), Q says "My name". The latter implies that Othello sees Desdemona's purity as confirming his own purity (I, II, 30); her deception as blackening his reputataion. Hence, more than love is lost if Desdemona is impure. In either case, Othello expresses self-loathing and a concern for reputation: his/her name is as "begrim'd and black as mine own face".

- (III, III, 447) "Now do I see 'tis true." - The handkerchief finally convinces Othello of Desdemona's guilt and a jealous passion takes over: "O blood, blood, blood!" The self-control he had exhibited up to this point is gone and passion is now in charge of his actions. His rage contrasts sharply with the delicate love he expressed for Desdemona earlier (II, I, 181). That love had held his aggressive emotions in check, but it's no longer able to do so.

- (III, III, 456 – 465) "Never, Iago. Like to the …" - Othello compares himself to the Pontic Sea. He has an inflated ego and often engages in over-the-top language in describing himself. He "sees the world as a theater for his professional reputation; this most valiant of soldiers has no fear of literal death-in-battle, which only would enhance his glory. But to be cuckolded by his wife with his subordinate Cassio as the other offender, would be a … death-in-life, since his reputation would not survive it" (Bl 449).

  Othello has been faulted for not demanding an explanation from Desdemona instead of planning her death. But an argument in his defense can be mounted based on the fact that "Othello regarded Desdemona's love for him as a dream too beautiful to be true. Hence, when it's suggested that her love isn't true, it's what he has been ready to believe all along. … When we wake from a dream, we don't go around searching for material evidence that it wasn't a dream" (Go 88). Othello has also been criticized for trusting Iago and not Desdemona. In his defense, it can be said that (Br 192) (1) Iago had been his companion in arms and is trusted by everyone, (2) Othello didn't know Desdemona very well, (3) coming from a different culture, Othello had little knowledge of the morality of Venetian women and Iago took advantage of that by poisoning his mind on the subject, and (4) Othello saw how Desdemona had deceived her father.

- (III, IV, 58 - 69) "That's a fault." - The handkerchief "is a symbol of women's loving, civilizing, sexual power." It had been passed from one woman to another (Sybil (72), an Egyptian charmer, his mother, Desdemona) and has a mystical origin that enables women to use and control sexuality. It encourages "marital chastity – sexuality transformed by loving fidelity. Its function is to chasten and control men's love and desire" (Bl8 98). Othello demands it of Desdemona, but she foolishly and courageously insists on pleading Cassio's case (95). Her innocence, "a frank childlike boldness" (Br 205), causes her to persist in helping Cassio. Her inability to sense Othello's concerns is the flip side of his inability to recognize her innocence, and they are the source of the tragedy. They illustrate the kind of interpersonal problems that can arise not because people disagree, but because they misunderstand each other's needs and motivation. In this case they both agree on the importance of fidelity in marriage and their affection for Cassio (II, III, 244).

- (III, IV, 145 - 162) "Men's natures wrangle with ..." - Desdemona is a realist. Men aren't gods, they're sometimes focused on major issues and ignore the niceties of polite behavior. She completely misunderstands Othello's actions and blames herself for causing his anger. Emilia's analysis of jealousy (160) describes Othello. He's not jealous for a cause, but jealous because he's prone to jealousy.

- (IV, I, 35) "Lie with her?" - Othello reaches a peak of rage and confusion, his language becomes disjointed and he falls into an epileptic fit. "Earlier in the play he was supremely in command of himself and others" (Bl8 136). At this point he's completely out of control.

- (IV, I, 49) "What's the matter?" - Cassio arrives on the scene while Othello is unconscious and this bit of chance allows Iago to set up an incriminating encounter (57) that Othello can observe and misinterpret (75, 105). Bianca arrives (145) to further the deception. Iago delivers blow after blow, allowing no time for Othello to recover (Br 196). Taken together with the loss of the handkerchief and its recovery by Emilia, chance enables Iago to move his plot forward. We get the sense that Othello and Desdemona are dragged down by a fate from which they cannot escape, as opposed to a flaw in Othello's character.

- (IV, I, 178) "Ay, let her rot and perish ..." - Othello is a man of extremes – his emotions swing from intense love to intense hatred. Later he says, "I will chop her up into messes" (196). Contrast this with his language in the first half of the play. He's torn between the Venetian civilization into which he has assimilated and the image of pagan Africa. Desdemona's love, in contrast, is constant, as indicated by her use of the endearment "sweet" (239). Shakespeare assigns "less sense and less sensibility to the heroes than to the heroines ... Desdemona, Emilia and Bianca are all cast aside by their men ... and all three give themselves to love more unstintingly than their self-centered men" (ArO 54). Although Iago had not planned Desdemona's death (179), he makes no effort to stop it and even participates in planning how it is to be done (204). He seems to treat it as an unforeseen dividend.

- (IV, I, 239) "Devil!" - Othello strikes Desdemona. This is so out of character that Lodovico asks (264): Is this the "nature whom passion cannot shake?" Othello's self-control, symbolized by the line that he used to stop the brawl, "Keep up your bright swords ..." (I, II, 59), has been shattered.

- (IV, II, 48 - 65) "Had it pleased heaven ..." - Othello speaks eloquently of his pain. He compares himself to Job. He can bear any kind of hardship or scorn, but to lose his love – "the fountain from which my current runs" – is more than he can endure. Othello has so closely identified himself with Desdemona that he cannot dissociate himself from her corruption. Hence, her apparent sensuality becomes his sensuality, and since sensuality is associated with black Africa, he's not the Venetian that he aspires to be.

- (IV, II, 91) "I took you for that …" - Another reference to adultery in Venice.

- (IV, II, 108) "And call thy husband hither." - Desdemona calls for Iago to comfort her. If we think of Iago as representing evil and Desdemona as representing good, then the conclusion we can draw from this meeting is that not only does good "not resist evil, it is unaware of its presence" (Go 95).

- (IV, II, 120) "Am I that name, Iago?" - Shakespeare emphasizes Desdemona's innocence by showing her unwilling to repeat the word "whore".

- (IV, II, 154 – 163) "If e'er my will …" - Desdemona's words can be interpreted as either a statement of subjection to Othello no matter what he does to her, or as a commitment to her marriage vow. In the latter case it shows Desdemona's strength, not her weakness.

- (IV, II, 199) "if she will return me …" - Roderigo plans to ask Desdemona to return the jewels that he believes Iago has given to her on his behalf. This is a problem for Iago, since he simply pocketed them. Hence, Roderigo has to die.

- (IV, III, 17) "So would not I: …" - Desdemona declares her love for Othello and then anticipates her death (22). The wedding bed has been referred to throughout the play, reminding us of their unconsummated love. Here the wedding sheets anticipate the play's tragic ending. The following lines suggest an "intimate togetherness" and "feminine tenderness and communion" (ArO 55) between Cordelia and Emilia, with Emilia serving more as a mother than an attendant.

- (IV, III, 50 - 102) "Let nobody blame him, ..." - Desdemona makes a Freudian slip in singing the willow song (51). Initially the verse tells of a maiden who doesn't want her lover to be blamed for scorning her. This is acceptance of male scorn and perhaps indicates that Desdemona doesn't want Othello to be blamed for what he might do. The alternate verse (56) speaks instead of resisting such treatment. Emilia and Desdemona discuss adultery. Desdemona, in her purity, denies that a woman could be adulterous (64). Emilia takes an earthy point of view. She'd be unfaithful if the rewards were great enough (70) but, more importantly, she speaks out forcefully against the double standard that condemns unfaithful woman and not unfaithful men (85 – 102). Shakespeare takes a strong feminist view here. Emilia "combines sharp-tongued honesty with warm affection" (Bl8 87) and in this way balances Desdemona's purity.

- (V, I, 19) "He hath a daily beauty in his life that makes me ugly; ..." – Iago describes Cassio. "These are the most consciously self-revealing words that Iago speaks. Ugliness cannot tolerate beauty" (Go 76). He is jealous of Cassio. Perhaps this relates to his lower-class origins. Iago's feelings towards Cassio mirror similar feelings towards Othello and serve as motivators for his actions. Here we have another example of plotting on the fly.

- (V, I, 42) "Two or three groan." - Shakespeare mocks male pretensions of valor: Lodovico and Gratiano are afraid to be involved in the fight between Cassio and Roderigo.

- (V, II, 1 - 6) "It is the cause, ..." - Othello claims that he must kill Desdemona in order to save her from further dishonor, to do justice (17), and to prevent her from betraying other men. (His view is reminiscent of a view taken by some in the military during the Vietnam War that certain villages had to be destroyed in order to save them from the Vietcong.) Some commentators (Br 197) (K 123) believe him, while others feel that he's deceiving himself and finding a justification for an action which he does out of hatred and revenge (ArO 84). He speaks of her skin as whiter than snow and as smooth as monumental alabaster. This is his idealistic view of womanhood and there's a coldness about it. He says that he'll love her when she's dead, perhaps because then she'll be passive and pure (18). If so, this is an admission that her sexuality stood in the way of the chaste union that he preferred (Bl8 56).

- (V, II, 26 – 28, 53) "If you bethink ..." - Othello's heritage is not Christian and, like many converts, "he can't allow himself the moderately flexible adherence that most ordinary men have to their own formal beliefs" (Bl8 50). Assimilation requires that he be more observant than those whose relationship to the religion is not suspect.

  Confession is a central act in Christianity and Othello mentions it in a general way early in the play (I, III, 123). But it becomes central later. Before killing Desdemona, he demands a death-bed confession. When she refuses "he feels the outrage of the thwarted system that needs to imagine itself merciful and sacramental, when it disciplines"

(63 – 65). Othello had not viewed Desdemona's death as murder, since Old Testament doctrine called for the killing of adulterers and some 16th Century Protestant clerics had called for a return to this doctrine for the "tranquility and commonwealth of the church". "Putrified and corrupt members" should be cut off "from the whole body, lest they poison and destroy the body" and this is the "law of love". "It is in the bitter spirit of these convictions that Othello enacts the grotesque comedy of treating his wife as a strumpet and the tragedy of executing her in the name of justice" (Bl8 51 - 52).

Othello's orthodoxy showed up earlier (IV, I, 2 – 9) when he tried to distinguish between a venal sin, one that can be pardoned by the church, (an unauthorized kiss) and a mortal sin, one that cannot be pardoned and is punishable by death (naked with a friend in bed). Such sins were precisely defined in religious manuals of that time.

- (V, II, 76) "Alas, he is betrayed, and I am undone." - Othello misinterprets Desdemona's statement as a confession of guilt.

- (V, II, 122) "Nobody. I myself." - Desdemona has lived a chaste life and her reputation is unstained. Here she tries to protect Othello with her dying breath by saying that she herself is responsible for her death. This is exceptional. She realizes that she hasn't convinced Othello of her fidelity and hence she will be reputed to have deceived her husband, a devastating stain, and she goes even further and claims the infamous reputation of a suicide.

Desdemona's attitude towards her reputation stands in contrast to the attitudes of the men, who are so concerned with their good names. Cassio bemoans the loss of his reputation (II, III, 258). Othello speaks highly of Montano's reputation (II, III, 188) and regrets the blackening of Desdemona's name (and/or his own) (III, III, 389). In his final speech (V, II, 350), he tries to salvage some of his reputation. The fact that Iago is not concerned with reputation indicates a correlation between concern and a vulnerability to manipulation.

- (V, II, 129) "And you the blacker devil!" - Emilia reveals hidden racism.

- (V, II, 158 - 163) "Thou hast not half ..." - Emilia achieves heroic stature by defying Othello, saying that she can endure more hurt than he can administer and that she's not intimidated by his sword.

- (V, II, 192) "Good gentlemen, let me have ..." - Emilia addresses an issue discussed by Renaissance scholars. Is it necessary to obey an immoral command given by an authority figure? The scholars feared that disobedience can lead to chaos and so must always be discouraged. Emilia's answer, "'Tis proper I obey him – but not now", is probably Shakespeare's view: under some circumstances, disobedience is appropriate.

- (V, II, 214) "It was a handkerchief, ..." - Othello reveals that the handkerchief was the crucial piece of evidence that condemned Desdemona and he contradicts the story he told her about its origin. He apparently was trying to scare her.

- (V, II, 217) "'Twill out, 'twill out!" - Emilia realizes that her desire to please Iago has led to Desdemona's death. Emilia reveals Iago's villainy. Although she is portrayed throughout the play as rather common, we see here that she's capable of defying her husband and performing a heroic act. She is "one thing without, another within", an attribute shared by others in the play: "Roderigo, the fine young gentleman, rotten at the core; Bianca, the courtesan who falls in love; Brabantio, the harsh father who dies of a broken heart; Cassio, the profligate with a pure heart" (Go 75). And finally, Iago.

- (V, II, 235) "Ay, ay; O lay me ..." - Emilia asks to be laid next to Desdemona, creating an image of feminine loyalty and defiance to the tyranny of their husbands. The marriage bed, which had been the symbol of the (possibly unattained) union of Desdemona and Othello, becomes, instead, the site of the union between Desdemona and Emilia.

- (V, II, 257 - 279) "Behold, I have a weapon, ..." - Othello is not beyond boasting of his abilities as a warrior at this terrible time. And then he goes on to blame fate (263), minimizing his guilt (and later uses the adjectives "ill-starred" (270) and "unlucky" (339)). "Cold, cold, my girl" (273) refers back to his words (III, IV, 39) "Hot, hot, and moist", which was a reference to Desdemona's suspected infidelity. It reinforces his earlier description (5) of her skin as whiter than snow and as smooth as "monumental alabaster", and the way he idealizes women. The fact that this doesn't describe Desdemona is an indication that he never understood her. Knowing that she wasn't unfaithful to him, the phrase "Even like thy chastity" (274) might imply that the marriage was never consummated.

- (V, II, 336 - 349) "Soft you, a word or two ..." - Othello tries to explain the inexplicable: He is "One that loved not wisely, but too well". He then blames the two poles of his nature: "one not easily jealous but, being wrought, perplexed in the extreme". Once he's brought to a passionate state, he's "likely to act with little reflection, with no delay, and in the most decisive manner conceivable" (Br 186). He's defending his honor here. He has stopped thinking "about Desdemona and is thinking about himself ... Nothing dies harder than the desire to think well of oneself." (quote from T. S. Eliot (ArO 83)). But finally, he shows his generous nature with "one whose hand ... threw a pearl away richer than all his tribe".

- (V, II, 353) "I took by th' throat ..." - Othello is the Venetian who defended the honor of his state by killing the circumcised Turk. (Since Moslems are circumcised and Christian aren't, Othello implies that he is uncircumcised and hence we can conclude that he was born a Christian.) But by killing himself, he also associates himself with that Turk. He thus acknowledges the "two contradictory self-images that have haunted him throughout the play" (Bl9 56): assimilated Venetian and barbarian. His inability to see himself as a whole human being is a character flaw that contributes to his destruction. "Othello leaves the play exactly as he had entered it, affirming his services to the state, confessing (I, III, 125), asking for justice and judgment, telling stories about his past, and putting his 'unhoused free condition' (I, II, 25) into its ultimate 'confine' for love of Desdemona" (Bl8 102).

- (V, II, 356) "I kissed thee ere I killed thee: ..." - In a sense love triumphs over evil, but only in death: Desdemona dies loving Othello, Othello dies loving Desdemona, and Iago is to die a horrible death.

- (V, II, 359) "For he was great at heart." - Cassio acknowledges Othello's stature - "he was great at heart" – but the play ends on a note of "destruction without catharsis" (Bl8 104). Lodovico has the last word, saying the corpses should be hidden because "the object poisons sight" (362).

Discussion

Themes – *Othello* is primarily a domestic drama about one particular man. There's not much dialogue that directly addresses issues that aren't related to the action. "*Othello* differs from *Hamlet, King Lear* and *Macbeth* in being more insistently ... concerned with the here and now rather than with eternal verities" (ArO 107). For example, *King Lear* consistently goes beyond the immediate confines of the story to deal with questions relating to the nature of man, to justice and to the universe.

Within the confines of the story, however, it's still possible to isolate some themes that *Othello* addresses. An obvious one is the imperceptibility of evil and its power over innocence. Desdemona, the personification of goodness, fails to see the evil in Iago and Othello only recognizes it when it's explained to him after the murder. And connected with this is the sense that "the moral order and the intellectual order are in conflict with one another" (K 125). Iago is intellect run wild, with no notion of morality to give it direction.

A subtler theme is the divided nature of the male psyche. Both Othello and Iago touch on this subject early in the play. Iago speaks of the balance between reason on the one hand and sensuality, including male sexual desire, on the other (I, III, 319). Othello says (I, II, 25) "but that I love the gentle Desdemona I would not my unhoused free condition put into circumspection and confine for the sea's worth", a statement that addresses the conflicting demands of domesticity and a more masculine agenda. And finally, there's the conflict between Othello's passionate nature, which is associated with his pagan roots, and his commanding self-control, which is associated with his assimilated Venetian sensibility. Although these conflicts are exaggerated in Othello, Shakespeare implies that they are typically male.

Race - The effect of race, alienation and assimilation is a central theme of the play. Othello is a rootless wanderer who has cut his ties to his cultural past. Roderigo calls him "an extravagant and wheeling stranger of here and everywhere" (I, I, 134). He "never defends his blackness; nor does he defend the religion or culture that lies behind him" (Bl9 50). In "his aspirations towards assimilation and anxieties about his blackness" (Bl9 57) he internalizes a contradiction that dehumanizes him. He sees himself as the Venetians see him, either "as an exotic European", in other words fully assimilated, or "as a barbarian, worthy of destruction". Or, "in the final paradox of his death, both" (V, II, 353) (Bl9 57).

Shakespeare's most penetrating insight concerns alienation. It's not so much that Othello is a Moor in Venice, it's that the racial atmosphere that he breathes determines his response to being an alien. The most disastrous consequence of racial alienation for Othello is not the hostility of the Venetians, but "his own acceptance of the framework within which they define him" (Bl9 57) and the split that this causes in his self-image.

"In representing Othello's 'Africanness' without resorting to negative stereotyping of racial difference" and without ignoring racial differences entirely, "Shakespeare stretched the mental framework of the age, thrusting upon audiences a more sympathetic understanding of the alien than was customarily available" (Bl9 57).

Is *Othello* a tragedy? – Classical tragedies are often characterized by a protagonist who is a great and noble man, but whose character contains some flaw. He's faced with a situation in which he has to make a choice, and because of that flaw he chooses badly. He's dragged down to his destruction as a result, but in the process, he undergoes an education which gives him, as well as the audience, a better understanding of the human condition. This structure is most evident in *Hamlet* and *King Lear,* two of Shakespeare's greatest tragedies.

In *Othello,* Shakespeare presents us with a noble man who is socially unsophisticated and with no great insights into human nature. His tragic flaws are this simplicity, which renders him easily manipulated, and an overly passionate nature, which causes him to act rashly. His downfall isn't so much the result of a bad choice as the result of the ease with which he yields to an externalized evil. We see no struggle in Othello's soul. Evidence that he has undergone a transformation at the end of the play or has gained new insight into the human condition is weak, consisting of only a few lines in his final speech. This raises the question of whether the play fits the mold of tragedy.

"Of all of Shakespeare's tragedies *Othello* is the most painfully exciting and the most terrible" (Br 176). "What comes to us most forcefully from the stage is not mystery but the agony of loss, loss all the more tragic for not being inevitable. ... The love that these lovers shared before Iago's corruption sets in commands a power that sets it far above the commonplace, as Desdemona is in the radiant generosity and innocence that makes her vulnerable, and as Othello is in the 'free and open nature' that makes him vulnerable ... It is precisely the loss of a love as rare and magical as the fabled handkerchief by a pair of lovers whose vulnerabilities are inseparable from their beauties that tears at the feelings throughout this play and brings to any audience listening to Othello's comparison of himself to 'the base Indian' who 'threw a pearl away richer than all his tribes' ... a shock of self-recognition" (Bl9 89). Othello's fall from the heights of total happiness, where his "soul hath her content so absolute" (II, I, 189), to the depths of savagery has no "meaning and that is the ultimate horror of it" (Ba2 114).

Chapter 12

MACBETH

Background

Wilson Knight describes *Macbeth* as Shakespeare's most profound and mature vision of evil (Kn 140), Harold Bloom says that it is his "personal favorite of all the high tragedies" (Bl 545), and Harold Goddard speaks of it as possibly Shakespeare's most sublime work (Go2 108). A. C. Bradley says that "It is the most vehement, the most concentrated, perhaps we may say the most tremendous, of the tragedies" (Br 333).

The play was probably written in 1605 or 1606, during the reign of James I, and at roughly the same time as *King Lear*. James was king of both England and Scotland, so it's not surprising that Scotland appears in a positive light in the play: Macbeth is defeated by a combined Scottish and English army. In contrast, *Henry IV* is an Elizabethan play in which Scotland opposes the English crown. *Macbeth* is the shortest of all Shakespeare's tragedies, about half the length of *Hamlet*, and the scenes are short, so the action moves along quickly. The primary source of the story is *The Chronicles*, written by the 16th Century historian Holinshed, which describes the murder of a Scottish king that might or might not have some factual basis. The murderers in the original story were Macbeth and Banquo. In *Macbeth*, Shakespeare transformed Banquo into a hero, apparently because James was reputed to have been his descendant.

The Play (line numbers from (ArM))

- (I, I, 1) The witches set the tone of the play: a storm, the heath, filthy air. "Lost and won" and "fair is foul" (11) are examples of the kind of contradictions that appear in much of the play's dialogue and serve to lend a sense of confusion and mystery to its atmosphere. The scene is immediately followed by the arrival of a "bloody man" (I, II, 1) and this introduces blood as a recurrent image.

- (I, II, 16 - 24) "For brave Macbeth ..." - Macbeth is introduced as brave, his sword smoked with bloody execution. He unseamed Macdonwald "from the nave to th'chops and fix'd his head upon our battlements", to which Duncan, king of Scotland, replies that Macbeth is valiant and a "worthy gentleman". This is the universe in which the action is played out. Macbeth is presented to us as a powerful defender of Duncan's throne, and hence the regicide described in the next act is a reversal. Ambition has transformed him.

- (I, III, 48) "All hail Macbeth! hail to thee, Thane of Glamis!" - The witches tempt both Macbeth and Banquo. They greet Macbeth as Thane of Glamis, Thane of Cawdor and "King hereafter". He knows he has attained the first title but is shocked at the last two. Perhaps he has thought of the crown and this might be a sign of a guilty conscience. Banquo notices his reaction (51). The witches speak in riddles to Banquo (65 – 67): He will be "lesser than Macbeth, and greater", "Not so happy, yet much happier", and "get kings, though thou be none". They equivocate: They don't tell Macbeth that he'll have to kill to become king and they don't tell Banquo that he won't live to see his heirs as kings.

- (I, III, 105) "He bade me, from him, ..." - Rosse confirms that the witches' reference to him as Thane of Cawdor is true, giving credence to their prophesies. Macbeth's aside, "the greatest is behind" (116), is evidence that his ambition for the crown has preceded the witches' words, although we do not know if his thoughts included regicide.

- (I, III, 120 – 126) "That, trusted home, ..." - Banquo foresees the trap into which Macbeth will fall.

- (I, III, 127 - 142) "Two truths are told ..." - Macbeth seems to be almost in a trance here, drawn to the crime against his will. "This is temptation, presented with concrete force" (BlM 40). He's "driven along by the violence of his fate like a vessel drifting before a storm" (H 11) and he's aware from the beginning that the deed he contemplates is evil. His speech touches on several themes of the play:

  - (128) "the swelling act of the imperial theme" – This is a reference to his mounting desire for the throne.

  - (131) "cannot be ill; cannot be good" – The witches' message cannot be intended to promote evil, since it promised him a good thing that turned out to be true. The play presents an atmosphere of ambiguity and uncertainty which leaves us on edge.

- (134) "why do I yield to that suggestion" – But the witches' message cannot be good because it suggests an evil action. Macbeth's battle with temptation is a major issue in the play.

- (135) "whose horrid image doth unfix my hair" – Fear permeates the play. It's evident that Macbeth is contemplating regicide and he fully recognizes the horror of the act. Macbeth is proleptic: he imagines and responds to the future as if it has already happened. His imaginings demonstrate his acute sensitivity to the immorality of what he contemplates.

- (137) "against the use of nature" – The act he contemplates is unnatural.

- (137) "present fears are less than horrible imaginings" - What Macbeth imagines is more horrible than any fears he currently experiences.

- (139) "My thought, whose murder yet is but fantastical [imaginary], shakes so my single state of man that function is smother'd in surmise" – Macbeth's imagination of what is to come is so vivid that it smothers his ability to act. He "scarcely is conscious of an ambition, desire, or wish before he sees himself on the other side or shore, already having performed the crime that equivocally fulfills ambition" (Bl 517).

- (142) "nothing is but what is not" - Anticipation of the crime has created a world of confusion and unreality for him.

With these words "Macbeth introduces us to the extraordinary nature of his imagination" (Bl 535).

- (I, III, 144) "If Chance will have me King, ..." - Macbeth hasn't committed to doing the crime. He hopes that the crown will come to him without his taking any action.

- (I, IV, 7 - 11) "Nothing in his life ..." - This is a succinct description of the act of accepting one's fate.

- (I, IV, 11) "There's no art ..." - Duncan speaks truly: one is easily deceived, there's no way to tell what a man is thinking. Ironically, Macbeth immediately enters.

- (I, IV, 22) "The service and the loyalty I owe ..." - Macbeth's words can be understood as simply hypocritical. Alternatively, they show a man who is torn between his ambition and his acceptance of the ordered world (who gives, who receives) that Duncan represents.

- (I, IV, 38) "Our eldest, Malcolm; ..." - Macbeth's hope to ascend the throne on Duncan's death is dashed. This undoubtedly fuels his drive to perform the crime. Although it's still possible that Macbeth could ascend in the normal course of events (accession was not necessarily heredity), he doesn't want to wait. He invokes darkness (50 - 51), a symbol for evil and the interruption of the natural processes. And he hopes to separate his "eye", meaning his conscious mind with its conscience, from his hand, the instrument of the crime: "The eye wink at the hand" (52). This is a wish for self-division. Unfortunately for him, but fortunately for us, this doesn't work.

- (I, V, 10) "This have I thought good …" - Macbeth calls Lady Macbeth "my dearest partner" and later (58) "my dearest love". Shakespeare presents them as a happily married couple.

- (I, V, 16 - 29) "Yet do I fear thy nature: …" - Lady Macbeth acknowledges Macbeth's essential morality. She is well aware of the evil she promotes. She says that "illness" (20), the willingness to commit crime, should accompany ambition, a rather twisted view of life. She fears that Macbeth is inhibited by the "milk of human kindness". Milk is a symbol of nature and goodness and contrasts with her later reference to gall (48) and the numerous references to blood. She recognizes that Macbeth is not without ambition, but sees his approach as a losing combination: "what thou wouldst highly, that wouldst thou holily" (20), and "wouldst not play false, and yet wrongly win". He wants the throne, but he doesn't want to commit the crime that is necessary to get it.

- (I, V, 40 - 53) "Come, you Spirits …" - Lady Macbeth invokes "the powers of darkness to take possession of her. The invocation is not metaphorical or symbolical, but in deadly earnest" (ArM lviii). She calls for some supernatural force to enter her body and act on her behalf. But as the play progresses it becomes clear that the responsibility for the crime lies not with the supernatural, but entirely with Macbeth and his wife. Her call to be "unsexed" (41) is a direct violation of the procreative dimension of nature and hence an attack on the natural progression of life. This is consistent with the regicide, which is an attack on the natural progression of rule in an orderly society. Her desire to "Stop up th' access and passage to remorse" (44) and block "compunctious visitings of Nature" is an acknowledgment that man has an innate morality based in nature.

Lady Macbeth is concerned with the distinction between desire and will. This was also a concern of Player King, Claudius and Hamlet himself in *Hamlet.* The intention ("purpose" (46)) to perform an act doesn't always result in the act itself ("effect") being performed. Hamlet expressed this as "the native hue of resolution is sicklied o'er with the pale cast of thought" (*Hamlet* (III, I, 83)). She wishes for the same self-division that Macbeth had previously requested - that "my keen knife see not the wound it makes" (I, IV, 52).

- (I, V, 60 - 66) "O! never shall sun that morrow see!" – Lady Macbeth fears that their murderous intentions can be read in Macbeth's face. Again, the issue is deception (see (I, IV, 12)).

- (I, VI, 3 - 9) "This guest of summer ..." - Banquo's imagery dwells on nature - the martlet (swallow), the fragrance of the air, summer, the bed (sleep), procreation – and contrasts with the imagery used by Macbeth – blood, night. The natural order is wholesome, and Macbeth is about to violate its equivalent in the human sphere. Banquo's imagery also contrasts with Lady Macbeth's earlier mention of a raven and battlements (I, V, 38). The scene provides dramatic effect. It separates the earlier scene containing Lady Macbeth's invocation of the powers of darkness (I, V, 40) and the later scene in which Macbeth decides to commit the crime (I, VII, 80). "It is from the 'life' images of the play, which range from the temple-haunting martlets to Macduff's 'babes', his 'pretty ones' and include all the scattered references to man's natural goods – sleep and food and fellowship – that we take our bearings in the apprehension of evil" (BIM 52).

- (I, VI, 10 – 30) "See, see! Our honour'd hostess." - Duncan is the opposite of Macbeth. "Meek" and "clear" are words used to describe him. His mind is incapable of suspicion (I, IV, 12). He uses the word "love" four times in this conversation with Lady Macbeth.

- (I, VII, 1 - 28) "If it were done, when 'tis done, then 'twere well it were done quickly: ..." – The opening line of this soliloquy has the same familiar ring as the opening line of Hamlet's soliloquy: "To be or not to be". Just as the words "no", "nothing", and "never" keep recurring in *King Lear* and emphasize the play's focus on life's emptiness and the lack of a moral order, the various forms of the verb "to do" keep recurring in *Macbeth* and emphasize the play's focus on the consequences that follow the doing of a deed.

  Macbeth is concerned with punishment in this life and says that he's willing to ignore the possibility of punishment in the afterlife. This contrasts with Hamlet, who worries about punishment after death: "The dread of something after death puzzles the will" (*Hamlet* (III, 1, 77)). But Macbeth does worry about guilt: "We still have judgment here" (8). The evil we do winds up poisoning us (10). It can be argued that the soliloquy shows that Macbeth is deterred only by fear of the consequences of the deed, not by its immorality, but it's clear that he is haunted by the horror of murder.

  Macbeth realizes that the deed is particularly wrong because he is both Duncan's kinsman and host, and because Duncan is a good king (13 - 28), thus demonstrating his complete moral awareness. This gives a tragic dimension to his character and separates him from Lady Macbeth. "Macbeth embarks on his career of crime with anguish and reluctance, 'as if it were an appalling duty'. He is humanized by his fears, which prove him to be a man, and not the monster his oppressed subjects believe him to be" (ArM lii). He expresses here his "inner awareness". Pity, pictured as a new-born babe – hence nature – cries out against the deed (21).

Macbeth struggles with his choice. The play shows us the "steps by which a noble and valiant man is brought to his damnation" and it presents the "process in such a way as to arouse our pity and terror" (ArM liii).

- (I, VII, 29) "He has almost supp'd." - Duncan has eaten and later (II, I, 12) he will sleep. He is at one with nature, something that is denied to Macbeth, who cannot eat (at the banquet scene) or sleep ("these dreams that shake us nightly" (III, II, 18)).

- (I, VII, 31 - 45) "We will proceed no further ..." - The struggle between Macbeth's ambition and his moral awareness breaks into the open with his declaration that he will not go forward with the murder. But whereas the witches merely tempt Macbeth to evil, Lady Macbeth actively persuades him. She appeals to his love for her and she taunts him with the accusation of cowardice, "a taunt no man can bear, and least of all a soldier" (Br 367). She draws the distinction between desire and will (39): Macbeth desires the crown but doesn't have the will to take it. Lady Macbeth does.

- (I, VII, 46 – 49) "I dare do all that may become a man; who dares do more is none." – Macbeth's reply to Lady Macbeth's taunt tells us that his notion of manhood places limits on the use of force. The play reinforces this with characters such as Macduff and Duncan, who see manhood as encompassing a wide variety of other attributes, like the ability to love and the desire to behave morally. The play raises the question: What is the nature of manhood? Shakespeare suggests that there are limits. Macbeth exhibits an awareness of this early in the play, but as the action progresses his view contracts into "a condition in which all faculties are attenuated to a male and murderous courage, noble and admirable only as the beast of prey is noble and admirable" (BlM 70). For Lady Macbeth, manhood implies force and courage unrestrained by notions of morality and pity - the direction of an active will towards some end. "When you durst do it then you were a man" (49).

- (I, VII, 54 - 62) "I have given suck, ..." - Lady Macbeth reveals the extent of her evil intent and her role as the instigator of the murder. She refers to the fact that she has had a child, although the play gives us no evidence of that. (Shakespeare based Lady Macbeth on her historical counterpart who had had a child by her first husband (Bl21 8).) The fact that Macbeth has no heirs is consistent with the symbolism that their marriage has not taken its natural course. Her description of the things she would do before forswearing what she had previously pledged is something "one does not dare speak aloud, for fear speech should give them reality. And yet determination in this woman has been fanned to such white heat that she can not only say it but contemplate the unnameable with an overwhelming actuality. ... There is an appalling grandeur in Lady Macbeth's complete subjugation of nature" (Sa 296).

- **Macbeth** - The question of what finally brings Macbeth to become a murderer is complex. Shakespeare deliberately doesn't make clear how the thought of murder took hold in Macbeth's mind. The witches don't suggest murder, although they tempt him. That the crime is not imposed on him by the witches is evident since Banquo doesn't commit a crime to make good his prophesy. Macbeth is certainly considering the crime after meeting with the witches (I, III, 128) and he might have thought of it before the play began.

  Lady Macbeth, however, clearly plays a major role in convincing him. His struggle with his conscience makes him an easy prey to her single-minded evil. Her admonition, "But screw your courage to the sticking-place and we'll not fail" (62), is frequently used to encourage a person to perform difficult or dangerous tasks. Her confidence stiffens his hesitancy.

  Shakespeare tries to make us feel a kinship with Macbeth and recognize that if we had been similarly tempted, we too might have fallen. Macbeth isn't simply an evil man (like Richard III, Iago, or Edmund). Early in the play he is shown to be noble, courageous and gifted with a vivid imagination. Duncan speaks of him this way; Banquo respects him at the beginning. Lady Macbeth says that his nature is "too full o'th'milk of human kindness" (I, V, 17). Milk is a symbol of the goodness of nature and a recurring image in the play that contrasts with blood.

  Although Macbeth doesn't have a predisposition to murder and he understands that he has no justification for the crime, he has an inordinate ambition that makes murder seem to be a lesser evil than failing to achieve the crown and disappointing his wife. His conscience succumbs in its struggle with ambition. "In his susceptibility to conventional human desires, and his momentary willingness to forget the reasons they must be suppressed, Macbeth is one of us. He shows us the logical extension, and the logical costs, of our own frailties. ... If we can recognize Macbeth's crime as essentially an extension of our own casual recalcitrance at the ways of natural and social order, a symbolic performance of our resentful impulses against the aspects of the world that inconvenience us, we may find it hard to hold him accountable for his sin" (BlM 138).

Macbeth's ambition arises from the natural desire of a person to shape his environment for good as well as evil ends. "The destruction of Macbeth ... can please us as humane justice on only the most superficial level. Conventional goodness is victorious [in the play], but it defeats an evil that Shakespeare invites us to recognize as a plausible extension of the things that make us human, and its weapons are the instruments of our oppression as well as our salvation" (BlM 159).

- (II, I, 4 - 9) "How goes the night, boy?" - The scene takes place at night, a symbol of evil. We begin to see a change in Banquo. Whereas up to this point he's depicted as simply brave, loyal and honest, his character begins to show a new dimension. He can't sleep, whereas Duncan sleeps easily (11). Sleep is an essential aspect of nature's goodness which is denied to those with evil intentions. The nature symbolized by the martlet yields to "cursed thoughts that nature gives way to in repose". What is he thinking about? Apparently, he's resisting the same temptation to which Macbeth succumbs. Hence, he serves as a contrast to Macbeth. He asks for his sword. Macbeth seems to be trying to get a sense of Banquo's loyalty (25), and we sense that Banquo is being cautious in his response (26 - 29). Perhaps he suspects that the witches' prophesy has caused a change in Macbeth's behavior. Banquo places limits on what he's willing to do. He won't do anything to jeopardize his honor. His words are similar to those Macbeth spoke earlier (I, VII, 46).

- (II, I, 22) "Yet when we can ..." – Macbeth's thoughts surface in an embarrassing way: he uses the royal "we" in speaking of himself, but recovers using "my" in the next line.

- (II, I, 33 - 64) "Is this a dagger, ..." - The knife that Macbeth apparently sees is the first of the visions which trouble him once he starts on his criminal enterprise (Banquo's ghost is another). This is an example of "horrid imaginings" that he had previously spoken of (I, III, 135). He recognizes that it proceeds from his "heat-oppressed brain" (38), and it is evidence of an acute awareness of the evil act he's about to do. He sees blood on the blade, imagining the effect of his action before it has actually happened. His words, "I go, and it is done" (62), show a profound ignorance of the guilt and consequences that will follow the act. The murder is performed at night (50), a time for evil, a time for "wicked dreams", a time when "Nature seems dead". Nature replaces God and heaven in the play as the source of all that is good, and its absence leaves room for the nightmares that both Macbeth and Banquo experience when they sleep.

In both *Hamlet* and *Macbeth,* the major action is the murder of a king and in both plays the protagonist needs to be convinced to do the deed. It takes only seven scenes to convince Macbeth, because Shakespeare is interested in the consequences of the deed, whereas it takes the entire play to convince Hamlet because Shakespeare is interested in the morality of the deed. Another difference is that whereas Hamlet is instructed by the ghost to murder Claudius, the witches only tempt Macbeth. The motivation for Duncan's murder arises from within the murderer. On the other hand, in both plays Shakespeare is interested in the psychology of the protagonists.

- (II, II, 1 - 13) "That which hath made them drunk ..." - Although "the greatness of Lady Macbeth lies almost wholly in courage and force of will" (Br 371), she isn't quite as evil a person as she first appears. She needs alcohol to fortify herself before the murder, she's frightened by the owl, and she admits that she couldn't do the crime herself since Duncan looks like her father. Unlike Macbeth, she shows little imagination or awareness of the moral dimensions of the deed. She sees facts, not visions. She's concerned with how the deed is to be done, not the consequences that will follow.

- (II, II, 14) "I have done the deed." - Macbeth's first words after the murder make memorable use of the verb "to do". And the fact that he refers to the murder as "the deed", instead of what it actually is, is the first indication of his shame. His exchange of words with Lady Macbeth conveys a breathless fear (14 – 20). Lady Macbeth dismisses Macbeth's moral concerns and, foreseeing the future, predicts that if he dwells on his guilt it will make him mad (33).

  Macbeth imagines that he's heard a voice that said "Sleep no more! Macbeth doth murder sleep", and he becomes obsessed with the thought that he has destroyed this essential element of nature (34 - 42). The ability to enjoy sleep and meals are natural parts of life. The inability to do so is a direct result of the crime and is referred to throughout the play. The king sleeps (II, I, 11), Banquo wishes Macbeth "good repose" (II, I, 29). But after the murder we see that Macbeth is unable to eat or sleep (II, III, 16), (III, IV), and Lady Macbeth's sleep is unnatural (V, I).

- (II, II, 45) "Go, get some waters, ..." - To Lady Macbeth the blood on Macbeth's hand can simply be washed off (45, 66). She seems unconcerned with the horror of the act. Her recognition of its enormity will appear later. Macbeth, however, lives in a world whose dimensions go beyond the literal. He's troubled by the fact that he "could not say Amen" (28). He's frightened by every noise (57). To him blood symbolizes the horror of the deed. It will redden the entire sea, and "all great Neptune's ocean" will not wash it away (59).

Macbeth refers again (I, IV, 52) to the division between his hands and his eyes (58). But now the deed has been done and the hand, the instrument of the crime, plucks out the eyes, his conscience. This is a much more violent separation, indicating the two cannot reside together in a sane person, a situation that he acknowledges by saying, "To know my deed, 'twere best not to know myself" (72). If he accepts the reality of the deed, he will be alienated from himself (Sa 290). He has the choice of overcoming his conscience and living "unblinkingly with the consequences of his own deed", or to apply "endless salves and plasters to [his] sick conscience" and disintegrate in guilt (Sa1 79). That disintegration is already apparent: The man who "unseam'd" Macdonwald now says "I am afraid to think what I have done: Look on't again I dare not" (51). The scene ends with Macbeth already expressing regret for what he has done (73).

- (II, III, 1) "Here's a knocking, indeed!" - Duncan's murder is a departure from normal life. Shakespeare emphasizes its horror by immediately following the murder scene with a scene showing normal activity. "The re-establishment of the goings-on of the world in which we live makes us profoundly sensible of the awful parenthesis that had suspended them" (DQ).

  The porter is awakened to answer a knocking at the gate. The knocking is perceived in three different ways (Go2 119). Lady Macbeth, all business, says: "Get on your night-gown" (II, II, 69). Macbeth, expressing tragic imagination and regret, says: "Wake Duncan with thy knocking: I would thou couldst!" (II, II, 73). And the porter, half drunk and imagining himself managing the gates of hell, expresses annoyance saying: "Here's a knocking, indeed!" (II, III, 1). The role that the porter takes is Shakespeare's way of suggesting that Macbeth has transformed his castle into a hell on earth (JS 183). The porter imagines welcoming an equivocator to hell (II, III, 9) and in so doing introduces the notion of equivocation as a significant theme in the play.

- **Equivocation** - The word refers to ambiguity and, more specifically, concealing the truth by saying something which, although true, hides a different meaning. This was a major issue in the political scene at the time *Macbeth* was written. Catholic terrorists had almost succeeded in destroying the entire English government, including King James, in an action called the Gunpowder Plot, and an atmosphere of fear and suspicion spread throughout the country directed against all Catholics. Government authorities found a manual that described a technique promoted by the Jesuit branch of the Catholic Church which instructed those being questioned under oath, often under the most extreme form of torture, to give ambiguous answers that seemed true even while they withheld the truth, and doing so without violating church doctrine. This was not simply a tool useful in hiding plots against the government. Catholics often found it necessary in Protestant England to equivocate: to deny their faith in public while maintaining it in private. The government saw this not only as a tool to be used to overthrow the government but, more generally, as a threat to the social fabric of the country (JS 155).

Although at that time equivocation was associated with Catholics, Shakespeare expands this to a universal condition and seems to be saying that we live with incomplete and ambiguous information. For example, early in the play the witches confuse Banquo saying that he will be "Lesser than Macbeth, and greater" and "Not so happy, yet much happier" (I, III, 65 - 66). It's true that Banquo will be greater than Macbeth, but they withhold the information that he won't live to see it. Later in the play (IV, I) they mislead Macbeth, encouraging him to believe himself invulnerable. In both cases, however, what they say is true, but incomplete.

- (II, III, 24 – 35) "Faith, Sir, we were carousing ..." - The porter gives his take on an issue that was introduced earlier, the difference between desire and will. He says that drink both provokes and unprovokes lechery by stimulating desire but taking away performance (28). One might call this bodily equivocation. And this leads us to a central fact of the play: Macbeth desires, Lady Macbeth wills.

- (II, III, 86) "What! In our house?" - The concern that Lady Macbeth expresses is not so much with the murder as with the fact that it occurred in her house. Banquo immediately rebukes her.

- (II, III, 89 - 94) "Had I but died ..." - Macbeth's words have a double meaning. On the one hand, he is equivocating because he is hiding the fact that he is the murderer. On the other hand, he genuinely regrets having done the deed. His words (91) anticipate the ending (V, V, 17): life has lost its meaning.

- (II, III, 133 – 139) "What will you do?" - Malcolm says that it's easy "to show an unfelt sorrow", and hence the assassin might be one of those who will appear to mourn Duncan's murder. Sensing that their own lives might be in danger, he and Donalbain decide to flee.

- (III, I, 1 - 10) "Thou hast it now, ..." - We see a different side of Banquo. He's now looking to the fulfillment of the witches' prophesy for him and his descendants.

- (III, I, 47 - 71) "To be thus is nothing, ..." - Macbeth fears Banquo's "royalty of nature" (49), the "dauntless temper of his mind" (51), and his wisdom. They are a reproach to his own character: "under him my genius is rebuked" (54). This is similar to Iago's remark about Cassio: "He hath a daily beauty in his life that makes me ugly" (*Othello* (V, I, 19)). Macbeth probably wonders why Banquo has never made public the witches' prophesies and he's concerned that Banquo suspects him and might try to avenge Duncan's murder. Perhaps Banquo hasn't revealed the prophesies because he doesn't want to disturb the forces that hopefully will give the succession to his children. By killing Banquo and Fleance, Macbeth hopes to assure the succession to his own, as yet non-existent, descendants (63).

- (III, II, 4 - 22) "Nought's had, all's spent, ..." - The effects of the crime are now evident. Macbeth admits failure. He keeps to himself. Apparently, he has even separated himself from Lady Macbeth. The outer disorder brings an inner disorder with it. He's troubled by thoughts and dreams, he can't sleep, meals are eaten in fear.

  Lady Macbeth now also recognizes the enormity of the crime: "Things without all remedy should be without regard: what's done is done" (11), another use of the verb "to do" with significant ethical implications. Unfortunately, this is not possible. Macbeth would rather see the universe fall to pieces than to continue to suffer from the inability to eat and sleep peacefully, to be deprived the beneficence of nature (16 - 22). The real punishment for an evil act is generated from within.

- (III, II, 38) "But in them Nature's copy ..." - Perhaps this is a suggestion that they should be killed.

- (III, II, 39 – 55) "There's comfort yet; ..." - Macbeth is now working alone; Lady Macbeth is no longer a partner to his crimes. Although his bond to her remains - he refers to her as "dearest chuck" (45) – and they feel sorry for each other, they no longer communicate. He has become totally isolated.

  Macbeth has undergone a transformation. There is no longer a debate between ambition and morality, no longer a conflict between the reality of the evil nature of his deed and his conscience. He has decided to subdue his conscience and not allow it to destroy him with guilt:

"Cancel that great bond which keeps me pale!" (III, II, 49). He demonstrates his strength by challenging the moral law and moving ahead with the additional crimes necessary to consolidate his position. In a perverse way, this elevates him to the level of a tragic hero. "That great bond" is another reference (in addition to (I, V, 44)) to the fact that a sense of morality is natural in man. Macbeth had thought that he could violate this bond with impunity.

Macbeth's brilliance is shown in the richness of the images that embroider his thoughts – in this case, images of night and evil. He ends with his belief that "Things bad begun, make strong themselves by ill" (55), a prescription that leads him further down the path to destruction.

- (III, III, 17) "O, treachery! Fly, good Fleance, ..." - Fleance's escape marks the turning point in the play. Macbeth's plans are thwarted, and Banquo's heirs are assured the succession to the throne. In particular, James I is presumably a descendant of Fleance.

- (III, IV, 1) "You know your own degrees, ..." - The guests are invited to sit in an orderly way, according to their rank, and Macbeth attempts to mix socially as well as partake in the meal. The murderer arrives and describes the wounds he inflicted on Banquo as "A death to nature" (27). The words have a double meaning: Each wound is enough to kill a man, but Shakespeare also intends us to understand that the act is an assault on the order of nature as well. Macbeth returns to his guests and speaks of the relationship between appetite, digestion, and good health (37). But the crime, in the form of Banquo's ghost, disrupts these natural processes and frightens Macbeth. Lady Macbeth, who does not see the ghost, taunts him by questioning his manhood

(57, 64, 73), and once again raises the issue of whether masculinity is based solely on raw courage. Macbeth is now socially isolated, he doesn't sleep, and he takes no pleasure in food.

- (III, IV, 74) "Blood hath been shed ere now, …" - Rather than expressing guilt over the murder, Macbeth seems to be outraged that Banquo has returned: "The time has been that when the brains were out the man would die" (77). This is an indication of the extent to which Macbeth has descended into evil. Macbeth defends his masculinity with the words that echo his earlier response (I, VII, 46) to Lady Macbeth's taunt: "What man dare, I dare" (98), and then goes on to define it as courage in battle. The notion that masculinity might involve more than that, or has limitations, is missing.

- (III, IV, 118) "Stand not upon the order …" - In contrast to their orderly arrival, the guests leave in disorder. The crime has not only disrupted the natural process of taking food, it has disrupted the orderly working of society.

- (III, IV, 121) "It will have blood, …" - One murder begets another and thus evil propagates itself.

- (III, IV, 130) "There's not a one of them, …" - The sense of fear that pervades the play is heightened by the admission that Macbeth has a spy in each noble's house.

- (III, IV, 135 – 140) "I am in blood …" - The image of blood appears again. Macbeth's ambition has been replaced by misery. He imagines the possibility of undoing his crime – "returning" - and says that doing so would be as "tedious" as continuing in the criminal enterprise. The implication is that he could undo what he's done and thus give up the crown, but it's not worth the effort. Morality doesn't seem to enter into the choice. One gets the sense that he is exhausted, overwhelmed by tedium, and insensitive to the effects of his actions.

He stresses the need to act and not allow thought – "things I have in head" - to interfere with action: "that will to hand, which must be acted, ere they may be scann'd" (139). The relationship between thought and action is an issue that obsessed Hamlet as well. Macbeth argues against that which makes us human: our ability to consider – scan - the moral implications of our actions. The scene ends with Macbeth attributing his vision of Banquo to the fact that he and Lady Macbeth are only beginners in crime and that they need "hard use", by which he means more experience. The implication is that when they commit more crimes, they will be able to control their reactions and continue on their murderous path more easily.

- (III, IV, 140) "You lack the season of all natures, …" - Lady Macbeth expresses her love for Macbeth in her concern for his inability to sleep.

- **Context** – The play presents a desolate and dark universe where everything is confused, unclear and filled with evil. This universe mirrors and reinforces the subject of the play. A few examples illustrate how Shakespeare conveys this atmosphere.

    - He creates an air of uncertainty by filling the play with questions. Probably in no other of his plays are so many questions asked (Kn 141). For example, the play opens with, "When shall we three meet again?" (I, I, 1). The second scene opens with "What bloody man is that?" (I, II, 1). Banquo's first words are "How far is't call'd to Forres?" (I, III, 39). More importantly, Macbeth asks, "Is this a dagger I see before me?" (II, I, 33) as he approaches Duncan's bedroom. Macbeth's and Lady Macbeth's mental state after the killing (II, II) is conveyed by a series of questions "Who's there?", "Didst thou not hear a noise?", "Did not you speak?", "When?", "As I descended?", "Who lies i'th' second chamber?", "But wherefore could I not pronounce Amen?" And later, "Will all great Neptune's oceans wash this blood clean from my hand?" (II, II, 59).

- Characters are in doubt and surprise is continual (Kn 142). Macbeth doesn't understand how he can be Thane of Cawdor; Lady Macbeth is startled at the news of Duncan's visit; Duncan is surprised that Macbeth arrived before he did; Lenox, Ross and the old man are surprised at the strange happenings on the night of the murder (II, III); and on and on. Why does Macduff leave his wife unprotected? Who is the third person involved in the murder of Banquo? What happened to the child that Lady Macbeth speaks of? Why do Malcolm and Donalbain flee to different countries?

- Compounding this is a repeated use of contradictory terms and ambiguity of meaning, which add a sense of confusion and mystery to the atmosphere. The witches open the play by describing the battle as "lost and won" (I, I, 4), then they prepare us for the uncertainty that is to follow by saying "fair is foul" (I, I, 11), and finally they predict Macbeth's and Banquo's future with "lesser than Macbeth, and greater" (I, III, 65), "not so happy, yet much happier" (I, III, 66). Macbeth describes the weather with "so foul and fair a day I have not seen" (I, III, 38), and he comments on the witches' predictions by saying they "cannot be ill, cannot be good" (I, III, 131) and "nothing is but what is not" (I, III, 142). Macduff says, "such welcome and unwelcome things at once" (IV, III, 138). And the porter, speaking of the effect of drinking, says it "provokes and unprovokes", and "it makes him and it mars him; it sets him on and it takes him off" (II, III, 25 - 35).

- Darkness permeates the play. Lady Macbeth prays, "Come thick night and pall thee in the dunnest smoke of hell" (I, V, 50). Macbeth says, "stars, hide your fires, let not light see my black and deep desires" (I, IV, 50), and he later invites darkness with the words "Come, seeling Night" (III, II, 46). During the play "light thickens" (III, II, 50), "dark night strangles the travelling lamp" (II, IV, 7), and there is "husbandry in heaven; their candles are all out" (II, I, 4) (because the moon and stars are not shining).

- All of this creates an atmosphere of fear. The word "fear" is used constantly, and fear leads to nightmares. Macbeth speaks of the "terrible dreams that shake us nightly" (III, II, 18) and Banquo speaks of "the cursed thoughts that nature gives way to in repose" (II, I, 8). Lady Macbeth relives the murder during her sleep-walk. This is the ultimate attack on sleep. Beyond this we have Macbeth's visions of the dagger and Banquo's ghost. And finally, Shakespeare gives us the witches, who are "nightmares actualized" (Kn 147).

There's a constant reference to blood. The play opens with Macbeth and Banquo "bathe[d] in reeking wounds"

(I, II, 40) in the fight reported by the "bloody" sergeant. Then we hear of the blood on Macbeth's sword, on the imaginary and real daggers, smeared on Duncan's grooms and the murderer's face, on Macbeth's and Lady Macbeth's hands. Lady Macbeth says, "make thick my blood" (I, V, 43) and asks, "who would have thought the old man to have so much blood in him?" (V, I, 37). Macbeth says, "I am in blood stepp'd so far that, should I wade no more, Returning were as tedious as go o'er" (III, IV, 135). Darkness and blood symbolize the realm of the unnatural. Predatory creatures are mentioned: Hyrcan tiger, armed rhinoceros, rugged Russian bear, wolf, raven, owl, rook, snake. Macbeth's mind is full of scorpions. Duncan's horses eat each other (II, IV, 14).

- The images are intended to give us the sense that we are "in touch with absolute evil which, being absolute, has a satanic beauty, a hideous, serpent-like grace and attraction" (Kn 147). The play is set in a cosmological emptiness (Bl 539), a godless wasteland in which evil is unrestrained. In that respect, the play anticipates the world described by the existentialist philosophers of the 20th Century and a play like *Waiting for Godot*.

- Just as Malcolm's and Duncan's goodness contrast with, and thus emphasize, Macbeth's evil, Shakespeare uses natural, nurturing images to symbolize a fully human way of life. He thinks of such a life as closely related to the wider setting of organic growth, as indeed "directly based on man's dealings with the earth that nourishes him" (BlM 43). Thus, sleep and milk contrast with blood and nightmares and the temple haunting martlet contrasts with the raven and rook. Lady Macbeth speaks of Macbeth as "too full o'th'milk of human kindness" (I, V, 17), she prays that her milk be taken for gall, and later says that she knows "how tender 'tis to love the baby that milks me" (I, VII, 55). Nature symbolizes the moral order in society. Sleep, meals, companionship are part of the natural world. The natural succession in government is also a part of this order. We submit to this order because it is "not only compatible with our humanity, but necessary for its survival" (BIM 159). We need to live in an orderly world. The crime is an attack on this order and it is therefore unnatural.

- (IV, I, 52 – 60) "Though you untie the winds, ..." - Macbeth describes a chaotic world.

- (IV, I, 69) "Tell me, thou unknown power, ..." - The apparitions deliberately equivocate. Macbeth doesn't question them and as a result is misled. Perhaps this is further evidence of the narrowing of Macbeth's awareness, imagery, and understanding. He later finds out that the armed head is his own (V, IX, 20), the bloody child represents Macduff torn from his mother's womb (V, VIII, 15), the child and tree represents Malcolm and Birnam Wood (BIM 103).

- (IV, I, 84 – 86) "But yet I'll make assurance ..." - Having rejected the idea of reversing direction on his path through blood as too tedious (III, IV, 136), Macbeth decides to move forward and murder Macduff in a vain attempt to alleviate his fears and bring some peace into his life.

- (IV, I, 121) "That two-fold balls ..." – Apparently this refers to the double coronation of James in Scotland and England.

- (IV, I, 144) "Time, thou anticipat'st ..." - Macbeth vows that there shall be no separation between desire and action: "be it thought and done" (149). The line recalls (II, I, 62) and (III, IV, 138) and is more evidence of the narrowing of his internal awareness. This is the ultimate assertion of power and resembles the description of the Creation in Genesis: "The Lord said let there be light and there was light". It also echoes Hamlet's vow: "From this time forth My thoughts be bloody or nothing worth", although Hamlet never makes good on this. But Macbeth does make good on this by arranging for the murder of Macduff's family in the next scene. This power to make words reality is the goal of the tyrant.

- (IV, II, 30) "Sirrah, your father's dead: ..." - Macduff has, inexplicably, left his family unprotected. Lady Macduff alludes to this when she tells her son that his father is dead.

- (IV, III) Malcolm tests Macduff's loyalty by denigrating himself to see if Macduff will still support him. He says that "there's no bottom, none, in my voluptuousness" (60), and Macduff responds with "we have willing dames enough" (73).

- (IV, III, 216 - 227) "He has no children." - The simplicity of Macduff's comment speaks eloquently of the horror of what has happened, but it's not clear who the "he" is that Macduff refers to. If he is speaking of Macbeth, he means either that Macbeth has no children on whom he can take revenge, or possibly that, if Macbeth had children, he would not have done such a horrible thing. If he is speaking of Malcolm, he means "if he had children of his own, he would not suggest revenge as a cure for grief" (ArM 135) or be so quick to use Macduff's grief to further his own military plans (213).

Malcolm urges Macduff to "dispute it like a man" (220) and Macduff responds by reminding him that there are two aspects of manhood, the willingness to fight and the ability to feel sympathy and love. This contrasts with Macbeth, who only understands the first. Macduff understands what Macbeth hints at in (I, VII, 46): manhood is more than unrestricted strength and courage. And then (223) he raises the question of an empty universe by asking why heaven didn't protect his family.

- (V, I, 21) "Why, it stood by her: ..." - Lady Macbeth requires light. This is a pathetic reversal of her call for darkness to envelop the act of murder (I, V, 50) and symbolizes her desire to return to the natural progression of day and night that has been interrupted by that act.

- (V, I, 40) "The Thane of Fife had a wife: ..." - Lady Macbeth's depravity emerges in her sleep: she recites a rhyme that mocks the murdered wife of Macduff. She then re-enacts her participation in Duncan's murder. She unconsciously understands what Macbeth saw initially. "A little water clears us of this deed" (II, II, 66) is now replaced by "will these hands ne'er be clean" and "what's done is done" (III, II, 11) is now replaced by "what's done cannot be undone" (64). She has undergone a total transformation. The lesson is that we are accountable for what we do. "Her sleepwalking ... complements her hand-washing: both represent a futile effort to erase the consequences of a deed that murdered sleep both in Duncan and in her" (BlM 149).

Lady Macbeth's madness is a measure of the humanity that she tried to negate in her attempt to invoke the powers of darkness to take possession of her. It is a residue of the modicum of humanity that was apparent at the time of the murder: she needed alcohol to blunt the horror she felt, and she admitted that she couldn't have done the murder herself because of remembered filial ties. The murder would have been second nature if the powers of darkness had really taken hold. It's ironic that Lady Macbeth suffers a guilty breakdown, since she was the person whose strong will instigated the murder. Macbeth, who had to be convinced to perform the act, hardened as the play progressed, while her recognition of the horror of the murder has finally emerged.

Shakespeare seems to follow the rule that characters "whose state of mind is abnormal" speak in prose (Br 398): Hamlet when playing the madman, Ophelia when mad, Lear when insane, Lady Macbeth when sleepwalking, the porter when drunk. Presumably the regular rhythm of verse is inappropriate when the mind has lost its balance.

- (V, III, 19 - 28) "Take thy face hence." - Macbeth speaks with resignation of the coming battle. He might lose and, if so, he has lived long enough, his life has withered. His enumeration of the losses he has suffered because of the crime all fall into the category of natural human relationships: "honor, love, obedience, troops of friends". These are his deepest needs. He's now reduced to a brutal warrior who will fight to the end (32).

- (V, V, 9 - 28) "I have almost forgot ..." - "Everything that Macbeth says in the course of the drama leads into its most famous and most powerful speech" (BlM 4). His criminal enterprise has come to nought. He has lost his humanity. He has lost his beloved wife and can express no grief for her (17 - 18). He cannot even feel fear (9). "There would have been time for such a word" might mean that death has no meaning in a world where life has no meaning – a point he makes in the next few lines. His crimes have reduced his view of life to "an affair of absolute inconsequence" (ArM lii) consisting of pointless repetition.

Macbeth is describing cosmological emptiness, the meaninglessness of life and its ephemeral nature (19 – 28). It is the view of a man who has broken the moral bond that is needed to hold humanity together, a man who "has directed his will to evil, towards something that of its very nature makes for chaos and the abnegation of meaning" (BlM 56). But it also "speaks the great annihilating truths that we all, sometimes, live with, and all know we live with sometimes" (Sa1 90).

Thus, the play ends on a decidedly un-Christian note. Macbeth's words express contempt for the entire enterprise of life and are a fierce declaration of nihilism, as signified by the last word of the speech, "nothing" {28). This is the view of a man who has attacked the natural flow of life and who has suffered the consequences.

- (V, V, 35) "The wood began to move." - The approach of Birnam Wood can be taken to symbolize nature's eventual triumph over the forces that had disrupted it, and Dunsinane Castle, the "prize of Macbeth's ambition, represents ... all of man's futile stays against his moral limitations", an "emblem for the futility of humanity's ambitious projects" (BlM 159). Macbeth recognizes the witches' equivocation (43) and wishes the destruction of the universe (49 – 50).

- (V, VIII, 4) "Of all men else ..." - Macbeth shows an "unsuspected reserve of sympathetic and spontaneous humanity" (BIM 102), reminding us of his former better nature. The lines have the same effect as the sleepwalking scene had for Lady Macbeth. In both cases we see that the evil façade is not a complete picture of their characters. The play starts and ends showing us Macbeth the warrior, but there is a difference. In Act I he's fighting in defense of a good king trying to preserve an orderly society. He destroyed that order over the course of the play and at the end he's fighting for nothing.

Discussion

Ambition, Conscience and Evil – *Macbeth* deals with the conflict between ambition and conscience, forces that are present in us all. Ambition wins out, as it often does. A regrettable act follows and the protagonist suffers from a guilty conscience. All of this is commonplace. The elements of the story that distinguish it from normal life is the devastating nature of the crime and, more importantly, the intensity of the guilt that results. Shakespeare is interested in showing us the consequences of choosing evil and by exaggerating the crime and the guilt he's better able to expose this. The play "leaves on most readers a profound impression of the misery of a guilty conscience and the retribution of crime ... But what Shakespeare perhaps felt even more deeply ... was the *incalculability* of evil" (Br 386); that evil acts produce unexpected results. "The soul ... is a thing of such inconceivable depth, complexity, and delicacy, and when you introduce into it

… any change, and particularly the change called evil, you can form only the vaguest idea of the reaction you will provoke" (Br 386). The play suggests that morality is an essential part of human nature that cannot be removed and the consequences of violating it cannot be avoided.

The play makes evil seem palpable. The notion that good and evil are two real and competing forces in the universe is referred to as a Manichaean view. It is rejected by Christian theology, which views evil as simply the absence of good, not a force in its own right (Sa 275). Furthermore, the evil in *Macbeth* doesn't emanate from hell or carry with it damnation. Evil comes from a denial of nature. It carries with it the inability to sleep or eat and it is represented by night and the crow and, most of all, by blood. Lady Macbeth's call to "unsex me" is a call to the devil. In contrast, grace is embedded in nature, not in heaven. Sleeping, eating, socializing and procreation are a part of this, and light and the temple haunting martlet and, most of all, milk symbolize it. Feelings such as remorse, pity and kindness are expressions of grace. Duncan's murder is an assault against nature.

A Hostile Universe – Shakespeare has filled the play with "words, acts and situations which may be interpreted or taken in two ways at the peril of the chooser and which in aggregate produce an overwhelming conviction that behind the visible world lies another world, immeasurably wider and deeper, on its relation to which human destiny turns. … Not only the plot and characters of the play, … but its music, imagery and atmosphere … unite in giving the impression of mighty and inscrutable forces behind human life" (Go2 118). These forces often act to draw man to grief. The witches' prophecies are an obvious example of this. Just as Oedipus misinterprets, and is unable to evade, the Delphic prophesies, Macbeth is fooled by the witches. They tell the truth but hide the meaning. Macbeth says to Banquo, "fail not our feast", and Banquo replies "My lord I will not", but he arrives in a manner that Macbeth hadn't anticipated. Macbeth arrives the moment after Duncan says that treachery cannot be read in the face. Lady Macbeth arrives just as Macbeth laments the lack of a spur to commit the murder. The conviction is ultimately produced "that there is something deep in life with power to reverse all its surface indications, as if its undercurrent is set in just the opposite direction from the movement on its surface" (Go2 119).

Macbeth* and *King Lear – Both *Macbeth* and *King Lear* are bleak in the extreme. But the bleakness in *King Lear* is moderated by the fact that we have been shown a towering character who assumes greatness over the course of the play. That reassures us of man's potential for nobility. In *Macbeth,* on the other hand, there's nothing to redeem the triumph of evil. Furthermore, there's a significant difference between the evil characters in the two plays. Although Edmund delights in his evil, Macbeth suffers intensely from knowing that he has committed a crime (Bl 517).

Both plays end on a positive note: the evil characters are defeated and Malcolm and Edgar, two good people, take the thrones. But the new kings are one-dimensional and it's clear that Shakespeare isn't very interested in them. One is left with the feeling that in both cases a happy ending has been tacked on to blunt the effect of the play, which is meant to be devastating.

Macbeth is the character that Shakespeare is interested in and at the end of the play Macbeth is convinced that life is meaningless. At this point, however, he is consumed with guilt and has been reduced to a shell of a man. He has rejected nature and the bounty that a natural life can offer but his view of life is peculiar to his situation. Clearly Duncan, a good and kind man, would have expressed a different view of life had he lived, and we certainly shouldn't assume that Shakespeare agrees with Macbeth. But we would be foolish to dismiss Macbeth's judgment that life is meaninglessness out of hand. We each form our views based on the life that we have lived, and Macbeth's view has as much validity as any other.

Similarly, Macbeth gets what he deserves, but we shouldn't be too quick to celebrate. The play is a tragedy that records the descent of a good man into evil, something that should give us pause. And ambition, the trait that brings Macbeth down, is not a bad thing. It is something we all share and the driving force behind the progress of civilization. *King Lear* ends on a similar note of meaninglessness, but Lear is an entirely different protagonist, both admirable and wise. In contrast to Lear, Macbeth has not developed as a person or come to some new understanding of life as the play progresses. He has simply disintegrated. The dedication to evil kills the possibility of transformation; it's in conflict with growth.

Chapter 13

KING LEAR

Background

Percy Bysshe Shelley, Samuel Coleridge and John Keats were three of the greatest early 19th Century English Romantic poets and all commented on *King Lear*. Shelley said that Lear "may be judged to be the most perfect specimen of the dramatic art existing in the world" (T 98). Coleridge called the play "the most tremendous effort of Shakespeare as a poet" (M xlvii). Keats said, "The excellence of every art is in its intensity, capable of making all disagreeables evaporate ... Examine *King Lear*, and you will find this exemplified throughout" (M xlvii). The 19th Century critic William Hazlitt said "To attempt to give a description of the play itself or of its effect upon the mind, is a mere impertinence: yet we must say something. - It is then the best of all Shakespeare's plays, for it is the one in which he was most in earnest" (H 94). More recently Edward Tayler, a distinguished professor of English literature at Columbia, said that "This is the greatest thing written by anyone, anytime, anywhere" (DD 305). And Harold Bloom, an eminent critic at Yale, said "Of all of Shakespeare's dramas [*King Lear* and *Hamlet* show] an apparent infinitude that perhaps transcends the limits of literature ... [it] well may be the height of literary experience" (Bl 476).

But the play has also been said to be impossible to perform on the stage: too big and too emotional, and – since the actor playing Lear must be an older person - too demanding. The play is filled with physical and emotional pain: violence, murder, madness, degradation, nakedness, humiliation. While violence was an integral part of English life in the 17th Century, the play is so grim that it was considered inappropriate for the stage. As a result, from the late 17th Century to the early 19th Century, virtually all performances of the play used a rewritten version (by Nahum Tate) that gave it a happy ending: Cordelia survives and is united with Edgar at the end.

In constructing his plays, Shakespeare often adapted the plots of earlier work. *King Lear* is composed of two intertwined plots, taken from two different sources. The main plot, taken from a play entitled *King Leir* (author unknown), involves Lear and his three daughters; the subplot, taken from a prose romance, involves Gloucester and his two sons. Both Lear and Gloucester come to tragic ends; Gloucester's suffering is primarily physical; Lear's is mental. It's reasonable to ask why Shakespeare combined two tragedies in one play. One possible explanation is that the subplot reinforces the main plot by suggesting that what happens to Lear is no accident. Hence, the tragedy is not so much the story of a particular person, but has more universal significance.

Despite the horror it portrays, *King Lear* has been called the Shakespearean play of our time. The 20th Century saw a sequence of events that has shaken our faith in the ability of mankind to survive: The carnage of two world wars, the unspeakable horror of the Holocaust, the destruction visited on Hiroshima and the threat of nuclear war are but a few. The play reflects this loss of faith, since it is open to nihilistic and existentialist interpretations that show "not the potentially heroic journey … of Man through life, but rather a progression towards despair or mere nothingness" (ArK 2).

In contrast to *Hamlet*, *Macbeth* and *Othello*, Shakespeare's other great tragedies, which tend to be more narrowly focused, *King Lear* deals with universal themes and a wide variety of issues concerning all aspects of life:

- The nature of love: Can it be purchased? When is it controlling?
- The relationship between parent and child: What does a parent owe his or her child and what does a child owe his or her parent? Should a parent make demands on a grown child? As a parent ages, does he reach a point where he should become subject to the control of his child?
- The relationship between one generation and the next: Do the young learn from the old or vice versa?
- The proper response to legal authority: Should it always be obeyed?
- The tragedy of old age: Does loss of power imply loss of identity? Are you still respected when you retire?
- The nature of the forces that govern the universe: Is there some absolute power governing the universe, for example, God, the gods, or the stars. And if there is such a power is it moral, amoral or immoral? Or is there nothing (nihilism, existentialism)?
- The nature of the legal system: Does it enforce justice or is it simply a structure that allows some people to control others?
- Human nature: Is man a noble animal capable of heroic action, or is he a beast held in check by the laws of society?

- The relationship between suffering and wisdom: Does one lead to the other?

Lear is a towering figure. His mind ranges over the largest of subjects and passions. He doesn't hide his feelings and Shakespeare conveys his greatness through his eloquence. "Lear's utterances establish a standard of measurement that no other fictive personage can approach" (Bl 513). His mind's grandeur baffles his daughters and contends with the storm. We watch him undergo a painful transformation, marvel at the strength he demonstrates as he battles the forces that oppose him and mourn as he ultimately succumbs. With all his faults and frailties, he serves as a monument to the nobility to which man can aspire.

The Play (line numbers from (ArK))

- (I, I, 1 – 4) A major political issue at the time the play was written was King James' attempt to unify Scotland and England to form Great Britain against the wishes of Parliament. The play deals with this issue from the opposite point of view: Lear divides his kingdom up and chaos results. To further make the point that the play should be viewed in the light of the political debate at that time, Lear's sons-in-law are the Dukes of Albany and Cornwall, the titles of James' two sons. While the words "England" and "English" appear frequently in Shakespeare's Elizabethan plays they are used far less frequently in the Jacobean plays. Similarly, the words "Britain" and "British" are used far more frequently in the Jacobean than in the Elizabethan plays (JS 41).

- (I, I, 12 – 32) "Sir, this young fellow's …" - Gloucester's words establish his promiscuous nature and the fact that he's been a poor father: "the whoreson must be acknowledged". Edmund has been living in exile and it is Gloucester's intention that he continue to do so. These experiences might explain Edmund's behavior and they add depth to his character. One of the issues addressed in the play is the parent/child relationship. What do a parent and a child owe to one another? Is a parent allowed to make demands on a grown child? The fact that Gloucester keeps Edmund abroad indicates that he controls him despite the fact that Edmund is a grown man. This is a part of an abusive father/son relationship and grounds for Edmund's resentment.

- (I, I, 33) "Attend the lords …" - The scene shows the orderly and hierarchical social structure that exists in Lear's court before chaos sets in. Lear occupies the highest position, Gloucester reports to him and is to attend to the needs of France and Burgundy, Lear's children are also present in subservient positions. This structure disintegrates as the play progresses.

- (I, I, 37 - 40) "and 'tis our fast …" - Lear introduces one of the issues that the play addresses: What is the place of the elderly in society? Although Lear is portrayed as a vigorous man, here he relinquishes his power and his purpose in society so that he can "crawl towards death". There's more than a bit of drama and self-pity in this statement since he has every intention of maintaining control over his life and enjoying a full and energetic retirement. Note that he expresses no concern with death or the afterlife.

- (I, I, 51) "Which of you shall ..." - Lear sets up a contest in which his daughters are asked to proclaim their love for him. The daughter expressing the most love is to get the largest parcel of land. This is merely ceremony, since he has already divided his kingdom. Although clumsy in the extreme, Lear's desire for expressions of love and approval from his children is a need common to all parents, particularly as they age, and hence the contest is rooted in the parent/child relationship.

- (I, I, 82, 123) "But now our joy ..." - Lear speaks openly of Cordelia as his favorite and hence expects the most from her. This explains the extent of his anger when she refuses to cooperate and also explains the antagonism that exists between him and his other daughters. The fact that he openly speaks of favoritism shows him to be a poor father.

- (I, I, 87) "Nothing, my lord." - Cordelia's response, "nothing", is an assertion of independence and a revolt against his humiliating demand for expressions of love in a public forum. The scene raises the questions: Can love be purchased? Is it a transaction? When is it controlling? The use of the word "nothing" by Lear and Cordelia and its continuing use throughout the play has been interpreted as symbolizing the emptiness of life (Edmund/Gloucester (I, II, 32), Lear/Fool (I, IV, 129), Edgar (II, II, 192)). Lear's world disintegrates into nothing as the play progresses.

- (I, I, 96 - 104) "You have begot me ..." - Cordelia describes the love a child owes to a father before and after marriage. Her words are another view of the parent/child relationship and raise the question: What does a child owe to his or her parents? Cordelia is proud and obstinate (102). She makes the same mistake as Lear when she speaks of dividing her love the way he divides his land: "Half my love with him ..." The rationality of Cordelia's answer mirrors the numerical calculation that Lear used in dividing his kingdom and is exactly the cold answer that is inappropriate in this situation. Both seem to deny that a loving parent/child relationship is an essential part of human nature.

Instead of responding with a rule-based rigidity, Cordelia could have indulged her father and, by so doing, the catastrophe could have been easily avoided. Truth is not the only good in the world, nor is the obligation to tell it the only obligation. She also had an obligation to care for her father. She subordinates human kindness to a contractual view of human relations. Lear's desire for public testimony of affection is at worst a harmless folly, not an outrage. But, together with the flaws in his character, it's sufficient to propel the story to a disastrous ending. Small mistakes can yield huge consequences. Cordelia is often compared to Desdemona in *Othello*. They both have a similar view of the parent/child relationship after marriage. And, in the way that Cordelia stubbornly argues her case despite increasing signs that disaster approaches, she resembles Desdemona pleading for Cassio.

- (I, I, 105) "But goes thy heart with this?" – Lear is desperate for an expression of love and asks "is this what you really feel?". Cordelia loves Lear but is unwilling to say so (I, I, 78) and coldly decides that honesty is of more value than generosity. This raises the question of Cordelia's responsibility for the chaos that follows. A kind word might have been enough to reassure an elderly father with an uncertain future. Edgar repudiates this position in the last line of the play saying: "Speak what we feel, not what we ought to say" (V, III, 323).

Lear's demand for protestations of love (I, I, 51) is an assertion of power, particularly since he wants them to do it in front of the court. It's also a plea for the reassurance that the elderly need when they face loss of power, the decay of old age and death. He wants to measure their love, but love can't be measured in the same way as land (I, I, 198) (II, II, 447). Lear doesn't understand what love is, and this is the underlying cause of his tragedy. He sees it as a transaction, land for love, instead of an emotion freely given by one person to another. Lear's demand corrupts not only his capacity for loving but the spontaneity with which his daughters can respond. The play is an indictment of love that is not selfless. It's a story of love gone wrong and of love unable to redeem a situation that goes out of control.

- (I, I, 109 - 121) "Well, let it be so." - One of the major issues dealt with in the play is the nature of the forces that control man's actions and here we see Lear giving his view. The heavenly "orbs" are in control and he sees himself as being able to command them to do his will: "By the sacred radiance of the sun... By all the operation of the orbs...". This is a pagan version of religion. (He does this again (I, IV, 268)). (That heavenly bodies control events on earth was not such a laughable position. At about the same time as *Lear* was written, Johannes Kepler, one of the foremost scientists of that time, said that he was under the control of Mar's "rage controlling force" (NY Science Times, 11/30/2010)).

- (I, I, 136) "We shall retain the name and all ..." - Is this possible? Can status be split from the power? Once you have given up your position in society can you expect to be treated in the same way?

- (I, 1, 147) "What wouldst thou do, old man?" - One of the questions that concerned Renaissance thinkers was whether there were "limits to the obedience that inferiors owed their social and political superiors" (St 104). Disobedience can lead to social unrest and ultimately to open rebellion against authority, an outcome much to be feared. On the other hand, obedience to immoral commands is the same as supporting those commands. "It is in Kent's behavior that the theme of virtuous, morally mandated disobedience, even interference," is fully displayed (St 113). He tells Lear the unpalatable truth despite the threats to his own person.

  Shakespeare emphasizes the foolishness of Lear's action by having Kent refer to him as "old man" and, even worse, as "thou". The latter would have struck contemporaries as shocking, since in Jacobean England the word "you" was used to address someone of equal or greater rank, "thou" to address someone of lower rank (JS 59).

- (I, I, 158 – 159) "Out of my sight!" - The symbolism of "seeing" recurs in the play. Lear doesn't see what's happening, Gloucester only "sees" after he's been blinded.

- (I, I, 198) "But now her price is fallen." - Lear again speaks of love as something that can be quantified.

- (I, I, 235) - "Better thou hadst not been born than not to have pleased me better." - Lear feels that a child's primary job is to please his/her parent. This is his answer to Cordelia's earlier declaration of what she owes her father and her future husband (I, I, 95).

- (I, I, 294 - 300) "'Tis the infirmity of his age, ..." – Regan's analysis of Lear is accurate: The effects of aging have compounded a problem that always existed: "He hath ever but slenderly known himself". He believes his power is such that he can command both love and nature.

- (I, I) However unlovable Lear is in the first scene, we will see as the play progresses that he's loved by all the good characters (Cordelia, Kent, Gloucester, Edgar, Albany, Fool) and we come to identify with him.

- (I, II, 1 – 22) "Thou, Nature, art my goddess; ..." - Edmund rejects the Elizabethan notion that filial piety (love) and intrinsic kindness are not only natural, but necessary to support the social order. That order has rejected him and he feels wronged. He doesn't believe that conventional morality governs the universe and instead appeals to an amoral Nature that acknowledges sexual appetite ("lusty stealth of nature") and asserts itself against the social order. He sees survival of the fittest as a guide to action. This may be a rationalization, since what he really wants to do is steal Edgar's inheritance. His biological makeup, as opposed to the social conventions that support the older generation over the younger and that reject bastardy, support his claim. He sees man's actions as guided by self-interest. Edmund endorses the use of one's wits to get ahead and, in contrast to Lear, he doesn't see himself bound by morality or capable of invoking the gods to get his way (Ha 78, 80).

- (I, II, 32 - 36) "Nothing, my lord." - The word "nothing" is exchanged by Gloucester and Edmund and once again has major implications.

- (I, II, 46 - 51, 72 - 76) "'This policy, and reverence ..." - The letter defines the case that a child can make against a parent. Although the outcome of the play doesn't endorse this, Montaigne made a similar argument (GT 80). Gloucester refers to Edgar as unnatural, since he sees the filial bond as a part of human nature.

- (I, II, 90 - 93) "If your honor judge it meet, ..." - Edmund will set up a meeting with Edgar that Gloucester can observe and that will provide him with "auricular assurance". This is similar to the meeting that Iago sets up with Cassio in *Othello* to provide Othello with "ocular proof" that Desdemona is unfaithful.

- (I, II, 103 - 117) "These late eclipses ..." - Gloucester is a simple, well-meaning man. In a manner similar to Lear, he accounts for Edgar's apparent treachery by appealing to the movement of heavenly bodies. Planetary movements break the (natural) filial bond. Love is natural, its withdrawal yields chaos.

- (I, II, 118 - 133) "This is excellent foppery ..." - Edmund mocks the belief that the stars control our destiny. He recognizes that man is responsible for what happens in life.

- (I, II, 177) "A credulous father ..." - Edmund's evaluation of Edgar is similar to Iago's evaluation of Othello.

- (I, II, 181 - 182) "Let me, if not by birth ..." - Edmund appeals to a notion of nature which produces a man governed by self-interest. "Let me, if not by birth [*i.e.*, in accordance with the rules of a hierarchical state], have lands by wit". He speaks the language of Machiavelli (Bl22 42). His (perhaps pagan) view of nature contrasts with Lear's anguished question "is there any cause in nature that makes these hard hearts" (III, VI, 77), which argues against cruelty as being natural in man. Edmund's notion of nature centers on the survival of the fittest. He sees the ends as justifying the means: "All with me's meet that I can fashion fit."

But Edmund is not a one-dimensional, evil character. We sympathize with him more than we do with Iago: He has had to deal with his bastardy and he's been exiled by his father (I, I, 31). And, as we'll see later, he's found to be attractive by both Regan and Goneril. He's given three soliloquies in this scene to explain his situation, and hence he is allowed to establish a bond with the audience.

- (I, III) The first two scenes set out the main theme and the subplot and introduce the characters. We're asked to accept the premise of the plot and subplot (the gullibility of Gloucester and Edgar, the foolishness of Lear). Given that, the drama unfolds in a believable way.

- (I, III, 4 - 8) "By day and night ..." - Goneril has reasons for her anger at Lear.

- (I, III, 17 – 21) "Idle old man ..." - Goneril argues for children controlling their parents. She thinks it natural that, once one renounces power, one must give up status as well. Age returns one to childhood

- (I, IV, 10) "A man, sir." - Kent's answer, is recognition of something that Lear has yet to learn: that a person isn't defined by his status (rank).

- (I, IV, 55 - 111) "My lord, I know not ..." - The action illustrates two views of the relationship between an inferior and a superior. Lear's knight excuses himself, but says it's his duty to speak plainly concerning the lack of "ceremonious affection" that Lear is receiving at the hands of Goneril and her court. In presuming to advise his superior, and thus breaching decorum, he violates his inferior status, but gives honest service. Lear also senses something's wrong, but he's careful with his words (65 - 69).

Oswald, by identifying Lear as "My lady's father" (77), offers a different notion of service. He slavishly obeys Goneril's instructions on how to behave to Lear, despite their cruel intent. He stands in stark contrast to Kent who had earlier risked his life in contradicting Lear in defense of Cordelia. Fool is the ultimate truth-teller. He mocks Kent for obeying someone who is out of favor (98). Lear threatens to beat him with a whip (108), but Fool is undeterred in his determination to tell Lear that he has acted foolishly (141 – 144, 163 – 169).

- (I, IV, 126 - 130, 178, 185) "This is nothing, fool." - The word "nothing" is used repeatedly. Lear has reduced himself to nothing and as a result has lost all power.

- (I, IV 145 - 149) – "No, faith, lords and ..." - Fool complains that the nobility won't let him have a monopoly on foolish behavior.

- (I, IV, 210 - 221) "Come, sir, ..." - Goneril reminds Lear that having given up his power he is no longer the person he was. Lear essentially agrees when he complains that he is now unrecognizable. He asks, "Does any here know me" and Fool replies "Lear's shadow". The play asks the questions: Is a man's identity based on his status and context in society? Or is it based on who he is as a person?

Is he still the same person after his status has been relinquished? What is essential in human nature?

- (I, IV, 231 - 239) "As you are old ..." - The power relationship between Goneril and Lear has been reversed. She speaks sternly to Lear, mocking his advanced age. But she has a valid complaint against Lear's knights. She threatens to "take the thing she begs".

- (I, IV, 267 - 280) "Hear, Nature, hear, ..." - Lear and Edmund both refer to Nature as their goddess (I, II, 1). But their view of her is different. Edmund sees her as someone who has set up the rules of existence and is no longer active, whereas Lear sees her as active, someone to whom he can appeal. Edmund sees her as having created a world in which men need to behave as animals to further their interests, whereas Lear believes that some basic notions of morality should govern human behavior. Here he mourns Goneril's lack of filial gratitude. "More hideous when thou show'st thee in a child" (252) and "How sharper than a serpent's tooth it is to have a thankless child" (280). Consistent with his nature, he goes to extremes in appealing to his goddess to inflict terrible punishment on Goneril.

- (I, V, 41) "Thou shouldst not ..." - Fool gives his judgment of Lear's problem. Lear fears madness, the ultimate manifestation of the chaos into which his situation is descending.

- (II, I, 44 - 50) "Persuade me to ..." - Edmund speaks sarcastically of the natural filial relationship and the gods who presumably enforce it.

- (II, I, 83) "and of my land ..." - Gloucester, as well as Lear, sees love as part of a transaction, and equates it with land. He speaks of loyalty as being "natural", an essential human characteristic.

- (II, II, 14) "A knave, a rascal ..." - Shakespeare sets Kent and Oswald against each other, both in the service of their masters. Kent calls Oswald a "super-serviceable, finical rogue" and later compares him to a dog who knows nothing but how to follow his master (68). Kent's meaning is that he has no independent moral compass and will perform any service demanded by his master, no matter how immoral. Shakespeare again speaks of the need for appropriate disobedience.

- (II, II, 172 - 192) "I heard myself proclaimed ..." - Edgar's soliloquy touches on the themes of the play: chaos (nakedness and madness) takes hold when the bonds of love are broken and it destroys the natural hierarchy that places man above beast. Edgar returns to nature: "penury in contempt of man brought near to beast" implies that when civilization is removed (penury), man is returned to a natural (bestial) state. This is a third view of nature (next to Lear's and Edmund's) which asserts that civilization is required to elevate man from his bestial roots (Ha 80). Chaos also destroys identity: "Edgar I nothing am" (192). (Bedlam (185) is a shortening of the name of a mental hospital in London: St Mary's of Bethlehem.)

- (II, II, 318 - 321) "Regan, I think you are." - Lear sees the bond between father and daughter as natural. If Regan is not glad to see him, she cannot be his daughter and therefore his wife must have been an adulteress who united with another man to father her.

- (II, II, 335 - 345) "O, sir, you are old: ..." - Regan raises the question of the role of the elderly in society. Her position is that they must be governed by their children because they no longer know what's good for them. This is consistent with the biological view that old age serves no purpose (GT 83) because the elderly are weak and beyond reproductive age. Hence, their presence on earth doesn't enhance the probability that the species will survive. And it is consistent with the feelings of many elderly people that their lives lack meaning and purpose. Lear (sarcastically) acknowledges this when he says, "age is unnecessary" (344). Coupled with Edmund's view that resources controlled by the elderly could be put to better use by the younger generation, we have strong argument for relegating the elderly to the ash heap. On the other hand, society in Shakespeare's time "proclaimed that by every natural impulse and moral code, honor and reverence were due to the elderly" (366) (GT 74).

- (II, II, 354) "You nimble lightnings ..." - Lear calls down the wrath of the gods on Goneril, but praises Regan for respecting "the offices of nature, bond of childhood" (366). Thus, the filial bond is a part of Nature.

- (II, II, 379 - 390) "If you do love old men ..." - Lear faces the realities against him: Goneril, Regan, Cornwall and Oswald. On his side are only Fool, Kent and Gloucester. He calls on the heavens for help. He alternates between pathos and calling down the wrath of the gods. Goneril speaks of his dotage and Regan says that with no power, Lear shouldn't expect to be treated with respect (390).

- (II, II, 407) "Now I prithee ..." - Lear fears madness – the ultimate chaos, the chaos of the mind.

- (II, II, 439) "And in good time ..." - Regan says that the division of the kingdom was not a gift. The time had come for Lear to give it to his children. This is consistent with Edmund's view (I, II, 46).

- (II, II, 448) "Thy fifty yet doth ..." - Lear measures Goneril's love by the number of knights she will allow in his entourage.

- (II, II, 453 - 475) "O, reason not the need!" - Lear speaks about the minimum needed to separate human life from the life of a beast. He echoes Edgar's earlier statement that penury brings man "near to beast" (172). Putting man and beast at the same level violates the hierarchy commonly accepted in English society that orders living things. Lear is speaking of more than the need for his knights. He says, "true need", but breaks off. He doesn't need the knights to protect him any more than an elderly person sent off to a nursing home needs his or her own chair and rug (Sny 145). Without them, however, that person feels diminished.

  Lear wants his knights and the adoration of his daughters as a way of reassuring himself of his importance and as a comfort in his old age. The extent of his rage is a measure of his fear that his self-image is being stripped away. The reality of his being a mere man is too frightening to contemplate. Cordelia subordinated kindness to rationality in response to Lear's request for love; here Regan and Goneril subordinate kindness to their desire for power.

  At this point (463), Lear makes the choice which is central to the structure of tragedy. He wants justice and he wants to preserve his dignity. He chooses to fight, although he is powerless. He threatens revenge (468), although he has no idea how he can make good on that threat. His situation is pitiful, but he chooses not to give up his independence and become subservient to Goneril and Regan. This is the heroic stance that characterizes the struggle of tragic heroes. It leads to his transformation and ultimately destroys him. It's an exaggeration of the choice faced by the elderly today: How do you retain your independence as you become physically frail?

Lear's language is a weapon in his fight. It is grand early in the play, broken here (459, 469), and simple with a lot of repetition at the end (G 270) (IV, VII, 60). The simplicity reflects his transition to an understanding of his place in the world. Here, he alternates between self-pity (461) and summoning up courage. He uses the word "unnatural" (467) in describing his daughter's lack of filial devotion, reflecting the positive view that he holds of what is essential in man.

- (III, I) **Hierarchical Orderings** - One theme of the play concerns the importance that 17th Century England placed on hierarchical orderings in the world. The order among living things was God, man, woman and then animals. The family ordering was father, mother and then children. The social ordering was king, nobles, and then peasants. Each ordering imposed rules of behavior that keep society functioning. The social ordering decreed that Gloucester must obey Cornwall. The family ordering decreed that Edmund must obey Gloucester. Power maintains the social order; love maintains the family order. Lear is a central figure in both.

These hierarchies have been destroyed at this point in the play. The social order was broken when Lear gave up the throne and became subject to his daughters. In a failure of love, Lear's and Gloucester's children oppose their fathers, breaking the family order. The moral order is broken as a result, and chaos follows. Identity is lost: Edgar and Kent are in disguise, Lear says "Does any here know me?" (I, IV, 217). Lear becomes a homeless wanderer, and eventually goes mad. Gloucester suffers horrible punishment. War breaks out. Shakespeare amplifies the chaos by introducing the storm. The disruption of the hierarchies is reflected in the disruption of weather.

- (III, II, 1 - 24) "Blow winds ..." - Lear's behavior in the storm demonstrates the powerlessness of outward calamity to subdue him. Ignoring the plea of Fool to submit and take shelter from the storm, Lear roars his defiance. His lines at the beginning of the storm are limited to expressing anger and self-pity in grand terms. He's concerned with the injustice that he has suffered and does this with exalted language, demonstrating his own large spirit and heroic nature.

  Lear is an emotional man, a man who feels much, and a man who expresses those feelings openly, forcefully and eloquently. In this respect he contrasts sharply with Hamlet, who might best be described as cerebral, analytic and not given to express his feelings in public (Bl22 1).

- (III, II, 49 - 68) "Let the great gods ..." - Lear begins his transformation. His call for justice is for the punishment of all criminals, not just justice for himself. He plaintively says that he is "a man more sinned against than sinning", a statement that admits some guilt on his part. He shows concern for Fool (68).

- (III, IV, 6 - 14) "Thou think'st 'tis ..." - The storm is nothing compared to filial ingratitude.

- (III, IV, 18 - 22) "Pour on; I will endure." Lear demonstrates his towering stature. He challenges the universe. He recognizes that dwelling on the offences that he has suffered will lead to madness (21), a lesson that is as relevant today as it was in Shakespeare's time.

- (III, IV, 23 - 36) "Prithee go in thyself ..." - Lear shows concern for Kent and then turns from his own suffering to the injustice and wrongs of the world and the responsibility of the haves to help the have-nots (28). He kneels in prayer, but he's not talking to the gods. The implication is that if justice is to exist on earth, man must create it, since it is not imposed on us by the cosmos. He accepts responsibility for not having done so. His acknowledgment, "Oh, I have ta'en Too little care of this" (32), implies that he has known of this suffering, perhaps even pitied those who experienced it, but has simply ignored it. Now he suffers and is moved to action. It follows that pity is insufficient to motivate compassionate action.

- (III, IV, 48) "Didst thou give all ..." - Apparently the shock of seeing Poor Tom brings on Lear's madness. Lear had mixed up the true nature of himself - a man - with society's view of the attributes of a king. He can't reconcile his former view of himself as all-powerful with his current recognition of his weakness, his former conviction of his own wisdom with the reality that he was wrong, his former belief in the love of his daughters with their treatment of him. All of this leads to a split in his psyche and results in madness. The lack of justice, his vulnerability, his dependence on others and the absence of love all contribute to this. This is the ultimate chaos of the mind.

- (III, IV, 64) "Nay, he reserved ..." - Fool points out that it's fortunate that Poor Tom kept a blanket. Otherwise, they'd all be embarrassed.

- (III, IV, 77) "This cold night will turn us all to fools and madmen." - The cold night can be interpreted as a reference to an empty universe, and the quote to the fact that it causes life to be absurd – a nihilistic view (see (K) for an extensive discussion of the relationship between the play and nihilism).

- (III, IV, 99 - 107) "Why, thou wert better ..." - The play raises the question of what is normal in human nature. Lear said earlier that the parent/child bond is natural (II, II, 367) and had rejected Regan and Goneril as unnatural (II, II, 467). Here, referring to Tom, he asks the question: "is man no more than this", the ultimate "nothing", the "thing itself". Stripped of the furnishings of civilization, "unaccommodated man is no more but such a poor, bare forked animal..." This goes further than Lear's earlier statement that if you deny man all but the barest essentials, his "life is cheap as beast's" (II, II, 453). Here Lear is saying that man is like a beast, a part of nature. Contrast this with Lear's view of himself in Act I, on top of the social hierarchy, all wise and all powerful. This is a radical thought for someone of Shakespeare's time, which assumed, as stated in Genesis (1:27), that man was created in God's image.

The play is a reminder that not only are we little more than a beast but, in contrast to a beast, we are particularly fragile: we can't survive outside of society. Shakespeare was very likely to have been familiar with Montaigne's essay *An Apology for Raymond Sebond,* in which Montaigne said something similar:

> "We are, they say, the only animal abandoned naked on the naked earth; we are in bonds and fetters, having nothing to arm or cover ourselves with but the pelts of other creatures; Nature has clad all others with shells, pods, husks, hair, wool, spikes, hide, down, feathers, scales, fleece or silk, according to the several necessities of the being; she has armed them with claws, teeth and horns for assault and defense; and, as is proper to them, has herself taught them to swim, to run, to fly or to sing. Man, on the other hand, without an apprenticeship, does not know how to walk, talk, eat or do anything at all but wail."

As a result, we must depend on each other. "If society will not protect us, then we shall have no protection at all; we cannot live outside society. We must have our clothes, our fires, our beds, and our kitchens – unlike other animals. The essence of human existence is therefore fragility" (CM 123). Society brings security, which in this scene is represented by clothing (which Lear had referred to earlier (II, II, 457)). In *Waiting for Godot*, Beckett places the tramps in exactly this situation. They are vulnerable, without any of the protections that society offers. He does this to force them to directly confront the apparent emptiness of the human condition.

In Lear's case, the bonds within family and society have been broken and he is barely surviving. He has come to see that he shares an essential humanity with Poor Tom, and he wants to identify with him. This commonality is denied by the difference between the quality of the clothing that they wear, an artificial social barrier that Lear wants to breach. He attempts to remove his clothes (106), which he refers to as "lendings", in recognition of the fact that they are not a part of his essential self. Lear's new understanding of human nature is a crushing blow to his sanity and produces the madness that he has feared.

Hobbes and Rousseau (who both wrote after Shakespeare's death) had opposite views of the essential nature of man. Hobbes viewed man as brutish and, as a result, saw society as necessary to place limits on his behavior. Edmund's attitude is consistent with this view, although he regards himself as unconstrained by these limits. This is survival of the fittest. Rousseau took the opposite view. He believed that man is naturally kind and good, and that he is corrupted by society which generates a need for power, office, wealth and mastery. Lear in the storm scene seems to adopt Rousseau's view.

- (III, IV, 144) "My duty cannot suffer ..." - Gloucester speaks of the need to disobey an immoral authority. It is his duty to ignore what he feels are Goneril and Regan's "hard commands".

- (III, IV, 150 - 168) "First let me talk with this philosopher: ..." - Lear rejects all civilized life. He sees Tom, a naked, gibbering, totally uncivilized wretch, as the essential man, a philosopher. He wants to learn from him. Tom is honest and he is what he appears to be, as opposed to Regan and Goneril who say one thing and do another.

- (III, IV, 180) "I smell the blood ..." - In an act of political correctness, Shakespeare changed the word "Englishman" to "Britishman" in the familiar rhyme (JS 44) in deference to King James' efforts to unify England and Scotland.

- (III, VI, 35) "I'll see their trial first." - Lear wants justice for himself (revenge).

- (III, VI, 73) "Then let them anatomize ..." - Lear questions what is natural in human nature: "Is there any cause in nature that makes these hard hearts?" Regan doesn't conform to the Elizabethan notion that cruelty is unnatural. This is an anguished question and it frustrates and maddens Lear. He is being forced to recognize that evil, like good, is indeed natural.

  Both Lear and Edmund speak of nature but mean different things. To Lear, nature is the source of all goodness in the world. It cements the filial bond and moves us to moral action. Edmund's view of nature (I, II, 1) has no moral component. It operates at the animal level of sexual urges and ruthless competition for selfish ends.

- (III, VI, 98) "Come, come away!" - Fool disappears from the play at this point. His role had been to prod Lear into seeing the reality of his situation, but Lear now understands. Hence, Fool no longer has a dramatic role to play.

- (III, VI, 99 - 107) "When we our betters ..." - Edgar's pain is lightened by seeing that Lear suffers similarly: the love between Edgar and Gloucester mirrors the love between

Cordelia and Lear. In both cases it is love gone wrong. Edgar's remark "he childed as I father'd" might refer to this or to the fact that Lear has been rejected by his children and he has been rejected by his father. In both cases love's failure has brought on the pain, and so one can argue that the play contains Shakespeare's indictment of love.

- (III, VII, 24) "Though well we may not ..." - The play raises the question of whether civil society enforces justice or whether justice is simply a façade that is used by some to control others. Cornwall answers this: Power rules (see also (V, III, 156)).

- (III, VII, 53) "I am tied to the stake ..." - Gloucester is referring to bear baiting.

- (III, VII, 71) "Hold your hand ... " - Justice (Cornwall's death) in this scene is brought about by a man (not the gods) and furthermore by a peasant, as noted by Regan (79). The servant articulates the thought that true service to a superior might involve opposing that person's actions. The cruelty that Shakespeare depicts on the stage is difficult to watch. It's worth noting, however, that an audience in 17th Century London was more accustomed to such acts than we are today. It was not uncommon for incredibly cruel punishments to be rendered publicly by the government.

- (III, VII, 85) "Edmund, enkindle all ..." - Gloucester sees nature as abhorring horrid acts.

- (IV, I, 1 - 13) "Yet better thus ..." - Edgar says that it's better to be openly despised as Poor Tom, since one can assume that the ill feeling is due to the disguise, than to be flattered in court as Edgar and know that you're despised anyway.

Contrast this view with Lear's, who sought flattery at the outset and didn't question whether or not it was honest.

Edgar thinks things are at their worst and hence can only get better ("the worst returns to laughter"), but by (28) he realizes that things have gotten worse still. The message is that things can always get worse. The world's "strange mutations", represented by his mutilated father, make us realize that aging isn't so bad; the real disasters of life make aging seem acceptable. Without such disasters, "Life would not yield to age" (12) and suicide would be seen as a reasonable solution to aging. In contrast to Lear, Edgar doesn't rage against adversity, rather he seems to accept it.

- (IV, I, 20 - 23) "I have no way ..." - Gloucester recognizes his responsibility for his actions and his true blindness: "I stumbled when I saw". His high position made him over-confident ("our means secure us"); his blindness is actually an advantage.

- (IV, 1, 33 - 39) "He has some reason ..." - Gloucester has come to understand that man is little more than an insect and - "As flies to wanton boys, are we to th' gods ..." - that the universe is governed by gods with no moral sense.

- (IV, I, 55) "Poor Tom's a-cold." - It's not clear why Edgar does not reveal himself to Gloucester at this point.

- (IV, I, 70 - 74) "Let the superfluous ..." - Gloucester echoes Lear's new social conscience (III, IV 23) by calling for a new tax structure: "distribution should undo excess, and each man have enough". Both are motivated to social justice by experiencing the pain of the impoverished. He criticizes the person "that will not see because he does not feel", thus mirroring Lear's recognition of the inadequacy of pity as a motivator to take action against the world's suffering (III, IV, 32). But his appeal to Heaven's ordnance contradicts his earlier claim (38) that the gods don't care about man.

- (IV, II, 30 - 59) "O Goneril ..." - Albany's view is that violation of the filial bond (33) causes man to behave "like monsters of the deep" (51). This is the Hobbesian state. Shakespeare's point is that this violation is what has triggered the disaster in the play. Goneril taunts Albany for being weak and, in a reference to Christianity, for turning the other cheek. She calls him a moral fool for failing to recognize offences that cannot be honorably borne and for being afraid to punish a villain before he actually commits a crime (55). This is a new notion of justice.

- (IV, II, 79 - 81) "This shows you are above ..." - Albany applauds the servant's act in opposing and then killing Cornwall. He sees a just universe in which the gods punish evil.

- (IV, III, 33) "It is the stars ..." - Kent's view of the forces that govern the world (the stars) is similar to Gloucester's view expressed earlier in the play.

- (IV, VI, 34 – 41) "O you mighty gods ..." - Gloucester addresses the gods. If he could accept the catastrophes that have befallen him without quarreling with the gods he would continue to live: "My snuff and loathed part of nature [the remainder of his life] should burn itself out". But he cannot.

- (IV, VI, 60 – 65) "Alack, I have no eyes." - Gloucester speaks of the value of suicide as the ultimate power in man's hand, an act of resistance against either a tyrant or god. Hence, suicide has meaning only if god exists. Otherwise it has no meaning - it just accelerates the inevitable. It's a protest against undeserved suffering and injustice and only counts in the final reckoning between god and man.

- (IV, VI, 67) "Upon the crown …" - Edgar imitates the technique of exorcism to try and rid Gloucester of his desire for suicide. "Edgar tries to create in Gloucester an experience of awe and wonder so intense that it can shatter his suicidal despair and restore his faith in the benevolence of the gods" (Bl10 111). He tells Gloucester that what he thought was a beggar at the top of the cliff was in reality a devil who has now been exorcised by the gods. Shakespeare is mocking the practice of exorcism, which was still in use at the time and is exposed as phony in this scene.

- (IV, VI, 72) "Therefore, thou happy father …" - Edgar speaks of the "clearest gods" who have preserved Gloucester's life, when in fact the good deed is his own doing. Gloucester gives up on suicide (75 – 77) (but then changes his mind later (227)). This is an example of the older generation learning from the younger.

- (IV, VI, 85) "O thou side-piercing sight!" - Shortly after Edgar says the gods are just, Lear – mad – enters. The one hundred lines starting from this point "constitute one of Shakespeare's assaults on the limits of art, largely because their pathos is unprecedented" (Bl 513).

- (IV, VI, 96 - 104) "Ha! Goneril with a white beard?" - Lear learns from the storm that he is not all-powerful – he is not "ague-proof". He has come to a new understanding of himself.

- (IV, VI, 107 - 127) "Ay, every inch a king." - Lear looks below the veneer of proper behavior and sees the sexual realities that underlie it. His attitude is similar to Edmund's in this regard (I, II, 13, 118, 128). Lear praises adultery because "Gloucester's bastard son was kinder to his father than were my daughters". He (and perhaps Shakespeare) is not fond of women and sees intercourse as lechery, unrelated to love. Edgar later expresses the same view (V, III, 170): "The dark and vicious place ..."

- (IV, VI, 129 - 131) "Let me wipe it first ..." - Gloucester offers love and Lear responds by expressing shame, saying his hand "smells of mortality". This is a far cry from Lear's words Act I when he demanded love. To be loved requires recognition of one's own faults and weaknesses and a willingness to expose them to others, something Lear was unable to do earlier. He does that here by speaking of his mortality. Gloucester refers to Lear as a "piece of nature", implying perhaps a masterpiece and that the world will "wear out to nought" the best that nature produces.

- (IV, VI, 146 - 168) "What, art mad?" - Lear is no longer seeking revenge. He's concerned with how justice is enforced in society and finds it lacking. He asks the question to what extent do the laws and social structure impose ethical behavior as opposed to simply being a disguise behind which some exert power over others? In the storm and in the trial scene (III, VI, 35), Lear had called for justice more as a matter of revenge (III, II, 50). Later, he recognized the injustice of wealth and spoke of shaking the "superflux" to the "poor naked wretches" to "show the heavens more just" (III, IV, 33). Here he addresses the failure of the system of justice (147, 155): the judges are corrupt, money protects the rich, punishment is meted out by those who are guiltier than the people they punish. His comment, "a dog's obey'd in office", emphasizes this as well as asserting that authority is a function of the office rather than the intrinsic worth of the office-holder. If the system of justice is rotten then it enforces power, not justice, and "none does offend" (164). Actual justice in the play isn't achieved by the judicial system, but by individuals (the servant kills Cornwall, Edgar punishes Edmund, Goneril kills Regan and then commits suicide). There's no sense that divine action is involved.

- (IV, VI, 168) "Now, now, now, ..." - The removal of boots is picked up in *Waiting for Godot.*

- (IV, VI, 174 - 183) "We came crying hither: ..." - Suffering is not punishment for one's actions; it is at the core of the human condition: "Thou knowest the first time we smell the air we wawl and cry." This is a nihilistic position. The reference to "this great stage of fools" brings to mind Macbeth's metaphor for life: "a poor player, that struts and frets his hour upon the stage". The repetition of "kill" mirrors the earlier repetition of "now" and is characteristic of Lear's language in the latter part of the play.

- (IV, VI, 247) "I know thee well ..." - Edgar condemns Oswald for being "duteous to the vices of thy mistress". Duty is not always a virtue. He addresses the issue of the need to oppose unjust commands from a superior.

- (IV, VII) Shakespeare's audience would naturally have sympathized with the British in their effort to defeat the French invaders. By placing Cordelia at the head of the

French forces, rather than her husband, it's possible that Shakespeare was trying to blunt this sympathy (JS 44).

- (IV, VII, 52 - 84) "Where have I been?" - Whereas at the beginning of the play Lear is confident and arrogant, at the end he's unsure of the simplest things (55). (This recognition of his ignorance is comparable to a similar transformation in Oedipus (CM 131).) He has recovered his sanity and has a new view of himself: "I am a very foolish, fond old man" (60) and "as I am a man" (68). He speaks simply. Lear's dialogue with Cordelia (72 - 75) reveals his newly acquired ability to give and accept love without conditions and to admit his dependence on others and his weakness (84). He accepts responsibility for his actions and the punishment that's due him: "If you have poison for me, I will drink it" (72). Earlier he had claimed that punishment is unjust - "None does offend ..." (IV, VI, 110, 164) – but that was part of his criticism of the system of justice.

  Cordelia's grant of forgiveness can be viewed as Christian, which teaches that mercy supersedes justice. Her response, "No cause" (75), is obviously untrue and contrasts with her need to be brutally honest in Act I. It is an indication that Cordelia has undergone her own transformation. "Kind words can sometimes be better than true words" (CM 128).

  Bloom describes this scene: "The love of daughter and father achieves absolute expression. I cannot think of another place in Western literature that is so luminous and poignant" (Bl22 126).

- (V, II, 9) "Men must endure ..." - We suffer in life and then die, you can't control the timing, "ripeness is all". The one important thing we must know about death is to be ready for it. "This statement stands apart from Edgar's affirmation of a just providential order ... [It] has no moralistic overtones" (Ca 84). Although Gloucester and Lear have many similarities, one difference is their ability to express themselves. Lear's language is supreme, Gloucester's is simple: "And that's true too." Gloucester is instructed by Edgar, just as Lear is instructed by Cordelia. In both cases, it is the child instructing the parent.

- (V, III, 8 - 19) "No, no, no ..." - Lear is beyond seeking revenge or justice and no longer demands declarations of love. He sees happiness based on a simple life and on love. He's satisfied to live in a cell. His view of his position in life has changed radically from that of Act I where he saw himself as the center of the universe. He now submits to the "gods" (21) and even refers to himself and Cordelia as "God's spies" (17). It's not clear what Shakespeare meant here since the apostrophe is omitted in both the quarto and folio editions. If we assume that he intended "God's spies", it might be an evolution in Lear's view of religion from pagan worship to monotheism (Kn 190). Alternatively, if he intended "gods' spies", monotheism has not been introduced.

- (V, III, 31) "Men are as the time is; ..." – Edmund means that men are shaped by the social context in which they live.

- (V, III, 39) "I cannot draw a cart ..." - The captain agrees to follow Edmund's order without knowing what he is been asked to do. Once again, we have a servant who is unwilling to interpose his own moral judgment between an order and an act. He says that man cannot do the work of a beast, but he can do "man's work" and, ironically, that includes murder.

- (V, III, 156) "Say if I do ..." - Goneril asserts the arbitrary quality of the law. It is to serve her needs, not to do justice.

- (V, III, 168) "The gods are just ..." - Edgar claims that we're punished in accordance with our "pleasant vices", a view taken earlier by Albany (V, II, 79). Gloucester was punished for fathering Edmund illegitimately and the product of that vice, Edmund, is responsible for Gloucester's suffering. Edgar's attempts to justify what is happening generally fall short. He speaks a simple morality and displays a simple goodness, but lacks deep insight (he is similar to Job's orthodox comforters). He is, however, the man who accomplishes most in the play: he evades a death sentence, protects Lear in the storm, saves his father from suicide and from Oswald, fights in battle, kills Edmund and becomes the ruler. Perhaps this indicates the limits of profundity and intellect.

- (V, III, 172) "The wheel has come full circle ...". Edmund accepts his fate. He started out with nothing and he's going to die with nothing.

- (V, III, 230) "This judgement of the heavens ..." - Albany again speaks of a just heaven and appeals to the gods to defend Cordelia, but immediately afterward Lear enters, carrying her dead body (254). Shakespeare seems to be mocking the notion of just gods. Her death is troubling since it is unnecessary, it is the result of an accidental delay. Its only purpose seems to be to reinforce the plays nihilistic outlook (Gd 50). It seems to make the point that once evil is released, it can't be held in check. Even Edmund, who ordered her death, can't stop it.

- (V, III, 261 – 262) "Is this the promised end?" - The three survivors mourn the sad ending. Kent's question might be a cynical forward reference to the promise of a Judgment Day. Albany's "Fall and Cease" conveys the sense that life is hopeless.

- (V, III, 287) "All's cheerless, dark and deadly" - Kent asserts the nihilistic view. His words echo those of Fool (III, IV, 77).

- (V, III, 297 - 303) "For us, we will resign ..." - Albany, the eternal optimist, says he will return his earthly powers to Lear. He talks of justice but, as if to mock his words, Lear dies immediately afterward.

- (V, III, 304 – 308) "And my poor fool ..." - The play uses repetition for emphasis: "kill, kill, ..." (IV, VI 183), "howl, howl, ..." (V, III, 255), "never, never, ...", and "no, no, no". This recalls the repetition of "nothing" in the first scene and emphasizes the nihilistic view that the universe is empty (no redemption, no heaven). Kent emphasizes this. He sees "the world as a scene of torment" (Ca 100) when he speaks of the "rack of this tough world" (313).

- (V, III, 323) "Speak what we feel, not what we ought to say." - Edgar's final words repudiate the hypocritical love test at the beginning of the play and call for integrity over obedience (St 123). The play ends on a note of personal and social disaster. This is the "no", "nothing", and "never" that has been the drum beat behind the dialogue throughout the play.

Discussion

Lear's Transformation - In accordance with the typical structure of tragedy, Lear undergoes a transformation over the course of the play. He starts as a prideful, egotistical and supremely powerful man who believes that his power flows from who he is rather than the position he occupies. He even believes that he can invoke the forces of nature on his behalf. But this view is shattered by the treatment he endures from his daughters. His progress lies through a dissipation of egoism, a submission to the cruelty of an indifferent nature, and an acceptance of selfless love (G 265).

Lear's thoughts first center on himself and filial ingratitude. His strength is made evident by the degree of his rage, which assumes heroic proportions in the storm scene: "Pour on; I will endure" (III, IV, 18). He is powerless and has been stripped of everything, but he is unbroken and demands justice. As the storm scenes progress, however, his thoughts extend to a concern for others and an indictment of society. He learns humility and charity and that the world is a perpetual insult to our self-importance. He comes to an understanding of his own frailty and the difference between who he is and the trappings of his position: "They flatter'd me like a dog ..." (IV, VI, 96, 103). And he accepts man's insignificance in an unfriendly universe where suffering exists independent of one's actions: "We came crying hither" (IV, VI 174).

His education comes through suffering. He comes to understand the true nature of his place in the universe and his common humanity with others. "By heroically enduring a fate he is powerless to alter, by insisting, moreover, upon *knowing* it, man grows in stature even as he is being destroyed" (Do 71).

The transformation that has occurred in Lear's character over the course of the play affects his attitude towards the essential aspects of life:

- Love – Lear initially had no concept of love. He viewed it as a transaction: you fawn over me and I'll give you a portion of my kingdom whose size is based on how well you do it. At the end, we see selfless love between Lear and Cordelia with no strings attached. He learns that his real need is love, not power.

- Family – Lear initially didn't understand his daughters and his responsibility to them. His view was summarized by: "Better thou hadst not been born than not to have pleased me better", by which he means that a child's job is to please his or her parent. At the end of the play he asks for Cordelia's forgiveness (V, III, 11).

- Governance and justice – Lear comes to realize that a leader has a responsibility to work for the good of his subjects and rectify the injustices of society.

- Nature of man – Lear initially saw a hierarchy among men, with himself on top capable of controlling everyone around him and invoking nature in his defense. He finally accepts that all men are simply poor forked animals, not very different from beasts, and he sees himself as a "very foolish, fond old man".

The Tragedy of Old Age - In Shakespeare's world age carried with it status, power and a presumption of wisdom, and the young were required to defer to the old. Ultimately, however, the young come of age, the old deteriorate and a transition occurs in which the roles of the two are reversed. On the positive side, the reversal implies freedom over rigidity and permits society to renew itself with the vitality of the younger generation. But the anguish it causes in the older generation can be considerable. The play deals with this anguish. As Edgar says, "But that thy strange mutations make us hate thee, Life would not yield to age" (IV, I, 12), meaning that we wouldn't tolerate the depredations of age.

Lear retires and transfers his power to his daughters with the expectation that his status – the respect that he gets in society – will be preserved. He still wants to be treated as king (I, I, 136). But retirement puts a strain on the relationship between status and power. They go together, something Lear didn't anticipate. Lear's fate is the fate of anyone who survives his direct usefulness to the younger generation. We watch Lear struggle with his loss of status and become obsessed with loyalty and the signs of the respect he was formerly given. And we recognize that his loss is no different from what we all feel today at the same stage of life, even though the power we relinquish in retirement is a small fraction of what Lear had possessed.

Loss of power also carries with it a loss of identity. Who are we if we no longer occupy the position we had previously held? Lear asks "Does anyone here know me? ... Who is it that can tell me who I am?" (I, IV, 217). When power has been relinquished and status has been stripped away what's left? What is inherent in the individual? This is one of the most important questions that the play raises.

Related to this is the question of wisdom. We expect Lear and Gloucester, because of their age, to be wise. Instead they're foolish at the start of the play. In a violation of the familial hierarchy, we see as the play ends Lear learning from Cordelia and Gloucester learning from Edgar (IV, VI, 75) (V, II, 9).

Human Nature and the Human Condition - All the characters, either directly or indirectly, offer their views on what is inherent in human nature and the forces that seem to control their lives. Shakespeare doesn't necessarily endorse these views, but the play is concerned with them, since they say something about the characters who espouse them.

- Gloucester speaks of vast powers working in the universe against which man is helpless, for example the influence of the stars and the control exerted by amoral gods. The play seems to reject this explanation of man's behavior. Both Lear's and Gloucester's suffering are related to foolish decisions they made in their relationship with their children. The plot doesn't depend on such external forces, but instead is shaped entirely by the characters themselves. The tragedy could have been avoided by a saving word or a more considered action. The characters invoke the divine on occasion, but there's no evidence that the gods respond. Whatever goodness exists is the result of what the characters do themselves. And there's no mention of heaven: Goodness is its own reward. The gods seem to be "figments of the human mind rather than omnipotent ruling powers" (Kn 187). Invocations seem to "show at the most an insistent need in humanity to cry for justification to something beyond its horizon" (Kn 188).

- Edgar and Albany believe that poetic justice is a force in the world. Under this assumption, suffering is meted out in proportion to one's misdeeds. But the play doesn't seem to support this view either. Most would agree that the extent of Lear's and Gloucester's suffering is not justified by their actions, and Cordelia's death is totally undeserved. In fact, the play raises a contrary the question, "Is there *any* justice in the universe?" Lear addresses this in the storm and his answer is "no". Although the play is filled with a spiritual darkness, in the end the evil characters are dead and Edgar, a sensible and kind man, is triumphant. So, in this pagan play, a rough morality does seem to triumph.

It's natural to think of the *Book of Job* as a forerunner to *King Lear*. Both Job and Lear suffer horribly. Both challenge their god and both undergo a transformation over the course of their stories. But despite these similarities, the characters are quite different. Lear bears some responsibility for his suffering, while Job does not. Although Job initially questions God's justice, he never loses his faith and in the end his belief that God has imposed an ordering in the universe is strengthened. Lear's initial belief in a god-controlled universe, on the other hand, is destroyed by the end of the play. While the *Book of Job* justifies man's faith in God, *King Lear* opposes any such belief.

- The play touches briefly on the impact of social forces on our lives. In this view, Lear's actions and personality are shaped by the role he must play as king. Edmund endorses this when he says, "men are as the time is", meaning that we don't always behave in accordance with our principles, but instead tailor our actions to the needs of the times. A belief that Edmund's character was shaped by the mistreatment that he endured growing up a bastard, rather than anything intrinsic in his nature, would be consistent with this view. And when Lear says, "a Dog's obey'd in office", he means something similar: it doesn't matter who you are, it is the role you play that carries weight.

- Some take the view that we are endowed at birth with some essential personal qualities. This is referred to as an essentialist view. In the humanistic version of this, man is seen as capable of heroic action. The dignity and greatness that naturally exists at the core of human nature is stressed. Man is essentially moral, and any inclination to evil is a distortion of nature. Lear takes this view when he calls his daughters "unnatural hags" and asks if there is any cause in nature that makes their "hard hearts". Gloucester also takes this view in speaking of Edmund's filial devotion as "natural". This humanist view places man in control of his destiny. The universe plays a secondary role: It is "at best callously just, at worst sadistically vindictive" (Bl10 71) or simply uninvolved. Man suffers, and by enduring he reveals his essential courage and integrity. Lear is such a man and one can argue that his death counts for little. The greatness of his spirit - in spite of failure - is nearer to the heart of the play than his survival.

- In contrast to the humanistic version of the essentialist view, the Christian version focuses on man's soul, or spiritual core, as the site that shapes his actions. Both versions emphasize man's role in controlling events, rather than external forces. Man is a sinner, he is responsible for his sins and he suffers as a result of them. Suffering is intrinsic to God's redemptive design for man and brings out his intrinsic worth. Lear's progress through life is seen as illustrating this view: pride, fall, suffering, recognition of guilt, forgiveness and reconciliation. Cordelia's willingness to forgive is further evidence of it. Mercy supersedes justice.

  The Christian view of the play is hard to defend, since the play is set in a pre-Christian time and there's only one passing reference to God. There's nothing Christian in the ending, no notion of personal resurrection. We see only suffering on the stage, with no hope of rewards after death. Cordelia's death is totally unjustified, a senseless mistake, and the effect of either pure chance or malevolent fate.

"The play's values of love, forgiveness and fellow-feeling gained through suffering are indeed those preached by Christianity. The point is that rather than being handed down from on high, they take root in and grow up from the ground of human desperation. Furthermore, in an apparently random universe with no afterlife in which ultimate justice is meted out, following that ethic must be its own reward" (Sny 179).

At a more fundamental level, one can question whether Christian tragic theater is even possible. Within the system of Christian beliefs, success and disaster in this world cannot be the whole story, since punishment and rewards follow in the afterlife. Tragedy is supposed to inform us on how life is lived on the earth and doesn't take this into account.

- Edmund illustrates yet another view of what is essential in human nature. He believes that Nature is the controlling force in the world. He denies a noble or a spiritual essence. He sees man's actions as based on self-interest and survival of the fittest. Nature is cruel, there is no essential or god-given morality, and actions aren't controlled by supernatural forces. Man is who he is by his own choice and he's responsible for what happens to him. God can't be blamed. Both Lear and Gloucester echo this theme of personal responsibility in the latter part of the play.

- Finally, the argument can be made that the play presents a nihilistic view of the human condition. There is no external force shaping our actions and there is nothing essential in human nature. The randomness of the suffering experienced by the characters argues for a universe that is empty and amoral. Lear dies *after* he's repented his mistakes and repaired his relationship with Cordelia. Cordelia dies for no reason at all. Gloucester, a good but simple man, is horribly punished for his loyalty to Lear. This nihilistic view resonates with the post WWII generation and might explain the current popularity of the play. The use of the words "nothing" and "never" speak of the emptiness, illogic, terror and absurdity of the modern condition.

Most readers agree that the play presents a grim view of the human condition in a pitiless universe. Lear sees Poor Tom as the essential human being, a "bare forked animal", and comes to realize that unexplained suffering is in the very nature of the human condition: "Thou must be patient. We came crying hither..." But our situation is not hopeless. Lear and Gloucester have grown in wisdom, Edmund repents, Cornwall's servant (a nameless everyman) is heroic, Albany has become a force for good, the evil characters are dead, and Edgar's final words are not despairing: the state will be rebuilt, order will be restored.

The fact that the play presents so many views is a measure of its depth and richness and of Shakespeare's genius. But we're left with the question "What was Shakespeare's view?" Perhaps it's best to simply say that the play doesn't endorse any view. The views expressed by the characters are Shakespeare's way of describing who the characters are. He presents us with a picture of human relationships and the human condition in glorious language. "Tragedy never tells us what to think; it shows us what we are and may be" (Mk 117). We have to supply the answers ourselves. "What we are and may be was never more memorably fixed upon a stage than in this kneeling old man whose heartbreak is precisely the measure of what … it is possible to lose and possible to win. … [The play] begs us to seek the meaning of our human fate not in what becomes of us, but in what we become. Death … is miscellaneous and commonplace; it is life whose qualities may be made noble and distinctive. Suffering we all recoil from; but we know it is a greater thing to suffer than to lack the feelings and virtues that make it possible to suffer" (Mk 117).

Chapter 14

ANTONY AND CLEOPATRA

Background

Shakespeare wrote *Antony and Cleopatra* around 1607, a particularly productive period for the playwright since in about fourteen months he wrote *King Lear* and *Macbeth* as well. Harold Bloom says that *Antony and Cleopatra* is "notoriously excessive", "exhilarating but exhausting" and that teaching it is a "kind of glorious ordeal" (Bl 560). "I can think of no other play, by anyone, that approaches the range and zest of *Antony and Cleopatra*. If the greatest of all Shakespeare's astonishing gifts was his ability to invent the human ... then this play, more than *Hamlet* and *King Lear,* might be considered his masterwork, except that its kaleidoscopic shifting of perspectives bewilders us" (Bl 560). A. C. Bradley considered Cleopatra, along with Hamlet, Falstaff and Iago, as one of Shakespeare's most "inexhaustible" characters (Bl 546). And Mark Van Doren said, "Line for line it is perhaps the richest poetry Shakespeare wrote" (VD 236).

As with *Julius Caesar,* the play is historical in nature since it's based closely on Plutarch's book *Parallel Lives.* Hence, it can be grouped with Shakespeare's history plays. But Antony is often considered one of Shakespeare's tragic heroes, a towering figure who is forced to make a choice that ultimately leads to his destruction, and hence the play is generally considered one of Shakespeare's major tragedies. The play is large in many senses. It's one of Shakespeare's longest plays, it's composed of over forty scenes (although scene divisions were apparently not specified by Shakespeare and were supplied later by editors), it has a large cast, its scenes are set around the entire Eastern Mediterranean - including Rome, Athens and Alexandria - and its main characters, Antony, Octavius and Cleopatra, were the leading figures of Western civilization at that time. The play conveys an expansive sense of time and space, a sense of over-abundance. "Shakespeare's stage is always the world. But in this instance the world is not a metaphor; it is solid and differentiated, it is historical and geographical" (K 171).

Antony and Cleopatra continues the history of Rome from the point that the play *Julius Caesar* leaves off. Caesar had defeated Pompey the Great, assumed control in Rome and was then assassinated. Octavius Caesar, Julius Caesar's grand-nephew and designated heir, joined forces with Mark Antony and defeated Brutus and Cassius at Philippi. Together with Lepidus, they then divided the lands of the Roman Republic among themselves and ruled as military dictators. The eastern Mediterranean, including Egypt, was assigned to Antony, the western provinces to Octavius Caesar. Lepidus' stature didn't match that of his co-rulers and he was later eased out of power. A showdown between Mark Antony and Octavius Caesar, that would determine who was to control the Roman Empire, was inevitable. Independently, Pompey the Great's younger son, Sextus Pompeius, was also seeking power and revenge for the defeat of his father by Julius Caesar.

Egypt at this time was a client state of Rome, nominally independent but subject to the dictates of Rome. It was in the region assigned to Antony. Cleopatra, the last ruler of the Ptolemaic dynasty, was its queen. She was a descendant of Ptolemy I, who was a general in the army of Alexander the Great of Greece. Egypt had been conquered by Alexander and Ptolemy was made king of Egypt after Alexander's death in 323 BCE. Although Cleopatra had hoped to preserve the dynasty by passing control on to her children, it became a part of the Roman Empire after her death.

When the play opens, Cleopatra is twenty-nine years old and in the intimate relationship with Antony that would come to define them both. Antony is forty-three. Hence, in contrast with *Romeo and Juliet*, this is not a story of young love. She had previously had a relationship with Pompey the Great (or with his son – this is unclear) and later with Julius Caesar, to whom she bore a son, and she had just given birth to Antony's twins.

Cleopatra was clearly working her way through the leadership of Rome and for good reason: her hold on the Egyptian throne depended on her relationship to Rome. Hence, her affair with Antony had both a romantic and a political motivation and as a result might have been unstable. But her beauty and charm were legendary in the lands surrounding the Mediterranean Sea. Antony and Cleopatra were towering figures who played a central role in events that affected the direction of the history of the Western World. "They [were] conscious of and [sought] to perpetuate their legendary status. At the same time, they [were] intimately human." (ArAC 4)

In the play, Sextus Pompeius is referred to simply as Pompey and Octavius Caesar, who takes the name Augustus when he becomes the first emperor of Rome, is referred to simply as Caesar.

The Play (line numbers from (ArAC))

- (I, I, 1 - 13) The play opens with a presentation of the conflict that underlies the action. Philo speaks of Antony as he had been: his "goodly eyes that o'er the files and musters of the war Have glowed like plated Mars", "his captain's heart, which in the scuffles of the great fights hath burst the buckles on his breast". Philo then compares that with Antony as he now is: he has "become the bellows and the fan to cool a gipsy's lust". The "triple pillar of the world" – meaning Antony, the other two pillars being Caesar and Lepidus - has been transformed "Into a strumpet's fool". In Philo's view the ideal Roman has been reduced by Egypt to a wimp.

- (I, I, 15 - 41) "There's beggary in the love that can be reckoned." - Antony enters and says his love for Cleopatra can't be measured, that it goes out to a "new heaven, new earth". The arrival of a messenger from Rome annoys him since it reminds him of his responsibilities in Rome and interrupts the life he enjoys in Egypt (17). In the space of a few lines we get a sense of the size of the play: their love extends out into the universe, Antony's obligations extend to Rome. He then says, "in one of the most famous declarations of love in all of literature" (Bl17 114) (34 – 41), that his home is in Egypt, that Rome should "in Tiber melt and the wide arch of the ranged empire fall" as far as he's concerned. He says that kingdoms are only dirt (36) and dirt feeds both man and beast. The real difference between the two is that man has the capability to love and that love shows the "nobleness of life". There is an innocence in his plan to wander the streets of Alexandria with Cleopatra (according to Plutarch, in disguise) like two young lovers on a date and spy on the people that they see (53). "Here is the tragic excess, but with it the tragic greatness, the capacity of finding in something the infinite, and of pursuing it into the jaws of death." (Br2 293) The play contrasts two large attitudes towards existence: Egypt offers pleasure and love, Rome thrives in the exercise of raw power.

- (I, II, 49 – 87) "There's a palm ..." - Casual sexuality (49 – 80) and "mirth" (87) are associated with Egypt. Rome by contrast is serious.

- (I, II, 111 - 117) "Speak to me home; ..." - Antony understands how the Romans view Cleopatra and he recognizes that his stay in Egypt has violated the spirit of Rome.

- (I, II, 122 – 137) "These strong Egyptian fetters ..." - Antony is torn between the pleasure he enjoys in Egypt and the duty he feels to Rome and also by guilt over his treatment of his wife, Fulvia. He recognizes that she deserved better. He contemplates breaking off his relationship with Cleopatra, having previously compared his love to a "new heaven". This oscillation in his ardor continues throughout the play and mirrors a similar pattern in Cleopatra (III, XIII, 63).

- (I, II, 139 - 162) "I must with haste from hence." - "In most literature there is a convention that character is knowable as it rarely is in life, that characters act in accordance with certain constant, recognizable, and explicable principles which we and they can know" (Bl17 11). Shakespeare often violates this pattern. Particularly in his major tragedies, it's often unclear what motivates the protagonist's actions. Why does Lear divide his kingdom? Why doesn't Hamlet act to revenge his father's murder? Why does Macbeth murder Duncan? There are several reasonable explanations for these actions and the plays are so rich in dialogue and soliloquys that different positions can be defended.

The issue is different in *Antony and Cleopatra*. In contrast to these characters, Cleopatra is an actress who deliberately attempts to mislead. Enobarbus discusses this in relationship to Antony's planned departure from Egypt. He mockingly says it will kill her and then goes on, "I have seen her die twenty times upon far poorer moment" (148). Antony agrees, saying "she is cunning past man's thought" (152). But despite his obvious disapproval of Cleopatra and the effect she's had on Antony, Enobarbus recognizes what an extraordinary person she is: "her passions are made of nothing but the finest part of pure love" (153). As the play progresses, we will see that both evaluations are true. Cleopatra is a complex character, not easy to know. Enobarbus then goes on to philosophize on the role of the gods in replacing old wives with new ones (168 – 177).

- (I, II, 192) "Our slippery people, …" - The first of several comments on the fickleness of the populace, who do not give their love to a deserving ruler at the time he is giving good service.

- (I, III, 3 - 6) "See where he is, …" - The scene illustrates the nature of the relationship between Cleopatra and Antony. She doesn't want him to return to Rome and, consistent with her character, uses every deception at her command in an attempt to convince him to stay. First, she proposes to lie (4). Then she rejects Charmian's advice and proceeds to feign sickness (14). She blames him for betraying her (26) and doesn't let him explain why he feels he must return. She then tries to make him feel guilty, using hyperbolic language to describe the intensity of their former love (36 – 40). Hyperbole conveys the high emotion which Shakespeare attaches to Egyptian life and he contrasts this with the more reasonable and unadorned language style used by the Romans. She "expresses every possible emotion from rapturous joy and uncontrollable rage to suicidal despair, but seems incapable of moderation, the Roman 'measure' or golden mean" (ArAC 51).

When Antony finally gets a chance to speak (43) he does so in Roman style: "The strong necessity of time commands ..." He speaks of the problems of governing (48 – 55). And he says that, although the populace had formerly hated Pompey, he has "grown to strength, [and] newly grown to love", thus adding to his earlier comment on the subject (I, II, 192). He ends by telling of Fulvia's death (57). Cleopatra's first response is that at her age she's not naïve enough to be fooled by that claim. When she realizes that he's not fooling, she switches her strategy. First, she criticizes him for not mourning Fulvia and then she attacks him by saying that when she dies, he won't mourn her as well (63). He defends his love for her (74) but she says he's acting (79). The scene ends on a serious note: she wishes him well (93) and he says that even though he must leave, his spirit remains with her (105).

- (I, IV, 3 - 72) "From Alexandria this is the news: ..." - Caesar condemns Antony's profligate life in Egypt saying he "is not more manlike than Cleopatra, nor the Queen of Ptolemy more womanly than he" (5). Lepidus' defense of Antony uses an interesting construction: In his metaphor goodness is blackness and faults are stars (10 - 15). Caesar bemoans the fact that Antony's absence places greater weight on Lepidus and himself to defend the Empire against Pompey (24), to whom many Romans are transferring their support. Caesar comments that leaders aren't valued while they're in power, only after they've lost power (42). This complements Antony's earlier comment on that subject (I, II, 192). Caesar then bemoans the inconstancy of the Roman people (44 – 47). Finally, he recalls with admiration Antony's stoicism and courage and his ability to endure deprivation in his life before Cleopatra (56 – 72). This is the ideal to which the Romans aspire.

- (I, V) In this short scene we see multiple aspects of Cleopatra's personality. She jokes with Mardian the eunuch (whose presence reminds us of the excesses of Egyptian life) (10), she acts like a love-sick young girl (20), she hints at the sexual nature of her relationship with Antony (22) and speaks extravagantly of him (24), she remembers nostalgically her former beauty and lovers (28 – 35), she interprets what she hears to suit her feelings (56 – 64), she's prone to excess (66), she threatens violence (73) and she excuses her past actions (76).

- **Caesar** is a man devoted to power and capable of using devious means to attain it. In arranging for Octavia's marriage, he demonstrates his ability to sacrifice the emotional relationships that make us human in favor of the actions necessary to build an empire. He embodies the order and self-sacrifice that were at the heart of the Roman success in controlling the Western World.

Cleopatra, on the other hand, embodies the Egyptian view of life. She is a woman of infinite variety. She expresses love, anger, jealousy, courage, guile, sexuality, playfulness, fear, and showmanship. She instills desire, anger, and loyalty in others. She can be headstrong and promiscuous, she can lie. In some ways the Shakespearean character she most resembles is Falstaff. "Cleopatra has all the moral neutrality of nature. There she is, like the soil, equally ready to produce the most noxious weed or the rarest flower" (Go2 194). She has related herself so much to life that a positive value seems to emerge, independent of what she does. The question that arises is, however, does this justify the excesses that are involved?

Antony is torn between Rome and Egypt. He's a man with a generous nature, quite free from envy, capable of great magnanimity and stoicism, and naturally straightforward. He can admit faults, accept advice, and take a jest against himself with good humor. His soldiers are attached to him. But he's neither a mere soldier nor a mere sensualist. He has imagination, he revels in abundant and rejoicing appetites, he flings himself into mirth and revelry. He has our full sympathy, partly because he is never unmanly, partly because he himself is sympathetic. He was not born to rule: Power for him is chiefly a means to pleasure (Br2 295). "He refuses to sacrifice to the Roman Empire his heritage as a man" (Go2 206).

"Throughout the play, Roman attitudes and principles, expressed mainly by Octavius Caesar, are placed in opposition to Egyptian, represented chiefly by Cleopatra. Antony is in a similar position [to Prince Hal in *Henry IV*], equally at home in either world but compelled eventually to choose between them ... Rome and Egypt 'represent crucial moral choices and they function as symbolic locales ... For the Romans the ideal is measured in masculine, political, pragmatic, military terms, the subservience of the individual to the common good of the state, of personal pleasure to public duty, of private, domestic loyalties to the demands of empire. Alexandria, on the other hand, is a predominantly female society for which the ideal is measured in terms of the intensity of emotion, of physical sensation, the subservience of social responsibility to the demands of feeling" (ArAC 27).

- (II, I, 20 - 27) "But all the charms of love, ..." – Pompey uses lush poetry to describe the sensual life he imagines Antony enjoys in Egypt and hopes that it will keep him out of battle.

- (II, II, 187 - 193) "Ay, sir, we did sleep day out ..." - Enobarbus speaks of the excesses that he enjoyed while living in Alexandria.

- (II, II, 201 – 250) "The barge she sat in, ..." – Enobarbus describes the first meeting between Antony and Cleopatra (201 – 228), one in which she sailed down "the river of Cydnus" in a golden and perfumed barge like a "burnished throne", tended by mermaids with "flower soft hands", "pretty dimpled boys, like smiling cupids", the winds were "love-sick", the water "amorous" of the strokes of the silver oars, the rigging tended by mermaids. Cleopatra, more beautiful than Venus, "beggared all description". The entire city went to the wharf to see her arrival. Cleopatra made "defect perfection" (241), "Age cannot wither her, nor custom stale her infinite variety" (245), "she makes hungry where she most satisfies" (247). Enobarbus says that Cleopatra has overcome the effects of time, exhibits infinite variety unencumbered by custom, inflames passion endlessly, and can make even the most wanton actions seem virtuous.

This is the world in which Antony is now living, a largely feminine world of opulence and eroticism which contrasts sharply with the largely masculine world of Rome. It's also a world which threatens dissolution through sensuousness, a point which Agrippa makes with his coarse comment that Cleopatra made Julius Caesar "lay his sword to bed. He plowed her, and she cropped." (237)

- (II, III) The stage directions specifically say that Octavia enters between Caesar and Antony, symbolizing her divided loyalties. Antony's inclinations up to this point have been split between Rome and Egypt. Despite the fact that he has just married Octavia and promised to act honorably (4), he finally makes his choice and justifies it by saying "I'th' East my pleasure lies" (37). Although our sympathies in the play lay with him, he shows himself here to be dishonorable. Unfortunately, unlike Hamlet or Macbeth, Antony doesn't give us any insight into the thought processes that underlie this choice. Although this might be consistent with Antony's character since he's not a thoughtful person, it diminishes the depth of the play.

- (II, V, 15 - 80) "'Twas merry when you wagered ..." - Cleopatra is in a happy mood, recalling the games she played with Antony (15), but she loses control (72) when she hears of Antony's marriage. Charmian urges her to "keep yourself within yourself", essentially asking her to be more Roman. Cleopatra's remark, "Melt Egypt into Nile", is a sharp and mocking reminder of Antony's previous declaration "Let Rome in Tiber melt".

- (II, VI, 93) "You have been a great thief by sea." - Menas and Enobarbus acknowledge that their military service amounts to thievery. This is Shakespeare's comment on the morality of the power struggle between Antony and Caesar and, by extension, all such struggles. The tenor of the conversation lends a light touch to the play.

- (II, VII, 11 – 16) "Why, this it is to have …" - As is often the case in Shakespeare's plays, the comments of minor observers contain important insights. Here, the servants' comment on Lepidus' situation. Compared to the others at the banquet, he has no significant power. One of Shakespeare's purposes in the play is to show the reduction of the three ruling consuls to one, and here we get a forecast that Lepidus is not going to be that one (Br2 287).

- (II, VII, 71) "These three world-sharers, …" - Menas offers a plan to murder the triumvirate. Pompey declines, not because it would be wrong to do so, but because he doesn't want to share the guilt of the act. He then makes the ridiculous claim that his honor must come before his profit. Caesar speaks the Roman line that he'd rather fast for four days than drink so much in one (102), but they all wind up drunk and the party ends happily with a dance. Once again, the underlying hostility between the characters is mocked by the apparent bond between them at the surface. Shakespeare seems to be saying "behold the leaders of the Roman Empire".

- (III, I, 25 – 27) "I could do more to do Antonius good, …" - Once again, a minor character makes a meaningful comment on life. In this case, Ventidius advises that you don't want to outdo your boss.

- (III, II, 1 - 20) "What, are the brothers parted?" - Here and elsewhere, Enobarbus plays the role of the honest interpreter, cutting through appearances. He and Agrippa mock Lepidus and give us a cynical view of the proceedings. They go on to mock Caesar's and Antony's hypocrisy (54 - 59). When Agrippa recalls how Antony cried when Julius Caesar and Brutus died, he says, "That year, indeed, he was troubled with a rheum". One gets the sense in this and the previous two scenes that Shakespeare is contrasting the hypocrisy of the political actions of the powerful with the honesty at the lower level of society – Eros, Charmian, Iras, Enobarbus – and with the love between Antony and Cleopatra (Br2 291).

- (III, III) Another aspect of Cleopatra's personality is displayed – jealousy and vanity. It's notable that the description of Octavia that the Messenger gives paints her in a bad light and one is left to wonder if he has learned the lesson that if his message displeases Cleopatra he'll get beaten (II, V). That his description is subjective is borne out by the description of Octavia given by Maecenas in which he says she has "beauty, wisdom and modesty" (II, II, 251) and the description given by Enobarbus that she "is of a holy, cold and still conversation" (II, VI, 124). Shakespeare seems to be saying that the accuracy of a description is a function of the observer.

- (III, V, 13) "Then, world, thou hast ..." - Enobarbus points out that even though Lepidus has been ousted, Antony and Caesar will fight because half the world is not enough for them. Enobarbus is the realist who tells us how the world works and thirst for power is one of the themes of the play.

- (III, VI, 40) "Hail, Caesar, and my lord!" - The loving relationship between Caesar and Octavia gives a warm dimension to his personality, which otherwise comes across as simply a strong, efficient leader. He regrets that she hasn't been given an appropriate welcome (51) and that she's been wronged by Antony (66). He says that Antony has given up an empire for a whore, but he ignores the fact that he has given up his sister for an empire (67). He advises stoicism and acceptance in the face of destiny in memorable words (84 - 87).

- (III, VII, 3) "Thou hast forspoke my being in these wars ..." - Cleopatra is headstrong. She unwisely demands that she be present at the battle at Actium (5) despite the objection of Enobarbus, who says that this will simply distract Antony – the way male horses distract female horses in battle (7). Attempting to please her, Antony invites her into a strategy session calling her "sweet" (23). Perhaps feeling that she is being patronized, she taunts Antony for his relaxed management of the war, and he defers to her, acknowledging his mistakes (24 – 27). She supports Antony's unwise decision to fight at sea, although she has no knowledge of military tactics (28), and he justifies it by saying that Caesar has dared him to such a fight. Enobarbus, Candidius and one of Antony's soldiers (61) try to dissuade Antony with good reasons, but Antony stubbornly insists, offering no other counterarguments.

  Antony's intransigence seems to be the result of both a desire to please Cleopatra and a reckless overcompensation for his sense that his life in Egypt has cost him his military edge (Bl17 143). Caesar has challenged him to a naval battle and Antony doesn't want to appear weak by not accepting that challenge (29). He risks everything in a fight on Caesar's terms and thus lets his personal life interfere with his military judgment.

- (III, XI, 9 – 24) "On our side, like the tokened pestilence ..." - Cleopatra flees in the middle of the battle and Antony follows her. This despite the fact that the outcome will determine not only his future, but the future of the entire Roman Empire. "Excessive devotion to the business of being a lover has destroyed Antony as a soldier" (Sa1 112).

- (III, XI, 51) "O, whither hast thou led me, ..." – Antony is humiliated by his behavior at sea and blames Cleopatra, who should have known that he would follow her in flight since his "heart was to thy rudder tied" (57). He has defied the "bidding of the gods" (60) in order to be near her. He realizes that his devotion to Cleopatra has cost him his honor, but he quickly forgives her: "Fall not a tear, ... One of them rates all that is won and lost. Give me a kiss." (69)

- (III, XIII, 25 - 37) "I dare him therefore ..." - Antony, reduced to a lone warrior, challenges Caesar to single combat. He personifies the Roman ideal of courage and strength in contrast to Caesar who, with his "coin, ships, legions" and his ministers, plays the role of a corporate executive who directs activities rather than involves himself personally. The challenge, of course, is futile. Caesar has what he wants. Antony is an anachronism. Enobarbus has a clear understanding of the situation: Antony's judgement is tied to his fortune, and circumstances have affected his inherent quality to the detriment of everything (31 - 34). Antony's attempt to affirm his identity as a ruler of the world confirms exactly the opposite (Bl17 142). Enobarbus begins to question his loyalty to someone he thinks is foolish (42). His little sermon ends on a positive note by speaking of the value that comes from remaining loyal to a "fallen lord". Interestingly, the reward is that one "earns a place i'th' story". The goal of reputation is central to both Antony and Cleopatra.

- (III, XIII, 63) "He is a god and knows ..." - It's not clear what Cleopatra's strategy is here and whether she has decided to ingratiate herself to Caesar (through Thidias) or is simply engaging in a delaying action. She's a wily character. There is a political dimension to her motives that Shakespeare only hints at. In order to hold on to her throne she needs the support of whomever controls Rome. So, she agrees with Thidias, saying that she was forced to accept Antony's love and that she didn't enter into her relationship with him voluntarily. Not only does Shakespeare not explain what Cleopatra is doing, but two observers of this interaction draw different conclusions: Enobarbus thinks that Cleopatra is betraying Antony by making peace with Rome (69), while Antony thinks she's flirting with Thidias. The play traces Antony's disintegration, evidence of which is shown both in Antony's desperate challenge of Caesar for single combat and his frustration with his servants who don't respond quickly to his summons: "Authority melts from me" (95).

- (III, XIII, 162) "Not know me yet?" - Cleopatra's question provides a clue to Antony's love/hate relationship with her. "Cleopatra rules his life, but he remains uncertain as to just who she is" (Bl17 49). The reader is similarly mystified.

- (III, XIII, 200 - 206) "Now he'll outstare the lightning." - Another sermon from Enobarbus: fury drives out fear and courage thrives when reason diminishes. He ends by deciding to desert Antony.

- (IV, I, 1) "He calls me boy, ..." - Both Coriolanus and Caesar are deeply offended when they are referred to as "boy" and this is probably because they see some truth in the description. Caesar's reference to Antony as an "old ruffian" gives us some insight into his character. "There is a horrid aptness in the phrase, but it disgusts us. It is shameful in this boy ... to feel at such a time nothing of the greatness of his victim and the tragedy of his victim's fall" (Br2 289).

- (IV, II, 13) "What means this?" - Antony forms a natural bond with men at all levels of society. Cleopatra doesn't share this quality. Antony's words are so foreign to her that she can't even understand what he's saying.

- (IV, III) Antony's decline as a leader and warrior is confirmed by the gods. He believed that he had inherited the qualities of Hercules and that Hercules supported him in life. The music overheard by the soldiers is interpreted as indicating that Hercules was abandoning him.

- (IV, V, 12) "Go, Eros, send his treasure after." - Antony sends Enobarbus' possessions to him after he has defected to Caesar, demonstrating his generous nature, shaming Enobarbus (IV, VI, 31), and ultimately causing his death (IV, IX). His generosity stands in sharp contrast to the devious and calculating behavior of Caesar, Pompey and Proculeius, and raises the question of whether his ambivalence towards Rome can be interpreted as a condemnation of what it means to be Roman. Just as Shakespeare shows the seamier side of Egyptian life, he's equally critical of Rome.

- (IV, VIII, 19 - 22) "We have beat them to their beds." - Antony celebrates a victory over his Roman enemies. He credits the wisdom that comes with age for this: He has gray hair mingled with brown He speaks for the older generation when he says, "we have a brain that nourishes our nerves and can get goal for goal of youth".

- (IV, XII, 10) "This foul Egyptian hath betrayed me." - Antony accuses Cleopatra of ordering her navy to join Caesar's forces and this results in Antony's final defeat. Here, as elsewhere in the play, Shakespeare does not make clear what has happened.

- (IV, XIII, 7) "Mardian, go tell him I ..." - Cleopatra, out of fear of Antony's anger, sends word to him announcing her suicide. This is Cleopatra at her devious best. As in *Romeo and Juliet*, this false information causes his death.

- (IV, XIV, 1 – 21) "Eros, thou yet behold'st me?" - In a line reminiscent of Lear, Antony questions his own existence. He no longer knows who he is. He has lost his substance, his constancy, and his Roman soul, which demands fixed purpose and stoicism in the face of opposition. He compares himself to a shape-shifting cloud. Cleopatra, on the other hand, embraces change. She will adopt any persona or strategy which suits the current need. His relationship to her has destroyed him. Unfortunately, Antony doesn't give us any sense that he's learned anything or regrets his choice of Egypt over Rome. Unlike Hamlet, Lear, Othello and Macbeth, Antony is not given the soliloquys to explain to us his thoughts.

- (IV, XIV, 45) "I will o'ertake thee, Cleopatra ..." - Antony quickly forgives Cleopatra's treachery when he's told that she has committed suicide. His previous condemnation of her was an expression of anger, not a denial of the overriding love that he has for her. He speaks of his anticipated reunion with her in death (51).

- (IV, XIV, 79 – 140) "Come, then! For with a wound …" - Antony botches his suicide: First Eros refuses to kill him and kills himself instead (95), then Antony falls on his sword (103), but the act isn't lethal and the guards refuse to complete the job. Antony speaks of an association of love and death (100), a theme that Cleopatra later repeats (V, II, 294). Finally, Antony discovers that Cleopatra isn't dead (126). The scene demonstrates the depths to which Antony's fortunes have sunk and his disintegration as a person.

- (IV, XV, 44 - 65) "Give me some wine and let me speak …"- Shakespeare inserts comedy into the scene: After having told Cleopatra that he had little time left to speak, he has to fight with her to get a word in (44 – 49). It's exchanges like this that critics point to in arguing that the play doesn't fit comfortably with Shakespeare's tragedies. Antony's last concern before dying is on Cleopatra's safety, but consistent with his decline as an effective person, the advice he gives her concerning who to trust in Rome (50) turns out to be wrong. Significantly, he says nothing about Cleopatra's lie as the cause of his suicide.

Goddard (G02 198) argues that Antony's suicide transforms Cleopatra. We see an indication of that when she says honor and safety "do not go together" (49) and "my resolution and my hands I'll trust" (51). She's determined not to be manipulated by Caesar.

Cleopatra's reference to Antony as "the crown o'th' earth" (65) mirrors Antony's earlier reference to Cleopatra as "day (light) o'th' world" (IV, XIII, 13), and thus their unity as lovers carries over to a unity of speech. They view their love as embracing the entire world and this contrasts with the Roman view that Rome's military might embraces the entire world.

- (IV, XV, 66) "O withered is the garland of the war, ..." - Antony dies, and Cleopatra bemoans the passing of a time when individual heroism was celebrated, and charismatic leaders were in control: "There is nothing left remarkable Beneath the visiting moon". The implication is that Caesar is a mere manager. Caesar later echoes Cleopatra's thought (V, I, 14 – 19), but is he sincere or are his words meant to impress his Council or War? They would carry more weight if they were said in a soliloquy (Br2 290). "Shakespeare shows us that a world goes down with Antony, ... With Antony's death, the age of Julius Caesar and of Pompey [the Great] is over, an age that began with the death of Alexander the Great. For Shakespeare, it is the ... heroic age ... and Antony ... is already archaic, reflective of a time when charismatic flamboyance still could overcome every obstacle" (Bl 558).

Cleopatra faints (70) and when she wakes, she claims to be reborn as a new woman, no longer a queen but a simple milkmaid (77). This is comparable to Lear's recognition at the end of the play that he's "a very fond and foolish old man". She sees no value in a world without Antony. It would be appropriate for her to challenge the gods, but it's not worth the effort (79): "All's but naught" (82). "Through humility both Lear and Cleopatra discover their humanity" (Go2 207).

Finally, Cleopatra speaks of seeking death in "high Roman fashion" (91), indicating that if in fact she has undergone a transformation, it involves an acceptance of some aspects of the Roman view of life. It's questionable, however, whether a real transformation has taken place. It might be that Cleopatra's real concern is about being displayed as a captive in Rome. This is another question that the play leaves unanswered.

- (V, I, 61 – 66) "Come hither, Proculeius." - Cynically, having instructed Proculeius to tell Cleopatra that he will provide her with anything she requires in order to prevent her from taking her life, Caesar goes on to anticipate that "her life in Rome would be eternal in our triumph", meaning that he intends to use her as a grand symbol of his triumph. Caesar is trying to create a myth that will enshrine him in history. "He will fix the qualities of the story forever in his own terms, which are those of the strumpet and the gorgon, not the lass unparalleled and the Mars. Cleopatra will fade into a mere parody queen in the epic pageant of his own imperial greatness, and Antony become the brother-in-arms who deserted his superior for a light woman and got what he deserved" (Bl17 51). Antony, Cleopatra and Caesar all seek immortality and try to shape the story by which they will be remembered.

- (V, II, 78 – 91) "His face was as the heavens ..." - Cleopatra describes Antony in terms of nature: sun, moon, ocean, thunder, the music of tuned spheres, the abundance of autumn. This imagery is consistent with Antony's claim at the beginning of the play (I, I, 17) that his love extends to a "new heaven, new earth". Shakespeare uses this hyperbolic language to convey the sense that their love exceeds normal bounds, that they are "overreachers of life" (Bl17

72). Van Doren says of her description of Antony (83 – 91) "there is no better speech in Shakespeare" (VD 238). And her mention that "realms and islands were as plates dropped from his pocket" (90) conveys the sense that he had a careless attitude towards the extent of the Empire. Antony wanted both love and empire, but he wanted love more. Compare this "with Caesar's careful accounting of Marc Antony's distribution of empire" earlier in the play (III, VI, 70) (Bl17 72). The realms were no mere plates to Caesar.

- (V, II, 141 - 174) "This is my treasurer." - There are different interpretations of this scene. Cleopatra claims that she has honestly described to Caesar her wealth, but it turns out that she hasn't. Perhaps she's trying to reserve something for herself in anticipation of resuming her life under Caesar. Such a plan would discredit her presumed transformation and her love of Antony. Alternatively, she's planning suicide and she fears that Caesar will prevent her from doing that since he wants to parade her in disgrace in Rome. She's committed to preventing that from happening. She lies about her wealth, anticipating that Seleucus will reveal her subterfuge. Caesar will then believe that she can't be planning suicide if she's hiding money. In this way she defeats Caesar, preserves the possibility of suicide, avoids disgrace and remains loyal to Antony. Here, as elsewhere in the play, Shakespeare doesn't make clear what her real motive is. (Bl17 9)

- (V, II, 175 – 178) "Be it known that we, ..." - The meaning here is that heads of state are often misjudged as having been responsible for the crimes of others, and when they fall, they're blamed for them.

- (V, II, 189 - 191) "My master and my lord!" - After having parted from Caesar, Cleopatra says, "He words me". She recognizes Caesar's lies. Although Shakespeare doesn't tell us what Cleopatra whispers to Charmian, it seems reasonable to assume that it concerns the asps, making it clear that her conversation with Caesar in this scene is all an act. Furthermore, Dolabella confirms Caesar's plans for her (197 – 203) after she has decided on suicide, implying that the decision was made before she was sure she would be humiliated. This is additional evidence of her transformation, although her motive for suicide remains clouded. Is it to avoid humiliation or out of her desire to be reunited with Antony?

- (V, II, 226) "Show me my women, like a queen." - Cleopatra intends to thwart Caesar's plans: "fool their preparation and to conquer their most absurd intents" (224) through suicide, and she plans to do it in grand style. She asks for her "best attires", so in death she will be seen as a queen. This is how she had been dressed when she first met Antony at Cydnus. Further evidence of Cleopatra's transformation can be found in her words "I have nothing of woman in me. Now from head to foot I am marble-constant" (237). The image is Roman, hard and stoic, and contrasts with the fluidity of the Egyptian style.

- (V, II, 246) "Those that do die of it ..." - The clown brings humor to the impending suicide. Cleopatra wants to get rid of him and get on with her suicide, but he insists on having a little chit-chat (259).

- (V, II, 270) "Will it eat me?" - "Cleopatra's whimsical, childlike question ... charms us, and fills us with fresh wonders at her personality" (Bl 583).

- (V, II, 279 - 289) "Give me my robe." - Cleopatra sees death as bringing her several gifts in addition to thwarting Caesar. It echoes a theme first enunciated by Antony (IV, XIV, 100) that they will be reunited in death. Suicide also allows her to cement an image that will be remembered through history. She's an actress who thrives on grand gestures – the grandeur of her meeting Antony on Cydnus and now this. She wants to be seen as having made "a supreme and glorious sacrifice" (ArAC 47). She imagines that the suicide will launch her into a transcendent afterlife with Antony in a final speech that Bradley says is "surpassed in poetry, if at all, only by the final speech of Othello" (Br2 303). She says: "I am fire and air; my other elements I give to baser life" (288).

- (V, II, 306) "That I might hear thee ..." - Her reference to Caesar as "ass unpolicied" is both an assertion that she has thwarted Caesar's plans and an indictment of all Caesars: "the revenge of poetry, which is the politics of heaven, on empire" (Go2 204).

- (V, II, 354) "She hath pursued conclusions infinite ..." - Cleopatra is not brave in the Roman sense – she fears pain, she was afraid at Actium and she feared Antony's anger afterward. But in the end, we have a sense that she triumphs over Rome using devious strategies and exotic techniques appropriate to Egypt. "She puts her conqueror to scorn and goes to meet her lover in the splendour that crowned and robed her long ago, when her barge burnt on the water like a burnished throne, and she floated to Cydnus on the enamoured stream to take him captive for ever" (Br2 303).

- (V, II, 355 – 362) "Take up her bed, ..." - As with Antony, Caesar gets to say the last words on Cleopatra. He pays tribute to her seductive abilities, he acknowledges the fame that she an Antony enjoy, and he pays himself a compliment by saying that the extent of the pity that their story evokes is no less than the glory that adheres to him for bringing them down. He recognizes that with her orchestrated death Cleopatra has triumphed. The myth of Antony and Cleopatra as tragic lovers will go forward. She has defeated time and oblivion and he chooses to cooperate in that. The final image is reminiscent of a similar scene in *Hamlet*, with Caesar playing the role of Fortinbras.

Discussion

The atmosphere of the play is not that of darkness and hell as in plays like *Macbeth* and *King Lear*. There is no concentrated point of evil, such as the witches, Edmund or Iago. Instead, the evil seems to reside in the excesses of normal and healthy impulses – love and politics, self-control and pleasure.

Rome and Egypt seem to "struggle for domination over Mark Antony's spirit and will ... [he stands] at the crossroads of duty and sensuality, of self-denial and self-indulgence. Rome is duty, obligation, austerity, politics, warfare, and honor: Rome is public life. Egypt is comfort, pleasure, softness, seduction, sensuousness ... variety and sport; Egypt promises her children rich, languorous pleasures and satisfactions. Rome is business, Egypt is [abundance]; Rome is warfare, Egypt is love" (Bl17 58).

Since the Roman and Egyptian views of the world, as expressed by Antony and Cleopatra, are quite different, one might reasonably ask which of the two does Shakespeare support?

Unfortunately, his judgment of the characters is difficult to discern since “no character speaks with the voice of the dramatist” (ArAC 38) and they express different views of each other, sometimes contradicting themselves. We are made to admire Antony and the Roman qualities that he exhibits – his courage, his masculinity and the generous relationship he has with other men. “But there is something not just unattractive but maimed about the exclusively masculine world of Rome” (Bl17 40). We also admire the Egyptian way of life for its richness and its embrace of the sensual pleasures offered by nature. But there is something dissolute about its idleness and lack of purpose. The play portrays a clash of civilizations and values and Shakespeare might be simply offering us a comparison between the two without raising one above the other. The one thing that does come through is the enduring love between the two protagonists. Perhaps this is what Shakespeare endorses.

“With all its qualifications and all its defects admitted … the love of Antony and Cleopatra is nonetheless affirmed, the strumpet and the strumpet’s fool grow into the imaginative warrior and the theatrical queen. There is no denying their excesses … We learn that in such excess, life itself can reside. Though it threatens to rot and seems at times to have corrupted the lovers, their style of living affirms their life” (Bl17 83).

“It is plain that the love of Antony and Cleopatra is destructive; that in some way it clashes with the nature of things; that, while they are sitting in their paradise like gods, its walls move inward to crush them at last to death. … We sympathize with them in their passion; we feel in it the infinity there is in man; even while we acquiesce in their defeat we are exulting in their victory” (Br1 293).

Although *Antony and Cleopatra* is generally recognized as one of Shakespeare's mature masterpieces, its stature as a tragedy has been questioned. Bradley "valued Shakespeare's tragedies for their capacity to interpret the world and man's place in it without recourse to Christian theology" (ArAC 49). In Shakespeare's four major tragic plays, good and evil are precisely located, but in this play, "where the perfection for which the two principal characters strive is also shown to be a waste and a delusion, it seems irrelevant. Nothing purely good or evil can be found in the play and what seems admirable in one context is shown as ridiculous in another – or, rather, appears as both admirable and ridiculous at one and the same time" (ArAC 49).

Chapter 15

CORIOLANUS

Background

Shakespeare wrote *Coriolanus* shortly after completing *Antony and Cleopatra*. Taken together with *Julius Caesar,* the three plays form a trilogy that follows Roman history from its early days at the beginning of the Roman Republic, through the fall of the Republic and the beginnings of the Roman Empire. Despite the fact that the play deals with Roman history, it's considered one of Shakespeare's tragedies and, in fact, his last tragedy. T. S. Eliot considered the play "Shakespeare's most assured success" (ArC 3), but many disagreed. It is one of Shakespeare's "least frequently performed" play (K 179). It is a bleak play about harsh political division within Rome between plebeians and patricians. Neither group is presented sympathetically. And standing above both is Coriolanus, a most unsympathetic character.

In contrast to Julius Caesar, Brutus, Marc Antony and Cleopatra, little is known about Coriolanus. Shakespeare based his play on Plutarch's *"Life of Coriolanus"*, but historians question the accuracy of the information recorded there. Coriolanus apparently lived in the early decades of the 5th Century BCE at the time when Rome was transitioning from Tarquin, it's last king, to a republic. Tarquin's reign has been described as a brutal tyranny and Coriolanus might have participated in his overthrow.

Both Shakespeare's play and Beethoven's *Coriolan Overture* serve to keep Coriolanus' memory alive today.

The Play

- (I, I) *Coriolanus* was written at the time of serious unrest in England, called the Midland Revolt, over shortages of grain and corn that threatened famine. This was aggravated by grain hoarding, which further limited the stocks of grain brought to market. Shakespeare seems to have had this in mind when he wrote the play (ArC 56 - 68). It opens with a gathering of citizens discussing the possibility of famine. Scholars have spent a lot of energy trying to understand Shakespeare's attitude towards the lower classes, and the presentation of the group of citizens in this scene is a case in point. Are they an unruly mob capable of unreasoned violence, or does Shakespeare show them as individuals with differing opinions? In *Julius Caesar* the former description seems to apply. There the citizens are a fickle group, first convinced by Brutus' justification of the assassination and then swayed to violence by Antony's denunciation of Brutus.

  Here, Citizen 1 calls for Coriolanus' death (9) for his role in creating the famine. The citizen refers to him as Martius, his birth name, which honors the Roman god of war. (His name will be changed to Coriolanus later in the play to honor his courage at the battle at Corioles.) Citizen 1 speaks of the need for the patricians to "yield but the superfluity", a thought that was expressed in *King Lear* by both Lear and

Gloucester. He defends this position rationally and says that it is motivated by hunger, not revenge (13 - 23).

The case Citizen 1 presents is one of class warfare: "our sufferance is a gain to them [the patricians]" (20). The group as a whole at first agrees (26), but Citizen 2 says that Coriolanus' service to Rome argues against murder (27) and the crowd demands that Citizen 1 "speak not maliciously" (32). While Citizen 2 admits that Coriolanus is a proud man, he points out that he isn't "covetous". They argue about whether he is motivated by patriotism, pride or a desire to please his mother. As a result, in contrast to the way the mob is presented in *Julius Caesar,* where no one seems to have an opinion of his own, the citizens in *Coriolanus* are shown to be individuals, some of whom have reasoned views and are capable of showing restraint, others "as unstable, fickle, anarchical, deficient in vision" (Bl18 53, 127).

Interestingly, Citizen 2 says that Coriolanus' pride is a part of his essential nature and thus he cannot help it (32), an opinion that contradicts a view expressed later that Coriolanus is the product of Volumnia's deliberate effort to shape him, and thus the result of nurture.

- (I, I, 46) "Worthy Menenius Agrippa, ..." - Menenius is a patrician, an elder statesman, who is well regarded by the plebeians. He attempts to defend the government's handling of the famine. Whereas Citizen 1 sees class warfare at the root of the problem, Menenius presents a different view. He warns the citizens that rebellion against Rome is futile and he blames the famine on the gods, not the Senate (62 – 69). He urges prayer.

He then compares the state to the human body, with the Senate occupying the belly (91), a central organ since it disburses food to the other parts. Menenius is fond of food and this gives him a unique personality, one that is developed as the play progresses. In contrast to an argument based on class warfare, his argument is essentially the trickle-down theory of economics: he defends the wealth of the few because it will eventually benefit the poor. Although this is an organic image of the state, it is unidirectional and contrasts with an image based on interdependence, in which each part benefits from the actions of all others. Menenius assigns Citizen 2 to the big toe (150), furthest from the center of power and least important. This reflects his attitude towards the populace. Although Menenius appears to be a patrician who is sympathetic to the plebeians, his underlying attitude towards them is revealed when he's interrupted and indignantly responds, "Fore me, this fellow speaks!" (115) and later refers to them as "rats" (157).

- (I, I, 159 - 216) "Thanks. What's the matter ..." - Coriolanus enters and his first words tell us the kind of person he is: he calls the citizens rogues without listening to their complaints. He angrily berates them, claiming that they're worthless. He says that they honor someone who has been properly punished for some crime and then they curse the justice that punished him (169 – 171). "What they cannot tolerate except in the crisis of war is a greatness which lifts a man far beyond their reach" (171) (Bl18 12). He accuses them of being fickle (177). They should honor the government which maintains order because without it they would "feed on one another" (183) – an image that Albany used in *King Lear*. He ignores their plea to reduce the price of grain and outlaw hoarding. Those who complain deserve death (192 - 195).

Menenius plays a conciliatory role (196). Coriolanus tells him that the rioting has forced the government to grant the citizens' demand for tribunes to represent their needs (210), hence disproving Menenius' earlier warning to the citizens (64) that an attack on the government is futile. Coriolanus is unsympathetic to the use of concessions as a way of placating the citizens, since he thinks it sets a precedent that will lead to more demands in the future (213) and, unlike the other patricians who accept the concessions as necessary to keep the peace, Coriolanus never modifies his position. His words mirror those of a proclamation issued in 1607 at the time of the Midland Riots (ArC 61).

- (I, I, 220) "I am glad on't." - Coriolanus speaks a long-standing truism, that a foreign war is a good way to control rebellious masses.

- (I, I, 228) "Were half to half the world ..." - Shakespeare sets up the rivalry between Coriolanus and Aufidius. A fight with Aufidius is the ultimate test of Coriolanus' valor, the one thing that Coriolanus values above all else. "By the end of the first scene we are bewildered. Though the populace is ugly enough to throw our sympathies to Martius, his undignified fury cools those sympathies." (Bl18 54)

- (I, I, 258 – 265) "Fame, at the which he aims, ..." - Brutus understands that Cominius', the Roman general, has a problem. Even though he performs "to th'utmost of a man", he will be criticized for not doing as well as Coriolanus, who is his junior, would have done had he led the army. Shakespeare hints that the problem might be a general one.

- (I, II, 34) "If we and Caius Martius ..." - The scene is apparently set in Colioles, a Volscian city. In contrast to the Romans, who are centered in a single city, the Volscians have a second city, Antium. Both Coriolanus and Aufidius are great warriors and rivals. Shakespeare compares and contrasts them through the entire play. Here we see Aufidius advocating secrecy in the Volscian's preparations for war, a devious strategy that contrasts with Coriolanus' open, straightforward approach to everything.

- (I, III, 1 – 25) "I pray you, daughter, ..." - Volumnia's first words speak of her single-minded effort to make Coriolanus a warrior who seeks honor over all else. She's willing to see him die in pursuit of this goal. She sent him to war when he was only a boy. She imagines his actions on the battlefield (34). We get the sense that, unable to join the battle herself, she lives through the exploits of her son. She compares him in battle to a "harvestman" killing his enemies (38). The implication of her description of his upbringing is that he is the product of her nurturing rather than of nature.

  Virgilia, on the other hand, is concerned with his survival (40), drawing a rebuke from Volumnia who says, "blood becomes a man" and Hecuba's breasts were not lovelier than Hector covered with blood (42 – 45). Her passion for blood is nothing short of grotesque. The play is "a tragedy of some little boy being made into only one thing ... There's a whole mass of experience he's never been allowed to have. So, he becomes this rigid thing, he can only be a sword" (ArC 135). Shakespeare emphasizes the radical nature of her attitude by changing the tone abruptly with the arrival of Valeria, who speaks of Virglia and Volumnia as housekeepers (53).

- (I, III, 62) "I saw him run after …" - Valeria describes how Young Martius tormented and then tore apart a beautiful butterfly, and says he is "the father's son", and Volumnia adds, approvingly, that he shares his father's moods.

- (I, IV, 55) "He is himself alone …" - Coriolanus fights alone within the city, achieving his ideal of complete independence, and displaying towering courage and valor.

- (I, VI, 42 – 45) "He did inform the truth." - "The war confirms the class hierarchy which Marcius already perceived in peace time. Patricians and plebeians behave differently in war" (K 195).

- (I, VIII, 1) "I'll fight with none but thee, …" - For Coriolanus, the worst thing that a person can do is break a promise. But we will see that lying is exactly what he will be asked to do later in the play.

- (I, IX, 13 - 65) "Pray now, no more." - Coriolanus is embarrassed by praise, even from his mother (15), and is generous in sharing the glory of victory with the others who fought with him (16). In recognition of their different views of honor, Cominius asks that Coriolanus accept public praise "In sign of what you are, not to reward what you have done" (26). He then offers him an extra portion of the spoils of their conquest (37). Coriolanus refuses this since he sees the reward as demeaning, explaining that he didn't fight for money, he fought for honor and to defend Rome.

Accepting spoils is like working for hire and this admits a dependence on others, something he abhors.

Coriolanus refers to the extra spoils as a "bribe" (37), illustrating his penchant for speaking with excessive bluntness. His words amount to a "gratuitous insulting of his friend and benefactor as a briber, and of the army he has led to victory as a pack of liars" (Bl18 61). Cominius rebukes him for expressing more resentment at the monetary award he's been offered than gratitude to those who cheer him honestly (52). He then gives him the honor of the name "Coriolanus" for his role in subduing the city – and when the soldiers cheer him his response is "I will go wash" (66).

This is the culmination of self-authorship: Coriolanus has usurped the role of his parents by effectively naming himself (Bl18 81). But, "in accepting the name Coriolanus, Martius accepts public recognition for what he has done, and necessarily compromises himself" (Bl18 63). He cannot both insist on the privateness of his action and yet use a name whose purpose is to remind the public of that action.

"For Cominius ... honor is something that comes to one for one's achievement in the world; it is conferred by society, involved in good name and reputation, public praise and office; the unrewarded deed is the grave of its deserving. For Caius Martius, however, the deed is its own reward, honorable or dishonorable regardless of what people think of it; honor is a quality of action, not of action's effects; honest praise is flattery and lies because all words that describe what is ultimately personal and subjective must miss the point" (Bl18 62).

The debate goes back to the early Greeks who distinguished between a shame culture and a guilt culture. A shame culture promoted the idea that virtue is defined by "a certain kind of social approval" and hence was sensitive to communal standards. A guilt culture promoted the idea of an "internalized virtue responsible only to absolutes that lie beyond social jurisdiction" and saw "individual conscience and consciousness" as the "only standards the virtuous man can respect" (Bl18 62). Although he accepts his new name, Coriolanus subscribes to a guilt culture.

It's apparent from the praise and the gift, that Cominius thinks highly of Coriolanus (52). Menenius and Lartius (I, V, 20) think well of him too. It follows that, despite his uncivil behavior, Shakespeare is telling us that there is much to admire in Coriolanus.

- (I, IX, 81) "I sometime lay here in Corioles, ..." - Coriolanus shows another dimension of his personality in his concern for a plebeian who aided him in Corioles. Significantly, although the incident is mentioned by Plutarch, Shakespeare says he's poor whereas Plutarch said he was wealthy and says nothing about Coriolanus having forgotten his name (ArC 42). Although the incident makes Coriolanus a more sympathetic character, the fact that he has forgotten the man's name might reveal an aristocratic disdain for a plebeian.

- (I, X, 12 - 16) "Mine emulation hath not ..." - Aufidius says that if he can't best Coriolanus in a fair fight, he's willing to use "wrath or craft" to defeat him. He is less than honorable.

- (II, I, 143 – 156) "I'th' shoulder and ..." - Volumnia celebrates the number of scars on her son's body and applauds his wonderful ability to kill.

- (II, I, 157) "Know, Rome, that all alone ..." – Coriolanus enters Rome surrounded by Cominius and Titus Lartius and the Herald proclaims his glory. His response is "No more of this, it does offend my heart" (163).

- (II, I, 195) "There's one thing wanting, ..." - Volumnia has political ambitions for her son that he doesn't share. The "one thing" that she refers to is the position of consul. But Coriolanus has other ideas (196 – 198), and we see a split between them that will only get worse.

  Volumnia and Lady Macbeth are ambitious women who are unphazed by the fact that inflicting death through war or murder is necessary to advance the careers of their male relatives. Indeed, they encourage it with a bloodthirsty enthusiasm. However, their motivations are quite different. Lady Macbeth advocates an anti-social act (Duncan's murder) for her own personal gain, while Volumnia encourages socially acceptable behavior to gain office and the respect of her city.

- (II, I, 217) "Then our office may, ..." - The tribunes realize that if Coriolanus becomes a consul they will lose their power. Pretending to represent the people, their actions will actually be directed to protecting themselves. Their hypocrisy serves to highlight Coriolanus' honesty. Sicinius accurately predicts that Coriolanus' tendency towards intemperate behavior will ultimately bring him down (218) and they plan to help that along (239).

- (II, II, 33) “Make way, they are coming.” - The tribunes, since they are not patricians, sit apart. The stage directions specify that Coriolanus first stands, then sits (46), then “rises and offers to go away” (64) and finally, after being told to sit down (72), leaves abruptly (75). Shakespeare seems to be using the directions to hint at Coriolanus' discomfort and perhaps ambivalence in his pursuit of the consulship (Sa1 178).

- (II, II, 124) “He covets less than misery ...” - For Coriolanus, doing the deed is its own reward.

- (II, II, 130) “The senate, Coriolanus, are well pleased!” - The Senate wants to make Coriolanus a consul. He agrees (132) but refuses to follow the ceremony of showing his wounds, wearing the gown of humility and asking for the votes of the plebeians. Menenius advises accommodation with the citizens (140). Although he basically agrees with Coriolanus' position, he's more politic. This is Shakespeare's way of showing an alternative to Coriolanus' excesses. Coriolanus says, in front of the tribunes, that the whole electoral process should be eliminated (143), with the implication that the plebeians should have no role in the government. This would violate the Roman principle that all Romans had some role, however symbolic. He refuses to do anything which would imply that his actions in Corioles were taken as a part of a transaction to gain some reward for himself (148).

Shakespeare here raises a basic question: what is the role of the man of principle in politics? Can he be an effective political leader and retain his honor? “Or, if he must compromise his principles in order to gain the popular support he needs to give him force, can those principles remain operative?" (Bl18 65).

- (II, III, 4 – 12) "We have power in ourselves ..." - Although citizens had the vote, it was simply a rubber stamp that they placed on a candidate nominated by another process over which they had no control. In the current election their role is to validate the Senate's choice of Coriolanus (ArC 78, 94). Citizen 3 says that the plebeians tend to have different opinions (20). This gives weight to the idea that Shakespeare did not want to present them as a mob.

- (II, III, 35) "Are you all resolved to give ..." - Voting did not involve written ballots. Instead, the voter spoke the name of his choice. Hence, the term "voice".

- (II, III, 39) "Here he comes, and in the gown ..." - Coriolanus meets the citizens wearing the gown of humility, as custom demands. He finds it difficult to ask for their voices (42) and uses language reminiscent of the words used by Cordelia, who famously said, "I cannot heave my heart into my mouth" in refusing to speak her love for her father. Coriolanus says, "I cannot bring my tongue to such a place" (49). Both are "incorrigible truth tellers" (Go2 210). He's disgusted by the citizens (60), resents their involvement in the electoral process, and feels that he deserves the office of consul and shouldn't need to ask for their consent (64). He doesn't, however, desire the office (66) and he's not seeking power (ArC 80).

Shakespeare gives more dignity to the plebeians than he does to Coriolanus. One requests that Coriolanus ask for a vote "kindly" (74), another politely rebukes him for his attitude (89), another expresses the hope that he will be the plebeians' friend (102) and wishes him joy (109). Although he has followed some of the customs that are expected of candidates for the consul position, he refuses to show his wounds (104). He says that if we follow customs the "dust of antique time would lie unswept, and mountainous error be too highly heaped for truth to o'erpeer". But he decides to continue on the path to the consul's office, since he's already gone through half of the indignity and might as well see it through.

His "reluctance stems from a virtue ... He refuses to seem other than he is and refuses to change his principles to suit the situation" (Bl18 13). In the end he gets the reluctant support of the citizens (136) and, as a last step, has to meet with the Senate.

- (II, III, 152) "How now, my masters, ..." - The tribunes go back to the citizens to stir them up against Coriolanus. They had advised the citizens to use cunning in dealing with him (173 - 196). They now organize the opposition, but at the same time they want to be seen by the patricians as having supported Coriolanus' election (225 – 235, 248). Interestingly, the citizens report that "almost all" of them – apparently there were some dissenters - repent having given their voice to him (251). Shakespeare seems to be going out of his way to say that the citizens are composed of individuals who maintain their independence.

- (III, I) "Tullus Aufidius then had made ..." - Coriolanus gets into an argument with the tribunes who, he says, he despises (22). They say the people are angry with him (33). He accuses the tribunes of inciting them against him (38). They say that he mocked the people and that he complained when corn was freely distributed. Coriolanus warns the senators that in attempting to sooth the populace they sow the seeds of rebellion (70 – 76). He refers to them as the Hydra (93), the mythological many-headed snake. He had previously referred to them as a many-headed multitude (II, III, 15). In both instances he emphasizes the fact that they operate as a group, and this fuels his disdain. He is the man who revels in his independence, the man who takes pride in the fact that he fought in Corioles alone.

His tirade against granting the plebeians power (92 - 113) ends with the questionable political advice that, if there are two centers of power in government, chaos results. This contradicts a view of government which embraces checks and balances (repeated in (143 - 150). Through it all Menenius tries to act as a conciliator.

- (III, I, 143 – 162) "This double worship, where one part ..." - Coriolanus sees honor and strength in a government controlled by the patricians. He says that patricians "disdain with cause" the plebeians, whereas the plebeians "insult without all reason". Government cannot function if it depends on "the yea and no of general ignorance" (146). He speaks his mind without concern over who he offends and however impolitic his views. His motives aren't selfish, and his honesty and courage are admirable.

- (III, I, 163) "He's spoken like a traitor, ..." - Coriolanus is answered by Sicinius, who calls him a traitor for the crime of speaking his mind. This goes beyond opposing Coriolanus' ascendancy to the position of consul. Sicinius claims he speaks for the people (174) and takes on the role of prosecutor (175 – 177), saying that Coriolanus is an enemy of the people. Then, in spite of Menenius' plea for calm, he proceeds to inflame the crowd. He asks, "What is the city but the people?" (199). This smacks of populism, and denies all that Rome stands for, including the structure of its government and the ideals of honor, virtue and courage for which it stands. It is a call to anarchy. And, beyond that, it is a denial of Coriolanus' view of the city as the embodiment of the Roman ideal.

Finally, acting as both Judge and jury, Sicinius denies Coriolanus his right to trial and sentences him to death (268 - 272). What started off as a legitimate reaction against a government that was not providing basic necessities to its citizens has disintegrated into mob rule. Shakespeare shows us the fragility of the rule of law and the demagogue in action.

- (III, I, 257 – 262) "His nature is too noble ..." - Menenius speaks of Coriolanus' honesty, but the underlying message is that it's foolish to wave a red flag in front of a raging bull.

- (III, I, 272) "He shall well know ..." - Citizen 1 takes Menenius' earlier metaphor comparing the state to the human body (I, I, 91) and reassigns the people and tribunes to dominant body parts.

- (III, II, 8) "I muse my mother ..." - Coriolanus wonders if Volumnia supports his treatment of the plebeians. This is significant because he had thought that they both had the same view of honor and that his actions would please her. He says that she disdains the plebeians, as he does, and viewed them as commodities, "things created to buy and sell with groats" (10). But we see that she is more political than he and he senses this. He asks, "Would you have me false to my nature?" (15) and she responds that he should have waited until he had their votes before he antagonized them (18), that "You might have been enough the man you are with striving less to be so" (20 – 24, 30 - 32) and that "you are too absolute" (40).

Volumnia then reminds him that he has said that in war honor and policy go together. Policy refers to practical steps – steps that might be devious - that should be taken to achieve a goal. She concludes that it must be so in peace as well (40 - 46). And she makes it clear that she would not place honor above her bonds to friends: "I would dissemble with my nature where my fortunes and my friends required I should do so" (63 – 65). This is exactly the issue that Coriolanus faces when the play reaches the final crisis.

Volumnia also makes an interesting observation. She wants him to be politic in both word and action saying, "Action is eloquence and the eyes of th'ignorant more learned than the ears" (77).

Menenius points out that the current crisis can be easily resolved: the plebeians will pardon him willingly if he follows Volumnia's advice (87). Coriolanus wants to maintain his integrity, but finally agrees to speak to the plebeians again, an action he regards as debasing himself (101). He "is well aware that [Volumnia has asked] him to betray an ideal and to sell himself" (Bl18 24). This is the first time Volumnia convinces her son to go against his instincts; there will be another.

The relationship between Coriolanus and Volumnia is central to the play. She is the strong mother and he the dutiful son. She calls him her "sweet son" and says, "To have my praise for this, perform a part thou hast not done before" (108 – 111). He wants to please her, but he also wants to fulfill the ideal of masculinity and independence that she has inculcated in him since childhood. It is this ideal that explains his rigidity and his hatred of the plebeians. Hence, he is conflicted. It is ironic that both Volumnia and the plebeians, who hate one another, ask him to compromise his idealism. He has accused the plebeians of being cowards, exactly what he wishes not to be. Perhaps subconsciously, Coriolanus fears that he doesn't measure up (Bl18 82).

- (III, II, 130) "Thy valiantness was mine, ..." - Volumnia takes credit for instilling "valiantness" in her son, but denies that she shares his pride.

- (III, III, 12 – 30) "Assemble presently the people hither, ..." - The tribunes plot to ensnare Coriolanus. Given their devious nature and his unbending and volatile nature, he is like a lamb being led to slaughter in their hands. He is banished (119) and in return he banishes Rome (122).

- (IV, II, 50) "Anger's my meat: ..." - Volumnia is a tiger, like her son.

- (IV, V, 86 – 94) "Then if thou hast ..." - Coriolanus offers up his services to Aufidius so that they can both take revenge on Rome. He views this as a sworn bond that he must honor (92).

- (IV, V, 222 – 234) "This peace is nothing, ..." - The Volscians prefer war to peace. "Peace is ... a getter of more bastard children than war's a destroyer of men" (227) and it makes men hate one another because "they then less need one another" (233).

- (IV, VI, 17) "All's well and might have been much better if he could have temporized." - Menenius is a compromiser.

- (IV, VI, 91) "He is their god." - Cominius describes a transformed Coriolanus as a "thing made by some other deity than nature". By single-mindedly demanding that her son place honor above all else, Volumnia has created an unnatural thing. Brutus (in *Julius Caesar*) is also a great warrior who values honor highly, but balances it with a deep concern for others, a concern that Coriolanus lacks.

- (IV, VII, 2 - 6) "He bears himself more proudlier, ..." - Although the relationship between Aufidius and Coriolanus begins on a high note (IV, V, 103), it ultimately degenerates into rivalry. Aufidius hints that he has a plan to bring Coriolanus down (18).

- (IV, VII, 28 – 57) "All places yields to him ..." - Aufidius evaluates Coriolanus' strengths and weaknesses. He says that Coriolanus won't have trouble defeating Rome, but he's not without weaknesses and he goes on to enumerate them. Too much success in the field has made him prideful (36). His poor judgment prevents him from taking advantage of the opportunities which he has earned (39). His rigidity, which enables him to be so successful in war, prevents him from handling peace, which he does with "the same austerity and garb as he controlled the war" (44). He enunciates a shame culture view of virtue: "So our virtues lie in th'interpretation of the time" (49). Aufidius points out that the person who has achieved a position of power destroys it by publicly proclaiming that he is powerful. Perhaps, one follows from the other because by proclaiming one's power, one stirs up opposition (ArC 363). The implication is that Coriiolanus is likely to do just that.

Aufidius goes on to say that rights and strengths have a way of destroying themselves (55), by which he might mean that too much of a good thing is a bad thing. Coriolanus is a good example of this – too much honor got him banished from Rome. He implies that, when Coriolanus is at the pinnacle of his power after having defeated Rome, he will be vulnerable. (A similar thought appears in *Julius Caesar* (III, I, 171).) He ends with the line, "When, Caius, Rome is thine, thou art poor'st of all; then shortly thou art mine." By making Aufidius devious, Shakespeare highlights the honesty of Coriolanus.

- (V, I, 11) "'Coriolanus' he would not answer to, ..." - Coriolanus has become a new person. He won't answer to his name, presumably because the name was awarded to him by Rome. He is hardly human. "He was a kind of nothing, titleless, till he had forged himself a name o'th' fire of burning Rome" (13). The fact that he is "kind of nothing" forewarns us that he does not view himself as being subject to the rules that constrain a normal person. He will not spare his family or friends saying "'twas folly for one poor grain or two [meanng his family and friends] to leave unburnt and still to nose the offence" (smell the plebeians) (26). Menenius agrees to plead for Rome but decides to wait until Coriolanus has eaten (56). He places great store on the importance of the belly and food (as seen in the analogy between the state and the body).

- (V, III, 24) "But out, affection! All bond and privilege of nature break!" - Coriolanus has vowed to destroy Rome (IV, V, 92) and honor requires him to adhere to that vow. But doing so is an attack on his family, and he recognizes that this is a violation of the bonds of nature (25, 33). Such bonds are a part of what it means to be human. Hence, Shakespeare has set up a confrontation between Coriolanus' honor and his humanity.

Volumnia, Virgilia and Young Martius enter and, interestingly, Coriolanus identifies Young Martius as Volumnia's grandchild rather than his son (24). This is evidence of her dominance in his life. He is torn by a conflict between nature and nurture. He does not welcome them at first, but instead waits for their greetings. Volumnia's bow and Virgilia's curtsy say something about their gender identification. His comment on Virgilia's "doves' eyes" (27), that they "can make gods forsworn", testifies to his love for her. Speaking of Young Martius, he says, "Great Nature cries 'Deny not'" (33). He says, "I melt, and am not of stronger earth than others" (28), an admission of natural human bonds, akin to Lear's acknowledgement of his humanity, "I am not ague-proof".

He has been nurtured from early childhood to believe that manhood requires a denial of these bonds, and he refers to this in his reference to the gosling's instinct (34). He strives to be a self-created man – a man who is "author of himself" (36) - one who depends on no other and thus is not bound by natural ties. He feels that any deviation from that is a sign of weakness. But his words describing Virgilia's kiss, "long as my exile, sweet as my revenge!" (45), signal his inability to maintain that position.

The role reversal signified by Volumnia kneeling before Coriolanus touches on another current that runs through the play. Coriolanus sees it as Olympus supplicating a molehill (30) and implies that chaos has engulfed the world (57 – 62). Volumnia has dominated his life – and reminds him of that by calling him "my warrior" (62) - and his dependence on her denies his determination to be the author of himself. Hence, her supplication satisfies his innermost desire to be independent (Bl18 86).

- (V, III, 70) "The god of soldiers, ..." – Coriolanus' advice to his son is significant. He tells him to live his life as he himself has lived (meaning in accordance with a guilt culture): to be invulnerable to shame. He should act on his own instincts, not try to do what others expect. And he should emulate "a great sea-mark" in war, standing firm and "saving those that eye thee". The latter is unexpected from someone who had been described as a great killing machine. Perhaps this indicates a tragic transformation in Coriolanus' attitude. He says that his denial of Volumnia's and Virgilia's request shouldn't be taken personally; it is the result of his oath to the Voscilians (80).

- (V, III, 102) "tearing his country's bowels out; ..." - Volumnia is horrified at the prospect of seeing her son destroy Rome. She speaks of her bond to Rome: "how can we for our country pray" (107), "The country, our dear nurse" (110). But "Roman patriotism counts for little to [Coriolanus], compared with a purely personal honor" (Bl 581). Volumnia takes control by making it clear that his attack on Rome is also an attack on her: he will tread "on thy mother's womb that brought thee to this world" (123), a threat of suicide. Coriolanus' reply (129) is that in order to hold firm in his resolve he doesn't want his family present to remind him of his natural bonds.

- (V, III, 135) "No, our suit is that you reconcile them: ..." - Volumnia had raised Coriolanus with a reverence for courage and honor. She now reverses herself and argues that he will be blessed for making peace and that wiping out Rome (145) and remembering the wrongs done to him by the Romans is ignoble (154). She focuses on the fact that he will destroy his name for all time. Hence, she adopts a shame culture view of honor and asks him to reject the direction of his life.

- (V, III, 158) "There's no man in the world more bound to's mother ..." - Volumnia reminds Coriolanus of his bond to her and of "the duty which to a mother's part belongs". She explicitly draws on what she knows to be his weakness.

- (V, III, 182 - 202) "O, mother, mother!" - Coriolanus must make a choice. Does he choose honor or mercy? He has vowed to destroy Rome and has sworn loyalty to the Volsces. Hence, in his mind, sparing Rome compromises his honor. For the second time Volumnia convinces him to compromise, and in both cases disaster follows. He agrees to spare Rome and he attributes this change of course to his mother saying, "O mother, mother! What have you done?" (182). His words, "The gods look down and this unnatural scene they laugh at" (184) refers to the fact that in order to preserve the natural order of kinship – which implies duty to his mother - he must sacrifice his ideal of honor. He relents, fully realizing that making peace might prove "most mortal to him" (189) and, perhaps significantly, Volumnia does not respond (Br1 15).

"Volumnia has simultaneously asserted his dependence on her and made the dangers inherent in his defense against that dependence [(V, III, 123)] horrifyingly clear. In the end it is the combination of her insistence on his dependency and her threat to disown him, to literalize his fantasy of standing alone, that causes him to capitulate. Finally, he cannot 'stand as if a man were author of himself and knew no other kin'" (Bl18 87).

Coriolanus' dependence on Volumnia undermines his view of himself as a self-made man. When he agrees not to destroy Rome, he realizes that he can't free himself from the bonds of nature. This destroys him spiritually. The rigid masculinity that Coriolanus finds in war is a defense against an acknowledgment of his neediness; he has become a grotesquely invulnerable and isolated thing. "His whole life is devoted to disproving the possibility that he is vulnerable" (Bl18 78). "The desperation behind his claim to self-sufficiency is revealed by his horror of praise ..." Praise is "soft as the parasite's silk" (I, IX, 44) and threatens the rigidity of the soldier's steel.

- (V, III, 194) "I was moved withal." - Aufidius, seemingly sympathetic to the choice Coriolanus has made, says he's moved. But, hypocrite that he is, he privately plans Coriolanus' destruction (200).

- (V, IV, 12 – 24) "This Martius is gown ..." – Menenius, unaware that Coriolanus has capitulated to Volumnia, describes the new Coriolanus. His overwhelming power (22) is portrayed in terms reminiscent of the description of God in Genesis: "and God said let there be light, and there was light". He needs only to say what must be done and it is done. "There's no more mercy in him than there is milk in a male tiger" (27).

- (V, VI, 85) "But tell the traitor ..." - Aufidius calls Coriolanus a traitor, but it is his use of the word "boy" (103) (a word that also infuriated Romeo), with its implication of dependence on his mother, that infuriates Coriolanus. Apparently,

Coriolanus himself recognizes that this dependence is evidence of his weakness. His exultant cry, "Alone I did it" (117) is both accurate and the goal to which Coriolanus has aspired throughout the play, a goal that denies the human bond that underlies civilized society.

- (V, VI, 131) "Kill, kill, kill, ..." – "The Shakespearean tragic universe offers no guaranteed connexion between integrity and survival-value" (Sa1 184).

Discussion

Coriolanus can be viewed as both a political play and as a tragedy. From a political perspective we are shown two extreme approaches to the mechanism and the purpose of government. On the one hand, we see government by an unruly mob directed by cynical leaders whose purpose is to give the populace what it demands. On the other hand, we see government by an aristocracy that is insensitive to the genuine needs of the people, but supportive of the notion that Rome stands for certain ideals. Coriolanus is associated with this latter position, but Shakespeare doesn't endorse either one. In fact, the play never converges on a single attitude that defines its politics precisely.

Political interpretations of the play center on class warfare. They take either the workers' point of view, emphasizing the positive aspects of Shakespeare's portrayal of the citizens and Coriolanus' arrogance, or a reactionary point of view, emphasizing the negative aspects of Shakespeare's portrayal of the citizens and the corruption of the tribunes. As a result, the politics of the play is essentially the politics of a particular production (Bl18 102). The director chooses what to emphasize. "As always, classical narrative is grist to the mill of ideological argument" (ArC 104).

Harold Goddard took a cynical view of the history described by the three Roman Plays *Coriolanus, Antony and Cleopatra* and *Julius Caesar*. If we take them as a single history of the Roman Republic, "there is little but disillusionment and a sense of the predestined tendency of freedom, when it has once been wrested from slavery, to return again to slavery as if in a perpetual circle" (Go2 208).

It's more interesting to view *Coriolanus* as the tragic story of its hero, rather than as political commentary. Shakespearean tragedy generally assumes that we live in a universe that is governed by a natural order, perhaps imposed by the gods, that specifies certain rules of behavior. These rules define what is called the human condition. A tragedy centers on a protagonist who is in many ways an admirable person, but whose character is flawed. The flaw leads him to violate a rule. He struggles and suffers as a result and, in the process, he is transformed. He comes to a new understanding of himself and/or the universe. In the end, however, he is overcome, and he dies a wiser man. The struggle illuminates the harshness of the human condition that embraces us all and the protagonist's behavior during the struggle uplifts us by showing man's potential for strength and nobility.

The question is, does *Coriolanus* fit this pattern of a tragedy? In many ways, it does. The protagonist is an admirable person, more than just a great warrior. He acts honorably and courageously, and he seeks no rewards for his actions. He speaks his mind honestly and forcefully, no matter what the consequences. He is the only character in the play whose principles are presented as worthy of respect, even if we don't always agree with him, and he stands out along with Shakespeare's other tragic heroes.

Ironically, his tragic flaw is his uncompromising adherence to the characteristic that makes him great. His "virtue – his passionate sense of honor and allegiance to principles - is also his vice" (Bl18 73). He is a proud idealist who is too conscious of the virtue he is trying to live. He carries moral goodness as far as it can go and, as a result, he's unwilling to recognize the natural bond that connects him to his fellow human beings.

Coriolanus confronts this problem when he's forced to choose between making peace with the Romans or making war. The former involves recognition of this bond and the latter allows him to rigidly adhere to his code of honor. He reluctantly chooses peace. Is his choice evidence of new wisdom or is he simply a broken man?

Unfortunately, Shakespeare doesn't give us easy access "to the self that lies within [Coriolanus'] character" (ArC 47), "the audience must itself bridge the gap ... between his actions and a credible motivation for them" (ArC 48). In contrast to Hamlet, for example, who is given multiple soliloquys to tell us what he's thinking, Coriolanus tell us little about himself. Hence, there's little evidence in the play that Coriolanus has undergone a transformation. Instead, his acceptance of the bond of nature has simply influenced a particular choice he must make. "It is almost inconceivable that he should deny the claims made by Volumnia ... He avoids an act of shocking inhumanity and thereby surrenders control of his world to the forces of policy and compromise – the enemies of the 'noble heart'" (Bl18 28). "We are witnessing only the conquest of passion by simple human feelings" (Br1 12).

That there has been no transformation is implied by his words at the end of the play, "Alone I did it" (V, VI, 117), drawing attention to his valor and independence in the victory at Corioles, as he did at the beginning of the play. It is evidence that there is no new understanding that it is his single-minded focus on honor that has brought about his downfall. Coriolanus' death is the result of his rivalry with Aufidius, not the result of a bad choice he has made due to the flaw in his character. The flaw has driven him into an impossible situation and the choice he makes, to save Rome, can hardly be viewed as bad. He embodies "the heroism that fights alone and wins alone, and that can find no place in the world of the commonal and the communal" (Bl18 7).

As a result, one can question whether the play qualifies as one of Shakespeare's great tragedies. Coriolanus' recognition of his bond is perfunctory: we are shown no acknowledgment of the love that connects him to his family and that motivated him in his decision. Perhaps because he is a difficult character with whom to sympathize, we feel little emotion when he grants his mother's wish. The reconciliation marks only his total collapse. Tragedy should provide consolation to the audience, an acknowledgment that the suffering we feel in our lives is shared by others, shared even by the towering protagonist we see on the stage. Tragedy should provide a cathartic experience. One can question whether *Coriolanus* succeeds in this way. It does, however, acknowledge both our mutual dependence and the fact that that dependence can interfere with the abstract ideals that we set for ourselves.

Beyond the question of whether *Coriolanus* fits the mold of a Shakespearean tragedy is the question of what Shakespeare sees as a better alternative to the way the protagonist pursues his honor. The play doesn't seem to recommend compromise as a possibility. In fact, it's Coriolanus' decision to compromise that destroys him. Shakespeare shows us three other characters as possible models of behavior: Cominius, Menenius and Volumnia. (Bl18 68) They are all compromisers, and all are flawed. Cominius depends on Coriolanus to win his battles for him. Coriolanus is passionate, Cominius isn't, and passion wins battles. Menenius is a peace maker. His goal is nothing more than to preserve the domination of his social class and that isn't an attractive alternative.

Volumnia requires a more complex analysis. Rome is more than just a city to Coriolanus, it's an ideal of courage, honor, and valor. When he's banished, he loses more than his home. He realizes that Rome doesn't embody that ideal. Hence, he banishes Rome because it has failed him. For Volumnia, on the other hand, Rome comes first. It "is not, as it is for Martius, an abstract ethical idea, but a city, a people, a state, a history ... For Volumnia honor is the glory that Rome can confer on its loyal servants, and that honor can therefore employ policy, political expediency" (Bl18 68). Since honor is not an ideal for her, it can be compromised. She subscribes to a shame culture view. Her notion of honor requires that "Coriolanus see his virtue not in terms of what he has accomplished, but in terms of what it can get him" (Bl18 69), and that inevitably involves how others see him. Her notion of honor "concedes that value is dictated not by the nature of the object but by the tastes of the valuer, so that Coriolanus is honorable not so much when he rescues Rome as when he receives the accolades of its worthless citizens" (Bl18 69).

Coriolanus has been described as Shakespeare's grimmest play. Whereas in *Hamlet, Macbeth* and *King Lear* we're left with the sense that the characters who survive at the end of the play offer some hope for the regeneration of society, *Coriolanus* offers no such hope. The Romans are celebrating their survival at the same time that Coriolanus is being murdered. The devious Aufidius undergoes a sudden conversion and orders drums to beat mournfully for the hero he has murdered, but he delivers no final tribute.

Cleopatra's words over the dead Antony seem to apply here: "The soldier's pole is fallen! Young boys and girls are level now with men. The odds is gone, and there is nothing left remarkable beneath the visiting moon" (*Antony and Cleopatra* (IV, XV, 67)).

Chapter 16

The Tempest

Background

The Tempest was written in 1611, probably the last complete play that Shakespeare wrote. Except for *The Comedy of Errors*, it's Shakespeare's shortest play. It's been speculated that when Shakespeare wrote it, he had already planned his retirement and that Prospero speaks his valedictory message.

Meaning in the play is "not self-evident". Mark Van Doren said that "One interpretation of *The Tempest* does not agree with another. And there is deeper trouble in the truth that any interpretation, even the wildest, is more or less plausible. This deep trouble, and this deep truth, should warn us that *The Tempest* is a composition about which we had better not be too knowing" (VD 280).

The play's action takes place between 2 PM and 6 PM of a single day – practically the same amount of time as an actual performance. The play is "less the story of the shipwreck, island refuge, murderous cabals and happy ending than it is a study of its vibrant but ambiguous central characters: the admirable or detestable Prospero, ... the bestial or noble Caliban, the loyal or resentful Ariel, the demure or resilient Miranda" (ArT 1). The island setting gives Shakespeare what's been called a second world structure similar to science fiction, which allows him to portray human relations without reality's constraints. It allows him to construct a social context within which he can better expose and isolate the basic forces that influence human behavior. In this artificial environment, Prospero controls the action within the play in the same way that Shakespeare controls the play as a whole.

Perhaps it's no coincidence that two years before the play was written England sent a fleet of boats to Virginia in an attempt to set up what was to become a colony. The colony was named Jamestown in honor of King James I, who was the reigning monarch at the time. Hence, questions concerning the challenges of living in an uncivilized land among uncivilized natives were very much on the mind of theatergoers in London.

The Tempest's characters "embody the most basic human relationships: father and daughter, king and subject, master and servant. In all three interactions, the play emphasizes the dynamics of freedom and restraint, obedience and rebellion, authority and tyranny" (ArT 74).

The Play (line numbers from (ArT))

- (I, I) The first scene introduces the Neapolitans: Alonso, king of Naples, Sebastian, his brother, Antonio, Duke of Milan and Gonzalo, his councilor. In a few words, Shakespeare gives us a clue to the character of each one: Alonso encourages the sailors (10), Sebastian and Antonio curse them (40), and Gonzalo speaks reasonably (53).

- (I, I, 16 - 26) "What cares these roarers for the name of the king?" - The boatswain condenses all of *King Lear* in that question. Nature is all powerful and pays no heed to social rank.

- (I, I, 27 - 32) "Methinks he has no drowning mark ..." - The dialogue draws on a proverb that asserts that someone born to be hanged will never drown. Since the sailors look like they'll hang, the boat will survive the storm.

- (I, II, 66 - 186) "My brother and thy uncle ..." - Prospero tells his story. He was Duke of Milan, but he neglected his duties while he buried himself in his studies and he allowed his brother Antonio to run the government. Antonio lied so much that he came to believe his own lies and thought that he was the duke (100). Having gathered the reins of power (97) he made a deal with the King of Naples, Alonso, to assist him in overthrowing Prospero (120). He then set Prospero and his daughter Miranda adrift in a small boat. Fortunately, Gonzalo, a minister in the government, outfitted the boat with provisions and with Prospero's books (160). They landed on the island twelve years ago. Prospero's story is the first of several in the play that centers on violence and a struggle for power in society. Prospero's books teach him the magic he uses to control the natural world. Magic can be viewed as a metaphor for science, a discipline which was growing rapidly during the Renaissance and which serves the same purpose.

- (I, II, 189 - 193) "All hail, great master; ..." – Ariel arrives with a declaration of his willingness to serve Prospero. He has just performed Prospero's bidding: he created a tempest, terrorized the king's ship, forced the king's party ashore, and parked the ship safely with all the sailors asleep (226). Prospero is pleased: "Ariel, thy charge exactly is performed" (237).

- (I, II, 245 - 280) "What is't thou canst demand?" – Ariel now wants Prospero to grant him his freedom (193). Prospero's relationship with Ariel is mixed. Here, Prospero seems unreasonably angry. He claims that Ariel is insufficiently appreciative, considering what Prospero has done for him. We will see later that there is a friendly side to their relationship. We sympathize with Ariel. He does his job well and asks only for the freedom he has been promised. Once again, Shakespeare presents us with a situation involving violence and a struggle for power.

- (I, II) **Ariel** is a spirit associated with air and fire (Bl 671), gifted with magical powers. He's not human, but he exhibits some human qualities. He speaks of "doing his spiriting gently" (298). He's visible only to Prospero and the audience (303) and he's under Prospero's control. He was originally the servant of the witch Sycorax, the previous ruler of the island, who punished him by imprisoning him painfully in a tree when he refused to obey her "abhorred commands" (273). Prospero freed him, but treats him as his slave (270).

  "Ariel's joy as Prospero's helper is to enact in spectacular dramatic form the thoughts of his master. Thus, we can understand Ariel as the spirit of instantaneous imaginative embodiment, as quick as thought itself, the spirit that, in the famous terms of Theseus's speech in *A Midsummer Night's Dream*, makes 'apprehension' into 'comprehension'" (Bl14 76). Theseus was referring to poetry which takes the abstract concept of joy and gives it substance, makes it temporal (*i.e.,* something that happens in time). Here, it is Ariel who gives substance to Prospero's thoughts.

- (I, II, 322 - 350) "As wicked dew as e'er ..." - Caliban is described as a "deformed savage", the child of Sycorax's union with the devil. In contrast to Ariel, he's associated with earth and water. He is, presumably, basically human, but he's not a "Noble Savage". "Shakespeare does not shrink from the darkest European fantasies about the Wild Man. Indeed, he exaggerates them: Caliban is deformed, lecherous, evil-smelling, idle, treacherous, naïve, drunken, rebellious, violent, and devil-worshipping" (Bl14 67). When Prospero took over the island, he treated Caliban well (334) and Caliban responded in kind. Prospero educated him and Caliban showed Prospero how to live on the island. But then Caliban attempted to rape Miranda (348) (Caliban admits this (350)), and Prospero enslaved him (320).

  Prospero uses Ariel and Caliban to satisfy his needs. For example, Caliban makes the fire and fetches wood (312), while Ariel implements Prospero's magic. Here, Caliban enters with a curse (322) and Prospero responds in kind. But Caliban has some justification for his anger since, as the son of Sycorax, the island was originally his (332). Thus, Prospero has deposed Caliban just as he was deposed by Antonio. We are still in the first act and Shakespeare has now described three violent power struggles that preceded the start of the play. It wouldn't be unreasonable to see the play as suggesting that this type of behavior occupies a central role in society.

  Prospero is a harsh master of both Ariel and Caliban. In the former case, he's extracting payment from Ariel for freeing him from the tree in which he had been imprisoned by Sycorax. In the latter case, he's punishing Caliban for his attempt to rape Miranda.

- (I, II, 418) "I might call him ..." - Ferdinand and Miranda are immediately smitten with each other. "They represent the world's youth. They don't see the world as it is and the evil that surrounds them. They see only each other" (K 337). Prospero approves of the romance and might even have planned it (421), but he doesn't want Ferdinand to succeed too easily, and so he tests him by forcing him to do some punishing work. Miranda's remark, "This is the third man that e'er I saw" (445) tells us that she regards Caliban as a man. The romance creates a dilemma. Prospero can't punish Alonso and at the same time promote a marriage with Alonso's son. Hence, the need to reform Alonso instead. Prospero again shows his anger (461).

- (II, I, 129) "You were kneeled to ..." - Alonso forced his daughter to accept marriage to the King of Tunis. This contrasts with Prospero's choice of Ferdinand for Miranda.

- (II, I, 138) "The truth you speak doth lack some gentleness, ..." - Gonzalo displays his gentle nature.

- (II, I, 148 – 168) "I'th' commonwealth I would by contraries ..." - Gonzalo's description of a Utopian society appears to be taken directly from Montaigne's essay "On Cannibals". He's the well-intentioned, reasonable advisor who clings to a hopelessly idealistic vision of a golden age. In this vision, everyone is beautiful and kind, free of original sin and uncorrupted by civilization, a premise carried forward in the Enlightenment by Jacques Rousseau. In Gonzalo's Utopia, rank will be abolished. This is particularly objectionable to Sebastian and Antonio, so it's not surprising that they mock Gonzalo. "The latter end ..." (159) refers to Gonzalo's imagining that he'd be king of a colony that doesn't honor rank (ArT 61), an apparent oxymoron. Poverty would be abolished and justice would prevail and in that sense his Utopia is a natural evolution from Lear's and Gloucester's call for justice and a redistribution of wealth.

Montaigne had also said "that barbarousness is determined by behavior, not by rank or family" (ArT 61). Shakespeare confirms this in his portrayal of Sebastian and Antonio, whose behavior is barbarous despite their rank. Caliban may be a savage, but "he proves to be more rational and sympathetic than the two Neapolitan conspirators or the two drunken servants who represent European culture's corrupt underside" (ArT 62).

Although Shakespeare might wish for Gonzalo's Utopia, there's no evidence in either *King Lear* or *The Tempest* that he shares Gonzalo's rosy view of mankind or of the benevolence of nature.

- (II, I, 178) "Who, in this kind of merry ..." - Gonzalo proclaims his own nothingness. Shakespeare is preparing us for Prospero's revels speech, which asserts the individual's insignificance and ultimate nothingness (Bl14 90).

- (II, I, 208) "My strong imagination sees a crown ..." - Antonio encourages Sebastian to murder Alonso in a manner remarkably similar to Lady Macbeth's temptation of her husband. Antonio suggests that Sebastian has subconsciously imagined such an act (221 - 225) and, like Macbeth, Sebastian is concerned about his conscience (276). The murder itself, were it to happen, would be similar to the betrayal of Prospero by Antonio. Thus, the evil that existed earlier in Naples exists as well on Prospero's island. The island becomes a microcosm of the larger society and a laboratory for Prospero's efforts to root out evil. The murder plot is crazy, since they're stranded on the island and there is no benefit to be gained by assuming Alonso's position.

- (II, II, 29) "There would this monster make a man; ..." - Shakespeare puts in an extraneous (because Trinculo comes from Italy) gibe at Englishmen.

- (III, II, 29 - 143) "Lo, how he mocks me." - Caliban proposes a scheme to Stephano, the drunken butler, and Trinculo, the court jester, to murder Prospero. This would be a second violent act in the island experiment (50). This time, however, it's played out as pure farce and it originates at a different level of society. The two plots mock Gonzalo's vision of an ideal society populated by noble savages living peacefully. This raises the question "which is more barbarous, the educated European who makes a sham of his Christian upbringing, or the 'savage' who responds honestly to his natural instincts? Does civilization uplift or corrupt?" (ArT 36)

- (III, II) **Caliban** - Although Prospero sees Caliban as pure evil, Shakespeare presents a more complex character. Caliban hates Prospero, but he exhibits a simpleminded goodwill to Stephano and offers to be his servant (55). Caliban is "childlike in his fears and passions (29, 31), ingenuous in the immediacy of his responses to nature and man, open in the expression of feeling" (Bl14 17 - 18) (36, 44, 80, 83, 116). He loves the island and knows it well. He appreciates the music of the island. His poetic description of the music is evidence of this (135 – 143). He has learned a foreign language, and he displays a strong resistance to tyranny. To Hazlitt "his deformity ... is redeemed by the power and truth of the imagination displayed in it". He's like a caged wild beast. All this gains our sympathy and at the end of the play we're glad to see him free and master over his island. But his attempt to rape Miranda and his plot to kill Prospero negate this.

While some critics see in him humankind's most bestial qualities, others see him as a "symbol of human nature, not as we know it, but as we might have found it at the beginning of time ... [they] see in him all man's possibilities in their undeveloped form, ... and a longing for brightness and beauty as no less real than a tendency to darkness and evil" (Bl14 18).

Caliban's presence as a character in the play raises the question of what makes one human. "The presence of a real monster acts as a scale figure, allowing us to measure bestiality in the other characters" (Bl14 60). But although Caliban's shape isn't human, some of his instincts are. Similarly, Ariel is essentially human in all respects other than his physical abilities. The other characters exhibit humanity in degrees, with Stephano at the bottom and Miranda at the top. Prospero is a special case. He's human in all ways except when he wields his magical powers, and then he's god-like (Bl14 125).

- (III, III, 18) "What harmony is this?" - Just as Prospero has used his magic to create the illusion of a tempest to set the stage for his revenge, here he creates the illusion of a banquet to punish and hopefully reform the survivors of the shipwreck.

- (III, III, 31 - 36) "Who, though they are of monstrous ..." - Gonzalo differentiates the human shape from human behavior and finds more humanity in the spirits that set the banquet table than he does in his fellow citizens of Naples.

- (III, III, 68) "But remember …" – The banquet has suddenly disappeared and Ariel appears, accuses Alonso, Antonio and Sebastian of their crime against Prospero and pronounces "ling'ring perdition, worse than any death" as punishment.

- (IV, I, 5) "All thy vexations were but my trials …" - The action on the island is a trial that Prospero has set up. Here Prospero praises Ferdinand for passing the test of service.

- (IV, I, 48) "Do you love me, master?" - Ariel is a complex character. Here he asks for Prospero's affection.

- (IV, I, 51) "Look thou be true." - Prospero's concern for Miranda's virginity is linked to his hopes for a fruitful marriage and the legitimacy of his dynasty (ArT 70).

- (IV, I, 60 - 137) "Ceres, most bounteous lady, …" – Prospero uses his magical powers to create another illusion, this time in the form of a masque. Whereas the banquet was directed at the sinners, this illusion celebrates Ferdinand's and Miranda's betrothal. But it also teaches them a lesson: It's a message emphasizing the importance of purity and chastity, and stands in sharp contrast to Caliban's attempt to rape Miranda. It's also a warning of the threat of sexual desire, represented by Venus and Cupid, to the sanctity of the marriage. Juno represents fecundity and the maternal side of marriage (103). The question is, can magic, which represents science and knowledge, play a role in eliminating evil from society?

Masques in Jacobean time were elaborate events involving painting, music, mechanical devices, dancing, acting and costumes. They could be exceedingly expensive events to stage, and so their purpose was limited to entertaining the court at weddings, birthdays and the like. Although they didn't compete with productions at the London theaters, they attracted Shakespeare's interest probably because they began to displace the central position that he enjoyed in providing court entertainment.

The masque *Hymenaei,* written for King James's entertainment and celebrating the wedding of the children of two important court families, was a high point in the development of this form. It "was one of the most expensive entertainments ever staged in England" (JS 158). It was conceived and written by Ben Jonson who, along with Shakespeare, was one of the leading playwrights of the time. Shakespeare borrowed liberally from *Hymenaei* in writing Prospero's masque.

- (IV, I, 139 - 190) "I had forgot that foul conspiracy ..." - Prospero's masque celebrates that part of the world uncontaminated by evil. But his recollection of Caliban's plot makes Prospero realize that his knowledge (magic) is insufficient to control evil. Caliban isn't a threat to Prospero – he's easily controlled. But Caliban's plot, together with Antonio's plot to kill Alonso and his earlier conspiracy against Prospero, causes Prospero to abandon his hope for purity in the world and to abort the masque with the line, "Our revels now are ended" (148). This is the turning point in the play.

Prospero now believes that evil underlies all of life and that everything noble, beautiful, and good – the works of man, the liberal arts, the aspirations represented by the "cloud capp'd towers, the gorgeous palaces, the solemn temples, the great globe itself", and the beliefs and hopes by which he had ordered his life – all are insubstantial and unreal compared to the baseness in man's stock (148 – 158). The crux of his self-criticism lies in the phrase, "the baseless fabric of this vision," and perhaps especially in the word "baseless". The vision is not only insubstantial but, together with his statement "We are such stuff as dreams are made *on*", can be taken to mean that our dreams are made on top of human material that is itself base, as represented by Caliban.

Prospero's assertion that Caliban is a devil "on whose nature nurture can never stick" (188) is an admission that both the magical (scientific) power that he possesses as well as his earlier attempt to nurture Caliban, were insufficient to control his evil inclinations. The dreams allow man to deny the base reality of his nature. The best man can hope for is to have his little life rounded with sleep (157). Prospero expresses his – and perhaps Shakespeare's - view of life: short, insubstantial, evanescent, and therefore meaningless.

- (IV, I, 225) "Let it alone, thou fool; ..." - This is the third show put on by Prospero, and in this case the audience is Stephano and Trinculo. Prospero "is able to divert the assassination attempt by hanging theatrical costumes on the clothesline for Stephano and Trinculo to dress up in, like adult-children unable to imagine anything more than present gratification" (Bl14 78, 117). Even Caliban sees the stupidity of their behavior. Prospero then frightens them with dogs.

- (V, I, 17 - 30) "Your charm so strongly works 'em ..." - Prospero, with Ariel's encouragement, agrees to forgive his courtier enemies. Perhaps he has to do this since Miranda is to marry Ferdinand. And perhaps he intended forgiveness right from the beginning, since he was careful not to allow the tempest to cause any permanent harm (I, II, 15). With this act Prospero performs his last, and greatest, miracle: he has the power to take revenge but chooses forgiveness. The choice defines him as human (Go 284).

- (V, I, 33 - 50) "Ye elves of hills, ..." - Prospero's soliloquy speaks of the extent of his magical powers. But over the years his magic has come to symbolize knowledge and the soliloquy has been interpreted as an assertion of the power of the human mind to control the elemental forces of nature (K 322).

- (V, I, 50 – 87) "But this rough magic I here abjure; ..." - The soliloquy concludes with Prospero's decision to relinquish his powers. This can be interpreted in many ways. Perhaps it's an acknowledgment of the inability of magic to change human behavior and eliminate evil. If we interpret magic more generally as a metaphor for science and man's use of knowledge to control his environment, there's an interesting parallel between *The Tempest* and *Oedipus Rex*. The latter celebrated the growing and seemingly unlimited power of man, while at the same time it recognized that, in the end, the gods, for good or ill, preside over man's fate.

  Prospero now sees that "the rarer action is in virtue than in vengeance" (V, I, 27). Vengeance is something he can achieve through magic but, since virtue is preferable, magic can be dispensed with. Perhaps it's an acceptance of his humanity, particularly since he's returning to society.

Perhaps he recognizes that, in contrast to his obsession with his books twelve years earlier, he must govern in the real world trying to improve society in small ways rather than transforming it entirely.

Prospero is retiring and it's been suggested that Shakespeare had his own retirement in mind when he wrote this, his last play. There is a sense of lost illusions. Prospero's hope of a happy result of his effort to reform his mini-world has turned out to be just a dream and the soliloquy ends with his turning his attention to the sinners with no real hope of having accomplished anything.

- (V, I, 62 - 82) "Holy Gonzalo, honourable man, ..." - Prospero makes his peace with his Italian visitors, praising Gonzalo and forgiving the courtiers.

- (V, I, 102) "I drink the air before me ..." – This is Ariel's response when told to make good speed by Prospero. It is something like Puck's boast (*A Midsummer Night's Dream*) on a similar occasion: 'I'll put a girdle round about the earth in forty minutes." Ariel is imaginary power, the swiftness of thought personified. But Ariel differs from Puck by forming a human bond with the person he interacts with (16 - 20).

- (V, I, 126) "But you, my brace of lords, ..." - Prospero threatens Sebastian and Antonio by warning them that he will reveal their aborted plot to kill Alonso. This is an acknowledgment that magic is insufficient to the task of reforming the evil in man. Prospero has to resort to brute force – in the form of blackmail - to control an evil that cannot be eliminated.

- (V, I, 130) "For you, most wicked sir ..." - The shock is in the language, the stark sequence of contempt and forgiveness.

- (V, I, 181- 184) "O wonder! How many goodly creatures ..." - Miranda's amazement at the "Brave new world" and its "beauteous people" is a result of her naivety. Prospero's comment, "'Tis new to thee", reflects his new cynicism (VD 286).

- (V, I, 197) "I must ask my child forgiveness." - Alonso must ask for Miranda's forgiveness, since he had exiled her as well as Prospero.

- (V, I, 208 - 213) "In one voyage did ..." - "Gonzalo's assertion that all the Neapolitans have 'found' themselves during their afternoon on this enchanted island is overly optimistic" since Sebastian and Antonio show no signs of repenting.

- (V, I, 275) "This thing of darkness I acknowledge mine." - The line is ambiguous. Is Prospero simply saying that Caliban is his servant, or is he acknowledging an evil element in his own person?

- (V, I, 295 - 298) "Ay, that I will; ..." - Caliban regrets his stupidity in following Stephano, and in so doing he shows himself to be superior to him. We don't know what he means when he says that he'll "seek for grace", but it's a hopeful sign. Both he and Prospero have lost their illusions.

- (V, I, 312) "Every third thought shall be my grave." - At the end, Prospero is a wiser man. By giving up his power, releasing Ariel, forgiving his enemies, and accepting the inevitability of death he recognizes his humanity and the limitations it imposes on him. He prepares to leave the island, the home of illusion, and return to Milan, the home of reality, and take up the position he had held twelve years earlier. Alonso has repented, regained his son and will return as king of Naples. Ariel gets back his earlier freedom. Caliban regains his island and is perhaps a little wiser. Since neither Sebastian nor Antonio has indicated any remorse, we can assume that they are unreformed. So, despite Prospero's efforts, not much has changed since the time he was overthrown and this is a bitter result. The only bright spot is the union of Ferdinand and Miranda and perhaps this can be taken as hope for the future.

- **Epilogue** - Prospero, having given up his magical powers, asks the audience for help (in a manner similar to Puck in *A Midsummer Night's Dream*). He's weary (his strength is "faint") and he wants applause to send him on his way. This is a conventional appeal to the audience to recognize that it has been well entertained. But he also says that he needs their prayers to avoid ending in despair. He's human and he needs forgiveness, just as he has forgiven the court party, Alonso has asked forgiveness from Miranda (198), and even Caliban has expressed remorse (295). And furthermore, when he says, "As you from crimes would pardoned be", he reminds the audience that they too need forgiveness.

Discussion

Prospero presides over his own island universe using magic. His magic is strong enough to allow him to control both nature and the one evil character on the island, Caliban. He now plans to use the magic to reform the characters who wronged him before he was exiled from Milan. Sadly, he discovers that this is impossible. The play shows us the divergence between the greatness of the human (Prospero's) mind, on the one hand, and the intractability of evil in the world, on the other.

Prospero's anguish goes beyond this failure, however. In his revels speech (IV, I, 148), he speaks of the evanescence of life. All of man's achievements, the "cloud capp'd towers, the gorgeous palaces, the solemn temples, the great globe itself" will ultimately dissolve and "leave not a rack behind". Under such circumstances, there is little incentive for man to build for a better future. Prospero sees life as meaningless and, as he says in the Epilogue, his "ending is despair". Kott speaks of the play as a "great Renaissance tragedy of lost illusions" (K 327). With all of this in mind, it's not hard to see why the play is often thought of as a tragedy, despite the fact that the protagonist is still alive when the curtain falls.

The play has been interpreted in several ways (Bl14 14, 85 - 91). A Christian interpretation emphasizes Prospero's act of forgiving those who have harmed him rather than taking revenge, since forgiveness is an act that conforms to New Testament (as opposed to Old Testament) theology. A Freudian interpretation sees Caliban and Ariel as "embodiments of Prospero's subconscious mind: Ariel is his superego, Caliban his libido" (ArT 110).

A tragic interpretation emerges by comparing the play to *King Lear*. Lear is the king of Britain. He presides over Britain just as Prospero presides over his island. He initially believes that there is order in the universe and justice on earth and that they guarantee some basic decency in life. He is brought down from his all-powerful position through his own foolishness, and he struggles and suffers over the course of the play in an attempt to obtain justice for the wrongs he experiences. But he finds no order in the universe, nor justice on earth and he dies on a note of profound despair. He is a true tragic hero.

Both Lear and Prospero are forced to confront their impotence in a world in which evil is an integral part of human nature. They come to similar conclusions, with the difference that, unlike Lear, *The Tempest* ends with Prospero leaving his island on a note of acceptance rather than despair. By accepting the universe as it is, Prospero transcends the tragic situation in which he finds himself. He doesn't allow himself to be destroyed by it. He comes to realize that evil resides in all men, but he's able to remain engaged in life despite that realization. He returns to Milan to govern, presumably with wisdom and with the limited goal of bettering a flawed society. He's well aware that although evil can't be eliminated, firm action, such as he has used against Caliban, can control it.

Prospero takes an existentialist stance that mandates that man must set his own goals and take the actions that he thinks are necessary without the help of any external force. Lear had hoped that the intervention of the gods or the wholesomeness of nature would provide him with the relief he thought he deserved, just as Prospero had hoped that his magic would be strong enough to overcome evil. Both were disappointed. But Prospero goes one step further. He recognizes that magic is not a solution to the problem of evil and discards its tools. He thus transcends the need for a belief in supernatural forces and instead chooses to live in a disordered world that he knows he can never fully control or predict. His statement, "we are such stuff as dreams are made on", recognizes the insubstantial nature of life, and his statements, "our little life is rounded with a sleep" and "Every third thought shall be my grave", contemplate death with no illusions about an afterlife.

Bibliography

(ArH) – *The Arden Shakespeare, Hamlet,* Ann Thompson and Neil Taylor, ed., third series, 2006

(Arch) –*The Harper Edition of Shakespeare's Works, vol XVII,* 1908

(ArA) – *The Arden Shakespeare, As You Like It*, Juliet Dusinberre, ed., third series, 2006

(ArAC) – *The Arden Shakespeare, Antony and Cleopatra*, John Wilders, ed., third series, 1995

(ArC) – *The Arden Shakespeare, Coriolanus,* Peter Holland, ed., third series, 2013

(ArH1) – *The Arden Shakespeare, King Henry IV Part 1,* David Kasten, ed., third series, 2002

(ArH2) – *The Arden Shakespeare, King Henry IV Part 2,* James Bulman, ed., third series, 2016

(ArJ) – *The Arden Shakespeare, Julius Caesar*, John Wilders, ed., third series, 1995

(ArK) – *The Arden Shakespeare, King Lear*, R. Foakes ed., third series, 1997

(ArM) – *The Arden Shakespeare, Macbeth*, Kenneth Muir, ed., third series, 1951

(ArN) – *The Arden Shakespeare, A Midsummer Night's Dream,* Harold Brooks, ed., third series, 1979

(ArO) – *The Arden Shakespeare, Othello,* E. Honigmann ed., third series, 1997

(ArR) – *The Arden Shakespeare, King Richard II,* Charles Forker ed., third series, 2002

(ArRJ) – *The Arden Shakespeare, Romeo and Juliet*, René Weis, ed., third series, 2012

(ArR3) – *The Arden Shakespeare, King Richard III*, James Siemon, ed., third series, 2010

(ArT) – *The Arden Shakespeare, The Tempest,* Vaughn and Vaughn, ed., third series, 2011

(Ba1) – Harley Granville-Barker, *Prefaces to Shakespeare, vol. 1*

(Ba2) - Harley Granville-Barker, *Prefaces to Shakespeare, vol. 2*

(Be) – Mary Beard, *SPQR: A History of Ancient Rome*

(Bl) – Harold Bloom, *Shakespeare, The Invention of the Human*

(Bl1) – *Bloom's Modern Critical Interpretations, William Shakespeare's Hamlet,* Harold Bloom, ed.

(Bl2) – *Modern Critical Interpretations, William Shakespeare's Hamlet,* Harold Bloom, ed.

(Bl3) – *Modern Critical Interpretations, William Shakespeare's Richard II,* Harold Bloom, ed.

(Bl4) – *Modern Critical Interpretations, William Shakespeare's Henry IV Part 1,* Harold Bloom, ed.

(Bl5) – *Modern Critical Interpretations, William Shakespeare's Henry IV Part 2,* Harold Bloom, ed.

(Bl6) – *Modern Critical Interpretations, William Shakespeare's A Midsummer Night's Dream,* Harold Bloom, ed., 1987

(Bl7) – *Bloom's Modern Critical Interpretations, William Shakespeare's A Midsummer Night's Dream,* Harold Bloom, ed., 2010

(Bl8) – *Modern Critical Interpretations, William Shakespeare's Othello,* Harold Bloom, ed.

(Bl9) - *Bloom's Modern Critical Interpretations, William Shakespeare's Othello,* Harold Bloom, ed.

(Bl10) - *Modern Critical Interpretations, William Shakespeare's King Lear,* Harold Bloom, ed.

(Bl11) - *Modern Critical Interpretations, Book of Job,* Harold Bloom, ed.

(Bl12) – *Bloom's Modern Critical Interpretations, William Shakespeare's As You Like It,* Harold Bloom, ed.

(Bl14) – *Modern Critical Interpretations, William Shakespeare's The Tempest*, Harold Bloom, ed.

(Bl15) – Harold Bloom, *Falstaff, Give Me Life*

(Bl16) – *Modern Critical Interpretations, William Shakespeare's Macbeth,* Harold Bloom ed.

(Bl17) – *Bloom's Modern Critical Interpretations, William Shakespeare's Antony and Cleopatra*, Harold Bloom, ed.

(Bl18) – *Modern Critical Interpretations, William Shakespeare's Coriolanus*, Harold Bloom, ed.

(Bl19) – *Bloom's Modern Critical Interpretations, William Shakespeare's Romeo and Juliet*, Harold Bloom, ed.

(Bl20) – *Modern Critical Interpretations, William Shakespeare's Richard III*, Harold Bloom, ed.

(Bl21) – Harold Bloom, *Macbeth: A Dagger of the Mind*

(Bl22) – Harold Bloom, *Lear: The Great Image of Authority*

(Br) – A. C. Bradley, *Shakespearean Tragedy*

(Br1) – A. C. Bradley, *Coriolanus*, Second Annual Shakespeare Lecture, British Academy, 1912

(Br2) – A. C. Bradley, *Oxford Lectures on Poetry*, 1909

(Ca) – Joseph Carroll, *An Evolutionary Approach to Shakespeare's King Lear,* Critical Insights

(CM) – Colin McGinn, *Shakespeare's Philosophy*

(DD) – David Denby, *Great Books*

(Do) – Jonathan Dollimore, *King Lear and Essentialist Humanism*

(DQ) – Thomas De Quincey, *On the Knocking at the Gate in Macbeth*

(G1) – Harley Granville-Barker, *Prefaces to Shakespeare, Volume I*

(G2) – Harley Granville-Barker, *Prefaces to Shakespeare, Volume II*

(Gd) – S. L. Goldberg, *An Essay on King Lear*

(Go1) – Harold Goddard, *The Meaning of Shakespeare, Volume 1*

(Go2) – Harold Goddard, *The Meaning of Shakespeare, Volume 2*

(Gr) – Stephen Greenblatt, *Will in the World*

(Gr1) – Stephen Greenblatt, *Shakespeare Explains the 2016 Election*, Op-Ed article, New York Times, Oct 8, 2016

(GT) – Stephen Greenblatt, *Shakespeare and the End of Life History,* The Tanner Lectures on Human Values, Princeton University, 2012

(GS) – George Santayana, *Introduction to "The Complete Works of William Shakespeare"*, Harper & Brothers

(H) – William Hazlitt, *Hazlitt's Characters of Shakespeare's Plays*

(Ha) - *Critical Essays on Shakespeare's King Lear,* J. Halio, ed.

(HC) – Hiram Corson, *Introduction to the Study of Shakespeare*

(HH) – *King Lear*, Henry Norman Hudson, ed.

(JL) – John Leo, *A Geographical Historie of Africa*

(JS) – James Shapiro, *The Year of Lear*

(K) – Jan Kott, *Shakespeare Our Contemporary*

(Kn) – G. Wilson Knight, *Wheel of Fire*

(Le) – Alexander Leggatt, *Shakespeare in Performance – King Lear*

(M) – Kenneth Muir, Introduction, Arden Shakespeare, *King Lear*, 8th edition, second series, 1952

(Mk) – Maynard Mack, *King Lear in our Time*

(Sa) – Wilbur Sanders, *The Dramatist and the Received Idea*

(Sa1) – Wilbur Sanders and Howard Jacobson, *Shakespeare's Magnanimity*

(SJ) – Samuel Johnson, *Preface to Shakespeare*

(Sny) – Susan Snyder, *The Comic Matrix of Shakespeare's Tragedies*

(St) – *The Historical Renaissance,* H. Dubrow and R. Strier, eds.

(STA) - *Shakespeare Through the Ages, Julius Caesar*, Harold Bloom, ed.

(T) – Albert Tolman, *Falstaff and Other Shakespearean Topics*

(Ta) – Tony Tanner, *Prefaces to Shakespeare*

(VD) – Mark Van Doren, *Shakespeare*

(WC) – Winston Churchill, *The Birth of Britain*

46734588R00254

Made in the USA
Lexington, KY
31 July 2019